The Territorial Dimension of Politics

Within, Among, and Across Nations

About the Book and Author

This comparative study examines the dialectical tensions between global and regional interdependence and the fragmentation of humankind into territorial entities. Political authority may remain territory-bound, but borders increasingly are penetrated by pollutants, individuals, noncentral governments in search of foreign trade and investment, and transnational corporations, as well as the traditional exchanges of trade, media, and culture. The result of these transborder flows, accelerated by new technologies, is a new variety of international relations among "perforated sovereignties."

Dr. Duchacek analyzes the territorial organization of political authority in both democratic and authoritarian frameworks as well as in unitary and federal systems. Case studies focus on new forms of transborder interactions between neighboring countries, especially in North America and in Western Europe. The book is of major interest to scholars in the fields of political science and political economy. Quotations from a variety of political theorists and practitioners, illustrative diagrams, and maps make the book suitable for students of comparative politics, international relations, comparative federalism, and public policy.

Ivo D. Duchacek, professor emeritus of political science of the City College of the City University of New York and visiting scholar at the Institute of Governmental Studies, University of California, Berkeley, is the author of several books on comparative politics, federalism, and international relations.

The Territorial
Dimension of Politics
Within, Among, and Across Nations

Ivo D. Duchacek

Westview Press / Boulder and London

Copyright © 1986 by Westview Press, Inc.

Published in 1986 in the United States of America by Westview Press, Inc.; Frederick A. Praeger, Publisher; 5500 Central Avenue, Boulder, Colorado 80301

Library of Congress Cataloging-in-Publication Data
Duchacek, Ivo D., 1913–
  The territorial dimension of politics within, among, and across nations.
  Bibliography: p.
  Includes index.
  1. International relations. 2. Territory, National.
3. Regionalism (International organization) I. Title.
JX1391.D83 1986   320.1'2   85-52109
ISBN 0-8133-7112-0

Composition for this book was provided by the author.

Printed and bound in the United States of America

 The paper used in this publication meets the requirements of the American National Standard for Permanence of Paper for Printed Library Materials Z39.48–1984.

6   5   4   3   2   1

Contents

Part 1:
Territorial Politics

Part 2:
Federal Systems

Figures

Preface

Tension between the complex interdependence and the territorial fragmentation of humanity is the main theme of this comparative study. Within territorial corrals, paradoxically, universalistic creeds and ideologies tend to become captives of their own spatial conquests. Individuals and groups continue to live, think, and act primarily as members of their various territorial communities.

Yet, while political authority and loyalties remain territory-bound, boundaries are being buffeted and percolated by various transfrontier flows. These flows are made up of migrating individuals and groups, products, energy and technology transfers, drugs, pollutants, corporate transnational activities, cultural exchanges, media messages and signals, as well as—a relatively new phenomenon—international activities initiated by noncentral governments in search of foreign investment, trade, and tourist currency.

These transborder streams pass through but do not destroy the walls of national sovereignties; the territorial boundaries are both respected and disrespected. The frequency, intensity, and speed of these various perforations have been enhanced by modern technology and also by new centrifugal or neopopulist trends. One of the results is—as this study argues and documents—a new variety of international relations: interactions between "perforated sovereignties." These interactions do not represent a dawn of global unity leading to world government; neither do they mean that politics within, among, and across sovereign nations is "business as usual."

In the free systems in particular but also in other parts of the world there has also emerged the concept and practice of the territorial state as a "multivocal actor"; i.e., the state speaks abroad with more than one central voice, especially in matters other than national security and diplomatic status. Since antiquity, of course, governments have listened and reacted to the arguments and claims promoted by other nations' subnational communities in their quest for power, above all the political opposition that may be the government of tomorrow. Like a magnet, internal dissent in a country has always invited international meddling in that country's internal affairs. In our era of rapid communications, the various voices and noises, including the drums of the opposition, are quite audible outside territorial limits. Sometimes these noises are recorded by outsiders as strident cacophonies; at other times, as relatively harmonious composites of regional and other subnational nuances. The role of other than central state actors was initially described by Robert O. Keohane and Joseph S. Nye in their "world paradigm," to which this study adds the new international roles of noncentral governments. The sum total of these various international activities raises the possibility of chaotic, segmented, "marbled," or, on the contrary, more tightly centralized conduct of foreign policy.

If boundaries in the free world and a portion of the Third World tend to become sieves, their frames, however, as this study shows, remain quite solid. Buttressed by tradition and security considerations, these intersovereign walls are certainly not about to crumble despite their meshlike features. Nevertheless, as the case studies in this analysis illustrate, much more than a camel passes through the eyes of the boundary.

The first three chapters of this study reexamine the causes, persistence, and consequences of the territorial organization of political authority in both democratic and authoritarian portions of the world and their centralist, decentralized unitary, or federal systems. These chapters represent a newly focused synthesis of concepts, initially developed in three of my books in the fields of international relations and comparative politics (*Nations and Men, Comparative Federalism,* and *Power Maps*). In particular the concept of "revocable" unitary decentralization and the usual yardsticks of federalism are reevaluated and, as a result, modified.

Chapters 4 and 5 deal with federalism. Chapters 6 and 7 deal with confederal associations of sovereign states and challenge the usual assumption that the world of perforated sovereignties and multivocal states imposes on humanity a clear and urgent choice between either continuing suicidal fragmentation or all-saving universalism. A more probable scenario of both change and continuity is untidy and inelegant. As has always been the case, political realities tend to bypass "either/or" dilemmas by improvising novel or makeshift devices, as is described or suggested in this book. The title of Chapter 7, "Consociations of Sovereignties" illustrates the potential for, but also the limits of, change in a territorially segmented world. In light of the U.S. confederal experience more than 200 years ago, the chapter also explores the confederal features of international organizations, including those of the United Nations. Every so often, as the study documents, the multiplying international functional organizations serve their creators and managers—the territorial governments—to make the world safer for their spatial parochialisms.

The last two chapters examine the new forms of regional, transregional, and global microdiplomacy that are conducted by other than central governments, and these new forms are illustrated by comparative case studies in the trifederal area between the Beaufort and the Bering seas to Belize—connecting Canada, the United States, and Mexico. The discussion also includes the regional "cooperatives" or transborder "regimes" in Western Europe, especially along the once hostile "great divide," the river Rhine, where today, not a Lorelei, but nuclear reactors tend to overheat the water.

Each of the ten chapters is introduced by epigraphs that present conflicting statements by political theorists and practitioners, ranging from Aristotle to the *Beijing Review*. The maps and diagrams will facilitate the reader's journey through the labyrinth of the many layers of modern international relations among perforated sovereignties.

Ivo D. Duchacek

Acknowledgments

Although written by a single author, a study of such a broad comparative scope necessarily reflects and is indebted to the thought, concepts, and suggestions emanating from or communicated by many scholars in both comparative and international fields, particularly when, as in this study, one attempts to bridge the fields of comparative politics and international relations. Although I must state the obvious, namely, that the responsibility for the views in this work are mine alone, I should also like to acknowledge the encouragement and advice received from Ernst B. Haas, Victor Jones, Martin Landau, and Kenneth N. Waltz at the University of California at Berkeley; Ronald L. Watts at Queen's University; Elliot J. Feldman, whose critical suggestions concerning Canada and Québec have been eminently helpful, Lily Gardner Feldman, and Panayotis Soldatos at the University Consortium for Research on North America at Harvard; Irving L. Markovitz at the City University of New York; Arend Lijphart at La Jolla; Joseph S. Nye, Jr., at Harvard; Robert O. Keohane at Brandeis; James N. Rosenau at the University of Southern California; André Bernard and Edmond Orban in Montréal; Martin Lubin at Plattsburg; John Kincaid at Denton; Jiri Kovtun in Washington, D.C.; Oscar I. Martinez at El Paso; Hans Briner in Basel; and Marcel Merle and Pavel Tigrid in Paris. My indebtedness to my two friends and mentors Daniel J. Elazar in Jerusalem and John H. Herz at the City University of New York is truly academic-life-long; none of my various publications could have been begun or completed without their advice and guidance.

My field research in Western Europe and the U.S. Southwest was supported by two grants from the Research Foundation of the City University of New York; without them the book could not have started. A four-year grant from the University Consortium for Research on North America, Harvard University, permitted me to explore the transborder tensions and cooperation between Canada and the United States, with a special emphasis on the Québec issue.

All of the diagrams, which illustrate the various political interactions in politics within and across territorial states, were designed by Helena Kolda whose computer skill and patience with my repeated demands for changes are here gratefully acknowledged. Jerry Kokoshka of Interdynamics Data Systems in New York offered his advice and help in preparing the computer designs for reproduction.

I conceived the idea of this volume and prepared the first and final draft of the manuscript during the three spring semesters I spent as a visiting scholar in the stimulating atmosphere of the Institute of Governmental Studies at the University of California at Berkeley and I am indebted to Eugene C. Lee, Todd R. La Porte, and Martin Landau for their invitations to work there. Warm appreciation is due to Kathy Streckfus and Megan Schoeck at Westview Press, two vigorous and vigilant editors turned friends. The book was completed among the silos and grazing cows of Kent, Connecticut. My deep thanks are addressed to my word processing assistant there, Mary Brink, who, with a smile and extreme patience, dealt with the many successive drafts of the manuscript and its many "absolutely final" versions.

I.D.D.

Part 1
Territorial Politics

1

Components of International and National Systems

Territory: the land around a town, a domain . . . Etymology unsettled: usually taken as a derivative of terra earth, land . . . but the original form territorium v. terratorium suggests derivation from terrere to frighten . . . a place from which people are warned off.

—The Oxford English Dictionary

The union of several village-communities forms, when complete, an actual state [polis], attaining, so to speak, the limit of perfect self-sufficience: at the outset a union for a bare livelihood, it exists to promote good [higher] life.

—Aristotle (384–322 B.C.)

Phenomena observed either as political or geographical appear to have four permanent characteristics in common: (1) they develop in the same space, that is, in the space available to human activities; (2) they reckon the diversity of that space; (3) they develop according to decisions influenced by the perception of spatial circumstances; (4) they reckon with a considerable diversity of the ways in which these circumstances and what should be done about them are perceived by people.

—Jean Gottmann
("Confronting Centre and Periphery" 1980)

Ideally, humankind is one and indivisible. In fact, the human race has lived for millennia in separate territorial compartments—local, tribal, or national— and organized its work, set common goals, and progressed toward them within geographically delineated areas, large or small. The political organization of the world is still primarily based on territorial divisions and subdivisions of the land surface and its imaginary extensions into the seas and air space. The territorial segments both reflect and shape geographically delineated territorial interests. The central concept of this study is a territorial community, a territorial interest group, by which I mean an aggregate of individuals and groups who are aware of their bonds of identification with each other as well as with the past, the present, and hopes for the future of their area.

The territorial segments of the earth's surface are fenced off from one another by either natural borders, such as rivers and mountain ranges or artificial boundaries established by political will or whim. "We fashion sensibilities, extract our sense of wants and needs, and locate our aspirations with respect to a geographical environment that is in large part created,"[1] David Harvey rightly noted in another context. The territorial compartments compete with but rarely fail to tame such nonterritorial challenges as economic interdependence, universalist creeds and ideologies, and cross-border movements of persons, products, and pollutants. Today, territorial communities, not humankind as a collective whole, try to handle and manage the contemporary complex interdependence, including modern technology that makes global destruction and global construction possible. In Reinhold Niebuhr's words uttered forty years ago, "Technical civilization has created an economic interdependence which generates insufferable frictions if it is not politically managed."[2]

For the past 350 years, the most durable and relatively efficient unit to ensure internal order and welfare has been the *territorial state*. Since individuals and groups usually give their effective allegiance to such a state and emotionally identify with it (the usual terms for such collective allegiance and emotional identification with a territory and its inhabitants are "nationalism" and "patriotism"), the unit is generally labeled the nation-state, clearly, an emotion-laden term. In the case of many federal and multinational states, however, especially in languages other than English, the term "nation" is quite misleading. Many territorial nation-states are composed of ethno-territorial communities that may be perceived by their inhabitants and other people as "stateless nations." This situation exists in the cases of the Soviet Union, Israel, Yugoslavia, India, Czechoslovakia, Malaysia, and Canada.

Today, the human race is divided into over 160 nation-states. The law-giving and law-enforcing limits of the various governments, central and noncentral, as indicated by national boundaries, are considered in principle as impenetrable. The territorial nation-state is still the largest political community people identify with, both pragmatically and emotionally; it is endowed with adequate authority to establish and enforce laws within clearly defined geographic boundaries in order to ensure domestic tranquillity, general welfare, preservation of territorial culture and/or language, and security (often illusory) against external threats. Today, people also expect their state to handle the contemporary challenges of economic, technological, and ecological interdependence. Despite some groups' claims to the contrary, a territorial state is still considered a more efficient instrument than any other alternative (such as world government) for coping with humankind's collective problems.

The spatial two-dimensionality of the territory is of cardinal importance. Speaking of the nation-state, Kenneth E. Boulding noted that the dimension of simple geographic space is perhaps "the most striking characteristic of the national state as an organization, by contrast with organizations such as firms or churches, that it thinks of itself as occupying, in a 'dense' and exclusive fashion, a certain area of the globe."[3]

On the Importance of Being Fenced In

If we view a territorial community as being primarily a geographically delineated *social communication system*, its decisive boundaries are identified by a relative discontinuity in the frequence of communication.[4] People do not communicate as often across a border as they do within a territorial community. Some of the reasons for the frequency or intensity of communication are language, habit, and the fact that the boundaries of communicative efficiency and administrative authority usually coincide, although, as we shall see in Chapters 9 and 10, in some border situations people often tend to communicate across international borders more intensively than with their own but too distant national centers (along the U.S.-Mexican border, for example). The coercive apparatus that sets limits to communications takes the form of frontier guards, customs officers, passport requirements, censorship, or the jamming of foreign radio broadcasts and television programs. Yet a territorial state may still in John H. Herz's words,

> salvage one feature of humanity which seems ever more threatened by the ongoing rush of mankind into the technological conformity of a synthetic planetary environment: diversity of life and culture, of traditions and civilizations. If the nation can preserve these values, it would at long last have emerged as that which the philosophers of early nationalism had expected it to be: the custodian of cultural diversity, among groups mutually granting each other their peculiar worth.[5]

Anthony D. Smith's words concerning nationalism in general also apply to its twin brother, the territorial nation-state:

> The very attempt to eradicate nationalism actually helps to entrench it further . . . and it would appear more sensible and appropriate to try to live with it, taming its excesses through mutual recognition and legitimizations, in so far as these seem practicable in given stress.[6]

Singly, the approximately 160 nation-states own and administer their portions of the world; collectively, they influence the whole of it. No inhabited territory has escaped direct or indirect control by territorial states. The colonies, protectorates, and dependencies that existed or still remain in Africa, Asia, Latin America, the Caribbean, and the Pacific represent administrative extensions of territorial states, mostly West European. Although the high seas and outer space do not belong to any territorial state, the question of where the nonterritorial limits of those seas and outer space begin is a matter of either specific agreements or controversy among the territorial masters of the earth. Within nation-states, internal boundaries determine the extent of administration and political control that are exercised by noncentral units of authority: towns, cities, counties, cantons (in the Swiss terminology), *Länder* (in German), *chous* (in Chinese), regions, provinces, or, in the federal terminology of North and South America and India states—a term that tends to introduce some terminological confusion in many comparative analyses dealing with nations, "States," and their sub-divisions, "states."

The number of territorial corrals into which humankind has split varies with time and according to the various criteria we may choose to use. The United States can be counted as one territorial unit if our criterion is that of a constitutional monopoly to determine the nation's collective defense, taxes and diplomacy. In terms of territorial authority with respect to internal affairs and some external affairs, the United States may be, for some purposes, counted as an aggregate of over fifty units (fifty states, Washington, D.C., Puerto Rico, and several dependencies) or as an aggregate of over 38,000 units of local government—nearly 90,000 if we add the well over 50,000 school and special districts. According to one criterion, Canada is a ten-province territorial state (to which the Northwest and Yukon Territories have to be added); according to another, it is a binational state composed of the two founding peoples, the anglophone and the francophone com-munities. The political organization of the whole world remains primarily based on territorial divisions and subdivisions, which reflect as well as shape territorial interests. "We have our created spaces," noted E. Gordon Ericksen, "as reflections of life styles, sentiments, values held dear."[7] Political parties, even when committed to nonterritorial creeds, are usually organized to reflect or manipulate the interests of territorial electoral districts. Functional interest groups, from labor to chambers of commerce, although formed to promote or defend nonterritorial specific interests, cannot escape the grav-itational pull of territoriality: the interest groups are bound to be organized into local cells or chapters. Dividing and subdividing the world according to the territorial principle seems inescapable. The process may have begun with the first delineation of boundaries between two clusters of inhabited caves and their respective hunting reservations. As political animals, humans seem to be inevitably also territorial ones.

How and why do people identify, rationally or emotionally or both, with a given territory and its values and goals? Several explanations will be suggested. Although they will be discussed separately, it should be kept in mind that they are intimately interconnected, each conditioning, causing, or reinforcing the other.

Duty and Habit to Obey

Humans often identify with a territory and with each other because they *must.* A territorial authority that asks for and enforces obedience within its boundaries is sometimes based on both past and present consensus, at other times, it is based on the results of a successful coup d'etat or conquest. In either case, "the existence of a political boundary is itself a major contribution to a sense of solidarity. . . . Among the most important experiences that can unite a group is that they share the same unit of government."[8] This unity clearly exists when the authority represents a territorial consensus. The point is that a certain degree of solidarity—a solidarity based on collaboration due to fear—may also result when the unit of government has been artificially or forcibly imposed, is intensely disliked, but within its boundaries must be obeyed.

Usually only an activist minority chooses to oppose an illegitimate government or to emigrate. In the latter case, the people who choose exile place themselves under a different territorial authority whose goals and methods they deem preferable. In order to physically survive, the majority may not see any rational choice other than to address its demands for order, services, and means of survival to the administrative authority—thus cooperating with it—which, however artificial, illegitimate, and therefore resented it may be, is in charge of territorial tranquillity and welfare.

Survival and Submission

Such a dilemma between resistance against insuperable odds (and possible death) and partial collaboration with the illegitimate territorial authority (and life) was met by the majority of the French after the defeat of their armed forces by Nazi Germany in June 1940. (A similar dilemma confronted the Hungarians in 1956 and the Czechoslovaks in 1968 following the Soviet invasion and occupation of their respective national territories.) The French national territory was divided into two zones to suit the defense and security requirements of the occupying Nazi forces. Northern France was administered by the German military government which was also in charge of Paris and the French Atlantic coast. Southern France and central France were administered by a French puppet government in Vichy presided over by Marshal Henri Philippe Pétain. Some French went into exile and formed the Free French movement under General Charles de Gaulle; others formed an underground resistance movement that operated behind the German lines and disregarded the Nazi-imposed territorial boundaries. A few actively collaborated with the territorial authorities and their concept of a divided France.

The majority of the French considered the imposed and entirely artificial division of their country a temporary arrangement pending the victory of the Allied or the Axis Forces. But having chosen to live as best or as honorably as they could under the circumstances, they had to obey the territorial authorities and even respect the new territorial boundaries. From those authorities, and only from them, were the French able to obtain their food rations, work permits, and permission to travel between the two zones of divided France.

This entirely artificial division of France, imposed by a superior force as a temporary measure, was of such short duration that no real habit or significant vested interests in the division had time to develop. But had the German Third Reich lasted for 1,000 years (as Hitler had predicted), it is conceivable that the initial reluctant acceptance of the temporary division would have been transformed into an unenthusiastic habit—tempered, of course, with the hope that in the future some external events or the decay of the ruling authority would restore French territorial unity.

A "Psychocide"?

Similarly, over 100 million Eastern Europeans have to live and therefore reluctantly accept the Russian military occupation and the related communist rule. There is only a vague hope for a change in the long run (for example, if and when the Russian center of the whole system collapses), but there is also the need to survive in a short run—that is, to live as well as one can, unfree yet enjoying many physical amenities of life. Such a philosophy of consumerism under communism tends, of course, to create a bad conscience of monumental proportions. This bad conscience clearly exists in Czechoslovakia, Hungary, and East Germany, less so in Poland on account of its redeeming Solidarity movement. The "short-run" perspective (one, five, ten generations) is typical for people when their leaders, the masters of the national economy, have the absolute power to determine jobs and welfare for everyone, and therefore life itself. In such a situation, the line between nonopposition and collaboration is a thin one and therefore the cause of many bad consciences. From the survivors of the Holocaust, we know that the people who managed to survive a death camp have not been subsequently free of pangs of conscience.

In modern authoritarian and totalitarian territorial systems (such as the nation-states forming the Soviet socialist bloc), the major levers for commanding mass conformity include not only secret police and political control of all the media but, even more important, total control over the territorial economy. The last gives a regime absolute power to withdraw employment from adults and education from children. In contrast to old-fashioned dictatorship which relied mostly on police repression, a modern garrison/welfare state can and does make an individual absolutely dependent on absolute political power since the state has a total monopoly over jobs.

Usually only a very small minority of the people chooses to emigrate abroad or to oppose the system by emigrating internally into the penumbra of a few harassed dissenters. The absolute majority of the inhabitants of authoritarian socialist or fascist countries is not composed of Joans of Arc or Andrei Sakharovs; neither do these people emigrate abroad, nor do they rebel. They choose to live as best and as honorably as their concern for their employment and for their children's future permits, but by choosing optimal survival within the totalitarian framework, one cannot avoid collaboration with, and occasionally even publicly manifest one's approval of the system, since visible or audible signs of conformity may be required for promotion. As Mussolini used to say, "Everything through the State, nothing outside the State, everything for the State."

A commitment to control one's own life, and therefore a commitment to the "life-giving" regime, necessarily lead to various degrees of pangs of conscience, for example, a feeling of guilt for having acquired a better apartment, a weekend cottage, or a better education for one's children by either pretense or cooperation. The final result may be called a "psychocide" (soul assassination) of relatively well-fed humans. Hannah Arendt once called the huge proportion of such an organized guilt in modern totalitarian systems "universal complicity" because it helps to hold the system together. Cynicism for the purpose of cleansing one's soul may prove less easy to espouse than an outsider may surmise. In Arendt's perceptive words:

> There are very few people who have the strength of character to remain "cynical" enough to keep their personalities intact. And even people who did not comply at all but only lived in the country that happened to be totalitarian are trapped in universal complicity. As Karl Jaspers said in 1945: "Our guilt is that we are still alive." This is not a sentimental exaggeration, but a precise description of the situation as it really is. . . . One must eat, and in modern societies one must work to eat, and in totalitarian societies *working is a political act.*[9]

Homogeneous Nations Subdivided by External Forces

After World War II, the following four nations were forcibly divided into communist and non communist sectors by external powers and interests: Germany (West Germany and East Germany plus the West Berlin enclave); Korea (North Korea and South Korea), China (mainland China and Taiwan), and Vietnam (North Vietnam and South Vietnam). While divided Austria was reunited and neutralized by diplomacy in 1955, Vietnam's reunification in 1975 was the result of a costly war. The continuing divisions of Germany, Korea, and China remain, imposed and maintained by the balancing needs of great powers. Despite the artificiality of the framework, an emergence of real and separate territorial identities is no longer beyond imagination, even though all concerned insist that the divisions are temporary. If the divisions last for several generations, the externally imposed divisions may harden into general acceptance. It would not be the first time in history that the temporary became permanent.

It is quite conceivable that the German language and culture, from Goethe to Heine, will remain common, not only to Austria and a portion of Switzerland, but also to the two, otherwise quite distinct, German states, eastern and western. Some aspects of the German language, however, may in the long run differ in the two German states. Even today, one would look in vain in the new official East German dictionary for the old German term *armenhaus* ("poorhouse") since under socialism there is allegedly no poverty and no capitalist charitable institutions to take care of it; nor does one find in the official West German dictionary terms, current in East Germany that are derived from Marxist-Leninist phraseology. On the other hand, the intrusion of modern "Americanisms" into West German usage is quite significant.

Other examples of a political superimposition of new boundaries upon formerly unified territories can be found in Canada, the United States, and

Latin America where geometrically straight lines across prairies, pampas, forests, and jungles are now often viewed by the inhabitants as being "natural" boundaries. In a study of the modern ramifications of this phenomenon, Sharon O'Brien cited the example of the Blackfoot Indians' surprise at the effect of the U.S.-Canadian border (which cut across the Blackfoot territory):

> Again and again Blackfeet warriors fleeing northward after a raiding attack watched with growing amazement as the pursuing troops of the United States Army came to a sudden, almost magical stop. Again and again, fleeing southward, they saw the same thing happen as the Canadian Mounties reined to an abrupt halt. The tribes of the Blackfeet Confederacy living along what is now the United States-Canadian border came to refer to that potent but invisible demarcation as the "Medicine Line." It seemed to them a supernatural manifestation . . . nearly impossible to comprehend: Man did not divide a land, rather, rivers and mountains interrupted the land's unity.[10]

Heterogeneous Societies Forced into Unity

In contrast to the subdivision of homogeneous nations, there are instances in which unity has been imposed on heterogeneity. One major example of such an imposition is the continent of Africa, where territorial units have been created without much regard for such factors as linguistic, tribal, or geographic boundaries. When the British, French, Spanish, Italian, Portuguese, German, and Belgian states were in the process of establishing their colonial empires in Africa, they subdivided the whole continent arbitrarily among themselves, usually proceeding from the coast into the interior, and in doing so they cut across all traditional boundaries. Africa was divided in such a way as to translate the European balance of power into African territorial terms. The resulting units, created to accommodate the competing colonial powers, were administered as territorial units by colonial officers and eventually these units began to be viewed as homogeneous polities to be liberated by the revolutionary elites. The administrative centers of colonial oppression were to become the capitals of the liberated territorial nation-states.

Although the African and Asian independence movements have been conducted in the name of national self-determination often understood in its ethnic or linguistic sense, they have been, "in fact, demands for political independence not in accord with ethnic distributions, but along the essentially happenstance borders that delimited either the sovereignty or the administrative zones of the former colonial powers."[11] Territories that initially were artificial creations are now in the painful, not always successful, process of becoming nation-states in the European sense of the word.

Even though, at least at the outset, awareness of the national territorial identity of countries such as Gambia, Nigeria, or Tanzania might have been limited to a thin top layer of the ruling elites, it is conceivable that in due time, the territorial authority in each of these countries, based on the glory of liberation and on the power to coerce will be able to transform the habit of obeying into positive, rational (as well as emotional) support. The problem of creating a community—that is, an aggregate of "people who have learned to communicate with each other and to understand each other well beyond the mere interchange of goods and services"[12]—has been called the primary crisis of developing nation-states, their identity crisis. It requires time before the people of a new state recognize their territory as a true homeland and before they feel "as individuals that their own personal identities are in part defined by their territorially delimited country. In most of the new states traditional forms of identity [some nonterritorial] ranging from tribe to ethnic and linguistic groups compete with the sense of larger national identity."[13]

The conflict between the European imposed territorial division and the African-desired fragmentation was well-described by the Nigerian statesman S. O. Adebo, chief of the Yoruba tribe, whose one portion is also in the neighboring state of Dahomey. In a lecture presented in New York, Adebo stated:

> It is fashionable to lay the responsibility for Africa's fragmentation at the door of the European politicians who in 1885 partitioned the bulk of the continent into national shares for their respective countries. That that act was reprehensible there can of course be no question. But considering Africa as it was before that partitioning, and Africa as it has developed at and since independence, supposing it had been left to its own resources and there had been no Treaty of Berlin, would the continent have been less divided today than it actually is? I wonder. . . . Certainly in British West Africa there were fewer independent units at the end of colonialism than at its beginning. . . . What I know of the African colonies of the other European powers makes me feel able to submit, without an intention to excuse the fact of colonization, that if it had not happened, there might in fact be more rather than fewer separate countries in Africa today.[14]

As Figure 1.1 shows, Nigeria is a good example of a long-term process by which that what initially was artificial (a British unity), may in due time become either natural or at least a fervently desired goal for the ruling elites. In 1900, the British divided Nigeria into two protectorates and one colony, and in 1914, they imposed a unitary administration on the whole territory. In 1939, however, the British again decentralized their colonial rule by subdividing Nigeria into three administrative regions. Post colonial Nigeria (independent as of October 1, 1960) maintained the British tripartite formula, with minor alteration in 1963, while searching for a more flexible federal formula which would correspond to Nigeria's tribal, linguistic, and religious heterogeneity (there are over 250 different tribes in Nigeria, with the Hausas in the north, the Yorubas in the west, and Ibos in the east—these three being the largest). One of Nigeria's statesmen, Obafemi Awolowo (writing then in prison) argued for a federal formula according to which no one or two states should be so large in size and population as to be able to overrule the other states and bend the will of the federal government

Figure 1.1

Nigeria: Unification by Subdivision

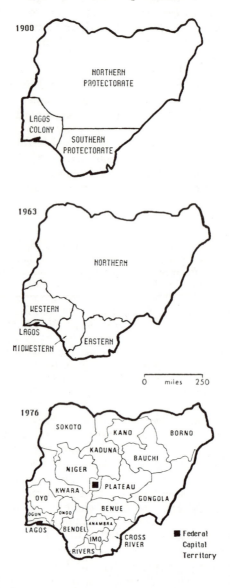

1900– Two protectorates and one colony under British rule.

1963 – Five units in independent Nigeria.

1976 – Nineteen states and a capital territory in federal Nigeria.

to their own, and no state should be so small as to be unable to maintain its independence within the sphere of functions allotted to it. At the end of his book Awolowo then concluded, "Our objectives are now clear and unmistakable: federalism, democracy, good leadership, socialism—these four. But the most urgent of them is—federalism."[15] In 1967, Nigeria was divided into 12 states and in 1976 into 19 states; instead of Lagos on the coast, a new capital city of Abuja was created in the heart of the country and formally opened in 1982. Nigeria's international boundaries underwent some changes with respect to neighboring Cameroon.

Artificial Units of Self-Rule
Created by Central Authority

Territorial units of self-rule may also be created by a central authority, not in response to corresponding territorial pressures, but in order to satisfy the administrative needs of the central authority. In these cases, too, habit and acceptance may follow the initial arbitrariness and result in the growth of a genuine territorial identity.

The history of modern France may serve as a good example of this phenomenon. Feudal and royal France was a composite of more or less self-administered provinces such as Burgundy, Normandy, Anjou, Poitou, Provence, and Brittany, and during the French Revolution, there was a strong awareness of provincial identity. In order to build the French nation so that it would coincide with the boundaries of the French territorial state and in order to eliminate provincial patriotism, first the Jacobins and then their heir, Napoleon, decided to replace the original revolutionary hope for decentralization and participatory democracy (a natural reaction against the former royal centralism) with a new, tight centralization of all power in Paris. Local implementation of national policies and programs was delegated from the center to eighty-three (later ninety-five) carefully supervised units of local authority called *départements*.[16] The *départements* were superimposed on the pre-existing provinces of feudal and royal France.

One of the purposes of the *départements* was to eliminate the former territorial loyalties and the provincial patriotism that could conceivably conflict with the French national interest.[17] The *départements* were small enough to permit their inhabitants to reach the seat of the higher territorial authority (that is, higher than the mayor of a city or a commune), attend to their affairs, and return home (presumably after a five-course luncheon in the restaurant of a *chef-lieu*, the seat of the prefecture) all in one day. Each *département* was presided over by a prefect, an experienced civil servant appointed by and responsible to the central authorities in Paris for ensuring the predominance of national policies over narrow parochial interests, budgetary irresponsibility, and where warranted, centrifugal tendencies. By raising the walls of sovereignty and national consciousness with regard to neighboring nations while breaking down the former provincial loyalties and interests, France became a relatively homogeneous nation; the side effect was a near end of local participation, responsibility, and self rule.[18]

With the advent of national economic planning and rapid transportation, the Napeolonic division of France into excessively small *départements* proved less useful and practical than before. In 1966, under General de Gaulle, a new administrative reform (again from the top down rather than in response to local grievances voiced from the bottom up) was enacted. Its purpose was to regroup the Napoleonic *départements* into much larger Gaullist *régions* for the purpose of better planning and administration. In the 1980s, under the Socialist President François Mitterrand, these *régions* were to be given a more significant degree of territorial autonomy—a quasi-federal democratic evolution, which was bound to evoke some separatist tendencies (in Corsica, for example) and conflict with the socialist concept of centralized national planning coupled with state ownership of key industries and enterprises.

The half-implemented reform of the borders and autonomy of noncentral governments in France well illustrates the phenomenon of both the artificiality and the *naturalness* of any territorial delineation when it is permitted or ordered to last. The new administrative *régions* in France, grouping from three to five *départements* into one unit, are now being criticized mostly on the grounds that they destroy an arrangement that had over 150 years become natural—although originally quite artificial. The *départements* had indeed become units that reflected not only the geographic limits of local administration but also the corresponding economic activities, transportation networks radiating from the *départemental* "capital," and a modest degree of vested interests. (For more about decentralization in centralist France, see Chapter 3.)

The United States offers a different, yet related, example of a transformation of arbitrarily delineated territories into bases of vested interests and loyalty. The original thirteen colonies grew into the present union of fifty states by successive additions of territories that were later broken into states. Most people who moved into the frontier territories did so *after* their nominal identities had been established, while they were still almost empty, so the boundaries of states could be drawn geometrically without much regard to natural or economic realities. Morton Grodzins, who called these boundaries "the worst inanities," added, however, the following: "The strong constitutional position of the states—for example, the assignment of two senators to each state, the role given the states in administering even national elections, and the relatively few limitations on their law making powers—[establishes] the geographical units as natural centers of administrative and political strength."[19]

The artificial boundaries of North Dakota and South Dakota are often used as a good example of the transformation of a synthetic creation into a natural one. Although it is indeed doubtful "that the two Dakotas warranted the dignity of separate statehood at the time of their entry into the union . . . who can deny now that, having lived as states for a number of years, they would look with disfavor upon any proposal to deprive them of their individuality by merging them into one?"[20]

Satisfactory Performance and Consent

People usually support, and identify with, persons and institutions that largely satisfy their fundamental demands for identity, internal order, external security, progress, welfare, and culture. Gratitude for benefits received and expectation of more to come constitute the foundations of political loyalty. Hans Kohn defined nationalism as the state of mind in which the supreme loyalty of the individual is due the territorial state that is recognized as the ideal form of political organization.[21] This nationalism may be viewed as a result of two interacting factors: the binding rules that come from the authority (and that people have the duty and the habit to obey) and supports that come from the people (that are based on their satisfaction with authority's performance). The same combination of authority's and people's supports also accounts for patriotism on a subnational level (that is, provincial or local awareness of separate territorial identity). Graphically, the political two-way traffic may be expressed as shown in the diagram in Figure 1.2, which uses David Easton's simplified model of a political system to depict *inputs* (supports and demands), which are addressed by citizens, parties, interest groups, and media to the political system, and *outputs* (policies and actions). By means of feedback loops, the outputs shape both supports and demands by either satisfying or suppressing them, the latter by instilling fear and compliance by means of economic, social or police terror.

Emotional identification with the territorial authority—be it a monarch or an abstraction such as a province, canton, nation or state—has often had an artificial beginning. Authority and the duty and habit to abide by its rules often come first; later, in response to the authority's satisfactory performance, rational and emotional consent follow. When the 1648 Peace of Westphalia pacified Europe by breaking it into hundreds of dynastic territorial states (which replaced the previous fundamental division of Europe between the Catholics and the Protestants), people were not consulted as to their territorial preferences. They began, however to identify with the new authorities, partly because they had no other choice, and partly because these authorities gave them what they desired (that is, internal order and external security) after they had suffered and bled for many decades under the blows of the intra-European religious strife.

Understandably, the initial identification with the territorial authority centered around the sovereign ruler and his or her court and administration; later, the inhabitants of a royal or princely territory proved able to transfer their allegiance and loyalty from their sovereign to the institutions and symbols of the territory. After Louis XVI was beheaded, the majority of the French began to identify with his abstract successor, the French Republic (*la France*). In the process of reidentification, the new abstraction was endowed with familiar human features. The symbol of the French Republic,

Figure 1.2

Supports and Governmental Performance

A Two-Way Traffic

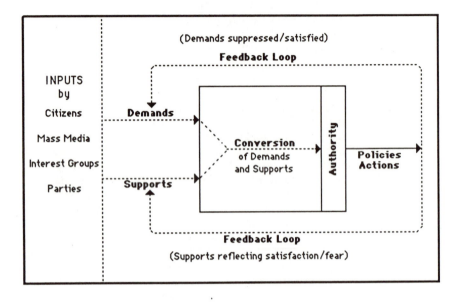

Based on Easton's "Simplified Model of a Political System," contained in David Easton, A System Analysis of Political Life (New York: Wiley, 1965), p.32.

as we find it on the French stamps or in the form of busts displayed in many town halls, is now a young woman, Marianne, with the revolutionary Phrygian cap on her head. The national territory—land—is combined in many languages with mother or father images (motherland, fatherland).

Territorial Indoctrination

People become attached rationally and emotionally to their territory, its way of life, its institutions, and its culture by a complex process that, in the present context, one may call *territorial socialization*, a term that emphasizes the geographic aspect of the general process of political socialization.[22] From a tender age, humans learn about values and goals, political authority and political culture, folk arts and entertainment, the existence of rewards and punishments, as well as the existence of geographic boundaries between their own territory and the external, alien world. The schoolroom maps that divide the world into colored shapes that are identified as nations are an important part of what is called territorial socialization.[23]

Political socialization, by which information about and values and feelings toward the territorial community are transmitted, is so gradual and often so imperceptible that some aspects of it seem latent. In contrast, there is also a manifest indoctrination that addresses itself to people's reason and heart openly and that does not conceal its aim to create territorial human beings.

All territorial authorities engage in verbal, visual, and symbolic propaganda to make identity with the territory separate from that with the rest of the world. From cradle to grave, a continuous display and manipulation of territorial symbols—flags, flowers, trees, birds, uniforms, emblems, slogans, and anthems—are meant to enhance local pride (and prejudice) and a sense of belonging forever to a given territory, be it a nation-state, a province, or a city.

Not only have all nation-states officially proclaimed their territorial mottoes, anthems, flags, and animal symbols—the last usually ferocious ones such as lions, panthers, tigers or eagles (see Figure 1.3)—but their subnational divisions—provinces, cantons, states, regions, and cities—have their territorial symbols too. The official songs (Nevada's state song, for example, sounds very territorial—"Home Means Nevada"), flags, and floral or animal symbols (the latter usually tame) are all meant to express a particular territorial identity.

The fiftieth state, Hawaii, for example, adopted "Hawaii Ponoi" as its state song, Life is Perpetuated in Righteousness as its state motto, the hibiscus as its state flower, the nene (Hawaiian goose) as its state bird, and the kukui (candlenut) as its state tree. Nebraska has passed legislation to make the mammoth the state fossil, and Ohio's seeming predilection for the color red (with apparently no political implication) is reflected in the state insect (ladybug), state flower (scarlet carnation), state bird (cardinal), and even state drink (tomato juice since 1965). In the 1950s, the states of Vermont and New York mildly disputed whether the state tree of Vermont, the sugar maple, could or could not also be adopted as a state symbol by New York. (It was.) The reason for the dispute, however, was eminently practical because New York's aim was to promote the sale of its maple syrup in competition with Vermont.

It is a familiar practice to enhance a positive identification with one's own territorial community by inducing hostile emotions and attitudes toward some or all outside groups. Feuds among regional and ethnic groups within nation-states often parallel in intense hatred those among nation-states. In biethnic or polyethnic states, an intramural hatred may be fanned into an all-devouring fire if the component units of such states are or have been made aware of their intimate links with blood relatives abroad who administer their own territorial states. International enmity between nation-states is thus transferred to the domestic scene; and domestic tensions, in turn, contaminate the international arena.

Figure 1.3. Territorial-National Emblems: Eagles, Lions, Panthers, and Tigers

INDIA

POLAND

SPAIN

U.S.A.

SRI LANKA
(formerly Ceylon)

KENYA

BULGARIA

SOMALIA

AUSTRIA

Source: Ivo D. Duchacek, *Power Maps: Comparative Politics of Constitutions* (Santa Barbara, Calif.: ABC-Clio, 1973).

Examples of such reciprocal contagion are numerous: the German minorities in Eastern Europe before World War II, the Chinese minorities in Southeast Asia, the Arabs in Israel, and the Turks and Greeks on Cyprus. Within the biethnic state of Cyprus, for instance, people are taught (indoctrinated) from childhood to extol the glory of their community and to debase the history and characteristics of the other national group. In the 1960s, a text for Greek sixth-graders described the Turkish massacre of the Greeks on Easter Sunday in 1821 as follows: "Turks with madness depicted on their faces seized, tortured, and hanged the patriarch and left his remains hanging for three days." Throughout the Greek texts, the Turks are depicted as "barbarians," "heathens," "ignorant," "avaricious," "mad," and "merciless." On the other hand, the Turkish textbooks extol the Ottoman Empire. A history text for Turkish sixth-graders concludes: "Our ancestors never attacked others unless they themselves had met with wrong and aggression. The sole reason why they won great wars was because they had right on their side."

Indoctrination by means of history textbooks is not, of course, a Greek or Turkish specialty. All communities engage in it. A recent study of biases in the U.S. and English textbooks showed that authors

> write unabashedly as Americans or Englishmen, standing squarely with feet planted in Boston or Washington or London. The result is distortion, often subconscious, but nonetheless dangerous. . . . Readers emerge from such accounts with the impression that the patriots (itself a biased word) lost only the Battle of Bunker Hill, and that because they ran out of powder. English writers dwell with equal affection on the triumphs of their generals, leaving the student bewildered that such a series of victories could have lost a war. . . . Not a single junior high school textbook used in the United States fails to describe the burning of Washington by the British troops during the war, and not one tells of the American burning of the Canadian city of York [Toronto] that led to England's retaliation.[24]

Commenting on the task of transforming immigrant children into patriotic citizens, a school superintendent in the United States described how the children "catch the school spirit. . . . American heroes become their own, American history wins their loyalty, the Stars and Stripes, always before their eyes in the school room, receives their daily salute."[25]

Thus, through indoctrination and direct experience, people acquire a set of perceptions about and attitudes toward their territorial community and its values; the territory and its ways become familiar, comforting, and personal. In contrast, the rest of the world seems distant, exotic, and potentially hostile. The world is physically and psychologically walled off by boundaries, passports, visas, often unintelligible scripts and languages, and unfamiliar currency—"ugly Americans" abroad, inquiring about the price of displayed goods are sometimes heard to ask, What is it in *real* money? Real for them is only what has been previously experienced in life, however parochial such a life may have been. Schools, siblings, parents,

work groups, clubs, professional voluntary associations, and political movements all contribute to the never-ending process of territorial socialization.

Information about and feelings toward the territory and its political and
nonpolitical cultures that have been acquired and accepted may subsequently
be unlearned and rejected. An early attachment to a territorial community
and its values may later be replaced by a total rejection and identification
with, or even immigration to, an alien country; one then attempts to make
the alien country one's own by a new, partly self-socialization process.
Although such cases are frequent, the early conditioning (with modification)
in one's native country usually lasts a lifetime and remains very intensive.

A succinct but tragic example of an unsuccessful search for identification
with a new community is a statement made by Sirhan Bishara Sirhan, the
assassin of Robert F. Kennedy. During Sirhan's trial in Los Angeles (March
4, 1969) he spoke about his unassimilated life in the United States:

> I was sick and tired of being a foreigner, of being alone. I wanted a *place*
> of my own, where they speak my own language, where they eat my own
> food, share my own politics. I wanted to have something I could identify
> with as a Palestinian and an Arab. I wanted my own *country*, my own *city*,
> my own business. I wanted my own everything, sir.[26]

In the array of territorial values, absorbed through the process of socialization,
the territory itself—the spatial area—appears as an important element by
itself because of its assumed durability. Willa Cather spoke of the universal
human yearning for something permanent, enduring, without shadow of
change; a slice of the surface of our planet indeed seems so much more
permanent than everything else; people, institutions, beliefs, values, and
laws change, but the territory undergoes changes that are perceptible only
to geologists studying millennia of evolution. In defining a nation, Abraham
Lincoln identified its main ingredients—its territory, its people, and its
laws—and then added, "The territory is the only part which is of certain
durability."[27] An area, of course, may be perforated and infiltrated, lost,
divided, or conquered, and now, there is also the possibility that it could
be transformed into a heap of radioactive dust. Yet, by comparison, everything
else is even more perishable.

Instinct

Ethologists stress that instinct is a possible explanation of the observable
drive of humans to possess, defend, and politically organize a delineated
geographic area.[28] The ethologists argue that possession of, and identification
with, a territory are prerequisites for the fulfillment of people's basic needs
such as security (as opposed to anxiety), stimulation by border quarrels (as
opposed to boredom), and above all, identity (as opposed to anonymity).
Robert Ardrey expressed the concept of personal identity derived from
territorial identity as follows:

Figure 1.4. Territorial Imperative?

Source: Drawing by W. Steig; copyright 1973 by The New Yorker Magazine, Inc. Reprinted by permission.

"This place is mine; I am of this place," says the albatross, the patas monkey, the green sunfish, the Spaniard, the great horned owl, the wolf, the Venetian, the prairie dog, the three-spined stickleback, the Scotsman, the skua, the man from La Crosse, Wisconsin, the Alsatian, the little-ringed plover, the Argentine, the lungfish, the Chinook salmon, the Parisian. I am of this place which is different from and superior to all other places of earth and I partake of its identity so that I too am both different and superior, and it is something that you cannot take away from me despite all afflictions which I may suffer or where I may go and where I may die. I shall remain always and uniquely of this place.[29]

Accordingly, the ethologists maintain that all the following result from people's innate (genetically determined) behavior: chasing trespassers from private property, defending one's province against the national central authority, and defending one's nation against an external threat. Local patriotism and nationalism are viewed as nothing more and nothing less than the human expression of the animal drive to territory. Indeed, Ardrey's book *The Territorial Imperative* has the subtitle, *A Personal Inquiry into the Animal Origins of Property and Nations.*

It seems debatable, however, whether human instincts play a more decisive role than the duty and habit to obey and the concomitant territorial indoctrination. The instinctive theory of territoriality cannot explain human rationality and ambitions that may result in either giving up one's own territory or, on the contrary, acquiring more of it than one needs. As one can know from Ardrey and from his or her own gardens, a territorial bird par excellence, the wren, never needs more than two and a half acres for its family; unlike humans, wrens need neither less nor more. In contrast, many national leaders have often conquered territories that are unnecessary for their people's survival. Conquests have been often undertaken in order to fulfill some messianic dream, to realize some ideological goal, or to obtain absolute security, that is, a world in which all actual or potential rivals would be destroyed—e.g., a world absolutely safe for democracy, communism, or Islam.

But leaders can also give up a good portion of national territory in order to attain some ideological objective. In 1918, for example, at Brest Litovsk, Lenin signed a humiliating peace treaty with imperial Germany. He had reached the conclusion that the preservation of a territorial basis, however limited (a major portion of the national territory and its important resources was surrendered to the Germans), was more important for the future of communism than the whole of the Ukraine and Russia's western provinces. Animals apparently do not reason in such a fashion; they can only be forcibly deprived of their territory and transferred to a cage.

When Ardrey compared the territorial nationalism of men with animal territorial urges (which are not so general; our closest relatives, gorillas and chimpanzees, do not defend territories), he added that nationalism differs from the social territoriality of the primates only by the degree of man's capacity to form coalitions, and I would add, and federations; this is an important qualification. Unlike the lion, the lungfish, or the little-ringed plover, who do not seem to have any rational choice in the matter, human groups may select either to establish or to not establish broader territorial coalitions such as alliances, confederations, common markets, federal unions, and transborder regionalism—each based on an agreement to engage in a new, cooperative territorial venture. A federal state represents an aggregate and a coalition of several territorial communities and institutions, and unlike animals, territorial communities can either close or open their boundaries to let foreign persons or products in.

It may be concluded that in contrast with territorial animals, humans are both worse off and better off than the primates with respect to territorial behavior. This situation exists because people's instincts have to compete not only with their capacity to reason, which is good, but also with their irrationality and complex ambitions, which is often quite bad.

Language and Territoriality

Unlike most animals, humans learn complex patterns of social behavior by means of verbal communication, and the language barrier usually either creates or raises the walls separating territorial states to considerable heights. The reality of territorial identity is then obvious at the first sound, even though political and linguistic boundaries often overlap.

On the other hand, many territorial communities lack the additional dimension of a separate territorial language.

> Linguistic choices . . . affect frontiers during key moments in the history of the rise of ethnic and national grouping . . . the decisions taken at that time . . . determine basic institutions, frontiers, patterns of access, political culture, and ideologies for centuries. . . . Political elites take the language fashioned by their cultural allies and make it a banner of challenge.[30]

Examples include the United States and all the English-speaking members of the Commonwealth; West Germany, East Germany, Austria, and a portion of Switzerland; France and portions of Belgium, Canada, Switzerland, and the Caribbean; and Spain, Portugal, and Latin America. But in many other parts of the world, the territorial boundaries coincide with the linguistic ones, and the language then appears to be only one of the most important ingredients in one's awareness of territorial identity, but also the most effective instrument of territorial socialization and the most treasured heritage of the common past. Often, after a long sojourn abroad, hearing one's native tongue again—or hearing the home accent again after being in another territory that shares the same language—gives one a high degree of personal gratification and an upsurge of emotional identification with the culture, way of life, and history of one's own nation. After reading Boris Pasternak's *Doctor Zhivago* in the original, the Russian-educated daughter of a Georgian father, Stalin, Svetlana Alliluyeva who had defected from Russia, wrote in the *Atlantic Monthly*, "This encounter with the Russian tongue at its most powerful went through me like a shock, like a surge of electricity."[31] Svetlana with her American born daughter, redefected back to Russia in 1984 but returned to the United States in 1986.

Within nation-states, territorial "linguism" may prove one of the most disruptive and centrifugal forces leading to demands of complete separation. In India, for instance, territorial and linguistic differences were submerged for centuries under the unifying lid of the common Hindu culture. This was the period of dominantly face-to-face relations; the problem of what language or languages to use in the mass media had not yet arisen. Furthermore, the common struggle against British rule added another unifying element to Indian nationalism. Today, the situation is different. Secularism has weakened the religious Hindu bonds, and the unifying enmity against the British has been only partly replaced by a common fear of China and a common anger directed toward Pakistan.

The national struggle against illiteracy has increased the role of the local schools; furthermore, local vernaculars have become important instruments of political communication and participation on a local level and in the assertion of local and regional interests vis-à-vis the federal central authority in New Delhi. It has become almost irresistible for a local politician, the product of postliberation education in a locally written language, not to utilize linguistic territorialism in his or her struggle for power and status. Writing with noticeable melancholy, a former nationalist delegate to two round table conferences in 1926 and 1932 defined Indian linguism as "a claim that Indians speaking the same language should have a state: *one language, one state.*" (Italics in original) He added, "Linguism has come to occupy the center of the stage. . . . The fissiparous linguistic communalism of today, when there is no British overlord to stoke it, is somewhat disillusioning to the ardent Indian nationalist."[32]

There are 845 languages and dialects in India, 14 of which, in addition to English, are recognized by the Indian Constitution (Eighth Schedule) as major and official.

The Linguistic Provinces Commission, appointed by the Indian Constituent Assembly in 1948, reported with melancholy: "Some of the ablest men in the country came before us and confidently and emphatically stated that language in this country stood for and represented culture, race, history, individuality, and finally sub-nation. . . . We were simply horrified to see how thin was the ice upon which we were skating."[33]

With respect to its francophone citizens, Canada faces two distinct problems. The first, quite acute, problem is that of Québec Province as to identity and political goals are based not only on the French language and culture but also on a compact and an economically viable territory.[34] The second problem is that of the "nonterritorial" francophones who live in either dominantly anglophone provinces (Ontario and Manitoba) or in bilingual New Brunswick. (For more about Québec, see Chapter 10.)

Many European scholars tend to discuss and analyze nationalism dominantly in terms of linguistic differences, but the situation is different on the North and South American continents. There, political antagonisms, distance, and the resulting different development over 200 years gave birth to well over twenty different nations, from anglophone Canada and the United States to Brazil and Argentina. Each of these now independent and nationalistic units initially shared the same language and culture with their respective homelands, despite their common cultural heritages, whether Shakespeare or Cervantes, highly self-defined territorial-political communities have developed in North, South, and Caribbean Americas.

Territoriality[n]

One factor can raise the intensity of territorial awareness to the nth power (to use mathematical terminology): contact with an alien group, especially if it is a hostile one. In his classic study of international law and relations, Charles de Visscher, a former justice of the International Court of Justice, wrote: "It is in contact with the world outside that any social group differentiates and becomes conscious itself. . . . Only against the stranger does [group] solidarity fully assert itself. National solidarities have triumphed over internal tensions, even the most deep-rooted such as between class and class."[35] Similarly, the Indian nationalist leader, Jawaharlal Nehru defined nationalism as an antifeeling, one that feeds and fattens on hatred and anger against other national groups.

Like two men who, when engaged in a street fight, readily gang up against a policeman or a would-be arbiter and, following the removal of the outsider, either make peace or resume fighting, groups and individuals are often able to discover harmony only when they become aware of a common external danger whether it originates in an external groups or in nature. External threat has often proved capable of subsuming internal concerns, however normally divisive they may be, into one overriding interest in the preservation of the community. According to one depressing, but nonetheless truthful, comment on human nature, "The brotherhood of man finds much of its working expression within the nation, though its other face is hostility to those outside."[36]

In his *Principles of Ethics*, Herbert Spencer described how tribal as well as civilized societies constantly carry on external self-defense and internal cooperation and amity. The phrase, "an amiable xenophobic whole," coined by Robert Ardrey with reference to his observation of rhesus monkeys and their instinctive tendency to establish proper hostility to neighboring groups, largely applies to human territorial group behavior. Somewhat facetiously, Ardrey expressed the amity-enmity relationship in a mathematical formula, $A = E + h$, in which amity (A) is equal to the sum of the forces of enmity (E) that originate in humans plus the forces of hazard (h, natural and supernatural dangers).[37]

It would, however, be wrong to imply a monolithic response of a community to an external threat. The exact meaning of the collective interest to be protected may be a matter of controversy. Should the people sacrifice their lives for the protection of their territorial integrity or should the people sacrifice their territorial integrity for the protection of their lives? There may also be controversy as to the method of protection of territorial values, ranging from capitulation to nuclear retaliation. Furthermore, individuals and groups may disagree as to their perceptions and estimates of the gravity and imminence of an external menace.

Subnational and Supranational Loyalties

In addition, not all external threats are or are perceived as being aimed at the territorial nation as a whole. Within the nation-state individuals and groups are simultaneously members of various subnational communities, some of which may have intimate links with related groups or governments abroad. The interests and goals of different communities within the boundaries of a nation-state sometimes complement and reinforce each other, but often they are in conflict.

Competition or conflict between the various identifications and allegiances within the territorial state itself is both natural and inevitable because a nation-state is in itself a composite of many competing, functional, and geographically delineated interest groups, ranging from a street block or hamlet to districts, counties, cities, and provinces. A strong emotional identification with a subnational community, such as a province, frequently contains a secessionist potential. When viewed from the national or imperial center, a revolutionary "local-patriotic" quest for territorial self-determination often appears to be parochial localism posing as nationalism. Viewed from the ethnoterritorial perspective it is, simply, nationalism. Neglect or oppression may have endowed what originally was limited local patriotism aiming only at a larger autonomy, with all the explosive ingredients of fierce nationalism.

Serious internal conflicts have always been magnets for external lures or threats. Interference in the domestic affairs of territorial nation-states (see Chapter 8) often consists of offers of paradise to some related groups (ethnic minorities or workers) while promising hell to others. Previous injustices may give subnational groups reason to listen attentively to external promises.

Nevertheless, people's allegiance to other communities abroad is normally less intense and less unconditional than their devotion to their territorial nation-state. A relatively low intensity has so far characterized people's allegiance to supranational communities such as alliances or common markets or to universalistic creeds such as communism, Islam, or Christianity. Sadly, the weakest extraterritorial allegiance of all is people's identification with the abstract notion of the human race and its fragile habitat.

Notes

1. David Harvey, *Social Justice and the City* (Baltimore: Johns Hopkins University Press, 1975), p. 310.

2. Reinhold Niebuhr, "The Myth of World Government," *Nation*, March 16, 1946, p. 314.

3. Kenneth E. Boulding, "National Images and International Systems," *Journal of Conflict Resolution* 3 (1959), p. 123.

4. Peter H. Merkl, "Federalism and Social Structure" (Paper read at the Sixth Congress of the International Political Science Association, Geneva, 1964), p. 7.

5. John H. Herz, "The Territorial State Revisited," *Polity* 1:1 (1968), p. 34.

6. Anthony D. Smith, *Nationalism in the Twentieth Century* (New York: New York University Press, 1979), p. 196. See also Anthony D. Smith, *Theories of Nationalism* (New York: Holmes and Meier, 1983), chap. 7.

7. E. Gordon Ericksen, *The Territorial Experience: Human Ecology as Symbolic Interaction* (Austin: University of Texas Press, 1980), p. 163.

8. Leslie Lipson, *The Great Issues of Politics* (Englewood Cliffs, N.J.: Prentice-Hall, 1965), pp. 288–289.

9. From Hannah Arendt and Ivo D. Duchacek discussion in Carl J. Friedrich (ed.) *Totalitarianism: Proceedings of a Conference Held at the American Academy of Arts and Science*, March 1953 (Cambridge: Harvard University Press, 1954), p. 337 (italics added).

10. Sharon O'Brien, "The Medicine Line: A Border Dividing Tribal Sovereignty, Economies, and Families," *Fordham Law Review* 13:2 (November 1984), p. 315.

11. Walker Connor, "Self-Determination: The New Phase," *World Politics* 20:1 (October 1967), p. 31.

12. Karl W. Deutsch, *National and Social Communication: An Inquiry into the Foundations of Nationality* (Cambridge, Mass.: MIT Press, 1966), p. 91.

13. Lucian W. Pye, *Aspects of Political Development* (Boston: Little, Brown, 1966), p. 63.

14. S. O. Adebo, "Fragmented Africa" (Paper presented at the Ralph Bunche Institute of the City University of New York, May 26, 1969), p. 9.

15. Obafemi Awolowo, *Thoughts on the Nigerian Constitution* (Ibadan: Oxford University Press, 1966), pp. 97, 162.

16. *Départements* represent an intermediate level of authority between the national government in Paris and the local units of self-rule such as communes, municipalities, *arrondissements*, or cantons. I preserve the French spelling and accent aigu to distinguish territorial *départements* from the executive departments in the United States.

17. A French administrative expert, Councillor of State Hervé Detton, noted that the old royal provinces "had not been so fully broken up as some think. They had remained, to say the least, under the surface [*sous-jacentes*]" (author's translation of Hervé Detton, *L'Administration régionale et locale en France* [Paris: Presses Universitaires de France, 1964], p. 14).

18. Detton, *L'Administration*, p. 16 (author's translation): "All that had been marked by confusion in the administration of the Ancien Régime [Royal France] disappeared. But the former royal paternal centralization was replaced by an iron hand. This system of the postrevolutionary Year VIII, which had contributed to give France an internal peace, suffocated all local political initiative. . . . The spirit of the Year VIII still persists. It had been softened to a great extent during the last 150 years; local territorial authorities now have some independence, yet the administrative system of France basically remains the same as it had been organized by Napoleon."

19. Morton Grodzins, "The Federal System," in American Assembly, Columbia University, ed., *Goals for Americans* (Englewood Cliffs, N.J.: Prentice-Hall, 1960), p. 271.

20. William S. Livingston, "A Note on the Nature of Federalism," *Political Science Quarterly* 67:1 (March 1952), p. 95.

21. Hans Kohn, *The Idea of Nationalism: A Study of its Origins and Background* (New York: Macmillan, 1944), p. 16.

22. Compare Herbert Hyman, *Political Socialization* (New York: Free Press, 1959). See also David Easton, *A Systems Analysis of Political Life* (New York: John Wiley, 1965), in particular, pp. 278–343; Gabriel A. Almond and G. Bingham Powell, Jr., *Comparative Politics: A Developmental Approach* (Boston: Little, Brown, 1966), pp. 50–72; and Richard E. Dawson and Kenneth Prewitt, *Political Socialization* (Boston: Little, Brown, 1968), in particular, pp. 143–180 on education and schooling.

23. Boulding, "National Images and International Systems," p. 123.

24. Ray Allen Billington, "History Is a Dangerous Subject," *Saturday Review* (1966), pp. 60–61.

25. Quoted in Robert A. Dahl, *Who Governs?* (New Haven: Yale University Press, 1961), p. 317.

26. *The New York Times*, March 5, 1969.

27. Second Annual Message to Congress, December 1, 1862.

28. Ethology, a study of patterns of animal behavior with possible insights into human behavior, was pioneered by Austria's Konrad Lorenz and Holland's Niko

Tinbergen in the 1930s. A comparative study of animal and human behavior was popularized in the United States by Robert Ardrey in his two books, *The Territorial Imperative: A Personal Inquiry into the Animal Origins of Property and Nations* (New York: Dell Publishing, 1966) and *African Genesis* (New York: Dell Publishing, Laurel edition, 1967).

29. Ardrey, *African Genesis*, p. 178.

30. Brian Weinstein, "Language Strategists: Redefining Political Frontiers on the Basis of Linguistic Choices," *World Politics* 31:3 (April 1979), p. 362. The quote is based on Jiri Neustupny's sociolinguistic studies in which the period of linguistic/territorial choices is called "early modern."

31. Svetlana Alliluyeva, "To Boris Leonidovich Pasternak," *Atlantic Monthly* 219 (1967), p. 133.

32. P. Kodanda Rao, "Communalism in India," *Current History* 33 (February 1956), p. 84.

33. Ibid., p. 84.

34. See Gerard Bergeron and Rejean Pelletier, *L'Etat du Québec en devenir* (Montréal: Boréal Express, 1980); André Bernard, *La politique au Canada et au Québec* (Montréal: Les presses universitaires du Québec, 1980); Jacques Brossard, *L'Accession à la souveraineté et les cas de Québec* (Montréal: Les presses universitaires de Montréal, 1976); Pierre Guillaume et al., *Canada et Canadiens* (Bordeaux: Presses universitaires de Bordeaux, 1984); and William D. Coleman, *The Independence Movement in Québec: 1945-1980* (Toronto: University of Toronto Press, 1984).

35. Charles de Visscher, *Theory and Reality in Public International Law* (Princeton: Princeton University Press, 1957), p. 89.

36. Rupert Emerson, *From Empire to Nation* (Cambridge: Harvard University Press, 1960), p. 108.

37. The first chapter relies on and draws from the first three chapters of Ivo D. Duchacek's *Comparative Federalism: The Territorial Dimension of Politics* (New York: Holt, Rinehart and Winston, 1970; reprint, Washington, D.C.: University Press of America, forthcoming).

2

Universalist Creeds and the
Territorial Gravitational Pull

*In order to build socialism, we must first of all exist. . . . And to assure the
existence [of the Soviet State] compromise, humiliation, and retreat may become
necessary.*

—J. V. Stalin
(Message to the Communist International, 1926)

*Leaders of the Communist Party of the Soviet Union . . . pursued a policy of
great power chauvinism and national egoism toward fraternal Socialist countries
and thus disrupted the unity of the Socialist Camp. . . . The leaders of the
CPSU [Communist Party of the Soviet Union] regard fraternal parties as pawns
on their diplomatic chessboard. . . . They have made a mess of the splendid
Socialist camp.*

—Hongqui
(Red Flag, Beijing, January 1964)

*We observe a permanent seesaw between African unity, which fades quicker
and quicker into the mist of oblivion, and a heartbreaking return to chauvinism
in its most bitter and detestable form. . . . For the mass of the people competition
is represented principally by Africans of another nation. On the Ivory Coast
these competitors are the Dahomans; in Ghana they are Nigerians; in Senegal,
they are the Sudanese.*

—Frantz Fanon
(The Wretched of the Earth, 1968)

*States may be no more than collections of individuals and borders may be mere
facts. But a moral significance is attached to them.*

—Stanley Hoffman
(Duties Beyond Borders, 1981)

Many creeds that evoke sincere devotion on the part of their adherents
are nonterritorial in terms of their assumptions, goals, and promises. Political
ideologies, moral codes, Christianity, and Islam are examples of such
universalistic belief systems. They address their message to all humanity.

When these often idealistic doctrines and their central concepts about human nature and behavior are related to political action, they seem quite vulnerable to the gravitational pull of the existing territorial fragmentation of humankind. Even when a doctrine's central concept—God, brotherhood/sisterhood of humankind, continental unity,[1] or a socialist utopia of classless humanity—is nonterritorial and universalistic, its popular support and institutions still must be organized territorially within the existing national boundaries and its tactics, strategy, and message must be adjusted to territorial limitations, opportunities, and emotions. A socialist internationalist "must first take care of his domestic situation which he knows best," as Marx's Communist Manifesto of 1848 admonishes socialist revolutionaries; at the same time, they should follow the manifesto's nonterritorial class slogan, Proletarians of all countries, unite!

Clearly underestimating the magnetic force of territorial nationalism (calling it, as a matter of fact, a mere chimera) and fervently wishing for a single and final world wide revolution Marx did not take sufficient account of a possible paradox: A universalistic ideology conquers territorial state and so through its triumph becomes a prisoner. The simultaneity of ideological conquest and territorial captivity merits a closer examination of what may happen to universalistic creeds when they are transferred from the pulpits, coffeehouses, or conspiratorial cells to the battlefield of practical politics.

Political Ideology as a Guide for Action

By political ideology, I understand a more or less coherent system of concepts and beliefs that justify and demand political action on the basis of a particular analysis of history and current state of humanity and call for an organized effort to attain the proclaimed goal of transforming the human condition into a better one.[2] The various "isms" of our era are good examples. An ideology is, therefore not only an analysis and a declaration of intent and optimism about the future, it is also a guide for organization and action, as well as an instrument for mobilizing the mass support deemed essential for the attainment of its intermediate and ultimate objectives. The desirable link between the leaders and the masses places our concern with ideology clearly in the period of modern mass communications, mass rallies, and mass publications.

To sum up, using medical terms: A political ideology appears as a *diagnosis* of what is wrong with the present and past place of individuals and groups in society, combined with a *prescription* as to what the cure should be and crowned with an optimistic *prognosis* concerning the society's early and inevitable recovery if it takes the right kind of medication.

In his comparative study of the U.S., English, French, and Russian revolutions, Crane Brinton described an essential ingredient of all major revolutionary ideologies, the presence of some abstract, all-powerful force, a perfect ally: *God* for the English puritans, *nature* and *reason* for the French revolutionaries, and *dialectical materialism* for the socialists and communists. In Brinton's words: "Not only does God, nature, or dialectic materialism make the victory of the present underdog certain. The present upperdog can be shown . . . to have acquired its present preponderance by accident, or a particularly dirty trick, while God or nature was temporarily off duty."[3] The realization of the utopian dream, although lacking a blueprint, is presented as a not too distant possibility. Brinton called this element, present in most ideologies, "imminentism." The believers are assured that the better world is just around the corner but one must, of course, turn the corner with some effort.

Territorial Captivity of Ideological Conquerors

Given the variety of national histories, experiences, and political cultures, one single worldwide upheaval of human values and aspiration in every country and every corner of the world has proved evidently impossible. A universal ideology is therefore condemned to proceed toward its goals *territory by territory*, and it is this spatial circumstance that has exposed all universalist creeds to contamination by the territorial dimension of politics both within and among nation-states. Thus, by its very geographic expansion, a universalist creed becomes wedded to the various nation-states. A former ideological zealot now in practical charge of a triumphant yet territory-bound creed must necessarily adapt his or her strategy and tactics to the territorial nation's geopolitical position, history, political traditions, political culture, resources, development possibilities and drawbacks, and military capabilities as well as to the nation's territorial geographic neighbors and its general vulnerability to foreign pressure, blackmail, or attack. A common ideology is bound to be interpreted and applied quite differently by a small, underdeveloped, besieged Islamic country than by a large, highly developed, traditionally imperial and Christian Orthodox superpower.

Ideological utopia must prove its worth in the real world, especially in an anarchic and insecure system of mutually suspicious territorial states. Unlike the domestic scene, the international one is clearly beyond any individual actor's control. Whatever the ultimate goal may be—God's global village, world federation, or socialist classless and stateless commonwealth—the first requirement of any territorial base is self-preservation. If a threat seems to justify almost any means of defense, it more than justifies a short-term deviation from a long-term ideological commitment. What else? To sacrifice the state on the altar of ideological purity? "No prince is entitled," wrote Raymond Aron, "to make his nation the Christ among nations."[4]

Some of the examples of ideological betrayals caused by the imperative of territorial security are the cooperative agreements between Hitler and Stalin, Stalin and Churchill, Roosevelt and Stalin, Mao and Nixon, and devoted republican George Washington and the aristocratic representative of royal France, the Marquis de Lafayette. Islam may ideologically preach a holy war against all infidels in general and Israel in particular, but there may be situations in which an Islamic nation may accept peaceful cooperation with some infidels, including the state of Israel (e.g., President Carter's

Camp David accords). The Jewish creed may require that all activities cease on Yom Kippur, but an Arab offensive may impose a nonobservance of the holy day as one did in 1973.

True Believers and Opportunists

Three points of caution must be raised in this evaluation of the interplay between a sincerely held creed and territorial realities:

1. Thus far in this analysis, I have not calibrated the high or low degree of sincere belief on the part of leaders in what they ideologically preach to justify or promote their decisions. One should never exclude the possibility of a true ideological nonbeliever who uses an appealing ideology and its slogans as a "grass-for-the-mass," a hallucinogen for a collective trip to some never-never land.

2. If an ideology is also a message for mass consumption, its priests are and must be aware of the fact that their messages addressed to their adherents at home and abroad are naturally listened to and analyzed by their adversaries. This realization poses some problems for the ideological priests who, on account of a foreign audience, may soften or sharpen their message. Unlike secret military mobilization plans or the operational codes of a politburo or a Roman curia, a well-propagated ideology cannot help alerting or alarming its potential adversaries.

Within the ideological-territorial base, there usually is also quite a difference between the ideology as it is understood and applied by the elites, on the one hand and its simplified version fit for mass consumption, on the other. With regard to communism, for example, one observer of the Russian scene, Ralph K. White, noted that in the Soviet system, the leaders have access to certain types of information that are not shared with the general public. As a consequence, the leaders may have a less diabolical enemy image than the public, and a less innocent self-image. On the other hand, the leaders are apparently more deeply imbued with Marxism-Leninism— reared in it since infancy—than the general public is. And White concluded: "While [the leaders'] better access to information may make them less paranoid in their outlook upon the West than the general public is, their ideology probably makes them more so. The diabolical character of Wall Street is for them an article of faith."[5]

3. The third point of caution concerns the preceding definition of a political ideology as a guide for action. Generally, it is, but its specificity has to be taken with a handful of salt. No political ideology or moral code contains a precise navigational map or even less, a detailed blueprint for action in all future contingencies. The unforeseeable may and does happen. Although providing their adherents with a sense of direction and an optimistic faith in the final results, ideologies are, at best, guides for activities, not specific action. In a word, they are ambiguous and lend themselves to various interpretations by the activists.

As we all know, even laws that are written to eliminate ambiguity are not immune to conflicting interpretations as to their meaning and consequences—that is what lawyers thrive on—and ideological guidelines are even more ambiguous than either criminal or civil laws. Honest disagreements about their exact meaning among the leaders, militants, and factions are therefore both frequent and inevitable. Quite often, diametrically opposed conclusions have been drawn from the same body of ideological wisdom simply because of differences in the interpreters' characters, temperaments, personal ambitions, fears, experiences, ages, or mental and physical health. For example, a recognition of Martin Luther's constipation, Benito Mussolini's venereal disease, and Neville Chamberlain's stomach spasms may significantly help us to understand the crises in Christianity, Italian fascism, and prewar British foreign policy (Munich 1938), respectively.

Furthermore, it should be recognized that some highly publicized disagreements about the true meaning of an ideology have often been artificially fabricated for the purpose of a factional struggle for power by means of purges and heresy trials. One U.S. secretary of state, John Foster Dulles, however, did claim that "one would understand both the character of the Soviet leaders and the blueprint [!] of Soviet policy" by carefully reading Stalin's book *Problems of Communism,*[6] and in his answer to U.S. Kremlinologists, a U.S. scholar, Norton Long, facetiously suggested that we imagine that

> Moscow has established an Institute of Christology manned by renegade divines and dialectical students of comparative religions, to deduce logically what President Johnson, Prime Minister Wilson, and General de Gaulle will do because they are, after all, Christians, even though they may be bad Christians. It would be little more fanciful than some of the efforts in Marxology.[7]

Ideologies Seeking and Exercising State Power

More than a sinister purpose, loss of faith, cynicism, and honest disagreements about the true meaning of a creed, the simple facts of political life within and among territorial nations impose an often shattering burden of proof on political ideologies. All ideologies pay particularly heavy tribute to reality during the periods of their successful attainment and exercise of power. While opposing or subverting an existing order, ideologies usually reflect a high degree of idealism and utopianism, including an excessive idealization of people's reactions to a new order of things. But success and power induce a great intimacy with reality, which often has a devastating effect on both the optimism and some of the theoretical premises of the original theory.

Conceived during the period of revolutionary daydreaming, much of reality could be overlooked so as not to impede a bold vision of things to come. Exile, jail, and libraries afford time and opportunity for only one type of revolutionary "activity," ideological theorizing. When leaders of ideologies attain power, it is the primary and imperative need to preserve that power and use it, rather than the inherent hypocrisy of the leaders, that makes them relegate some of their erstwhile ideals to the role of decorative although useful accessories. A few principles have to be quietly discarded as the embarrassing burden of a dreamy past. Some concepts have to be rationalized into their near-opposites. A movement's enemies as well as its zealots label such compromises of theory with reality "betrayals."

In this sense, a "revolution betrayed," to use Trotsky's label for Stalin's successful consolidation of the Soviet state, is often, quite paradoxically, the twin brother of a successful maintenance of power. Napoleon, both betrayed *and* consolidated some of the gains of the French Revolution; and some people may argue that the conservative founding fathers at Philadelphia in 1787 also betrayed *and* consolidated the revolutionary thought of the signers of the Declaration of Independence.

From Universal Message
to Territorial Power Technique

The history of the communist movement is a success story if measured by square miles of territorial conquest and control. Ironically, it is also a story of the increasing decline of an ideology with each newly acquired square mile of territory. The ideology had to be successively distorted and disfigured to fit its fragmented application, territory by territory (instead of universalism), and its hierarchical authoritarian form (instead of the promise of freedom and equality). Today, communism's expansion and maintenance can be better explained by the might of the Soviet Union, the organizational skill of the Communist parties, the leaders' insights into mass psychology, and the inadequacy or gullibility of opponents than by Marx's theory of surplus value, proletarian solidarity, and class struggle. It may be said that communism has captured a large portion of the earth's surface from Berlin to Hanoi and Havana, not because of its universalistic ideology, but in spite of it.

In the case of communism, the constant need to twist its central dogmas to fit the facts, especially the interests of the Soviet state and its authoritarian regime has resulted in a situation in which, over the years, ideological zealots have been replaced by reckless and cynical practitioners. Today, seven decades after communism's first territorial triumph on November 7, 1917, there are very few people who truly believe in communist ideology as a universalistic supranational doctrine. Originally communist, revolutionary optimism may have appealed to some idealists and, in a popularized form, to downtrodden people who were aroused by the injustice and cruelty of early industrialism. Marxism and communism seemed to promise to create a happy life in a classless world polity, managing publicly owned means of production for the benefit of all on an equal basis.

Instead, dictatorship and inefficient economic policies have ensued wherever the Communist party has come to power. As communism has expanded territorially, it has made headway by coercion, military support, or invasion, not by example and persuasion. Nowhere has any nation voted itself freely into communism. Today, despite the rhetoric, which still tries to retain the heady flavor of 1848 and 1917, acquisition and maintenance of territorial power is the central goal and commitment of most communist leaders.

In politics *within* nations, communism has proved its worth as a technique and an organizational formula that allows its users to maximize the power of the territorial state. By means of totalitarian assignments of work, residence, education, and permissible thought, communism succeeds in making the opposition wither away, not the state as the doctrine had initially pledged.

In politics *among* nations, communism and its potential appeal have become instruments of the Soviet Union's foreign policy. The international system of states, first, and its nuclear dimension later, have also profoundly altered many a communist article of faith, especially Lenin's erstwhile assumption that intercapitalist wars were not only inevitable but desirable as springboards for proletarian revolutions. Clearly, Lenin's hopeful attitude toward intercapitalist wars required substantial amendment after Hiroshima and the advent of the nuclear age.

Mistaken Premises

Initially the central and allegedly scientific concept of the communist creed was that of class struggle (involving only two classes in a zero-sum type conflict) that would lead to a worldwide revolution based on transnational proletarian solidarity. In the resulting socialist global commonwealth (All-World Federative Soviet Republic in Lenin's terminology), not only the state but also the nationalism connected with it, would disappear.

The concept of transnational class unity was based on three premises—all incorrect. The first one explained nationalism as a class phenomenon belonging only to the era of capitalist states. The socialist president of Senegal, Leopold Sedar Senghor, rejected Marx's error succinctly:

> Marx underestimated political and national idealism, which, born in France upon the ruins of provincial fatherlands with the Revolution of 1789, won over the world. "Justice," Marx writes, "humanity, liberty, equality, fraternity, independence . . . these relatively moral categories . . . sound so nice but . . . in historical and political questions, prove absolutely nothing." I repeat: *independence.* If [Karl Marx] the creator of scientific socialism returned to this earth, he would perceive with amazement that these "chimeras" as he called them, and above all the concept of *Nation*, are living realities in the twentieth century.[8]

The second mistaken premise, derived from the first, was the Marxist belief that loyalty to a class is or may become the strongest of human bonds, stronger than a person's identification with his or her nation's history, welfare, and future. Marx not only underestimated nationalism but over-estimated the international solidarity of the working class irrespective of national boundaries, especially in the case of the imperialist nations and their colonies. As Senghor put it, Marx demonstrated a "blind confidence in proletarian generosity and conscience." As an African nationalist and socialist, Senghor could not help noting how limited was the feeling of solidarity on the part of the French working class while its well-being was partly the result of the French exploitation of the riches of Africa and Asia. "In a word," wrote Senghor, "the European proletariat has profited from the colonial system; therefore, it has never really—I mean, effectively— opposed it."[9]

The third premise of proletarian internationalism was the communist expectation that capitalism, in the process of its race to inevitable doom, would create everywhere, irrespective of national circumstances and traditions, identical conditions of oppression and exploitation. Common international misery was to lead to a common struggle against capitalism. "Modern industrial labor, modern subjugation to capital," proclaimed the Communist Manifesto, "the same in England as in France, in America as in Germany, has stripped the proletariat of every trace of national character. . . . National differences and antagonism between people are daily more and more vanishing."

Instead, the working-class movements could not have done other than to develop differently because their nations followed different patterns of economic development. As a consequence, instead of nations being socialized into a proletarian international commonwealth (Proletarians of all countries, unite!), socialism was nationalized, that is, territorialized. Or as the British historian Edward H. Carr put it:

> Their standard of living must be defended if necessary against the national trade (or political) policies of other states. . . . [A]s custodians of the living standard, employment and amenities of their whole populations, modern nations are, in virtue of their nature and function, probably less capable than any other group in modern times of reaching agreement with one another. . . . The socialization of nations has as its natural corollary the nationalization of socialism.[10]

These lines were written in 1945, long before the terms "national communism" and "socialist imperialism" became part of the political vocabulary.

The anational or antinational concepts were formulated by Marxist revolutionaries during the early period of their polemical overtheorizing (there was not much else to do), in relative isolation from the masses and practical politics.

Under such conditions, the "founding fathers" of communism were primarily concerned with strategy and tactics prior to acquisition of territorial control. The important questions posed and partly answered were, What was to be done in order to seize political power in the most advanced capitalist countries? How to transform inevitable intercapitalist wars into levers of international proletarian revolutions? and What were the capitalist countries' weakest spots that would make their doom inevitable? Much in the early communist doctrine was labeled "scientifically" inevitable. When, however, at a later stage, some occurrences were reclassified as no longer being inevitable—for example, wars in a nuclear age—one may wonder how anything can stop being inevitable unless it was not inevitable in the first place.

In Lenin's and other communists' writings, there is very little about the "day after," that is, how to manage the territorial domain, both internally and externally, after its conquest. The "scientific certainty" about the international dimension of the communist revolution and triumph did not encourage any consideration of what practical policies should apply in case communism were to triumph in only one backward country while the rest of the industrial world would refuse to follow the path prescribed by Marx and his followers.

Yet, what the doctrine and its rigid premises did not anticipate in fact happened. Only a part of European Russia fell under communist control, but it was immediately used successfully as a territorial base for the forcible reannexation of non-Russian territories (the Ukraine, the Caucasus, and Muslim Central Asia) and later became and was ideologically promoted to be the central base for world revolution, that is, revolutionary activities outside the former czarist domain. Nobody can guess today what would have been the shape and contents of contemporary communism had it first conquered a more advanced country such as Germany or England instead of being wedded, contrary to the doctrine's forecast, to Russia's economic and social backwardness, geography and history.

Such intertwining of the Russian territorial domain and communist ideology (and of their not necessarily compatible interests) was bound to become sooner or later a target for criticism by communists in other countries which eventually led to accusations of Russian's "great power chauvinism" on the part of the Yugoslav communists first and the Chinese later (see the second epigraph to this chapter).

Stubborn Facts Versus
Ideological Daydreaming

As pragmatic political leaders desiring to maintain and consolidate their power to manage their domain, Lenin, Stalin, and their successors down to Gorbachev had to make their dogmas conform or appear to conform to many unanticipated events—both inside and outside Russia.[11] Addressing the Eighth Party Congress on March 19, 1919, in the midst of serious difficulties facing the new Bolshevik regime, Lenin wisely warned against a wishful denial of adverse realities: "We cannot refuse to recognize what actually exists; it will itself compel us to recognize it."[12] Commenting on the Bolshevik adjustments to realities, Merle Fainsod described the territorial impact on the communist nonterritorial creed as follows:

Like many revolutionaries before them, [the Bolsheviks] found themselves
involved in a complex struggle to master the recalcitrant realities of their
environment. They pressed forward where they could, and they gave way
where they had to. The tragedy of unintended consequences overtook them.
As they sought to come to terms with the pressures which impinged on
them, vision of the future had to be modified or abandoned. Instruments
became ends; their retention and consolidation of power dwarfed all other
objectives. The party of revolution was transformed into the party of order.[13]

The international situation, in turn, resulted in other setbacks for the
communist ideology and its optimism. The "stubbornest" fact of all was
the failure of an international proletarian revolution to materialize. Although
the party heavily counted on communism in Western Europe for the survival
of Soviet Russia, it had to adapt itself to the reality of and need for survival
in a potentially or actually hostile environment.

In the early 1920s, the communist's attempts to seize and maintain
power—in Hungary, Bavaria, and Berlin—were defeated despite the optimistic
predictions of the dizzying speed Old Europe was going to rush toward
the proletarian revolution. But there was no such rush. Not even defeated
Germany, in which chaos, frustration, and misery proved to be such valuable
allies of communism, conformed to the theoretical anticipations; the defeat
of Germany in World War I finally produced a Hitler, not a Lenin.

On the other hand, this negative external development seemed at least
partly balanced by the capitalist countries' reluctance or inability to dislodge
Soviet communism from its territorial base and force it onto the periphery
of the political arena, as was the fate of the other Communist parties in
the rest of the world. However powerful and fearful of communist Russia
the Western powers might have been, Moscow was able to maneuver through
the hostile international environment as any other ostracized territorial state
would: by military deterrence, diplomacy, and splitting the enemy front.

Although the rest of the world was Soviet Russia's enemy (partly because,
in its capitalist form, it was marked by communist theory and practice for
total extinction), some of Russia's enemies were immediately more dangerous
than others. Although theory had taught the Russian leaders that capitalism
was an undiluted evil, the communist state had to treat some capitalist
countries as a lesser evil.

Some of the changes in Soviet foreign policy were truly dramatic and
sudden: for example, the shifts from cooperation with Western democracies
and the League of Nations to Stalin's pact with Hitler (1939) and then the
Stalin-Roosevelt-Churchill (1941–1945) cooperation. There is nothing to
indicate that communist theory has played any significant role in Soviet
decisions to oppose or align the Soviet Union with any particular combination
of foreign nations. The reversals of alliances can be explained, rather, by
the pragmatic considerations that any bourgeois or fascist state faces in the
process of maximizing its national interests. Nor is there any indication
that communist ideology has endowed communist leaders with any better
insight than noncommunist leaders into the potential developments of the

international situation. The Soviet leaders, however committed to communist ideology, seem to play it—no less and no more than other states' leaders—by ear.

Territorial Springboard of Global Expansion

Having captured the vast territory, population, and resources of Russia, the world communist movement could add the might of a great power to its conspiratorial and subversive underground techniques and to above ground agitation. Those branches of the national government that the communist leaders in the underground, in jail, or in exile had had to fear, dodge, or fight from a position of weakness could now be turned not only against their domestic enemies but also against the enemies of Russian and foreign communists. It was indeed "common sense," as pointed out by George Allen Morgan ("Historicus") in his excellent analysis of Stalin's concept of communist revolutions, "to use the foothold won in the Soviet Union as a base of world revolution."[14]

Until World War II, in a framework composed of a powerful and successful leader, on the one hand, and weak and unsuccessful communist parties, on the other, foreign communists rarely dared to question Soviet wisdom and right to inspire, criticize, purge, and guide the world communist movement. Formally, the Russian guidance was provided by the Comintern (Communist International), which tended to treat foreign communists as inept underlings who were expected to learn from Big Brother and follow his instructions.

Nevertheless, however united by a common creed, zeal, and dream the world communist movement was, it was an asymmetric association of the Soviet party in power and in control of a vast national territory with foreign parties striving in vain to acquire power in their respective national territories. Such an association between the powerful and successful, on the one hand, and the weak and unsuccessful, on the other, could not and did not avoid the three usual types of suspicion and doubt that characterize all asymmetric coalitions.

There is, first of all, the suspicion, so often fully justified, that the leading power may misuse its dominant position to promote its own interests at the expense of the other members; in its hands, the defense and promotion of the common interest of all participants may become a convenient garb to cloak the leading power's egoism. This suspicion has plagued all modern alliances. There is, second, a resentment against the tendency of the leading power to dictate the line of common policy or action to other member nations instead of consulting with them and treating them as coequals. And finally, there often is the feeling that the leadership exercised in behalf of all by the leading power is in the hands of inept and unskillful individuals, or at least that the leading power is negligent or ignorant of problems that are of immediate and pressing concern to some member nations but are deemed secondary by the power at the helm.

These doubts and suspicions appeared in various forms and and were voiced by various communist leaders or intellectuals long before World War II. One example was serious disagreements between the Soviet and Chinese parties in the midtwenties. Then during the first two years of World War II, there were some objections—ideological as well as national—on the part of Eastern European, Jewish, German, French, and American communists to the shortsighted Soviet cooperation with the Nazis (1939-1941) at the expense of peace and Poland. The prestige, power, sophistry, and apparatus of the Soviet party-state silenced, however, such dissent with relative ease and purged the critics into obedience or oblivion.

When the Nazis attacked the Soviet Union in 1941—and thus the power base of world communism—the identification of foreign communists with Russia acquired a renewed fervor. The previous Soviet cooperation with Hitler was soon forgotten or conveniently rationalized ("gaining more time for the Soviet base to be ready for war"). Yet, in its desperate fight against the German onslaught which by December 1941 had brought the Nazis to the heart of European Russia, Moscow deliberately toned down the previously dominant theme of world communism, that of proletarian internationalism, which ideologically included, of course, the German working class. In order to mobilize Soviet as well as foreign support for the total war effort, Moscow began using and propagating nonclass themes such as patriotism, Pan-slavism, religion, and ethnic hatred of everything German, Nazi or not.

The reasons for Moscow's encouragement of a nationalist reorientation of foreign Communist parties were, from a nonideological, pragmatic point of view, quite understandable. Despite their class-oriented ideology, the Soviet leaders simply could not risk relying on internationalism and pro-letarian solidarity to win the war: the German proletarians, now dressed in the uniforms of the advancing Nazi armies, did not show any inclination to desert to Russia as soon as their feet touched the holy ground of the ancestral land of socialism. In a natural reaction, dynamic nationalism and hatred of the Germans, not proletarian solidarity, were mobilized to help Moscow win the war and chase the Germans out of Russia: The war became a "great patriotic war." The German nation was no longer perceived through Marxist glasses as split into exploiting and exploited classes; thus, in his articles, the Soviet writer Ilya Ehrenburg was allowed to differentiate between only good Germans, who were dead, and bad Germans, who were still alive.

The process of "chauvinizing" proletarian internationalism reached its climax on May 15, 1943, when Stalin ordered the symbol and instrument of proletarian internationalism, the Comintern, disbanded. The decision to dissolve the Communist International as a guiding center of the international labor movement and to release "the 'national' communist parties of the Communist International from obligations ensuing from the constitution and decisions of the congresses of the Communist International" was signed by twelve leading members of the Comintern. The Communist International, as was pointed out in the announcement of its dissolution, "more and more outlived itself in proportion to the growth of this movement and to the increasing complexity of problems in each country." In the words of the communiqué, the Comintern "even became a hindrance to the further strengthening of the national workers' parties."[15]

Nationalist Boomerang

The public and publicized dissolution of the Comintern had a profound impact on both the leaders and the rank and file of Communist parties outside the Soviet Union, especially those who had participated since 1941 in their own patriotic wars against Germany. The merging of communism with territorial nationalism was not only permitted for the first time in the history of communism but actually ordered by Moscow under the conditions of war against a national enemy. The order fell on fertile soil, and foreign communists were never to recover from this wartime affliction. The combination of jingoism and communism that only the Russian communists had enjoyed until then was now to be emulated by all other Communist parties.

Following the Russian example, all the other Communist parties abandoned the previous stress on class loyalty and the proletarian movement. The French communists, symbolically and literally, placed the French tricolor over the party flag. From then on, in all countries the nation's anthem was to precede the proletarian song, "International" whereas before the war, national bourgeois anthems had never been played at any communist gathering.

Following the defeat of the Axis powers, European communists emerged from underground groups or from concentration camps endowed with an aura of patriotic respectability, heroism, or martyrdom. Although in Western Europe the communists were able to secure for themselves only minor cabinet portfolios, in Eastern Europe the presence of the Soviet armies catapulted the communists to leading positions in the national-front governments. Former agents of the Comintern became national prime ministers or ministers of foreign affairs, guerrilla leaders were promoted to positions of ministers of national defense or chiefs of staff, and former communist saboteurs obtained the portfolios of ministers of public works and national reconstruction.

As either leaders of or partners in the postwar coalition cabinets in Europe, the communists, willy-nilly, became involved in the promotion or defense of their own country's national interests vis-à-vis the interests of other states, whether bourgeois- or communist-led. The former links between the Communist parties were thus further weakened, and within national communities, the mutual interpenetration of communism and nationalism was accelerated. National communism became, in the words of the Yugoslav communist leader (later social democrat) Milovan Djilas, "a general phenomenon." In the opinion of Djilas, "in order to maintain itself, communism must become national"[16]—to which I would add, *territorial*.

But in an era of territorially fragmented communism, the drawbacks of automatically identifying the world communist movement with the national interests of the Soviet state were bound to catch up with the initial advantages of such an association. The drawbacks finally overtook the advantages in proportion to the territorial expansion of communism; the seeds of the nationalist territorial erosion of world communism were, ironically, the inevitable corollaries of the movement's geographic spread and success.

National Interests of Communist
Territorial States

In 1948, the clash between Soviet and Yugoslav nationalist communism came into the open: Long-accumulated tensions and irritations were dogmatized into new ideological positions. The Yugoslav revolt against Soviet leadership and policy was followed by Stalin's incapacity to initiate a purge of Tito and his associates from within the ranks of the Communist party of Yugoslavia, a procedure that under the Comintern had never failed to produce desired results within the then-nonterritorial Communist parties. A nation-state has other options and means of resistance than a party in the opposition or the underground has: It can mobilize territorial patriotism and foreign support—as Yugoslavia successfully did.

Inevitably, the question had to arise sooner or later as to which national communist interest would prevail in a clash with the Soviet state and other communist states. Nothing in previous communist theory or practice indicated exactly how international relations among the sovereign communist states would develop. The communist concept of vanguard leadership, elitism, and monolithic power does not allow for a give-and-take procedure among equals—a procedure proper to a democratic framework but alien to an authoritarian one. Communist Yugoslavia was the first party state to have the courage to oppose the Soviet imperial concept, according to which the interests of the Soviet Union as the base of world communism are under all circumstances primary and all other interests are secondary.

In 1948, under Stalin, Moscow did not dare to invade and streamline Yugoslavia. Three factors seemed decisive: the geographic location of Yugoslavia, not contiguous to the Soviet Union, Moscow's failure to purge the Yugoslav party from within, and the unfavorable international balance of power that existed at that time (the Soviet Union was to explode its first nuclear device only a year later on September 23, 1949). In 1956, however, under the conditions of mutual nuclear deterrence, Soviet tanks were dispatched by Khruschev to liquidate a national revolution in communist Hungary. And in 1968, under Brezhnev, Soviet tanks similarly crushed the Czechoslovak liberalization of communism, the so-called socialism with a human face, which Moscow replaced with a Russian one. In the wake of the Soviet military occupation of Czechoslovakia, the old Comintern and Cominform line regarding the primacy of the Soviet state as a base of world communism was reasserted in the so-called Brezhnev doctrine: "Each Communist party is responsible not only to its own people, but also to all socialist countries. . . . Whoever forgets this, in stressing only the independence of the Communist party, becomes one-sided. . . . The sovereignty of each socialist country cannot be opposed to the interests of the world socialism."[17] (See also Chapter 8, which deals with transborder interventions.) Clearly, the interests of world socialism, as well as Leninist doctrine itself, were to be interpreted by world communism's first territorial base, Russia.

In protest against the Soviet occupation of their country, the Czechoslovak communist leaders invoked the authority of Lenin, who had condemned any denial of the right of national self-determination. The Soviet leaders replied by quoting Lenin on the merits of proletarian internationalism. The Soviet tanks determined which quotation from Lenin should prevail (see figure 2.1). The Chinese communists condemned this imperial concept bluntly and succinctly by contrasting the limited sovereignty of the non-Russian communist states with the Soviet Union's unlimited sovereignty— leading to a "rule of the socialist community by the new tsars" and to an "international dictatorship over the colonies of social imperialism."[18]

The Soviet-Yugoslav dispute, like the later Sino-Soviet, Soviet-Albanian, and Soviet-Rumanian ones, brought to the surface what had been inherent in international communism since its spread beyond the territorial confines of the Soviet state: the inevitability of various conflicts of interests among communist nation-states.

Transnational Morality and Territorial Politics

Are religious doctrines and moral codes any more or any less vulnerable than political ideologies to the territorial fragmentation of humankind? No, even though in contrast to political ideologies, religious and ethical commands are not primarily concerned with the determination of political ends and means. Nevertheless, since the various religious and ethical codes claim to be guides for all human behavior under all circumstances, political activity should surely not be excluded from their strictures—or should it?

For more than three millennia, political writers and statesmen have been engaged in a controversy concerning the question whether there should be a difference between moral standards applying to an individual, acting on his or her behalf, and those applying to a king, prince, or statesman, acting on behalf of a territorial community. In other words, do moral codes address their commandments only to the conscience of an individual in his or her private capacity, or do they also provide guidance to political communities and their leaders? Two distinct schools of thought have conflicted with each other for ages with regard to this question.

First *moral perfectionists* (or idealists, including pacifists, conscientious objectors, and other nonviolent resisters) insist that the end can never justify the means. According to these people, even in a life-or-death situation,

Figure 2.1

"Which quotation from Lenin—the Russian or the Czech—will prevail?"

Source: Drawing by Jelinek in *Dikobraz*, Prague, August 6, 1968 (sixteen days before the Soviet invasion).

a noble goal can never ennoble ignoble means. The code of universal ethics is deemed to be absolute and, without any exception, should apply to all human actions in both the private and public realms regardless of the nature of the circumstances.

German sociologist Max Weber called nonresistance to evil the ethic of ultimate ends, in contrast to the political ethic of responsibility for foreseeable consequences. In Weber's words, a person who is guided by the ethic of ultimate ends, "does rightly and leaves the result with the Lord." If his or her action of good intent leads to bad results, "then, in the actor's eyes, not he but the world, or the stupidity of other men, or God's will who made them thus, is responsible for the evil. The believer in an ethic of ultimate ends feels responsible only for seeing to it that the flame of pure intentions is not squelched." And Weber concluded: "The proponent of an ethic of ultimate ends cannot stand up under the ethical irrationality of the world"[19] and, as I would add, under its territorial fragmentation, which also tends to fragment morality. The ethic of ultimate ends may indeed result in moral narcissism: The world may be aflame, but a moral perfectionist's hands remain clean.

After World War II, the English writer George Orwell urged on every pacifist: "a clear obligation to answer the following question: What about the Jews? Are you prepared to see them exterminated? If not, how do you propose to save them without resorting to war?"[20]

Moral Cynics

Second, *political realists and Machiavellians* insist that the people who make decisions on behalf of their communities may have to use all the means that are necessary to ensure the survival and way of life of their people, especially when threatened by the outsiders. In *The Prince* and *The Discourses* (A.D. 1532 and 1531, respectively), the Florentine political philosopher Niccolò Machiavelli expressed his realist concept, according to which, "In the actions of men, and especially princes, the end justifies the means." He then elaborated: "Where the very safety of the country depends upon the resolution to be taken, no consideration of justice or injustice, humanity or cruelty, nor of glory or shame, should be allowed. . . . The only question should be: What course will save the life and liberty of the country?"[21]

More than 1,800 years before those lines were written, Kautilya (a "Machiavellian" chancellor and writer who lived during the period of the Indian Mauryan Empire, 300–200 B.C.) similarly advised territorial rulers how to engage in dirty defensive wars and described the various methods a monarch should use when his overtures for peace have failed. Kautilya's list includes:

> Assassinating the enemy-king, seducing the enemy's chief civil and military officers. . . . Spies in the guise of vintners or of dealers in cooked food and meat are to poison enemy's military officers and men at camp; other spies are to poison the fodder for the enemy's elephants and horses. Others are to destroy the enemy at his fortified refuge by fire and poisonous fumes.[22]

Kautilya then added a long list of vegetable, mineral, and organic preparations that caused instantaneous and widespread death, blindness, deafness, numbness, or madness. Ethically speaking, humanity does not seem to have made much human progress in the past three millennia, and obviously, much more than centuries separate Kautilya's recipes for war from Gandhi's succinct "Morality is contraband in war."

In the 24,000 verses that make up the Hindu epic, *Mahabharata* (1500 B.C.)—another 1,000 years before Kautilya—we may read the following advice to monarchs: "There must be no hesitation to kill anybody, whether a relative or friend, for achieving one's end. Without cruelty, kings cannot attain felicity."[23] A modern Indian political scientist, K. Satchidananda Murty noted that "no Hindu thinker regarded it possible to moralize statecraft. Either one should choose to be in it and ignore ethics. Or if one wants to be ethical, he must remain aloof from statecraft."[24] Similarly, Max Weber argued, "He who seeks the salvation of the soul, should not seek it along the avenue of politics where the goal is the salvation of a community, not that of one's soul. . . . The genius or demon of politics lives in an inner tension with the god of love, as well as with Christian God as expressed by the church. This tension can at any time lead to an irreconcilable conflict."[25] A hermit meditating in some isolated spot cannot do much about the protection of national territory.

Approving of the political ethic of responsibility for the consequences of one's action, Weber admonished political leaders to take into account the average deficiencies of people without presupposing their goodness and perfection. In other words, political leaders' decisions are bound to be imperfect because the world in which they have to act is imperfect. Clearly, it takes both passion and courage to act in a framework of such constant imperfection and the resulting dilemma of choosing between two shades of gray.

Is there, or can there be, a middle position between the ethic of absolute ends and the ethic of political responsibility for foreseeable consequences? A U.S. scholar, Arnold Wolfers, suggested that most political decision makers are neither Machiavellian cynics nor moral perfectionists but "moral imperfectionists," who make the best moral choice the circumstances permit. Morality remains part of the process though not a decisive one. In Wolfers's words:

> Politics conducted in a multistate system is not necessarily any more immoral than average private behavior . . . the chief difference pertains . . . to the *circumstances* under which men are required to act. Much of what strikes people as the immoral practice of government may prove to be morally justified by the peculiar and unhappy circumstances that the statesman has to face and, as a rule, cannot hope to change.[26]

The controversy about morality in politics now clearly shifts to the operational framework. The question is, Who—on the basis of what information, among what options, and how reliably—can determine the imperative nature of a given *necessity* that justifies the use of measures that under less severe circumstances would be unacceptable, such as violence, blackmail, or deception? And there emerges also a preliminary political rather than an ethical question as to by whom and how has the situation that has made such painful choices unavoidable been brought about. Therefore, not only, Does a *correctly* perceived incoming nuclear salvo justify a first strike? but also, How have we reached this point of no return? These and related questions are clearly beyond the framework of this limited study; they are included in their rudimentary form only because they do directly touch upon our concern with the territorial aspects of all politics.

Choosing an Ethical Code

In light of the preceding points and controversies, it is clear that much of what has already been said about the role of political ideologies and their distortion due to the territorial fragmentation of humankind applies also to the various seemingly categorical moral and religious commandments. Morality, too, tends to be fragmented under the weight of conflicting territorial interests, and two nuances should be noted.

First, since the various moral and religious doctrines aim at being all-inclusive in the matter of human behavior, they prove even more ambiguous than political ideologies. Controversies about their true meaning and application to concrete situations have been very frequent throughout history, and continue to be so in the present. The most recent example was the controversy surrounding the U.S. Catholic bishops' 1984 proclamation favoring a nuclear freeze. In Christianity today the various and conflicting interpretations of the message of the Bible represent a broad spectrum ranging from Tolstoyan nonresisters, integral pacifists, Quakers, and Jehovah's Witnesses to high-church Protestants and Roman Catholics who occasionally feel authorized by the Scripture to bless the instruments of war, notwithstanding the Sermon on the Mount, which is often cited as categorically condemning any resort to violence. As a Jesuit political scientist, Joseph C. McKenna, noted:

> The Sermon on the Mount . . . in all literalness was addressed to individual persons in their individual capacities, not social collectivities or social leaders as such. Its admonitions . . . do not necessarily imply, therefore, that the statesman and his nation are morally obliged to sacrifice every other consideration and advantage for the sake of peace. . . . As long as some segments of mankind still find promise of gain in the use of threat of force, the other [territorial] segments of mankind must deal with a temptation of their own— to cancel out coercion's promise with a menace of counter coercion.[27]

The second point that merits attention is simply the fact that there is more than one code that claims universal validity yet some central issues conflict with each other. For example, Islam approves of offensive wars if they aim at converting infidels into Muslims. Protestantism approves only of self-defense of individuals and nations when there is no other way but sees in a violent defense a sinful, though inevitable, decision and action.

On the other hand, Catholic thinkers believe that "war can be morally justified in the light of both reason and revelation." McKenna explained:

Given the contemporary international setting, this judgment is to all intents and purposes only valid for defensive action. . . . For the Catholic thinkers war is not the lesser of two evils, but the lesser of two goods (one of which appears, at the moment of choice unattainable). . . . An act of self-defense . . . although imposed by circumstances which are regrettable, is morally good . . . if action is urgently needed and no other remedy is at hand; and only so much violence is allowed as will repel the unjust aggressor.[28]

To push the Catholic argument further: Is it moral when a Catholic *priest* kills his nation's enemies? An affirmative answer was given by the bishop of Verdun, the Most Reverend Pierre Boillon, at a conference of 120 French bishops held at the Shrine of Lourdes in 1968. Bishop Boillon said:

Personally, I have killed. I killed four Germans. I try to justify myself before God but I did not accuse myself at confession of sin. I had a conflict of duty of defending my country [Boillon was a resistance commander during the German occupation of France] and that of respecting human life. Killing those Germans was evil but not a sin. . . . If somebody came to me in confession and told me he had killed Hitler, I would tell him to go out and commit a sin so as to have something to confess.[29]

Summary

Should we then disregard moral values as possible restraints on the conduct of politics within and among nations? Not quite. Some political leaders, for instance, are personally much more committed to a transnational code of ethics than are others. Even if their vocation forces them to be moral imperfectionists, they often strongly prefer to act in accordance with their moral values if they can. Permeated by their strong moral convictions, their estimate of *if they can* is bound to shrink the range of what they consider the circumstances might force them to do.

On the opposite side of the morality-immorality spectrum, we find cynics who, paradoxically, may find it rewarding to act morally for nonethical reasons. It is indeed sometimes expedient to make political decisions conform to the moral standards that are strongly held by a decisive portion of the public. Thus, even cynics may be curbed by subliminal moral pressures so as not to antagonize those people those continued support is deemed necessary for the pursuit of their policies. "Ideals and self-interest are so interdependent," noted a critic of U.S. foreign policy, Robert Endicott Osgood, "that even on the grounds of national expedience, there are cogent arguments for maintaining the vitality of American idealism."[30]

In this connection, it should be also noted that moral arguments have often been an expression of self-deception. The capacity of people to rationalize their often predatory behavior, that is, to interpret it in such a manner as to make it seem just and reasonable, is frighteningly great. People incessantly seek to compromise with their conscience and, as E. A. Hooton sarcastically expressed it, they succeed in convincing themselves that their acts of grabbing are somehow noble and beautiful, that they can rape in righteousness and kill in magnanimity. "They insist upon playing the game, not only with an ace up their sleeve, but with the smug conviction that God has put it there."[31]

The adoption or rejection of many policies is often justified by references to moral or religious commandments; a close examination of the real motives may reveal that the decision was reached on other than moral grounds. What appears to reflect a moral motive has resulted from a very pragmatic calculation of the given pros and cons. Not infrequently, a policymaker discovers with a sigh of relief that what has been chosen as practical may also be viewed as ethical, especially if successful.

Conflicting Loyalties and Treason

Groups and individuals are simultaneously exposed to a great many pulls that originate in various, as it were, magnetic fields. Supranational creeds and ideologies, as just discussed, are one of them; emotional and pragmatic identification with one's own nation-state is another; and a citizen's own conscience, personal conviction, or egoism is still another. An explosive conflict arises when dissatisfaction with and hostility toward one's own national system is coupled with admiration for and identification with a foreign state that is viewed as an incarnation and a defender of a particular ideology or creed (liberal democracy, socialism, communism, Islam, or fascism). Loyalty to such a foreign state, perceived as a territorial base of political ideology, may then, in thought and action, take precedence over loyalty to one's own government, which may predispose a citizen to the crime of high treason. Not all betrayals, of course, are based on an assumed ideological kinship; some treasons simply reflect an individual's sordid financial motives (quite frequent in espionage cases), pathology, or a sick urge for revenge for some past wrong.

In the international system of territorial states the penalty of death is usually imposed on those people who have, as it were, betrayed a territory and its values. On this basis, constitutions and subsequent laws usually define the crime of treason as adherence to, collusion with, or giving aid and comfort to the enemy (U.S. constitutional terminology).

The key word is "enemy." It poses the question: Enemy of whom exactly? Enemy identified as such by a declaration of war (hot or cold)? Some citizens may consider their own national government to be their enemy and view a foreign government as their generous friend, ideological brother, or messiah. Spies in Canada and the United States (for example, Klaus Fuchs who kept Stalin well posted about atomic research in the U.S. laboratories in 1945) have reasoned in this way; at that time the Soviet Union was an ally, not a declared enemy. This problem is why various espionage and other laws extend the constitutional meaning of "enemy" to include all the potential ones, including friendly foreign states, and prohibit any transmission of classified sensitive information to foreign governments. (Unauthorized con-

Figure 2.2

"Admit it—your Motherland doesn't understand you."

tacts between individual citizens and foreign governments are further analyzed
in Chapter 8, dealing with the perforation of sovereign boundaries.)

One note of caution: In democracies, it would be, of course, suicidal to
treat every form of dissent, even if attuned to some foreign model, as
though it were sedition, subversion, treason, and collusion with the enemy.
And it would also be dangerous to deal with citizens' disloyalty at the
instigation or with the support of foreign powers as though it were merely
a passionate form of opposition and dissent.

National constitutions and criminal laws usually differentiate between the
crime of treason, on the one hand, and other less serious betrayals and
manifestations of disloyalty, on the other.[32] Two approaches can be found
in the texts of various national constitutions and laws: One is "all-embracing,"
the other is "limiting."

Communist constitutions have adopted the all-embracing concept. Article
133 of the 1936 Stalin Constitution for the Soviet Union (a model for

other communist constitutions) lists four general offenses—"violation of the oath of allegiance, desertion to the enemy, impairing the military power of the State, and espionage"—as being "treason to the motherland" and therefore "punishable with all the severity of the law as the most heinous crimes." No specific definitions are given for such vague acts as impairing the Soviet military power (by pacifist agitation?) or violation of the oath of allegiance (by dissent?). Practice indicates that additional criminal laws and the political authorities supply such definitions when deemed necessary for the suppression of dissent enjoying foreign sympathy.

The so-called limiting approach to the crime of treason is found in Western constitutions. The key sentence in the U.S. Constitution, (Article 3, section 3) reads, "Treason against the United States, shall consist *only* in levying War against them, or in adhering to their enemies, giving them aid and comfort" (italics added). Treason is also mentioned in Article 2, section 4, which speaks of impeachment and conviction of the president, vice-president, and other federal officers in cases of treason; and in Article 4, section 2, which stipulates the duty of extradition between the states in the case of a person charged with treason.

The U.S. Constitution (Article 3, section 3) limits the power of Congress to determine punishment of treason by excluding any "attainder of treason" that results in the "corruption of blood, or forfeiture except during the life of the person"—a practice under George III that resulted in punishment for crimes committed by one's ancestors or being prohibited from inheriting their property.

Today, the understanding is that for the purposes of defining treason, "enemies" are nations so identified by a congressional declaration of war. The constitutional provisions do not seem, therefore, to apply to "treason" in subbelligerent situations such as the cold war, Korea, Vietnam, Nicaragua, and El Salvador. Congress has, of course, passed acts concerning crimes of disloyalty other than high treason such as espionage, subversion, and communism to fill the gap, but their constitutionality has often been challenged.

There are two reasons for the West's reluctance to quickly label opposition or deviant behavior as treason. First, there is an awareness that past indictments and convictions of treason have frequently been used to stifle criticism, reform, and dissent. Second, the drafters of many postrevolutionary constitutions were the children of dissent and rebellion. Some of them were recipients of foreign suggestions, money, arms, and strategic advice— for example, American republican "traitors" welcomed the assistance of royal France and the Marquis de Lafayette. The government against which the American founding fathers rebelled labeled all of them traitors, and if they had lost the Revolution, they would have died as traitors.

U.S. high school textbooks are supposed to strengthen the patriotism and loyalty of young citizens by including Patrick Henry's glorification of treason, allegedly part of his address to the House of Burgesses at Williamsburg on May 29, 1765: "Caesar had his Brutus; Charles the First his Cromwell;

and George III may profit by their example. If this be treason make the most of it."

In her book *Treason in the Twentieth Century*, Margret Boveri noted how the meaning of treason changes as the wheels of history turn. "Men hanged yesterday as traitors, are today's heroes and martyrs." This statement occurred as she wrote about the hero of the anti-Nazi resistance, the chief conspirator preparing the assassination of Hitler, speaking to his fellow conspirators: "Look, let's go to the heart of the matter. I am engaged by every available means in the active practice of high treason."[33] To sum up, using Sir John Harington's (1561–1612) sarcastic epigram, written long before July 4, 1776, the day of history-making "territorial treason":

Treason doth never prosper; what's the reason?
Why, if it prosper, none dare call it treason.[34]

Chief Executive as Traitor?

The crime of adhering to a national enemy or of levying war against a legitimate government becomes more complex when the alleged rebel or traitor is the head of a national government. Many constitutions, including that of the United States, provide for impeachment in such cases. It is not easy to visualize how a president can levy war against his or her own country (except in a civil war, which may make a traitor or a rebel of the president who is defending the status quo). Constitutions do not elaborate on how a president can adhere to the national enemy, unless perhaps a decision to capitulate "unnecessarily," i.e., to surrender and accept foreign occupation, might be construed as "adhering to the enemy by giving him aid and comfort." How to define "grave and imminent danger" and how to evaluate the national interest in life-or-death situations are most difficult problems for statesmen in the conduct of foreign policy and people's ex post judgment thereof.

Laws cannot answer the question as to whether actions that appear treasonable might not have been simply lack of wisdom or foresight, and history may eventually judge deserters to be heroes and overcautious statesmen to be traitors, as in France during World War II. In June 1940, Marshal Pétain signed an armistice with Nazi Germany and continued at the helm of the French government in collaboration with the Germans. Anticipating German victory, he viewed his conduct as a proper patriotic duty. He labeled General de Gaulle's flight to London, association with Winston Churchill, and continued resistance to the Germans as the acts of a traitor and a deserter. The Allied victory eventually decided the issue. De Gaulle's adherence to a foreign nation, England, was patriotic and Pétain's adherence to Germany was treason. The verdict of history—and of the French trial of Pétain—may well have been different had Germany won the war.

Yugoslavia, which was subject to Nazi occupation during World War II (1941–1945), included a clear interdiction against capitulation and acknowledging any occupation of the country in its first postwar constitution (Article 254):

> No one shall have the right to sign or to acknowledge capitulation or the occupation of the country on behalf of the Socialist Federal Republic of Yugoslavia. Such an action is unconstitutional and shall be punishable by law. High treason is a crime against the people and shall be punished as a grave criminal offence.

How this article would be applied if the territory of the nation faced an atomic ultimatum, in which it were given a choice between national survival and slavery (which might not be permanent) or turning Yugoslavia into an atomic dust bowl (which would be quite permanent) is almost beyond conjecture.

Pangs of Conscience and Other Sanctions

Loss of life, profit, and job; social ostracism; and pangs of conscience represent a broad spectrum of sanctions that may follow as well as precede an individual's or a group's decision to sacrifice one loyalty or value for the sake of a conflicting one. Individuals and groups frequently experience the agony of choosing among their multiple allegiances to humanity, their nation, subnational community, and personal convictions, and they do so at least partly in the light of penalties that may be imposed on their violation of any related values. A conscientious objector would rather break the law than act against his or her deep convictions. A law-abiding citizen would rather experience the pain of violating his or her principle than break a law, however patently unjust or inhumane.

Figure 2.3 illustrates a three-way conflict between a citizen's own personal interests as opposed to or complementing national and humanity's interests. Each of the diagrammatic individuals is quite unrealistically depicted as either being 100 percent attached to (A) or 100 percent rejecting (R) each of the three values or interests. In real life these percentages are much less neat. The eight columns depicting the various value conflicts identify eight basic types of persons, ranging from traitors to patriots:

A-A-A: This column represents a person, probably a fool, who believes that personal, national, and supranational interests coincide perfectly.
A-R-R: This pattern represents the extreme egotist who places personal well-being above all collective (national and universal) interests.
A-A-R: A selfish patriot.
A-R-A: A selfish cosmopolitan or an agent who betrays his or her nation in favor of a foreign government for selfish reasons. This would be the case of a spy whose motive in working for a foreign government

Figure 2.3

Perceptions of Conflict or Coincidence
of Personal, National, or Other-than-national Interests

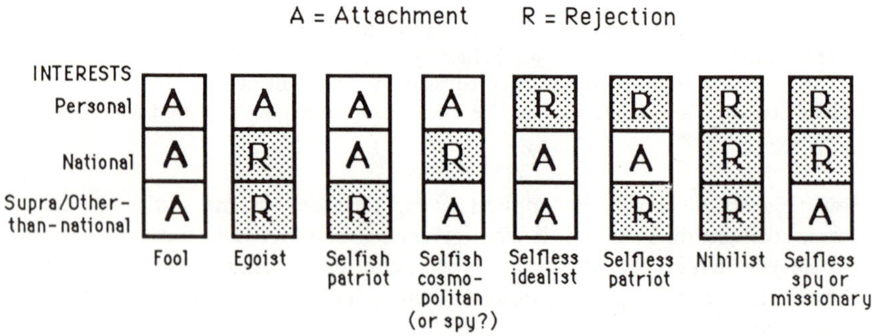

A = Attachment   R = Rejection

INTERESTS								
Personal	A	A	A	A	R	R	R	R
National	A	R	A	R	A	A	R	R
Supra/Other-than-national	A	R	R	A	A	R	R	A
	Fool	Egoist	Selfish patriot	Selfish cosmopolitan (or spy?)	Selfless idealist	Selfless patriot	Nihilist	Selfless spy or missionary

is financial reward (for example, the U.S. Navy warrant officer, John A. Walker, who for eighteen years transmitted vital U.S. secrets to the Soviet Union).

R-A-A: This rare selfless idealist, or fool, believes that his or her own nation's and foreign nations' interests are identical.

R-A-R: A selfless patriot.

R-R-R: The person who rejects all values whether personal, national, or supranational—probably a candidate for suicide.

R-R-A: The selfless missionary or saint who has none but supranational goals. The acceptance of another nation's goals as representing the interests of humankind describes selfless or ideological spies and traitors. For example, this category may describe those atomic scientists and spies who betrayed vital national interests to the Soviet Union, not for money, but because of the belief that Russia stood for the interests of humanity and peace more than their own government's did. The British top intelligence officer in charge of anti-Soviet counterespionage, Harold A.R. (Kim) Philby, classified himself in this category when, in a 1967 interview with *Izvestia*, (December 18, 1967) he explained the reasons why he worked for the Soviet Union. While in charge of British counterespionage and liaison with the U.S. Central Intelligence Agency, he had, in fact, worked for thirty years against England and the United States and for communism. During his period of service, he said, "There was no single case of Western consciously conceived operation against Soviet intelligence bearing fruit." He described his motives and his means of resolving the conflicting values between England and Russia by saying: "To betray you must first belong. I never belonged. I have followed exactly the same line the whole of of my adult life. The fight against Fascism and and the fight against imperialism were, fundamentally, the same fight. . . . I found the form of this struggle in my work in Soviet espionage. I felt, and I still feel, that by doing this work I have also served my English people."[35]

The diagram is merely a visual, oversimplified caricature of the actual and much more complex process of possible reconciliation or sacrifice of various values in actual individual decision making. Human behavior and its multiple causes obviously cannot be squeezed into eight neat columns and twenty-four squares and then be presented as a true portrait of human reasoning and emotions. But, in a way, the categories are not that much more approximate than those that are found in national constitutions and laws on the subject of disloyalty and treason. They all try to define for all time and schematically distinguish political and territorial loyalty from disloyalty, opposition with foreign support from foreign interference and dissent from treason.

Notes

1. The Algerian revolutionary Frantz Fanon warned against territorial nationalism in Africa, expressing a vain hope for the continent's unification and integration: "So, comrades, let us not pay tribute to Europe by creating states, institutions, and societies which draw their inspiration from her," (Frantz Fanon, *The Wretched of the Earth* [New York: Grove Press, 1968], p. 315). But Africa did do just that.

2. U.S., Soviet, and French definitions of the ideology are as follows: According to the *International Encyclopedia of the Social Sciences*, which focuses on selected internationally relevant ideologies in three areas—religious, democratic, and undemocratic—ideology is "the more or less coherent and consistent sum total of ideas and views on the life and the world (belief system, doctrine, *Weltanschauung*) that guides the attitudes of actual or would-be power holders: leaders of political units, such as nation-states or city-states, or of major organizations or movements, such as churches or political parties" (John H. Herz, "Ideological Aspects—International Relations," in *International Encyclopedia of Social Sciences* [New York: Crowell-Collier-Macmillan, 1968], p. 69).

Soviet (invoking the authority of Lenin): "Ideology is the consciousness of a society, class, or social group that is determined by the material conditions of their existence and provides the principal directions, principles, and goals of their practical activity. . . .

First, every ideology contains a generalised interpretation of the character and course of human social development, its foundations, and its motive forces.

Second, ideology as a whole indicates the goals, means and forms of practical, and, above all, political activities of classes, social groups, and individuals.

Third, ideology always contains a veiled or naked criticism of other ideologies," (Lev N. Moskvichov, *The End of Ideology Theory: Illusions and Reality—Critical Notes on a Fashionable Bourgeois Conception* [Moscow: Progress Publishers, 1974], pp. 66–68).

French: "Ideology is a sum total of perceptions that imply a coherent view of the reality, appropriate for explaining the totality of the phenomena, as well as an adherence to a system of values appropriate for justifying an action" (Marcel Merle, *Sociologie des relations internationales*, 3d ed. [Paris: Dalloz, 1982], p. 269).

3. Crane Brinton, *The Anatomy of Revolution* (New York: Random House, Vintage Books, 1965), p. 48.

4. Raymond Aron, *Peace and War: A Theory of International Relations* (New York: Praeger, 1966), p. 781.

5. Ralph K. White, "Images in the Context of International Conflict: Soviet Perceptions of the U.S. and the U.S.S.R." in Herbert C. Kelman, *International Behavior: A Social Psychological Analysis* (New York: Holt, Rinehart and Winston, 1965), p. 269.

6. U.S. Senate, Committees on Foreign Relations and Armed Services, *Hearings*, January 15, 1957, p. 176.

7. Norton E. Long, "Open and Closed Systems," in R. Barry Farrell, ed., *Approaches to Comparative and International Politics* (Evanston, Ill.: Northwestern University Press, 1966), p. 165.

8. Leopold Sedar Senghor, *African Socialism* (New York: Praeger, 1964), p. 47.

9. Ibid., p. 33.

10. Edward H. Carr, *Nationalism and After* (New York: St. Martin's Press, 1945), pp. 16–29. See also epigraph to Chapter 6 in this book.

11. This segment dealing with the territorial compartmentalization of world communism and then with morality in territorial politics draws upon the research and contains revised excerpts from Chapters 7 and 8 (pp. 219-312) in Ivo D. Duchacek, *Nations and Men: An Introduction to International Politics*, 3d ed. Copyright 1975 by the Dryden Press. Reprinted by permission of CBS College Publishing.

12. V. I. Lenin, *Selected Works*, vol. 8 (New York: International Publishers, 1943), p. 344.

13. Merle Fainsod, *How Russia Is Ruled* (Cambridge: Harvard University Press, 1953), p. 87.

14. Historicus, "Stalin on Revolution," *Foreign Affairs* (January 1949), p. 199.

15. *New York Times*, May 16, 1943.

16. Milovan Djilas, *The New Class* (New York: Praeger, 1957), p. 174.

17. *Pravda*, September 25, 1968.

18. *Beijing Review*, April 28, 1969.

19. H. H. Gerth and C. Wright Mills, *From Max Weber: Essays in Sociology* (New York: Oxford University Press, 1958), pp. 120–121.

20. George Orwell, "Reflections on Gandhi," *A Collection of Essays by George Orwell* (New York: Harcourt Brace Jovanovich, 1946), p. 177. In his comment on Louis Fisher's *Gandhi and Stalin*, Orwell quoted Gandhi's view that the German Jews ought to have committed collective suicide to "arouse the world and the people of Germany to Hitler's violence." After the war, according to Orwell, Gandhi justified himself by saying that the Jews had been killed anyway and they might as well have died significantly. Orwell added, "If you are not prepared to take life, you must often be prepared for lives to be lost in some other way" (p. 178).

21. Niccolò Machiavelli, *The Prince and the Discourses* (New York: Random House, 1950), pp. 64, 66.

22. Upendra Nath Goshal, *A History of Indian Political Ideas* (New York: Oxford University Press, 1959), pp. 144, 150, 153.

23. Satchidananda Murty, "Ethics and Politics in Hindu Culture," in Harold D. Lasswell and Harlan Cleveland. eds, *The Ethic of Power: The Interplay of Religion, Philosophy, and Politics* (New York: Harper and Row, 1962), p. 85.

24. Ibid., p. 85.

25. Gerth and Mills, op cit. p 126.

26. Arnold Wolfers, *Discord and Collaboration: Essays on International Politics* (Baltimore: Johns Hopkins Press, 1962), p. 50 (italics added).

27. Joseph C. McKenna, S.J., "Ethics and War: A Catholic View," *American Political Science Review* 54 (September 1960), p. 648.

28. Ibid., p. 650.

29. *Le Monde* (Paris), November 8, 1968 (*New York Times* translation, November 9, 1968).

30. Robert Endicott Osgood, *Ideals and Self-Interest in America's Foreign Relations* (Chicago: University of Chicago Press, 1953), p. 451.

31. E. A. Hooton, *Apes, Men, and Morons* (New York: Putnam, 1937), p. 151.

32. The treatment of the conflict of loyalties and treason contains excerpts from Ivo D. Duchacek, *Power Maps: Comparative Politics of Constitutions* (Santa Barbara, Calif.: ABC-Clio, 1973), by permission.

33. Margret Boveri, *Treason in the Twentieth Century* (New York: G. P. Putnam, 1961), p. 6.

34. Sir John Harington, *Epigrams*, 1618 (Menston: Scholar Press, 1970), p. 190.

35. *Izvestia* (Moscow), December 18, 1967. For an unofficial translation see *New York Times*, December 19, 1967, p. 18.

3

Territorial Power Maps: Decentralization

Were not this country divided into States, that division must be made that each might do for itself what concerns itself directly, and what it can so much better do than a distant authority.

—Thomas Jefferson
(autobiography, 1821)

It is a common error to attribute more cohesion to a state whose central government takes on tasks that subaltern bodies or individuals can do better. . . . The politics of a distant, vaster and more complex government and, above all, if it is Parliament, however inspired by the most benevolent of intentions, will never be so prompt, far-sighted and active to meet the needs of Sicily . . . which will disappear in the great mass of Italian affairs.

—Francesco Ferrara
(Brevi note sulla Sicilia, 1860)

Regional decentralization will not provide France with a federal structure. The particular conditions granted Corsica today will remain in the framework of the unitary constitution of the French Republic.

—Gaston Deferre
(in Ajaccio, August 7, 1981)

There are divisions in a democracy and so it is. . . . The question is to know at what point the risk of threatening national unity begins. I am the guarantor of this unity. . . . The president symbolizes the nation, the state, and the republic. . . . I'm here and nothing could stop me from being here. Is that clear?

—François Mitterrand
(Speech in Mulhouse, Alsace,
November 22, 1984)

The confidence of the American society in its citizens [may be found] in the authority delegated to local government to administer everyday aspects of life and to make decisions in the field of city planning, health, and education— decision-making powers our [French] central government would be terrified to put in the hands of [locally] elected officials.

—J. J. Servan-Schreiber
(The American Challenge, 1974)

58

No national government, whether democratic, authoritarian, or totalitarian, finds it physically possible, administratively effective, or politically wise to enact and enforce all rules from the center.The reason for any delegation or distribution of authority is simple enough: Political rulers can focus on some problems some of the time but cannot focus on all problems all of the time, on all levels, and in all localities. In political management, too, some division of labor is inevitable. In order to avoid being buried under an avalanche of legislative and executive details, the creators and managers of national governments distribute, divide, and subdivide (often minimally in essential issue-areas) their rule-making and rule-enforcing powers both *vertically* and *horizontally*, that is, hierarchically in terms of appropriate superordination and subordination and coordinately in terms of specific functional or geographically determined responsibility.

This and the following chapter will primarily focus on the *territorial* units of legislative and executive powers within national systems. These units represent territorial communities that either predate or result from the guarantee or grant of power. The scope of their authority varies, not only from system to system, but within the same system from time to time, from technology to technology, and from personality to personality. The spectrum of variations related to territorial power dispersion presents such extreme opposites as a totalitarian system with some territorial microautonomy, on the one hand, and a loose consociation of sovereign communities, on the other. The size, names, and degree of authority of these units also vary greatly as they might be hamlets, parishes, villages, towns, cities, municipalities, districts, or county boroughs (in England); *départements* (in France); provinces (in Canada and China); prefectures (in Japan); regions (in Italy and France); autonomous republics (in the USSR, Yugoslavia, and Czechoslovakia); *Länder* (in federal Austria and Germany); cantons (in Switzerland); or states (in the United States, India, Australia, and Latin American federations).

Although those various units of territorial authority deal with geographically confined clusters of functional issues, other nonterritorial *functional* institutions and agencies of a central government specialize and have expertise in such sectors of national concern as agriculture, industry, business, ecology, labor, education, and culture. Although these sectors are defined in all-national terms and responsibility, naturally, they too have geographically determined boundaries: first those of their home nation, separate and distinct from other territorial nations, and second, the territorial components of the nation-state. As noted in Chapter 1, we can never disregard the territorial dimension of anything we do: We create and are shaped by our spaces. Thus, in one way or another, the exercise of functional authority, although apparently independent of the territorial subdivisions within the national territory, has often proved to be confined and colored by those subdivisions.

The presence of various segments (agencies) of the central government within the components of the various decentralized or federal systems (such as the U.S., Canadian, Indian, and Swiss federal unions) is sometimes, and often rightly, viewed as making those agencies centralizing tentacles of the national government. Nevertheless, they too cannot help operating within, and therefore being influenced (or "corrupted") by, their specific, territorially defined environments. Even centralist and unitary France found that the centrally trained and appointed chief administrators in charge of territorial subdivisions, the prefects, could be deflected from their all-national concerns by regional interests and issues if they were allowed to stay too long in a particular *région*. Regular movement of prefects from one area to another, ordered and managed by Paris, was the result.

To Delegate or Not to Delegate

Assignment of specific duties either on a territorial or a functional basis, imposes a difficult task on the political leadership: to differentiate, however flexibly and approximately, between general, collective issues to be handled by the central authority, on the one hand, and special or territorial ones to be taken care of by either functional agencies or noncentral territorial authorities (provincial, state, cantonal, regional, etc.), on the other. All national problems are bound to have local ramifications, and all local issues may significantly affect other territorial communities as well as their sum total, the whole nation. Even modern authoritarian and totalitarian systems are not immune against the fundamental headache of assigning specific functional or territorial tasks to the appropriate decision-making administrative units.

Perhaps only some tribal territories or some of the modern microstates could conceivably be administered by a ruler as a personal fief on account of his godlike omnipotence and omnipresence. When, however, a nation-state is of some size, its leader and his or her immediate aides must organize power territorially; even modern detection and communication devices, coupled with extreme mobility of enforcing agents, necessitate some delegation of power, at least to those people who manipulate the devices and transports and command their immediate and local uses. Hitler, who had condemned the federal territorial diffusion of power under the democratic Weimar Republic, introduced another system of territorial subdivisions of Germany, all tightly controlled by Berlin. The Third Reich was divided into *Gaue*,[1] each headed by a *Gauleiter*, a Nazi "lieutenant" (which is, of course, another territorial term: person who holds a place—*tient un lieu*—in behalf of somebody else).

In the 1970s, several West German scholars, studied the extent of territorial elbowroom that had remained even under such a highly centralized and totalitarian system as the Third Reich.[2] Some territorial units (for example, Westphalia, Württemberg, and Lippe) were able to assert their territorial interests vis-à-vis the center. In the case of Lippe, for example, its integration with the neighboring Prussian provinces, as planned by Berlin, was prevented by local maneuvering.

A similar regional or ethnoterritorial resilience surfaced in the totalitarian framework of the Soviet Union in the late 1950s and prevented what presumably was Khrushchev's plan to replace Soviet intrafederal ethnic boundaries. Territorial subdivisions based on ethnic differences began to be viewed as a hurdle to a more rational distribution of authority within the framework of socialist long-term planning. Ethnic republics were to be replaced by supraethnic regions—such as "North-Center," Volga-Urals, "South," Central Asia, Kazakhstan, Siberia, and Far East. In the Khrushchev era, a few Soviet legal journals were even allowed to express the view that Soviet "federalism" had already fulfilled its historic—and temporary—role as a necessary step leading finally to a rational unitary system. There is, however, no trace of any departure from polyethnic federalism in the new Soviet Constitution of 1977 (the Brezhnev charter). The ruling elites fear of "decentralizing pressures from below," that is, ethnic discontent and dissent, seems to have played a decisive role.

In communist China, the only serious leadership crisis within the Chinese Communist party prior to the so-called Socialist Cultural Revolution of the late 1960s developed around the territorial ambitions of two party secretaries, Jao Shu-shih and Kao Kang, who were accused of having built personal territorial bases of power in Shanghai and Manchuria, respectively, for the alleged purpose of plotting against the center of the system and the party, Beijing (Peking).[3]

The history of all great empires is full of examples of crises precipitated by provincial lords who used their territorial power for the purpose of capturing the central imperial authority or of successfully seceding from it. Often, ancient empire builders who had personally, with sword in hand, conquered distant provinces finally had no choice but to transfer their administration to proconsuls and viceroys—usually relatives, friends, or trusted chieftains. And every so often, the empire builders came to regret their choice, because the people who had the organizational skill and political talent necessary to rule over the newly taken territory (that is, to command the local garrisons, legions, and police and to collect taxes) were quite capable of a rebellious bid for central or independent local power. Many rulers, when suddenly deposed by their inferiors and awaiting execution in prison, have realized, much to their surprise, that their fall stemmed from having delegated too much of their power. "We have kiss'd away kingdoms and provinces" is a famous melancholic statement made by Antony's friend Scarus in Shakespeare's *Antony and Cleopatra* (Act 3, scene 10).

On the other hand, many a ruler, dreading a dangerous dilution of power, has tried to concentrate authority in his or her own hands so excessively that their rule is undermined by the inefficiency of overcentralization. While choking all initiative, the ruler probably contributed to the assertion of the only remaining alternative, rebellion. The art of politics in many instances consists of maintaining an appropriately flexible compound of centralized and decentralized power.

There are two additional problems. First, power eludes any precise definition or measurement. When one says that political power has been divided fifty-fifty or delegated on a ninety-ten basis, the terms are at best allegorical expressions of intent rather than factual descriptions of reality. Even though James Madison spoke of "sums" or "quantities" of power, we cannot really quantify "all those activities which are or may become the subject of governmental control, we cannot presume that these activities are finite or infinite, and we cannot employ the idea of ratio except metaphorically."[4]

Second, in a world of constant economic, environmental, technological, social, and political changes, no division of labor responsibility or power can be considered immune to erosion, or explosion, as a result of those changes. New inventions, discoveries of new sources of raw materials, new means of transportation, and other technological innovations may catapult a backward sleepy province into the position with an energetic basis of power in a political system. Also, what has been delegated to institutions, groups, or men on the assumption of the province's marginal or purely local nature may be subsequently maneuvered into being a decisive area of power.

From the Top Down and/or from the Bottom Up

Territorial units of self-government within larger systems may issue from two distinct processes, each starting from an opposite pole. One process, *decentralization*, is a movement from the pole of a centralized unity to a situation of managed diversity. The term, "decentralization," logically presupposes the existence of a central authority whose leaders deem it useful, often inevitable, to delegate a portion of their centrally held power to subnational centers. A territorial self-government created from the top down by a central authority to suit its basic need to unburden its legislative and executive overload may be undone when the central responsibility once again becomes manageable or the decentralization leads to chaotic conditions. In principle, any delegation of power in a decentralized system remains revocable. As already noted, the task of dividing or delegating power is always delicate since the boundary between general and local issues is both blurred and changing. This problem is why a power-delegating center every so often prefers to err on the side of cautiousness than on that of trust and generosity, for example, socialist France in the 1980s (see the section "Decentralization in Centralist France" later in this chapter).

It should be noted that decentralization may also occur and has taken place within empires and that it can result in the replacement of the former imperial unity by a voluntary association or confederation of semisovereign or fully sovereign territorial communities. The evolution of the British Empire through the British Commonwealth of (semisovereign) Nations (Act of Westminster, 1931) to a very loose consociation of fully sovereign nations following World War II is a good example of this process.

The second process, *association*, starts *from the bottom up* (from dispersion to some degree of unity) when independent territorial communities agree to create a common central authority but reserve for themselves some specific powers. The scope of these powers is usually fixed and described in a compact (for example, in alliances, leagues, common markets, consociations or confederations) or a constitution (in the case of federal unions committed to creating a new "federal" nation).

An association of territorial communities may, of course, be based on central compulsion rather than on consent. The absence of consent distinguishes the territorial structure of an empire from a voluntary union based on an initial amicable agreement. (More about this matter is discussed in Chapter 4 in connection with the consociational cradle of federations and confederations.)

The processes of decentralization and territorial association by consent or conquest may be expressed graphically (see Figure 3.1). Territorial communities such as provinces, states, and cantons ("T" in Figure 3.1) delegate, in turn, portions of their power to local authorities such as municipalities, districts, counties, townships, and parishes ("M" in Figure 3.1). It should be noted that at a certain point, both movements, although contrastingly motivated and proceeding in opposite directions, may result in a similar pattern of spatial distribution of authority. It may be further noted that in the case of a significantly decentralized unitary system, the once-delegated and, in principle, revocable power may become politically, though not legally, irrevocable. It may become a political folly, if not suicide, to withdraw what, over the years, has become habit, tradition, and unwritten law.

In the association of territorial communities, the once-revocable membership and, in principle, revocable delegation of power from the territorial communities to a common center may in fact become permanent and significant. Figure 3.1 presents a "meeting" point that, in principle, may be reached, but the diagram cannot graphically capture the entirely different origin of the two movements, their constant changes, and the different dynamics of both configurations.

In some cases, both processes—the one from above and the other from below—may occur simultaneously, for example, a geographically distant or overburdened central or imperial authority invites, welcomes, or wisely yields to either a new or a resurrected sense of identity and of separate territorial self-rule. By a new sense of identity I mean a birth of collective awareness of separate destiny reflecting a distinct history, geography, or ideology—often a dose of all three ingredients. In the absence of racial, ethnocultural, and linguistic differences, one may speak of ideology or *ideoethnicity* as a possible basis of separate national identity and culture. This is the case in the United States, Canada, Australia, and New Zealand vis-à-vis their "mother country," England, and in Québec vis-à-vis France. By a resurrected sense of identity I mean the reawakening of old memories of independence once enjoyed and then lost. In many cases, an awareness of a territorially separate destiny *predates* the establishment of the central authority. This situation exists in the case of polyethnic systems (empires

64

Figure 3.1

Decentralization and Territorial Association

Delegation of Power by and from the Center

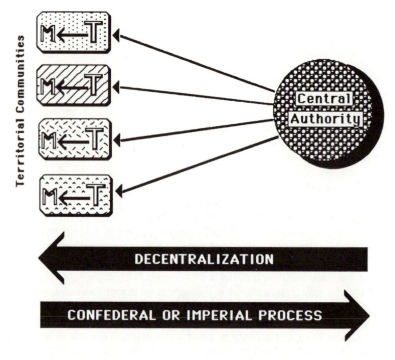

Delegation of Power to or Forcible Absorption by the Center

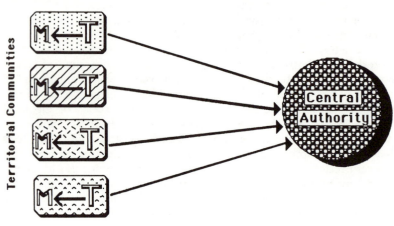

or states) that develop following a conquest or when dynastic agreements that attempt to incorporate alien groups into a system against their will.

For the past 125 years, the evolution of Canadian anglophone identity and federalism has been marked by a gradual yielding by a distant government (Westminster) to both distance and new ideoterritorial assertion. This mixed process, simultaneously proceeding from below and from above, culminated by the 1982 patriation[5] of the Canadian Constitution, which was presented to the distant authority and the world at large in terms that were basically characteristic of a mixed process. The resolution respecting the Canadian Constitution, as adopted by the Canadian House of Commons (December 1, 1981) and by the Senate (December 8, 1981), was forwarded to London in clearly nonrevolutionary terms, bearing little resemblance to, "If this be treason, make the most of it!" and other utterances by Patrick Henry in Williamsburg and Richmond in the 1770s. The Constitution Act of 1981 begins:

> To the Queen's Most Excellent Majesty:
> Most Gracious Sovereign:
>
> We, Your Majesty's loyal subjects, the House of Commons of Canada in Parliament assembled, respectfully approach Your Majesty, requesting that you may graciously be pleased to cause to be laid before the Parliament of the United Kingdom a measure containing the recitals and clauses hereinafter set forth.

The creation of several new states on the basis of lingual identity within the Indian federal union and the "federalization" of communist Czechoslovakia in 1968 are other examples of processes in which demands from the bottom up meet a central authority's goodwill (or yielding to a necessary evil) half way or at least a quarter of the way.

Basic Purposes of Decentralization

A territorial division or delegation of authority fulfills three basic purposes:

1. It unburdens the central authority and makes it more effective by transferring day-to-day concerns and the handling of local territorial matters to subnational units of rule making, such as villages, municipalities, counties, districts, or provinces. Even if there were no natural or preexisting elements of territorial identity, a rational distribution of the burden of rule making in itself would justify the maintenance or creation of units of territorial self-rule. But, as noted in Chapter 1, the very creation of a self-administering spatially defined unit, however artificial its origins, may over time give birth to genuine territorial identity and community (Chapter 1 notes the example of North and South Dakota).

2. A territorial distribution of authority also contributes to the mobilization of local initiative and responsibility on the assumption that people usually

care more about what is familiar and immediate in space and in time than about abstract, distant concepts and goals.

3. A unit of local territorial authority should also be viewed as an important channel for the transmission of political will and information in two directions: from the central authority to the local authority and from the local authority to the central authority. In democracies, especially the federal type, the traffic from the local authority to the central (national) authority may be heavy. But even in systems in which local units of authority are created from "above" by a dictator to serve as docile transmission belts in one direction only (from the central authority to the local authority), there is also a thin stream of messages in the opposite direction. This flow is often a mere trickle of political signals from "below"; they are usually contained in confidential reports of local representatives whose role it is to be not only the mouth but also the ears and eyes of the central authority in their assigned territories. Whether we have in mind local Communist party secretaries or local commanders in military systems in Asia, Africa, or Latin America, they all cautiously and discreetly inform the central authority as to where the national shoe locally pinches.

Mobilizing local initiative, responsibility, and supports; learning about local needs and discontent; and translating national goals and policies into local terms are the main reasons central authorities in democracies usually welcome and extol some form of territorial division of authority. It is a geographic expression of the core creed of a free society: to make authority responsible and responsive to the will of the people and enable the people to participate.

This analysis of the reasons for the territorial distribution of power leads to the preliminary conclusion that territorial identity, interest, and authority result from an interplay of two demands that tend to meet halfway. One demand is the desire of territorial interest groups to obtain or preserve their autonomy, and the other is the need of central authorities to rely on territorial units for local initiative, responsibility, and self-rule.

Territorial units of government (however created as is illustrated in Chapter 1) that give the people what they want but cannot achieve by individual efforts (such as welfare, security, order) may create or increase popular support for the territory and its political superstructure. Thus, political loyalty acquires well-defined geographic boundaries. The result is the territorial interest group or territorial community, which is defined in Chapter 1 as a group of people who are linked by particular bonds of territorial concern and advantage and who are aware of those bonds. An awareness of common territorial interest and destiny tends to aggregate competing political, economic, and social interests into a collective group interest, which is then defended against intrusion or manipulation by outsiders who are considered alien, hostile, or at least ignorant of local conditions.

Such a subnational territorial amalgamation of competing interests for the purpose of collective promotion and defense closely resembles nationalism (unity in relation to foreign nations); it differs from it in the choice of the primary target: Subnational territorial interests are asserted with vigor against the national center. As any well-organized group with a loyal membership, a territorial community has many political weapons and effective pressure techniques at its disposal such as petitions of grievances, propaganda, and professional lobbies. Some subnational, spatially well-defined territorial communities have an additional technique of pressure and blackmail, that is, a threat of secession (national self-determination)—a true time bomb that is not easy to defuse.

I use the terms "secession" and "self-determination" interchangeably since no modern nation can be born out of a total vacuum; a territorial community can obtain nationhood only by seceding from an empire or a nation-state. Secession occurs when a subnational territorial community becomes so alienated from a distant, neglectful, tyrannical, or hostile central authority (especially when decisive power is monopolized by a different ethnic, racial, lingual, or religious group) that it perceives secession and independent statehood as the only means of protecting and promoting all interests and claims.

The gravity of the possible dilemmas is obvious and explosive: Decentralization in a deeply divided society may compartmentalize it into feuding, intolerant, and egoistic communities that totally disregard the interest of the collective whole. In some situations, as noted above, a grant of local autonomy is viewed by tribes or ethnic groups as a first step toward secession at a later date. As this is often a distinct possibility in newly established territorial states, inhabited by unfinished nations, it is therefore a favorite argument on the part of the national leadership for not only a tightly centralized but also an authoritarian rule. Thus, just as diversity, if not tempered by a tolerant give-and-take, may fission an otherwise viable polity, so, in the name of unity, dictatorship may devour diversity, territorial as well as political.

Unity and Diversity

Unity coupled with diversity is a highly desirable goal and a very attractive slogan; it has been made part of many a political creed and constitutional text. The implementation of this goal in practice has, however, often been distorted in either direction. Instead of balancing each other, unity and diversity in frontal conflict may destroy one another: Commitment to the territorial unity may degenerate into extreme centralism or authoritarianism; commitment to diversity may encourage and lead to dismemberment and/or local tyrannies.

So far, institutional and constitutional efforts to strike a workable and enduring balance between unity and diversity have led to three basic formulas of territorial organization of political authority; these formulas represent a gradation of emphasis on territorial unity and diversity. More often than not, one formula shades into another to produce more hybrid systems than a comparative analyst may wish for. The three basic formulas to be discussed in this and the following chapters are: 1. unitary form of government, 2. federal unions, and 3. confederations ("consociations of homelands").

Unitary Delegation of Power

Out of the existing 160 or more territorial nation-states, over 90 percent have adopted the unitary form of government and, with it, the principle of the central authority's allocation of power to territorial subunits of self-rule. The other 10 percent of nation-states have adopted various types of federal systems of government. It should, however, be noted that approximately 10 percent of the nations that *claim* to be federal are the largest and most populous nations of the world (in parentheses, number of million square miles): the USSR (8.6), Canada (3.8), United States (3.61), Brazil (3.2), Australia (2.9), India (1.2), and Argentina (1.07); under 1 million square miles but above 350,000 are Mexico (761,000), Tanzania (362,000), Nigeria (356,000), and Venezuela (352,000). Although some relationship between size and the adoption of a federal system of government seems obvious, it should be noted that some very small nations are federal (nonunitary) too: Austria, Switzerland, and (with qualification) Belgium, Malaysia, Czechoslovakia, Yugoslavia, and the United Arab Emirates. (The varying institutions and practices of federal states is being analyzed in more detail in Chapter 4.)

A system of territorial distribution of authority is called *unitary* if the central authority has the constitutional right and political clout to centralize or decentralize more or less at will, that is, to delegate more or less power to territorial subunits such as provinces, regions, districts, counties, and cities. The extent of decentralization, which may or may not produce real local autonomy, reflects the central authority's estimate of how much and in which issue-areas various territorial communities should enjoy a degree of legislative or administrative autonomy. In a unitary system, any delegation of authority by the center is, in principle, revocable and amendable as to its scope. The balance between centralism and provincial or local autonomy may remain stabilized, be reversed, or be further tilted toward localism.

The nation center's estimate of the extent of power delegation usually reflects four basic considerations:

1. A response to local pressures and the ensuing political wisdom of yielding to them
2. Central authority's need for greater administrative and political flexibility by means of decentralization
3. Central authority's ideological or pragmatic commitment to pluralism and its expression in terms of territorial self-rule
4. An imitation of some successful examples abroad.

Usually, parts of all four considerations are present in the elite's approaches to decentralization. In other words, decentralization in a unitary system reflects the central authority's conclusion that its basic commitment to unity does not exclude some degree of local autonomy, within limits as determined by the central authority.

The power delegated by the central authority may, of course, be quite marginal—as, for example, authorization for a local government to determine the day and hour of local fiestas or market days in light of local traditions and customs. Or, on the contrary, the powers delegated by the national center may be substantial as well as relatively well funded—as, for example, the degree of self-rule enjoyed by counties and cities in the fifty states of the U.S. federal union.

In principle, the states that compose the United States are unitary and not federal; a contrast to the Soviet and Yugoslav federations which, on paper, not only federated the nation but also federalized some of its components (autonomous republics). With regard to the U.S. federal union consisting, in principle of unitary states, it should be noted that in the United States, since Missouri first introduced constitutional home rule in 1875, a total of thirty-six states have written constitutional home rule into their constitutions. At the very least, these state constitutions prevent the abolition of local governments and protect the boundaries of local authorities against any change without local consent. It may be argued that in a limited way, the federal principle of irrevocability of power division has been incorporated into the otherwise unitary framework of the various U.S. states—explicitly in the constitutions of the majority of states and perhaps implicitly in fourteen states by actual practice or impact of their neighbors' examples.

If, more than 140 of the 160 nation-states, have adopted the unitary form of territorial power arrangement (depending on the definition of true federalism), we should try to identify the reasons for their preference. Four are self-evident:

1. The political elites tend to find that a centralized unitary government better serves their fundamental goal of nation-building or nation-maintenance, including the maintenance of their own position at the helm.

2. The leading elites' fear of ethnoterritorial secessionism, present in so many unfinished nations of the Third World, further strengthens the elites' opposition to any significant decentralization or federalism (this tendency still exists in Nigeria, for example, despite its successful suppression of Biafran separatism). When the nation-state of Ghana was born, the preference for a unitary system over a federal one became a part of Nkrumah's eloquent promotion for the new constitution.

Ghana to be a Unitary State—The Government asks the people, by voting for their draft Constitution, to show that they believe in the unity of Ghana and reject any form of federalism. . . . The Government realizes that the present frontiers of Ghana, like so many other frontiers on the African continent, were drawn merely to suit the convenience of the Colonial Powers who divided Africa between them during the last century. The object of the draft Constitution is to provide firm, stable, and popular Government in Ghana . . . and [facilitate] the entry of Ghana into a union of African states.[6]

The last sentence is symptomatic of any situation in which supranational regional planning is on the agenda: National leaders prefer that their nations enter a regional consociation as national monoliths, not as multinational mosaics.

Western European national leaders have reacted quite negatively to their various ethnoterritorial regions (Brittany, Alsace, Occitanie [southern France including Provence] and the Basque area of France or Wales and Scotland in Britain) and their sometimes voiced desire to accede to a united Europe *qua* ethnic regions, not as integral parts of their nation-states. A French author, Marcel Merle, suggested that "maintenance of a country's unity is without any doubt a necessary precondition for its inclusion into an international community: thus, internal federalism appears as a possible obstacle to international federalism."[7]

3. Often, a centralized unitary system eminently fits some national elites' predilection for authoritarian rule.

4. Finally, many elites seem to believe that a unitary system is more manageable and effective in the era of modern warfare/welfare states, high technology, global and regional interdependence, and long-term national planning ensuring a *uniform* development and progress for all sectors of the national community.

Territorial Self-Rule in Unitary Systems

There is a great variety in the processes, structures, and institutions by means of which power delegated by the center may be exercised locally. Four very broad categories of territorial self-rule under a unitary system may be distinguished:

1. Agencies and officials are appointed by the central authority to run territorial subdivisions, take into account the local problems, solve them under central directives, and report to the center about the challenging ones. This type of central management of local affairs existed in imperial structures and in Nazi Germany. Rarely, however, is this arrangement used so blatantly; some appearances of local participation are usually added. The result is the second category.

2. Agencies and officials are appointed by the central authority, but the appointment is confirmed by a plebiscitary ceremonial called "elections," although there is no choice because only one slate of candidates is presented by the party or by the leader. This type of local administration exists in communist countries where all subnational levels of authority are in principle elected but are in reality appointed by the party and confirmed by an electoral ceremonial. Such units of local government are called soviets (councils) of working people's deputies in the Soviet Union, people's

committees or people's councils, in Eastern Europe, and people's congresses in China.

The fact of their appointment and fake nature of their election do not necessarily mean that these officials or agencies cannot be, in time, also responsive to local and special interest pressures, even though they primarily serve as channels for transmitting orders from the central authority to subnational groups. Thus, in authoritarian frameworks corporatist features may and do emerge.

3. In many countries there is a combination of centrally appointed officials in charge of local governments that have locally elected councils. Although the centrally appointed officials are responsible to the center, the locally elected bodies are responsible and accountable to their local electorates. This arrangement has existed in France and in a great many other countries that have followed its (Napoleonic) formula. In France today, however, on the immediate level below the national one, in the *régions* and *départements*, prefects the former instruments and symbols of French centralism have been replaced by commissioners (*commissaires de la République*). In comparison with the Napoleonic prefect, the supervisory and administrative supremacy of the commissioners has been somewhat curbed by the new economic powers of the now elected twenty-two regional assemblies (councils). Nevertheless, the administrative decentralization of France under Mitterand has not substantially altered the traditional French mistrust of locally elected representatives or the implied confidence of Paris in professional highly trained civil servants. One of the epigraphs to this chapter cites a well-known French political observer who is awed by the extent of legal and administrative elbowroom enjoyed by state and locally elected representatives in the United States.

4. Some unitary systems have rejected any form of central appointment in connection with provincial or local autonomy and prescribe an electoral basis for all subnational and national levels of government. This arrangement exists, for instance (under U.S.influence and pressure), in the case of unitary Japan. Its constitution proclaims the principle that there shall be territorial autonomy and that local officials must be elected by direct popular vote, although before World War II they used to be appointed by officials in Tokyo, like the prefects in France. The constitution further stipulates (Article 93) that local authorities have the right to manage their property affairs and administration and prescribes that "local public entities . . . establish assemblies as their deliberative organs." A special law, applicable to only one territorial unit, "cannot be enacted by the Diet without the majority of the voters of the local public entity concerned" (Article 95). This proviso represents a constitutional prohibition of territorial discrimination by the national center.

The preceding few selected examples can only suggest, but cannot describe, the extraordinary variety of territorial distribution of authority that we may find in the some of the 140 or so unitary national systems existing in the world today. They vary from country to country, and sometimes also from region to region within the same country, as to their source of power (election or appointment), scope of authority, and accountability. The nomenclature has created additional problems for comparative analysts since any translation of terms assigned to the hierarchy of subnational units of government is usually more misleading than illuminating; for example, identical terms such as "commune" in France or China and "county" in England or in a U.S. state represent contrasting distributions of authority.

"Indestructible" Units in Unitary Systems

The delegation of authority in a unitary system has so far been presented as being, in principle, always amendable and revocable by the center. This presumption now has to be qualified in two ways. First, what is revocable in theory, law, or constitution may not be so in practical politics. Although the central authority in a unitary system may curb local self-rule at will and can, acting quite constitutionally and legally (but perhaps quite unwisely), reduce it to zero, the center rarely does so. Why? No central government is really so blind as to totally disregard either the reality of territorial interests or the advisability of local initiative and participation. Central authorities do not operate in a weightless, nonpolitical atmosphere. Local centers of political gravity, as experience shows, exercise their magnetic pull whatever the constitutional arrangement may be.

A good example is the unitary United Kingdom in which the Parliament in Westminster is seemingly omnipotent. Theoretically, Parliament could replace the monarchy by a people's democracy and abrogate not only all local government in England but also the very divisions of the United Kingdom into Northern Ireland, Scotland, Wales, and England and could make all into a tightly London-dominated nation-state. It will not do so, being prevented, not by a written constitution but by an unwritten one: long-observed basic laws, tradition, and political culture.

Northern Ireland has its own Parliament and cabinet and has a modified form of nationalization of gas and electricity; Scotland, which has its own church and legal system, is represented in the British Parliament by elected representatives, who form a Committee of Scottish Bills,[8] and is represented in the cabinet by a secretary of state for Scotland, assisted by a minister of state for Scotland. In the 1960s, the Scottish Nationalists asked for their own Parliament and cabinet. Wales is represented in the British cabinet by a secretary of state for Welsh affairs, assisted by a minister of state who resides in Wales. The territorial distribution of authority in the United Kingdom, so solidly guaranteed by unwritten and written laws without a written constitution, has led many close observers of the British political practice to conclude that the unitary system of British government is, in fact, federal or quasi-federal.

Second, many constitutions that proclaim that their systems are unitary also proclaim the principle of territorial division of authority, describe and guarantee the formation and powers of territorial autonomous units, and often enumerate such units by categories or names, especially in the case of ethnoterritorial communities. Their "indestructibility" and autonomy are thus placed under special constitutional protection. Many scholars classify such arrangements as federal or quasi-federal.

"Regionalized" China

Such guarantees may be found in all the successive constitutions of the People's Republic of China, a unitary multiethnic state of 1 billion people, which, besides the Chinese, contains fifty-five ethnic groups, some truly minor but nearly all clearly territorial. The 1982 Constitution (similar to the 1958 one) and the Law on Regional Autonomy for Minority Nationalities of May 31, 1984, spell out some major principles of territorial self-rule combined with a heavy emphasis on China's unity to be protected and promoted by the central authorities (party and government).

China has established five major autonomous regions, thirty-one autonomous prefectures, and seventy-eight autonomous counties for the purpose of various degrees of limited self-rule by the ethnic minorities inhabiting these areas.[9] The five major regions are: Mongolia (to be distinguished from the Soviet-protected People's Republic of Mongolia, separated from Chinese Mongolia by the Gobi Desert), Xinjiang-Uygur (Chinese Turkestan), Ningsia (inhabited by the Muslim Hui people), Guangxi Zhuang (inhabited by Zhuangs, the most populous of China's minorities), and Tibet. In addition, other special areas or regions were or will be established on other than an ethnic basis.

For example, on the basis of different historic development, two special administrative regions were proposed by the Chinese leaders in the 1980s. First Hong Kong (Xianggang), when it returns to China on January 1, 1997, as a result of a 1984 Sino-British accord, will be a special region; the second will be Taiwan, if and when it is made a part of the People's Republic of China. The establishment of regions on other than an ethnic basis seems authorized by the 1982 Constitution.[10] A third case will be probably Macao, a Portuguese enclave on the South China coast, which, for the past 400 years, has been under Lisbon's administration. During the Portuguese president's visit to Beijing on May 23, 1985 (reported in *Beijing Review*, June 3, 1985), Portugal and China agreed to negotiate the transfer of administration back to China.

Clearly extraconstitutional, dominantly political motives induced the Chinese leaders to demonstrate its flexibility to the West. Such a demonstration is expected to prove helpful in arranging for the planned return of Hong Kong and Taiwan to China and to make the changes more palatable to the capitalist West. In August 1983, for example, Deng Xiaoping suggested that Beijing would recognize "the Taiwan local government's right to follow its own internal policy" as a special administrative region, "different from the other provincial and autonomous regional governments." Deng added that Taiwan would also "keep its own armed force so long as they do not impair the interests of the unified state" and promised that "the mainland would station neither troops nor administrative personnel in Taiwan," leaving it to the Kuomingtang party, army, and government to administer themselves. "Seats in the Central Government of China will be reserved for Taiwan," Deng concluded.[11]

In 1984, at the plenary session of the Central Advisory Commission, Deng introduced a new concept, referred to as "one country-two systems," which would allow Hong Kong and Taiwan to "adopt a political, economic and social system different from the main system,"[12] that is, "keeping socialism as the mainstay but allowing capitalism" in the two regions.[13] In a subsequent elaboration of Deng's proposal, Yan Jiaqi took pains to stress that China, although it would have "some characteristics of a pluralist system," would certainly not be federal: "Hong Kong and Taiwan do not have inherent powers. Their powers are granted by the central government." The writer did not mention whether these powers, once granted, could also be easily withdrawn. Yan specified that the central people's government would grant the two special regions "considerable diplomatic powers to handle some external affairs" (apparently foreign trade and investment); neither, however, could "exercise national sovereignty, carry out its own diplomacy or defence, and declare war or make peace."[14]

Although foreign policy considerations (reunification) clearly colored the concept of "one country-two systems," the establishment of the so-called special economic zones, which Beijing began authorizing in 1981 in coastal China, was clearly motivated by China's need to attract foreign capital and technology. Four such zones have been established in the cities of Shenzhen, Zhuhai, and Shantou in Guangdong Province and the city of Xiamen in Fujian Province. An official description of their functions stresses five reasons for this territorial decentralization:

1. Serve as "bridges for introducing foreign capital, advanced technology and equipment and as classrooms for training personnel"
2. "Promote competition between regions"
3. "Absorb foreign exchange"
4. "Serve as experimental units in economic structural reform and as schools for learning . . . the regulation of production according to market demands"
5. "To employ many young people waiting for jobs."[15]

The official weekly *Beijing Review* also emphasized that by establishing economic zones, China is doing basically what so many other countries are doing in this era of interdependence. In his justification of China's special zones, the vice-president of the Chinese Academy of Social Science and director of the Chinese Institute of Economics, Xu Dixin, pointed to "300 special economic zones established in about 75 countries and regions in the world today (some are called free trading zones, some processing-exporting zones and some tax-free trading zones)."[16]

Despite various partial departures from Chinese communist centralist rhetoric and unitary practices, Chinese leaders rarely miss an opportunity to emphasize the nonfederal nature of their system. In 1958, for example, the chairman of the Nationalities Committee of the National People's Congress, Liu Ke-ping, emphatically asserted that China was "not a federation of republics."[17] A quarter of a century later, *Beijing Review*, in commenting on the future of "special administrative regions," emphatically asserted again:

> There is only one China—the People's Republic. China is a single-system socialist country, not a federal state. . . . The special administrative regions are local units under the unified leadership of the central authorities. *They are not member-states of China.* They must exercise power within limits of authority prescribed by law . . . enacted by the National People's Congress. At the same time, the special administrative regions can be highly flexible . . . and are invested with special powers. For example, the Hong Kong Special Administrative Region . . . will enjoy a high degree of autonomy except in foreign and defense affairs, which are the responsibility of the Central People's Government. . . . The laws currently in force in Hong Kong will remain basically unchanged. . . . Using the name "Hong Kong, China," . . . the Region may maintain and develop economic and cultural relations and conclude agreements with states, regions and international organizations on its own[!] . . . The [1982] Constitution stipulates in Article 1 that . . . "China is a socialist state under the people's democratic dictatorship, with the socialist system as its basic system." This stipulation is not in contradiction with that allowing the special administrative regions to retain their capitalistic system. For the good of the whole country, it is necessary to maintain the socialist system. But for some localities [Hong Kong and Taiwan], it is better to let them keep their capitalistic system.[18]

The constitutional provisions for and official comments on territorial autonomy in unitary China[19] consistently avoid any terminology that could ever so faintly suggest to China's fifty-five ethnic communities that they ever had or could ever hope for true federalism or sovereignty. It is in this context that the mere mention of "federalism" appears to the Chinese leaders as "sacrilegious"—if I may take the liberty of using such a metaphor in an atheistic framework.

Regionalized Italy

Another unitary system utilizing a quasi-federal arrangement is regionalized Italy. The postwar 1947 Constitution of the Italian Republic, for instance, provides for regionalism in a detailed way. The names of all regions,[20] their financial autonomy, legislative councils, and executive organs (*giunta*) are described in the constitution. In all regions, the representative of the central authority (*commissario*) is to supervise the working of local self-rule. Only five out of twenty regions were granted special autonomous status right after 1947: the islands of Sicily and Sardinia, Trentino-Alto Adige (where there is a problem of German-speaking Italian citizens), Friuli-Venezia Giulia (a strategically important area contiguous with Yugoslavia; Trieste is part of that region), and Valle d'Aosta (adjoining France).

For twenty-two years the Italian political leaders representing the dominant force of Christian democracy in different combinations with democratic socialists hesitated to implement the constitutional provisions for the establishment of the other fifteen autonomous regions. Two reasons for the centralists' fear of quasi-federalism in Italy are worth noting. The experience with the first five regions had not been too encouraging; under the umbrella of local autonomy, they had proved quite scandal-ridden. Furthermore, the ruling majority dreaded that the autonomous regions might become convenient bases of power—and blackmail—for the Communist party, which in some cases could transform such regions into "soviet autonomous republics" of sorts.[21] Whatever the past and present fears might have been, the regional provisions of the constitution were finally implemented in 1970, and all twenty regions (five special and fifteen "ordinary") are now in full and successful operation;[22] the cohesion of Italy does not seem to be as threatened as some Italians feared. As one U.S. scholar summed up the experience:

> The setting up of regional units of government is a rather strong indication that Italian ruling elites are confident in the ability of the Italian polity to resist separatist tendencies. There could be no clearer vote of confidence in the existence and prospects of survival of an Italian nation than this erection of political subdivisions that are bound, by their very nature, to revive memories of political distinctions that existed in Italy during the Renaissance. To be sure, this regional arrangement is not federalism; the regions do not begin to have the power or prestige of the American states or German *Länder*. But there is definitely a departure from the rigid centralization of the past, when local initiative was discouraged and stifled and when all political roads led to Rome.[23]

Strong evidence of the regional governments' roles in the economic, social, and political life of Italy is documented in a study by an Italian expert on regionalism, Calogero Muscara. In his paper, "The Inner Boundaries of Italy," presented at the International Political Science Association in Paris (July 17, 1985), he confirmed the role of political institutions as creators of new political loyalties and habits or at least as tools for the reawakening of what had been dormant for decades or centuries. Muscara's study admits that regional identities and practices have asserted themselves in northern Italy with great vigor since they were grafted onto such powerful urban centers as Florence, Milan, or Venice, with their medieval histories of power and excellence, while the process has been hesitant in the rural south.

Some aspects of the Italian "federal political culture" that were present at the time of Italy's unification seem to have also been revived, as Filippo Sabetti's recent historical study documents. Quoting writers who had disagreed with Giuseppe Mazzini, in particular the then-leading Italian economist Francesco Ferrara (1810–1890), Sabetti concluded, for example, that Sicilians could become Italian nationalists only because of their hope for federal regionalism.[24] A few caveats some 125 years ago uttered by Francesco Ferrara, an Italian "federalist," form one of the epigraphs to this chapter. They are worth pondering still today both in Italy and in other countries.

Decentralization in Centralist France

In 1980, preparing for elections in alliance with the communists, the French Socialist party agreed on and in 1981 published a voluminous party platform. A book of 380 pages, it was entitled, *Socialist Project: For France of the 1980's*. It contained a plan for decentralization, which among other proposals included the following:

> For the socialists, decentralization means using the most powerful levers for breaking completely with capitalism. This lever will permit the citizens to participate most directly in the social transformation which will begin as soon as the national power is conquered by the Left. . . . A different division of tasks between the national government and local collectivities . . . will be assured. This is the sense of the triptych "planning-centralization-autogestion" which forms the very heart of our project concerning the organization of the established powers.[25]

The socialist project further promised the replacement of the powerful prefects by a new power to be enjoyed by an elected chairman of a regional legislative assembly. "Only a development of powerful and democratic regional communities can take away from the central authority [*l'Etat*] its dominance in deciding major issues." After enumerating the various future tasks of the regional authorities in matters of energy, industry, agriculture, health, communications, and education, the socialist document also suggested that decentralization would promote the various regional identities, especially in terms of regional languages and cultures. The text incorporated and fully endorsed a statement made by François Mitterand in 1973 (elected president in 1981), according to which the defense of a regional language is essential for the protection of the culture: "Recognition of the [regional] languages as a cultural fact leads to their acceptance as a political fact; this is preferable to stifling the soul of a people."[26]

The socialist platform gave assurance of an immediate grant of territorial autonomy to the island of Corsica. No other ethnoterritorial region (Brittany, Alsace, Basque country, or Occitanie) was so treated. The autonomy of Corsica granted in August 1981 did not satisfy that island's radical groups; the political situation there has remained highly unsettled ever since. When on August 7, 1981, the spokesman of the French socialist government, Minister Gaston Deferre, presented the principles of the new home rule in Ajaccio (the capital of Corsica), he stressed the *nonfederal* nature of the decentralization in terms that were almost identical to those the Chinese leaders have used speaking of special administrative regions. The same day,

Figure 3.2. France

Source: Ivo D. Duchacek, *Comparative Federalism: The Territorial Dimension of Politics* (New York: Holt, Rinehart and Winston, 1970).

the main daily of the French right, *Le Figaro*, entitled its highly critical editorial commenting on Corsican autonomy "A Bad Choice," and its main story had a mast heading "Corsica: A Dangerous Experience."

It appears that in France, from Robespierre and Napoleon through de Gaulle and Giscard d'Estaing to socialist Mitterand, "federalism" has been a dirty word. Another indication of the vigor of the antifederal and procentralist trends in France was the central government's hesitation to ratify the European Outline Convention on Transfrontier Cooperation

Between Territorial Communities or Authorities, which it helped prepare. Other European nations, federal and unitary (West Germany, Austria, Belgium, Italy, Netherlands, Ireland, and the Scandinavian countries) did so within a year following the convention's collective drafting and signing in 1980. France finally followed suit in February 1984, adding, however, important reservations that submit transborder regional cooperation to a preliminary authorization by Paris.

In French domestic legislation, a new law (no. 82-213, of March 1981) provides for the national government's authorization of "the new regional councils to organize regular cooperative contacts with foreign noncentral authorities across the national border." Only time will tell whether the borderland regions (from Alsace to the Basque country near the Pyrenees) will succeed in enlarging their autonomous elbowroom on the basis of such a vague pledge by a unitary government to delegate power. It should be also recognized that the socialist commitment to all-national planning and the nationalization of industries, inevitably involving central controls, nec-essarily conflicts with the alleged commitment to territorial political or economic *pluralism* (which conceivably could lead to the municipalization or regionalization of larger enterprises as British Fabians sometimes suggested) or workers' *autogestion* in industrial enterprises. The French socialist "trip-tych" slogan ("planification-decentralization-autogestion") misleadingly glosses over some inherent contradictions.

East Central Europe

In communist Eastern Europe, where the problems of ethnoterritorial or dispersed ethnic communities have traditionally been sensitive issues, the otherwise clearly unitary constitutions guarantee the autonomous devel-opment of those communities. The Socialist Republic of Rumania, for instance, assures (Article 22) the country's co-inhabiting nationalities the free use of their native language as well as "books, papers, magazines, theatres and education at all levels in their own language." Where a non-Rumanian group lives in a compact area, "all the bodies and institutions use the language of the respective nationality in speech and in writing and appoint officials from its ranks or from the ranks of other citizens who know the language and the way of life of the local population."

Curious is the case of Czechoslovakia. Until 1968, that country declared it was not and did not want to be a federation. Article 1 of its 1960 Constitution proclaimed that "the Czechoslovak Socialist Republic is a *unitary* state of two fraternal *nations*, possessing equal rights, the Czechs and the Slovaks" (italics added), and Chapter 6 of the constitutional text (Articles 73–85) spelled out the autonomy and reserved powers of Slovakia in some detail. There was a Slovak legislative chamber that had the authority to appoint a quasi-cabinet for Slovakia, but curiously, the constitution did not provide for corresponding organs of autonomy for the Czechs in Bohemia and Moravia. The common Czechoslovak organs were to serve the western

Czech half of the country while the eastern Slovak portion had its own political and administrative framework. At first sight, the system appeared to be a federal one heavily tilted to the advantage of the Slovaks. In reality, it was the opposite. The more advanced and industrial as well as the more populous Czech portion of the state has always played the decisive role in the direction of the republic.

The Czechs dominated the leading organs of the Czechoslovak Communist party and the Prague government. The Slovak resentment against this state of affairs was one of the triggers of the short-lived attempt to combine Czechoslovak socialism with pluralism ("socialism with a human face") in terms of both a multiparty system and federalism. The other triggers were the opposition of the youth and the intellectuals against the inhumanity of communism and the resentment of the workers and the consumers against the demonstrated gross inefficiency of the communist economy. Although the revolutionary ferment among the Czechs had dominantly liberal overtones—the central issue being the freedom of expression—among the Slovaks, nationalist self-assertion represented a decisive ingredient ("socialism with a Slovak face"?). A new constitutional change—commitment to a Czech-Slovak federalism—was announced on the fiftieth anniversary of the republic (October 28, 1968), two months and seven days after the Soviet occupation—a very strange framework indeed for an attempt at territorial pluralism.

Unitary Decentralization Qualified

Figure 3.3 presents a graphic "shorthand" summary of the preceding analysis. It also qualifies the earlier diagram of a unitary system (Figure 3.1), which only captures the power of the national center to delegate or not to delegate. The new figure is more realistic since it adds two barriers, or protective shields, against a centralist absorption of territorial self-rule: *constitutional* promises or guarantees of local autonomy and an *extraconstitutional* barrier against centralism, the "federal political culture." The arrows within the four territorial communities on the left side of the figure depict one possible form of delegation of power by territorial *subcenters* (T) to local communities such as counties, districts, and municipalities (M). For the sake of pictorial clarity, the other possible form of delegation of authority and funds to municipalities directly from the center to M bypassing T, is not depicted.

The first protective barrier (superimposed on the power-links between the center and the subcenters) is the national constitution when it contains clear guarantees of autonomy for territorial communities. The Italian and Chinese autonomous regions, discussed above, are so protected by their respective national constitutions.

The second shield represents an admittedly elusive but in practice often effective, brake on centralist tendencies at the national center: the habit and tradition of the political elites and people simply to prefer and practice a territorial division of powers over centralism regardless of labels and

Figure 3.3

"Guarantees" of Unitary Delegation of Power

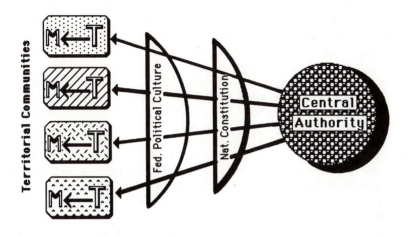

institutions. I have chosen to label such orientation "federal political culture," by which I mean, using Gabriel Almond's and Sidney Verba's terminology, attitudes, beliefs, values and behavioral propensities reflecting respect for and patterns of participation in more than one order of government and more than one territorial community (the subnational and national in this case).[27] These orientations toward the political process include knowledge (cognitive orientations), feelings (affective orientations, which, in this case, include a combination of nationalism and local patriotism), and judgments (evaluative orientations).

Political-Territorial Cultures: Unitary, Federal, and Confederal

The concept of political-territorial culture (the territorial aspect of political culture) admittedly is far from being empirically explored and tested. Its three general types—unitary, federal, and confederal—are used here tentatively and with a great deal of hesitancy. Yet, at this point, it is useful to record occasional manifestations of the three political-territorial general tendencies among elites and publics as they address their grievances to the various levels or orders of authority.

First, in some nations the public and the elites tend to turn to the national center solely or primarily for the solution of even minor local problems (which indicates what can be called a *unitary political culture*). Second, in other nation-states the national center is only one of two targets for the solution of issues (usually the "major" ones although the very concept of what is major is, of course, a matter of change and controversy); the second target for other matters is the local or regional authorities. In some cases, the elites and the public address their demands simultaneously to both orders of government—clearly, a *federal political culture*. Third, in still another framework, the elites and the public turn to regional-territorial authorities, the primary target for both grievances and loyalty except in the case of a major external threat to the associated or allied whole—a *confederal political culture*.

A unitary/territorial tradition tends to shape perceptions and the search for remedies even on the part of the people who oppose it. An illustrative example comes from Occitanie, an area of southern France that is often openly antagonistic to centralist Paris. In a discussion with an Occitan autonomist, the father of a ten-year-old child, I recorded his complaint about the dominant role of the French national language in all the schools around Avignon and the lack of education for his children in the Provençal language: "Why should my children get their education in the dialect of central France" (he referred to the French national language by a derogatory term, Le patois de l'Isle de France) "instead of the language of our great Mistral" (the great poet of Provence, Nobel laureate in 1904)?

When asked about a possible remedy, the Occitan's response was typical for a "unitary political culture": a priori he disregarded the possibility of local or regional self-help and said, "We will ask the French Ministry of National Education in Paris to reserve funds in the next budget for the Provençal language and literature to be taught in Provence and Langue d'Oc." This anecdote is illustrative of the nearly 200-year-old French unitary political tradition, which seems to have so far subverted any attempt at significant decentralization, even when occasionally advocated by reformist elites in both the provinces and Paris itself.

The opposite, a federal political culture, may be recorded in many a unitary framework, for example, in the United Kingdom. Despite the omnipotence of the central Parliament in Westminster, quasi-federal practices maintain themselves in the various regions of England itself and even more clearly in Scotland, Wales, and Northern Ireland.

Despite the lack of uniformity of terms used by students of federal/territorial politics, various authors often include emotional and evaluative orientations of the public and the elites toward noncentralized political processes and attitudes toward the role of self in one's territorial community as independent or intervening variables in their analyses of federalism. Morton Grodzins, for example, in discussing federalism as "antagonistic cooperation," coined the term "federal *creed*"; William S. Livingston spoke of "federal *qualities* of the society" (see the first epigraph to Chapter 5); Thomas A. Franck, "federal *feeling*" or "federal popular or elite *charisma*"; Daniel J. Elazar, a "*sense* of interdependent independence"; V. C. Wynne-Edwards, "*brotherhood* tempered rivalry"; and David B. Truman, "federalist *social factors* independent of the federal structure." In this context, Elazar appropriately posed the following question in 1977: "Many scholars have raised the question whether there is such a thing as a federal political culture . . . or at least political cultures that are more open than others to federal solution . . . which serves as precondition for the viable existence of federal institutions."[28]

As I have noted before, there may indeed be federal processes that not only predate federal institutions but also flourish in a unitary environment in the absence of corresponding federal institutions and structures. What is the cause? Is it the absentmindedness, neglect, or ineptitude of central elites who are outmaneuvered by diligent and intelligent local/territorial elites? Or is it a ruling elite's tacit commitment to significant decentralization in order to mobilize local initiative and responsibility—the federal "soul" of the elite and its political organization/party?

Similarly, when federal institutions and practices do coincide, why is it so? Can it be primarily a result of the constitutional imperatives and effects of political parties and government institutions and structures over a long period of time? Or has there been right from the beginning a mass and/ or elite federal "creed" because of geographic configuration and size? "Our country is too large to have all its affairs directed by a single government," Thomas Jefferson wrote to Gideon Granger in 1809.

When, on the opposite end of the spectrum, unitary and centralizing tendencies underlie—and undermine—the federal institutions and elite commitment, should we look for the causes in such environmental factors as the unitary/centralizing compulsion of modern economy, technology, and ecology, all of which conceivably enhance the power of the federal center at the expense of territorial components? Or is the cause the elites' betrayal of "people's federal sense"? Or is it simply the domino effect of the federal center's inevitable dominance in the issue-areas of defense, diplomacy, long-term planning, and modern technology? In our interdependent world, in which periods of major crises are more frequent than periods of normalcy, it is indeed possible that a welfare/warfare state has great difficulty in remaining not only fully democratic but also decentralized or federal.

As for the confederal political culture, four interconnected themes may be deemed to be its essential parts (see Chapters 6 and 7 for more discussion of confederalism):

1. Awareness of some common interests—external threat or opportunity—shared by the most influential participants in intra- and interterritorial politics
2. Explicit retention of territorial sovereignty and self-rule with the primary loyalty oriented toward the territorial community—a supra-community such as a "federal nation" is not deemed desirable or possible even though one may emerge and be occasionally emphasized for external purposes, especially as a symbol and barrier against a serious external threat
3. Cautiously specific delegation of some power to a decision-making body requiring unanimity for its major policies and actions

Figure 3.4. Interlocked Causes of Federalism

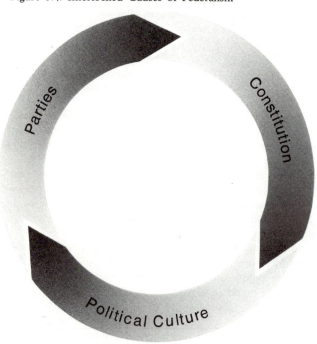

Source: Ivo D. Duchacek, *Comparative Federalism: The Territorial Dimension of Politics* (New York: Holt, Rinehart and Winston, 1970).

4. Self-definition and self-determination of participating territorial communities remain basically intact

From all the questions for which we do not have adequate answers as yet, we can perhaps detect a complex circular movement of causes-effects-causes that interconnects the constitutional institutions, parties, and the still-nebulous concept of habits, traditions, and commitments that I have tentatively called the federal political culture. In 1970, this concept of the three mutually reinforcing but possibly also eroding variables was expressed as in Figure 3.4;[29] today, it still raises more questions than it answers.

The next chapter deals with established federal systems that are generally deemed to be genuinely—politically as well as territorially—plural. Seemingly, that analysis will tread on firmer ground since it will consist of federal constitutions, structures, and practices, leaving the search for intervening variables, such as federal political culture, to academic adventurers better equipped for the task than I. For the time being, a white spot—the federal political culture, truly a *terra ignota*—will continue to mar our federal maps. Because of ignorance, I could have perhaps just as well followed a map-drawing custom of the Middle Ages and, like captains of old, affixed a panacean label to the uncharted blank: *Hic sunt leones foederales* (federal lions reside here). It might have been as explanatory as the term "federal political culture."

Notes

1. There were thirty-two *Gaue* in Germany proper, seven in annexed Austria, and one in the Sudetenland, which was detached from Czechoslovakia in 1938. Ultimately, the Nazi Reich was divided into forty-three *Gaue*. These were further subdivided into 920 districts (*Kreise*, under the control of a *Kreisleiter*). These, in turn, were territorially subdivided into about 30,000 communal groups (*Ortsgruppen*), which were broken down into blocks (*Blocke*) in urban areas and some 110,000 cells (*Zellen*) in rural areas. Harold Zink, *Modern Governments* (Princeton, N.J.: Van Nostrand, 1958), pp. 427–428.

2. Karl Teppe, *Provinz-Partei-Staat: Zur provinziellen Selbstverwaltung im Dritten Reich untersucht am Beispiel Westfalens* (Münster: Aschendorff, 1977); Paul Sauer, *Württemberg in der Zeit des Nationalsozialismus* (Ulm: Süddeutsche Verlagsgesellschaft, 1975), and Hans Jürgen-Sengotta, *Der Reichsstaathalter in Lippe 1933 bis 1939: reichsrechtliche Bestimmungen und politische Praxis* (Detmold: Naturwissenschaftlicher und Historischer Verein für das Land Lippe, 1976), p. 422.

3. In 1967, a Red Guard wall poster announced the purge of Ulanfu, a party leader, governor, and military commander of the Inner Mongolian province of China. The poster accused him of plotting to transform Inner Mongolia into an "independent kingdom." In 1968, Wang En-mao, the communist leader of the strategic Chinese province of Sinkiang, now spelled Xinjiang (Chinese Turkestan, inhabited by a Muslim people, the Uygurs), was purged. On December 22, the Sinkiang Revolutionary Committee, carrying out Mao's Cultural Revolution accused Wang of having a "mountain stronghold mentality" and of attempts to preserve "his independent kingdom."

4. Rufus Davis, "The Federal Principle Reconsidered," *Australian Journal of Politics and History* 1:2 (May 1956), p. 225.

5. The Canadian term "patriation," unusual to American ears, is supposed to differentiate between "repatriation," suggestive of a two-way journey (return to the country of origin), and the one-way process by which the amendments to the British North American act of 1867 (the first Canadian "constitution") were enacted by the "mother country" and its Parliament in Westminster to take its one and last journey from the constitutional fountain to Ottawa. The image of a one-way journey from London to Canada is not quite consistent with the fact that the constitutional text itself was drafted in Canada and by anglophone Canadians only. The then-Canadian Prime Minister, Pierre Elliott Trudeau, however, argued that he had rejected a purely Canadian endorsement of the constitution since it would represent a "revolutionary" step, involving too sharp a break with the original basis of Canada's constitutional system. A detailed description by two seasoned reporters of the triangular negotiations among Ottawa, the ten provinces, and London, which finally led to a compromise among nine provinces, excluding Québec, is contained in Robert Sheppard and Michael Valpy, *The National Deal: The Fight for a Canadian Constitution* (Toronto: Fleet Books, 1982). An analytical study of the amended

constitution is by Edward McWhinney, *Canada and the Constitution 1979-1982: Patriation and the Charter of Rights* (Toronto: University of Toronto Press, 1982).

6. Quoted in Egyptian Society of International Law, *Constitutions of the New African States—A Critical Survey* (Alexandria, March 1962), p. 65.

7. Marcel Merle, *Forces et enjeux dans les relations internationales* (Paris: Economica, 1981), p. 119.

8. See William S. Livingston, who analyzed the evolution of the Scottish Committee of the British House of Commons from a mere instrumentality into an institution that has become a thing of value in itself—"an essential part of the *federal* relation between England and Scotland" (Livingston, "A Note on the Nature of Federalism," *Political Science Quarterly* 67:1 [March 1952], p. 93, italics added).

9. An Zhiguo, "Regional Autonomy for Minorities," *Beijing Review*, June 11, 1984, p. 4.

10. Article 31: "The state may establish special administrative regions when necessary." In the framework of the present analysis, this reads like a classical statement of a unitary type of revocable and amendable delegation of power from and by the national center to subnational territorial communities.

11. *Beijing Review*, August 8, 1983, p. 5.

12. Ibid., February 4, 1985, p. 15.

13. Ibid., April 8, 1985, p. 22.

14. Ibid., April 8, 1985, p. 23.

15. Xu Dixin, "China's Special Economic Zone," *Beijing Review*, December 20, 1981, p. 14. The article suggests that "it is necessary to simplify procedures for entry and exit and make things easier for visitor." It adds that it may also prove necessary to "issue different currency" for such zones.

16. Ibid., pp. 15-17.

17. *Hsinhua* (New China News Agency) January 17, 1958. See also epigraph to Chapter 3 in this book.

18. Wang Shuwen, "Special Regions Leave Socialism Unchanged," *Beijing Review*, October 15, 1984, pp. 71-81 (italics added).

19. An unofficial insight into the provincial differences was offered by a Western journalist, Harrison Salisbury, in his retracing of the legendary Long March of Mao Zedong's armies, which marched 6,000 miles from Jiangxi to Yanan in October 1934 to October 1935: "In the Tibetan area of Sichuan [Province], the prayer flags wave over the Tibetan houses like a forest of streamers. Across the line in the Tibetan part of Gansu [Province], hardly one can be seen. The explanation? No official will venture one. My guess: Sichuan authorities are more tolerant than Gansu authorities" (*New York Times Magazine*, November 18, 1984, p. 44).

20. Piedmont, Valle d'Aosta, Lombardia, Trentino-Alto Adige, Veneto, Friuli-Venezia Giulia, Liguria, Emilia-Romagna, Toscana, Umbria, Marches, Lazio, Abruzzi, Molise, Campania, Puglia, Basilicata, Calabria, Sicily, Sardinia (Article 131). Chapter 5 of the constitution, which deals with regional autonomy, divides the national and regional powers and describes regional autonomy in great detail (Articles 114-133).

21. This was also one of the reasons why, after World War II, France did not experiment with real autonomy for its *départements*. The emergence of several "soviet" republics, administered by local communists in charge of the then still fully armed communist resistance groups, seemed a real possibility—and a nightmare—to de Gaulle's government.

22. Norman Kogan, "Impact on the New Italian Regional Governments and the Structure of Power Within the Parties," *Comparative Politics* 8:3 (April 1975), pp. 304-306. Robert D. Putnam et al., "Explaining Institutional Success: The Case of

Italian Regional Government," *American Political Science Review* 77:1 (March 1983), pp. 55–74.

23. Raphael Zariski, *Italy: The Politics of Uneven Development* (Hinsdale, Ill.: Dryden Press, 1972), p. 138.

24. Filippo Sabetti, "The Making of Italy as an Experiment in Constitutional Choice," *Publius* 12:3 (Summer 1982), p. 77.

25. Parti socialiste, *Projet socialiste: pour la France des années 80* (Paris: Club socialiste, 1981), pp. 252–253 (author's translation).

26. Ibid., p. 256.

27. The term and concept of political culture have been borrowed and adapted from three comparative studies: Gabriel A. Almond and Bingham J. Powell, Jr., *Comparative Politics: A Developmental Approach* (Boston: Little, Brown, 1966), p. 50; Lucian W. Pye, *Aspects of Political Development* (Boston: Little, Brown, 1966), p. 104; and Gabriel A. Almond and Sidney Verba, *The Civic Culture: Political Attitudes and Democracy in Five Nations* (Boston: Little, Brown, 1963), p. 12.

28. Daniel J. Elazar, "Dialogue on Comparative Federalism" (Roundtable discussion held at the Center for the Study of Federalism, Temple University, November 8, 1977), p. 5.

29. Ivo D. Duchacek, *Comparative Federalism: The Territorial Dimension of Politics* (New York: Holt, Rinehart and Winston, 1970; reprint, Washington, D.C.: University Press of America, 1986), p. 341.

Part 2
Federal Systems

4

Democracy's Territorial Twin: Federalism

Federalism is about the protection of spatially demarcated values and interests.
—Donald V. Smiley and R. L. Watts
("The Reform of Federal Institution:
Intrastate Federalism in Canada, 1985)

One of the special dimensions of the federal principle is that it starts with relationships rather than institutions and then concerns itself with structures and institutions on the basis of how they serve the desired relationships, rather than vice versa.
—Daniel J. Elazar
("Dialogue on Comparative Federalism," 1977)

To use the word "federalism" to classify . . . not fully constitutional [democratic] states . . . is like trying to classify cows by the number of petals. It is not useful.
—C. J. Hughes
("The Theory of Confederacies," 1964)

When is a republic no longer a republic; a democracy, no longer a democracy; constitutional government, no longer constitutional government; federalism, no longer federalism? Are we simply uttering sounds and scribbling marks without knowing how to associate words in a language with conceptual referents and how these conceptual referents relate to empirical referents in the world? Do many of the terms of political discourse mean anything, everything, and nothing, as John Adams is reputed to have observed about the term "republic"?
—Vincent Ostrom
(*Publius*, 15, 1985)

As water is for fish, federalism is the appropriate element for territorial communities that, conscious of their separate identities, desire self-government yet hope to achieve additional objectives by combining their efforts and domains into a composite national whole, both distinct from and interacting as a unit with other nation-states. The additional objectives to be attained through federal unification combined with a division of powers almost always are common protection against external military, economic, or cultural pressures and economic advantages to be derived from common planning, working, and exchanging products in a larger market. Military and economic concerns are usually not sufficient by themselves to create a composite federal nation: An awareness of a deeper affinity and hope for common destiny (an emotional federal impetus) is usually present too, that is, in William H. Riker's words, "some deeper emotion than mere geographic contiguity with cultural diversity."[1]

On the basis of correlated data, obtained from a study of four major federal failures, Thomas M. Franck identified two principal ingredients of the impetus for successful federation: the transmission of ideological commitment from charismatic leaders to the people (*elite charisma*) and/or the transmission of broadly shared values (culminating in a federal value) from the people to the leaders (*popular charisma*). "The leaders, and their followers, must feel federal; there must be a positive political and ideological commitment to the primary goal of federation as an end in itself."[2]

The federal process is often also a means of preserving rather than building a new national unity out of many components. By timely concessions to, and constitutional recognition of, territorial communities and their desire for self-rule, a formerly unitary nation-state may be re-formed and its national unity saved. Only the future will tell, for instance, whether the creation of additional states on a linguistic or religious basis in India after 1950 or the transformation of unitary Czechoslovakia into a federal state in 1968 were indeed timely measures in the right direction to channel centrifugal or outrightly secessionist tendencies into a cooperative and constructive framework of a federal division of authority.

The federal assertion of unity vis-à-vis other nation-states (often buttressed by an implicit or explicit elimination of the right of territorial secession on the part of any component) is coupled with a solemn commitment to a permanent internal division of political power between two sets (or orders) of government; one with jurisdiction over the whole national domain in some issue-areas, the other governments keeping their jurisdiction in other issue-areas in their respective territorial domains, whose sum total constitutes "nearly" all of the national territory. I say "nearly" since the national government usually administers directly some additional areas such as federal territories (for example, the Yukon and Northwest Territories in Canada or Guam and the Virgin Islands by the United States) or a federal district in which the national capital may be located (Washington, D.C., Canberra, Brasília, Mexico City, and New Delhi). The powers of the two sets of political authority—central and noncentral—are neither derived from nor dependent on each other. They are anchored in the federal constitution that expresses the preceding negotiation and amicable agreement among leaders of the territorial components.

The presence of two government layers superimposed on the same territory, neither being at the mercy of the other, is perhaps the shortest working definition of federalism and the one I intend to use in this study. The critical feature of this definition is, in Martin Landau's words, the *independence* rather than the interdependence.[3] Or as a truly shorthand definition of federalism (coined in 1869) expressed it when referring to the U.S. federal union, federalism is "an indestructible union of indestructible units."[4] The latter definition separates a federal from a confederal system by ruling out secession and also distinguishes a federal from a unitary system by ruling out elimination of subnational territorial autonomy.

It should be admitted at this point that, among scholars and constitutional lawyers, there is no generally accepted, satisfactory or simple definition of federalism. The Latin origin of the term *foedus* "compact" is recognized by all but not much more. The term "federalization," for example, is often used to describe the *process* of combining territorial communities that previously had not been directly joined into a new nation or a new unit of common interest, policy, and action. Federalization often describes the opposite process of a deconcentration of power that may endow territorial communities with *irrevocable* autonomy and so change a unitary, decentralized system into a federal one. In other contexts federalization is sometimes understood as absorption of provincial/state powers by the federal center (nationalization). Federalism is also often used to describe the *result* of the federalizing process, that is, specific federal institutions and structure.

Drafters of federal constitutions, sometimes unwittingly but often deliberately, blur the definitional boundaries between unitary (revocable) decentralization, on the one hand, and (irrevocable) *non*centralization (Elazar's subtle formulation), on the other. They may not want to commit their communities to either a federal or a unitary future, perhaps bearing in mind Walt Whitman's caution about the impenetrable blank of any future. Freely adapting Walt Whitman to the federal/unitary uncertainties, many a founding father may be inclined to say: "How can I perceive the impenetrable blank of the future [of federalism]? . . . I see thy light lighting and thy shadows shadowing . . . but I do not undertake to define thee—hardly to comprehend thee."

Three Hundred and Twenty-Six Federal Metaphors

One result of the lack of a clear definition is a jungle of qualifying adjectives, metaphors, and models to which scholars, political leaders, and the media keep on contributing by cheerfully coining such new ones as "quasi-military," "quasi-federal," "quasi-confederal," Nixon's "creative federalism," Reagan's "new federalism," "unitary system with quasi-federal gloss" (referring to Italy), "totalitarian federalism," "vertical federalism," and many others. William H. Stewart listed 326 metaphors and models of federalism![5] This study, alas adds two more: "osmotic" and "dyadic (or bicephalic)" federalism.

In the preceding chapter mention is made of the fact that out of the 160-odd existing nation-states only about ten percent have adopted a federal system of constitutional division of political authority. Depending on the definition of federalism that is used, however, the figure can be anywhere from 4 percent to 15 percent, an uncomfortably wide margin in our era of computerized statistics. The classification of federal states varies from author to author according to his or her criteria and definition, and the definitional controversy usually centers around two aspects of federalism: (1) federalism's incompatibility with dictatorship (see Suchecki's and Hughes's points in two of the epigraphs to this chapter), and (2) unitary systems whose decentralized nature appears quasi-permanent though not anchored in a federal constitution (e.g., the United Kingdom).

In one study,[6] Rufus Davis presented six authors (A. B. Hart, K. C. Wheare, B. M. Sharma, R. L. Watts, C. J. Friedrich, and I. D. Duchacek) and their contrasting lists of federal systems ranging in number from fourteen to twenty-one to thirty-six.[7] Despite their disagreements, these lists leave no doubt that at least the following seven states are definitely nonunitary and genuinely federal: Australia, Austria, Canada, Federal Republic of Germany, India, Switzerland, and the United States. Eight other nations are classified as "purportedly federal": Argentina, Brazil, Malaysia, Mexico, Nigeria, Venezuela, United Arab Emirates, and Yugoslavia. Tanzania (an association of Tanganyika with Zanzibar) has a potential for a federal union as well as for dissolution by secession.

At first sight, there seems to be some causal relationship between the large size of a nation and its manageability by a federal formula. Nations that are or merely claim to be federal are among the largest in the world: Of the six largest nation-states of the world (the Soviet Union, Canada, China, the United States, Brazil, and Australia), only China (3.7 million square miles) is unitary though decentralized to some extent (see Chapter 3).

Two observations, however, are in order. First, the Swiss, Austrian, and incipient Belgian federal systems are among the smallest in the world. Second, within the large federations, there are also a great many territorial subcenters, created not by the federal constitution, but by unitary delegation of either national or provincial/state/cantonal power. In the United States, for example, the national federal government and the state governments are only 51 out of nearly 38,000 territorial units of self-rule (counties, municipalities, townships, and towns); if school and special districts are added, the sum total is 90,000. Although the 51 governments reflect the principle of U.S. federalism, the other 89,949 spatially defined subunits represent more or less revocable decentralization by unitary delegation of authority. (The state constitutional guarantees of home rule are noted in Chapter 3.)

The United States, Australian, West German, and Swiss successes in federal practices may be the main reasons why, over the past two centuries, the word "federalism" has generally evoked a positive echo. Terms such as democracy, peace, progress, and federalism have often meant different things to different communities or individuals, who are sometimes inclined to interpret or distort a popular concept to their particular political needs. Occasionally, federalism may acquire a bad connotation when the federal center is perceived by the territorial components as being a centralizing agent and absorbing too much of local autonomy. This was the case in several Canadian provinces and especially in Québec under the Trudeau government in Canada in the 1970s until the mid-1980s. On the other hand, for the exact opposite reasons, the concept of federalization has often been viewed by the central governments in Western Europe, in centralist France in particular, as a threat to national unity because decentralization may favor the centrifugal tendencies of peripheral regions and ethnoterritorial communities (see Mitterrand's words in an epigraph to Chapter 3). Simultaneously, however, continental Western Europe, including many people in France, endows federalism with a hopeful and positive sound when it comes to the goal or ideal of transforming the European Communities into a federal union in which the majoritarian mode of collective decision making would replace the present confederal principle of unanimity, ensured by the right of veto reserved for each of its twelve members.

Nonterritorial Federalism?

The working definition of federalism used in this study emphasizes its territorial essence. It should be recognized that the terms *federalism* and *federalization* are also used in everyday parlance to describe any combination or balance between unity and diversity. They are therefore frequently used with reference to either nonpolitical or nonterritorial processes of institutions, for example, to describe ecumenical development or renewing unity among variants of a common creed or ideology. Other examples of nonpolitical associations of groups whose primary goals are service, production, or entertainment are the "federations" of consumer or producer cooperatives, chambers of commerce, veterans' posts, and sports, chess, and stamp collectors' clubs. Still other examples of nonpolitical federations are the commercial or industrial corporations that have been created by the association of previously independent companies whose autonomy and identity have been not totally obliterated but guaranteed in the merger or the complexes that, because of their successful growth and expansion, have found it necessary to decentralize and endow the new branches or sectors with financial and administrative autonomy. Such a "federalizing" process may be observed in both capitalist and communist economies; in both cases, flexibility and increased efficiency or service are the evident goals.

Examples of "federations" that are engaged in the political promotion and defense of nonterritorial *functional* interests, usually reflecting cooperative unions of diverse professional skills, are the American Federation of Labor, the United Federation of Teachers, the Trades Union Congress in Britain, the Swedish Federation of Labor, the Federation of British Industries, and the Federation of German Industries in West Germany. In France and Italy, labor and other functional federations are often so grouped as to represent extensions of political parties into different professional fields.

Churches usually represent a combination of territorial and ecumenical "federalism." In Protestant churches, for instance, the parishes represent the basic territorial units, and they are combined into higher regional, national, and international federations. But in addition, different Protestant denominational groups are federated in the World Council of Churches—a unity combined with both territorial *and* creed diversity. Some authors find federal institutions and habits even within the highly centralized Roman Catholic church, which is dedicated to dogmatic unity; the territorial autonomy of the bishops and some orders within the tenets of a common faith is often very real in practice. In 1964, at the Sixth World Congress of the International Political Science Association in Geneva, one of the participating scholars presented a paper that analyzed the autonomy of 200 Benedictine abbeys in terms of federalism.[8]

Dictatorship, Democracy, and Federalism

In its tightly centralized version, the unitary form of government has been adopted by the overwhelming majority of nations that are subject to communist, socialist-authoritarian, fascist, or military single-party rule. These nations today make up the majority of nations. As noted in Chapter 3, a number of truly democratic and pluralistic nation-states have also adopted a unitary form of government in combination with some decentralization by power delegation from the top to the bottom (France, for example).

Although the authoritarian and the democratic use and management of the unitary formula differ sharply, federalism, in my view, can never accommodate fascism or communism—and vice versa. Federalism is simply a territorial expression of the core creed of democracy, that is, respect for and management of political pluralism both *within* and *among* the territorial components of a nation-state. Democracy and federalism are indeed twin brothers, but the latter is more dependent on its kin than the others. Democracy can prosper without federalism, as it does in France or Norway, but a federal division of power, territorial political pluralism, is contrary to the concentration of all power in the hands of a single party presidium, junta, or fascist or military dictator. Any system whose basic maxim is a total concentration of all political and economic decisional power at a central point cannot reserve any significant portion of that central power for any group, whether ideological, functional, or territorial.

When in a politically centralized system and centrally planned economy regional pressures or the opinions of expert groups become apparent and have some effect, they represent manifestations of what we may call a movement toward *corporatism* in a dictatorial framework rather than a movement toward pluralistic federalism. Newer studies of the actual working of the Soviet system, for example, offer some indications of corporatist practices, especially in central environmental policies. In the case of the pollution of Lake Baikal (an emotion-laden issue), some regional interests that were critical of the official neglect were able to manifest themselves in this particular case and have some effect. The Soviet Union may well have become more corporatist, but it is not federal.

Each of the three socialist-authoritarian countries that claims to be federal (the Soviet Union, Czechoslovakia, and Yugoslavia) has based its claim on the Lenin/Stalin-blessed federal formula: territorial autonomy for every major ethnoterritorial community provided, of course, that the political and economic commanding heights remain firmly in the hands of the highly centralized one-party apparatus. The result has been a guarantee of cultural-linguistic autonomy to the extent that the various nationalities of the Soviet Union and Czechoslovakia have been permitted to express their political thoughts in appropriate languages and scripts—provided, of course, that the thought is the centrally approved one. For this reason, the Soviet and Czechoslovak federal unions cannot qualify as federations in the sense of political pluralism practiced within and among their territorial components: They are mere federal window dressing for basically tightly centralized unitary systems.

The evident incompatibility of federalism and dictatorship does not extend to the concept of confederalism (as we shall see in more detail in Chapters 6 and 7). Conceptually, a confederal association does not require that democracy be practiced either within or among the territorial components; some or all confederal components may make major decisions in an authoritarian manner within their boundaries; and, on the federal level, all-national decisions are reached either by negotiated consensus (consociationally) or by interdictatorial majoritarian modes of decision making. This situation seems to exist in modern Yugoslavia, a very special case of an interauthoritarian *confederation* of territorial dictatorships. With an initially tightly centralized system, Yugoslavia has indeed evolved into a confederal association of territorial communities, each of which governs itself in an authoritarian fashion in major areas of territorial import.

A severe critic of the Yugoslav system, Milovan Djilas, nevertheless acknowledged the significant degree of decentralization in Yugoslavia, labeling it "confederation" (one cannot be certain, of course, whether Djilas really intended to use the term "confederation" in this study's sense of the word, implying its interauthoritarian nature in contrast to democratic federalism):

> The relations between Yugoslavia's component republics have changed not only among themselves but also with respect to the state's central authorities in Belgrade. With the exception of power over national defense and foreign affairs, the republics to all intents and purposes acquired confederation status. While the ruling party itself has retained a monopoly on power, it too has undergone decentralization: Most political decision-making is now taking place in the republic's capitals.[9]

Attempts at Defining Federalism

A simplified diagram of a complex framework graphically illustrates the federal principle of noncentralization and the balance between two sets of government, one national and a number of subnational ones, independent

Figure 4.1

Federal Distribution of Power
and
Porosity of Intrafederal Boundaries

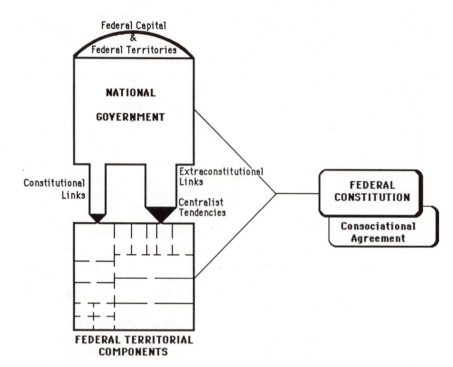

yet partly also connected (see Figure 4.1). In spatial terms, the jurisdiction of the national authority is depicted as being larger than the domain administered by the federal components. As noted previously, the federal center administers directly, federal territories as well as the federal district which, in some federal unions, is the location of the capital city so that the capital is not placed within or unduly influenced by a particular territorial community.

Although necessarily static, Figure 4.1 also tries to depict the inevitable linkages between the two sets of governments, which, in principle, are independent of each other. The left-hand, narrower channel suggests the shared or implied powers that are suggested or authorized by the federal charter itself. The other, boulevard-broad ("osmotic") link illustrates the numerous extraconstitutional linkages that often correct or distort the allegedly precise and permanent division of power. The constitutional wall between the national center and the various territorial subcenters has been pierced by such extraconstitutional, though not unconstitutional, developments as the emergence of all-national political parties, interest groups, and manufacturing and financial enterprises—as well as centralizing tendencies on the part of the national elites. The sum total of such extraconstitutional trends may conceivably lead to the emergence of a unitary political culture that undermines the federal institutions and structures.

Some scholars have argued that such unitary trends are inevitable in all modern federations committed to economic planning, welfare functions, and technological progress. This point has been quite eloquently argued by Edmond Orban in comparative study on the dynamics of centralization in federal states.[10] Orban's data indicate that an acceleration of the *centralizing* trends in determining essential national objectives and the means of financing their attainment is more often than not coupled with a decentralized implementation of common policies by noncentral governments. This assessment is evidenced by an increase of both personnel and funds earmarked for local and provincial/state administration of national programs and by a decentralization of expenses in the wake of centralization of receipts.

Figure 4.1 also indicates the open passages that connect the federal territorial components one with the other and so also permit transborder regional cooperative ventures (such as the New York–New Jersey Port Authority) within the national framework. (The possibility for territorial communities to establish contacts across the national borders will be analyzed and illustrated in Chapters 8–10.)

Neither the boundary line between federal and subnational territorial jurisdictions nor the intrafederal boundaries between the various autonomous components should be perceived as watertight. Their porousness should be assumed. Often it is explicitly or implicitly authorized by the federal constitution (e.g., federal/provincial joint jurisdiction and shared powers); at other times, the intrafederal borders are pierced by judicial interpretations. Whatever the method, times change and so do the intrafederal linkages without really altering the basic federal principle of jurisdictional divisions. Commenting on the necessary limits of the federal founding fathers' foresight, Rufus Davis wisely noted: "It is scarcely conceivable that all parties to the federal bargain at all times and in all places seek the same thing in the same proportions, for the same reasons. . . . At best the federal compact can only be a formalized transaction of a moment in the history of a particular community."[11] It is in this context of interpenetration between the two orders of government in modern federal unions that the concept of osmosis comes to mind and with it, still another metaphor applicable to federalism: "osmotic."

"Talk Until You Agree"[12]

The concept and term "consociationalism," which I use in this chapter to characterize the beginnings of federalism, has been borrowed from the analytical studies of the amicable decision-making modes that prevail in small West European democracies, notably the Netherlands, Switzerland, and Austria. The concept and practice of decision making based on a near unanimous consent among the leaders of all major segments of a polity (religious, ideological, ethnic, socioeconomic, and territorial) has been analyzed and contrasted with the majoritarian (elite or popular) mode of decision making. These studies show that in deeply segmented democracies, federal as well as unitary, stability and some slow progress have often been ensured over long spans of time by a grand coalition of major parties and interest groups promoting their specific interests but also seeking a general consensus on a give-and-take basis.

Some authors, such as Arend Lijphart and Val R. Lorwin, have described and analyzed such grand coalitions. The period of stability seemed to rest on the capitals (*chapitaux*) of the various pillars (e.g., Roman Catholic and Protestant *zuils* in the Netherlands).[13] Other authors observe that intersegmental interlacing has often involved the pillar bases, not only their tops. Herman Bakvis wrote for example, "Just as the watertight compartments metaphor as applied to federations may be highly inaccurate, so too may be the notion of the pillars in consociations being segregated."[14] Nevertheless, in the creation of federal unions and the management of confederal associations, it seems that the dominant feature of the consociational mode is the *elite* accommodation reached by a discussion going on "until a solution is found that is acceptable to all participants in the decision-making process,"[15] that is, "talk until you agree."

Praising the African intertribal decision-making process (*palaver*), Tanzania's President Julius Nyerere warned his fellow Africans against the English model of a two-party system and its majoritarian method of deciding important issues. Instead, Nyerere recommended that African leaders "sit under the tree until they agree." Similarly, in Muslim Indonesia, there has been a practice of extensive discussion to produce a synthesis of views, often only an implicit, generally felt consensus (*mufakat*). As George McT. Kahin noted, "Such a generally sensed agreement is reached not through a majority vote, but in a way somewhat reminiscent of the Quaker sense of the meeting."[16]

Interpreting the sense of a Quaker meeting is, of course, one thing. Interpreting the "implicit" sense of an interelite political discussion is another—especially if the "interpreter" happens to be an authoritarian leader presiding over some frightened or docile group of nodding individuals (as was precisely the case in Indonesia under Sukarno or in the Soviet Politburo under Stalin).

My reference to Sukarno and Stalin could appear to be misplaced here since nearly all studies of consociationalism have been concerned with segmented *democracies* in Western Europe. Nevertheless, there are fascist and socialist authoritarian systems in which leaders preside over parties or juntas that are internally, though not overtly segmented in the ideological and personal sense and over societies that are fragmented in the ethnic or religious sense. One can reasonably argue, for example, that the Soviet formula of "democratic centralism" initially contained a dose of consocia-tionalism. Under Lenin (but before Stalin), the various Communist party factions often argued and talked until they could find a synthesis of their conflicting Marxian approaches; votes were rarely taken except to manifest unanimity. The final interelite agreements reached in the Politburo and Central Committee were then binding upon the whole party apparatus and, through it, the whole society. Expressed in "consociationalese," an intra-communist elite cartel talked until its members agreed—not under Nyerere's symbolic tree but under the Soviet hammer and sickle in the Kremlin. Similarly, within Latin America juntas and some fascist regimes, the army, navy and air force commanders, together with industrial leaders and land-owners, usually engage in "dictatorial consociationalism."

In discussing the consensual, consociational decision-making, mode it is useful to distinguish between *consensus*, on the one hand, and *consent*. This distinction is necessary for two reasons. First, as Jürg Steiner perceptively noted, decision makers may pursue other values than the one to be maximized by a specific option to be agreed upon. For instance, another value might be the maintenance of "group solidarity and ideological rectitude" or even a desire to "minimize the time they invest in a particular decision situation."[17] In such a situation, consensus and specific consent would certainly be two different things. (As is well known to the participants of many a faculty meeting, boredom resulting from a long meeting and a need to hasten its end sometimes make participants go along with and consent to a proposed course of action without really thinking it through.) Second, as Douglas W. Rae noted, we should remain constantly aware of the difference—or abyss—between the consent of the governed (and, I am adding, their governors) to the existing regime (for example, federalism) and subsequent approval of future specific policies and actions of the regime.[18]

Confederal Consociations

In contrast to federal unions and their basic commitment to building a new nation, in a confederation there is no emotional or institutional commitment to building a suprasovereign community, a new "nation," only an amicable—temporary or perpetual—consociation of sovereign member entities. Insisting on full sovereignty, these confederal components cannot and do not accept subordination to a numerical majority of other sovereignties except in marginal matters. Veto reigns supreme.

In a confederation, the component communities combine into a cooperative association only for the purpose of executing some rather specific tasks in common, e.g., defense (see Figure 4.2). The confederal body has no inde-pendent life of its own; it is a mirror of its member communities which remain basically separate. Major decisions require that the component communities discuss the issue until they agree on common steps. The common decision-making body to which the component entities have delegated some specific powers is usually an assembly of delegates ("am-

Figure 4.2

Confederal Delegation of Authority

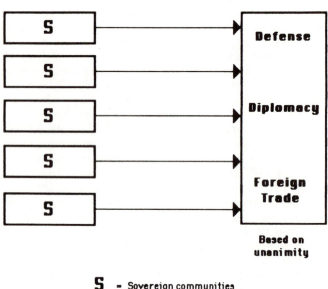

S - Sovereign communities

———▶ = Delegation of power

bassadors") sent to represent territories. This common body of confederation is not authorized to make decisions or enact rules that would directly affect individuals by central enforcement and taxation. Common institutions, when created, are accountable to territorial collectivities, not to individuals as citizens of a composite whole. In fact, the concept of confederal citizenship is generally absent, except for the free movement of persons across confederal boundaries. As succinctly expressed by Alexander Hamilton (*Federalist* Papers no. 25), "The great and radical vice in the construction of the existing Confederation is in the principle of LEGISLATION for STATES or GOVERNMENTS, in their CORPORATE or COLLECTIVE CAPACI- TIES, and as contradistinguished from the INDIVIDUALS of whom they consist." In *Federalist* Paper 19, both James Madison and Alexander Hamilton warned against imitating the then inter-sovereign German confederation, depicted as "agitated with unceasing fermentation" on account of its being only a community of sovereigns, not a federal nation.

Thus, a loosely structured, composite community (but nevertheless a community vis-à-vis external political, economic, or environmental challenges) is established without permitting the compounded concept to overshadow—politically, economically, or emotionally—the sovereign powers of the individual territorial components. In a confederal system, one's primary loyalty is still to one's home territory. "Right or wrong, my country" has quite a different connotation in a confederation—an aggregate of homelands—than in a federal union where federal loyalty (*Bundestreue; loyauté fédérale*) prevails. In 1774, for example, "our country" for John Adams basically meant Massachusetts, and for Thomas Jefferson, Virginia, even though the concept of America was beginning to assert itself ("I am not a Virginian, but an American"—Patrick Henry, October 14, 1774, in Philadelphia).

Lacking the central authority to mandate actions against the will of the territorial components, confederal systems, leagues, alliances, common markets, and international and intergovernmental organizations and agencies depend for their maintenance and operation primarily on consociational decision-making procedures rather than on a confederal "government" in the traditional executive/legislative/judicial sense. Intersovereign decision making in confederations therefore has contents and forms that correspond to all intersovereign *diplomacy* whether conducted in bilateral, conference, or summit frameworks (see Chapter 6).

Amicable diplomacy rather than the majoritarian mode of decision making necessarily also characterizes the various forms of transborder regional networks that link up noncentral (provincial, state, municipal, or cantonal) governments. In fact, when two or three contiguous federal or decentralized unitary systems develop and maintain new forms of transborder regional (formal and informal) networks on a noncentral government level, a rudimentary confederal overlap (a transfrontier consociation) between two or three subnations may emerge (Chapters 9 and 10 will deal with such overlaps in more detail).

Diplomatic intercourse and agreements are not only possible but frequent between dictators as well as between democrats and autocrats. Practicing tyranny in their respective home territories, dictators can easily engage in consociational or even majoritarian decision-making processes on the interautocratic summit level. Within the various Third World and communist blocs (confederal consociations sui generis) this is, in fact, a general practice. The same is true as Chapter 7 will document, in the United Nations.

Consociational Cradle of Federalism

The midwife of any association of territorial communities pregnant with a federal future is—and has to be—an amicable agreement reached by means of negotiation and bargaining among the leading representatives of these communities. The applicable term for an interelite summit that seeks and often finds a nearly unanimous agreement is *consociationalism* (a concept introduced mostly by Dutch scholars from Althusius and Grotius to Lijphart).[19] The consociational beginnings of most federations in which other decisional modes subsequently prevail is clearly a complex process.

A federal union is, as it were, both conceived and born in the same operation. No wonder that in its infancy federalism is usually a creature of rather delicate health.

Historically, this complexity certainly existed during the hot laborious summer in Philadelphia in 1787 when the Articles of Confederation were being transformed into a national federal constitution, endowing the thirteen states with a newly defined decisional autonomy to be limited by their reciprocal respect for the interests of their composite whole as well as for the particular interests of all the other constituent units. The process was roughly as complex during another hot summer on the Grütli meadow[20] in the canton of Uri where, in 1291 (and then in 1307), three cantons took the first steps toward the Swiss confederation and federation. Every successful federal birth is characterized by a consociational "overarching cooperation at the elite level,"[21] the aim of which is to counteract mutual suspicion and disintegrative tendencies on the part of the territorial segments.[22]

Nevertheless, no requirement or promise of continuing unanimity is ever contained in the final written document—the draft of the federal constitution—as it emerges from the constitutional interelite summit; no federation requires unanimous decision making in its central legislature or among its component entities. Nor does a federation even require unanimity to amend the constitutional compact itself despite its consociational origin. And rightly so. After all, the primary reason for replacing the preceding, usually confederal, association and its potential for immobilism because of minority vetoes is to adopt a simpler and more efficient majoritarian formula, fitting a unified polity and credited with the capacity to act and get things moving more expeditiously.

The need to protect the minority and prevent tyranny by a numerical majority is recognized in most majoritarian democracies, unitary and federal, by various declamatory safeguards, more than a simple majority on some issues, and a set of various checks and balances. The infallible protection against a tyrannical majority—the positive requirement of unanimity or the negative right of minority veto—is, however, not a part of federal charters.

Only a very few ingredients of the initial consociational bargain remain unamendable, except by another amicable summit. In the case of the United States, for example, the core principle of the Connecticut Compromise—equal representation of unequal states—seems beyond the amendatory process of Article 5 (two-thirds majority of the Congress first and ratification by three-fourths of the states afterward), although some constitutional lawyers have argued that even the last sentence of Article 5 ("no State, without its consent, shall be deprived of its equal suffrage in the Senate") could be eliminated by amendment, ratified by thirty-eight states out of fifty, and replaced, for example, by the Canadian or Indian formulas of weighted representation giving a favorable, but not equal, representation to very small components. Naturally, every federal component has the right to protect its "indestructibility" by a veto with regard to any change of its own boundaries within the federation (Article 4, section 3 in the U.S. Constitution).

The new Canadian Constitution (1982) allows the provinces to opt out from a new amendment passed by the appropriate majority if the amendment affects existing provincial powers (Article 38); in addition, if provincial legislative powers relating to education or other cultural matters are so transferred, the federal government has "to provide reasonable compensation to any province to which the amendment does not apply" (Article 40).

In 1984, following the defeat of Trudeau's Liberal party, Québec's linguistic-cultural veto became the subject of an interelite negotiation and bargaining involving the new Conservative government of Brian Mulroney, the other nine provinces, and the Québec leaders who in 1982 did not give their consent to the provisions and patriation of the new Canadian Constitution. The proposals announced by premier René Lévesque included constitutional recognition of the existence of the Quebeckers as a constituent people, the exclusion of Québec from the language provisions of the new Canadian Charter of Rights and Freedoms in exchange for a promise to modify the excessively strict "French only" provincial language law, and the right to veto Canadian constitutional amendments pertaining to education, culture, language, and Québec's decisive determination of its own economic development.

These far-reaching reservations, largely shared by both parties, the *Parti québécois* and the Québec Liberal party which, following the election of December 2, 1985, became the governing party of Québec, may conceptually be seen as a search for a guarantee for the Québec Community to renegotiate a consociational agreement in case of any far-reaching constitutional change. This may well be a precondition for harmony in any bicephalic (dyadic) federal union (Cyprus, Czechoslovakia, Belgium, Sri Lanka) in which two, and only two, communities face each other in a near-zero-sum game alley, which, because of lack of elbowroom, permits only the advance of one actor at the expense of the other, if no amicable agreement can be found somewhere in the middle.

Other observers may view such a dyadic feature as a constitutional veto—introducing into the Canadian federal union a *confederal* feature. To add to the confusion, it should be noted that for historical reasons, in Canada, as in Switzerland, the term "confederation" is often used in political discourses when federal union is meant—a slip of the tongue that, while possible in 1787, is hardly imaginable in contemporary United States.

In the case of Switzerland, both the existing constitution (Article 118) and the draft of the revised, but not yet adopted, constitution (Article 112) state that the federal constitution can at any time be revised in part or *totally*. Although the process of amending the Swiss Constitution is complex, again no unanimity but several majoritarian approvals at the federal, cantonal, and popular levels are provided for. Naturally, the whole process of altering the initial federal bargain is expected to be colored by the Swiss consociational practice, the so-called *Konkordanzdemokratie* ("concordant democracy"), which has, since the late 1950s united all the major political parties in a grand coalition. The elite cartel qua the founding fathers would most probably shy away from any proposal that could pass by only a bare majority against the opposite wishes of a substantive minority. This consociationalism is, as it were, tacitly present in many majoritarian procedures.

The inevitably consociational origin of federalism neither requires nor promises a continuation of consociationalism in the future management of the federal system. On the contrary, from the interelite summit there emerges a commitment to or an invitation for a majoritarian decisional mode. Whether, subsequently and extraconstitutionally, consociational practices will be adopted by the governing elites with regard to some or all major issues (in the center or the territorial components) will depend on factors other than the federal nature of the system. Most of these factors would lead to consociationalism in unitary systems as well. Lijphart[23] and other students of consociationalism have identified some of these factors as political culture, role structures, elite behavior, and new environmental factors; external pressures, threats, or opportunities should be added to the list. In national emergencies, for example, majoritarians tend to become (bipartisan) consociationalists.

Furthermore, following the initial consociational agreement, the subsequent decisional modes will most probably vary along a "finely graded continuum from amicable agreement to majority rule"[24] and their admixture[25]— differently at different times on different issues as well as in different frameworks of a federal system, that is, within and among the federal components as well as between the components, on the one hand, and the national center on the other. In other words, when practiced in an established federal union, consociationalism is a fortuitous feature of federalism; it is owing to factors other than the federal division of powers.

Consociationalism Within Majoritarianism

The consociational cradle of democratic federalism may form a subliminal framework for subsequent majoritarian practices; in other words, there could be such a thing as majoritarianism in practice restrained by the silent presence of an erstwhile consociational commitment. The spirit of the initial, one-shot consociational bargain (which, after all, did not and could not have reflected an awareness on the part of the elites of the depth of the various cleavages in the nation) may permeate subsequent majoritarian decision-making processes. Thus, the extreme form of majoritarianism, though mathematically attainable—winner take all—will be avoided by the majority for the sake of building and maintaining a diffuse support—as labeled by David Easton, that "reserve of support that enables a system to weather the many storms when outputs cannot be balanced off against inputs of demands."[26]

Diffuse support is deemed essential for the maintenance of any democratic system. Such support can be facilitated by the majority's acceptance of a common good transcending the particular good of any particular individuals or groups. In this spirit, by anticipating the minority's reaction even a large majority may not propose certain measures, or it may soften measures proposed by its militant wing or modify their enforcement so as to mollify the minority despite its voting or protesting against the principle or thrust of the measure. Such "consociationalism in majoritarian wrapping" may be called "*tacit consociationalism*,"[27] "implicit consociationalism," or simply wise politics on the part of the majority, which exercises pragmatic self-restraint by its enlightened anticipation of what will be the long-term consequences of too many crushing defeats inflicted upon the minority by a sheer weight of numbers.

An empirical illustration of the working of such tacit consociationalism is the long story of the current Swiss constitutional reform. In his study of this process, Charles F. Schuetz described the principal task of coordination between federal and cantonal jurisdictions, especially in the matter of social services and welfare. Schuetz then wrote: "There must be a broad national agreement on what is to be achieved, and on who would pay for it. The only way to accomplish this is through a process of tedious and time consuming negotiations . . . [leading] to a constitutional package that offers every major segment of society a fair deal."[28]

In this examination of consociationalism and federalism, it is important to bear in mind that the geographically delineated segments—whose existence and power determine and *define* federalism—are not the only cleavages, often not even the most significant, in a federal and plural society. Other cleavages separate socioeconomic, religious, racial, linguistic, and ethnic communities, which, because of their geographic dispersion (as the blacks,[29] Jews, Hispanics, or Asians in the United States), may have no other territorial dimension than town or barrio and cannot be accommodated by a polyethnic federal formula by which intrafederal and ethnolingual boundaries are explicitly meant to coincide as in India, Yugoslavia, Czechoslovakia, and the Soviet Union. Nonterritorial or local-territorial segments usually crisscross intrafederal territorial boundaries in a complex fashion.

In the United States, various militant groups have occasionally attempted to endow blacks with a territorial dimension. During the 1920s, for example, the concept of a Negro Self-Determination for the Black Belt by means of secession from the United States was promoted by one Harry Haywood, then a trainee at the School of Leninist Studies in Moscow. His proposal focused on those areas of the Deep South in which the blacks constituted a majority, and it was more or less endorsed by the Russian-led Comintern, the general staff of world communism. In a more racial than class form, the idea reappeared in the turbulent 1960s under the slogan, New Africa.[30]

In Canada, such ethnoterritorial reinforcement can be found in the dominantly francophone province of Québec and the dominantly anglophone provinces of British Columbia, Alberta, Saskatchewan, Newfoundland, Nova Scotia, and Prince Edward Island. New Brunswick, Manitoba, and Ontario are bilingual—New Brunswick constitutionally so. In plural Switzerland, too, only some linguistic boundaries coincide with the intrafederal (cantonal) boundaries. Several cantons are bilingual and one (Grisons/Graubünden) is trilingual. Some cantons are predominantly Protestant, others are Roman Catholic, and several are mixed. Today, for example, Calvin's Geneva is only about 40 percent Protestant. Even the Soviet, Czechoslovak, and Yugoslav federations, though in principle based on the Leninist-Stalinist formula of ethnoterritorial federalism—to each ethnic community its autonomous republic, region, or district—could not territorially accommodate all their minorities and grant them territorial autonomy because of their dispersion, small size, or nomadic quality—and, in some cases, because of their alleged ideological unreliability (Tatars, Ingush-Chechens, Volga Germans, etc.).

Communist and fascist federal systems are, of course, as stressed previously, "pseudofederations." Their internal operations are to some extent influenced but not codetermined by their cultural, ethnic, racial, and even religious diversities (for instance, the Muslims in the Soviet Union and Yugoslavia) and their respective territorial dimensions. No territorial or other segment of authoritarian societies can ever be endowed with any degree of decisional autonomy on account of the society's abhorrence of any division or diffusion of political power—as held by a single party in the Soviet Union and Czechoslovakia or by a junta in the Latin American context. The evolving and complex system of ethnoterritorial, interauthoritarian system of communist Yugoslavia places that country in a special category of rigid, dictatorial, one-party ideological centralization and ethnoterritorial confederalism.

In democratic federal systems, the territorial components may become, through time, less assertive than the nonterritorial cleavages. This situation may partly be a result of acquired self-confidence or of modern geographic mobility, which has made the citizens of territorial communities less sensitive about their segmental identity. Although the segmental pillars are separate and possibly antagonistic in the classical model of consociationalism, while their "capitals" engage in a consociational honeymoon, in federalism the territorial pillars may be quite intertwined at their popular bases while their competitive political elites (state politicians in the United States) may promote their states' rights and interests in a quite unconsociational or even unsocial manner.

In addition, new regional loyalties may emerge and politically, though not administratively, undermine the initial federal subdivisions.

The initially federal state of Pakistan, which in 1970 was reorganized to consist of five components—Sind, Punjab, Northwest Frontier, and Baluchistan in the west and Bengal in the east—split a year later on an East-West axis into two hostile units, West Pakistan and secessionist Bangladesh (East Pakistan). Another dramatic example of such a development was the North-South rift in the United States. In a system that was federally divided into thirty-four states (1860/1861), the rift finally led to a war between two hostile regions, consisting of the eleven Confederate States and their opponents. The fragility of the North-South axis, about which James Madison had warned in 1787, proved finally to be a veritable time bomb set to explode some seventy years later: "The great danger to our general government is the great southern and northern interest of the continent being opposed to each other. Look at the votes in Congress, and most of them stand divided by the geography of the country, not according to the size of the state."[31]

Notes

1. William H. Riker, *Federalism: Origin, Operation Significance* (Boston: Little, Brown, 1964), p. 35.

2. Thomas M. Franck, ed., *Why Federations Fail—An Inquiry into the Requisites for Successful Federalism* (New York: New York University Press, 1968), pp. 173-174.

3. Martin Landau, "Federalism, Redundancy, and System Reliability," *Publius* 3 (Fall 1973), pp. 173-196.

4. Texas v. White, 7 Wallace 700 (1869).

5. William H. Stewart, "Metaphors, Models, and the Development of Federal Theory," *Publius* 12 (Spring 1982), pp. 5-24.

6. Rufus Davis, *The Federal Principle: A Journey Through Time in Quest for Meaning* (Berkeley: University of California Press, 1978), pp. 217-219.

7. Daniel J. Elazar listed eighteen federal systems and eighteen political systems utilizing federal arrangements (unions and consociations) in his *Federalism and Political Integration* (Ramat Gan, Israel: Turtledove, 1979), pp. 19-21.

8. Leo Moulin, "Le fédéralisme dans l'organisation politique des ordres religieux," (Paper presented at the Sixth World Congress of the International Political Science Association, Geneva, September 21-25, 1964), p. 3, stated in his summary: "Benedictine life is based fundamentally on the principle of abbatial autonomy. The pressure of circumstances has led to the groupings of abbeys. . . . At the present about two hundred Benedictine abbeys are members of 15 Congregations, with very diverse regimes, but all with federal spirit" (p. 3; author's translation).

9. *New York Times*, November 12, 1983. Cf. Pedro Ramet, *Nationalism and Federalism in Yugoslavia: 1963-1983* (Bloomington: Indiana University Press, 1985), p. 299.

10. Edmond Orban, *La dynamique de la centralisation et l'Etat fédéral: un processus irréversible?* (Montréal: Québec/Amérique, 1984), p. 526.

11. Rufus Davis, "The Federal Principle Reconsidered," *Australian Journal of Politics and History* 1:2 (May 1956), p. 227.

12. This section reflects the argument developed in Ivo D. Duchacek, "Consociational Cradle of Federalism," *Publius* 15 (Winter 1985), pp. 85-98.

13. In the Dutch (Flemish) figure of speech, each of such nation's components—standing vertical and separate on its own base of religious or secular ideology—is indeed called a *zuil* ("pillar").

14. Herman Bakvis, "Structure and Processes in Federal and Consociational Arrangements" (Paper presented at the American Political Science Association Annual Meeting, Chicago, September 1-4, 1983), p. 8.

15. Jürg Steiner, *Amicable Agreement Versus Majority Rule: Conflict Resolution in Switzerland*, p. 5. Steiner's term for consociationalism, "amicable agreement," was apparently inspired by *amicabilis compositio*, which was used to describe a negotiated

compromise in deeply divided Europe at the time of the Peace of Westphalia in 1648. The term *consociatio* appears in Althusius and Grotius.

16. George McTurnan Kahin ed., *Major Governments of Asia*, 2d ed. (Ithaca: Cornell University Press, 1963), pp. 588–589.

17. Jürg Steiner, "The Consociational Theory and Beyond," *Comparative Politics* 13 (April 1981), p. 351.

18. Douglas W. Rae, "The Limits of Consensual Decision," *American Political Science Review* 29 (December 1975), p. 1274: "If (say by majority voting) n-1 people gain and one loses, we cannot claim to have done the group a good turn. *Any event in which some persons gain and some lose is indeterminate with respect to aggregate welfare* (italics are Rae's).

19. The consociational, concordant, or unanimous mode of political decision making has been, so far, the subject of numerous studies focusing on grand coalitions of heterogeneous small democracies in Western Europe such as the Netherlands, Switzerland, Austria, Belgium, and prewar Czechoslovakia. Important insights into consociational modes of decision making may be found in the following studies:

Bakvis, "Structure and Processes"; Thomas O. Hüglin, "Scarcity and Centralization: the Concept of European Integration," *International Political Science Review* 4 (Fall 1983), pp. 345–360; Gerhard Lehmbruch, *Proporzdemokratie: Politisches System und Politische Kultur in der Schweiz und in Österreich* (Tübingen: Mohr, 1967); Arend Lijphart, *Democracy in Plural Societies: A Comparative Exploration* (New Haven: Yale University Press, 1977); Arend Lijphart, *The Politics of Accommodation: Pluralism and Democracy in the Netherlands* (Berkeley: University of California Press, 1965); Arend Lijphart, "Consociational Democracy," *World Politics* 21 (January 1969), pp. 208–255; Val R. Lorwin, "Segmented Pluralism: Ideological Cleavages and Political Cohesion in the Smaller European Democracies," *Comparative Politics* 3 (January 1971), p. 142.

Eric Nordlinger, *Conflict Regulation in Divided Societies*, Center for International Affairs Occasional Papers no. 29 (Cambridge: Harvard University, 1971); Rae, "The Limits of Consensual Decision," p. 1271; Philippe C. Schmitter and Gerhard Lembruch, eds., *Trends Toward Corporatist Intermediation* (Beverly Hills, Calif.: Sage, 1979), p. 240; Charles F. Schuetz, *Revising the Federal Constitution of Switzerland* (Ottawa: Carleton University, Department of Political Science, 1983); Steiner, *Amicable Agreement*; Jürg Steiner and Jeffrey L. Obler, *Decision Making in Smaller Democracies: The Consociational Burden* (Beverly Hills, Calif.: Sage, 1977); Steiner, "The Consociational Theory and Beyond" (including Lijphart's comment).

20. A book by the Nouvelle Société Helvétique dealing with the shape of Swiss federal things to come by the year 2000 is bizarrely entitled *Anno 709 p.G.* (that is, post Grütli). The title simply means the year 1291 plus 709 equals 2000 A.D. The subtitle of the book is more prosaic: *Rapport final de la conférence de prospective de la nouvelle Société Helvétique* (Geneva: Edition Sonor, 1973).

21. Lijphart, "Consociational Democracy," p. 212.

22. Ian Lustick, "Stability in Deeply Divided Societies: Consociationalism Versus Control," *World Politics* 31 (April 1979), p. 334: "All consociational modes contain the assumption the sub-unit elites share an over-arching commitment to the perpetuation of the public arena within which they operate."

23. Arend Lijphart, "Non-Majoritarian Democracy: A Comparison of Federal and Consociational Theories" (Paper presented at the American Political Science Association, Annual Meeting, Chicago, September 1-4, 1983), p. 5. Lijphart found such a coincidence clearly only in the case of Switzerland since the 1950s and then less clearly and less consistently in the cases of Malaysia and Austria.

24. Steiner, *Amicable Agreement*, p. 6.

25. See Lijphart, "Non-Majoritarian Democracy," which describes how after 1966 Austria experienced both consociational and adversial decision-making modes simultaneously.

26. David Easton, *A Framework for Political Analysis* (Englewood Cliffs, N.J.: Prentice-Hall, 1965), p. 125. Cf. David Easton, *A Systems Analysis of Political Life* (New York: John Wiley, 1965), p. 273.

27. In using the term "tacit consociationalism," I mimic the term "tacit confederation" within a federal system as coined by Jack Rakove, a U.S. historian, in his analysis of two confederal eras in U.S. history: "The formal confederation of the 1780's and the tacit confederation which the Jeffersonians sought to restore" (Jack Rakove, "The Legacy of the Articles of Confederation," *Publius* 12 [Fall 1982], p. 65).

28. Schuetz, *Revising the Federal Constitution of Switzerland*, p. 181. At another point (p. 176), Schuetz described the seven-member executive of the Swiss federation and said, "There is simply no better instrument than a snall body of dedicated and capable people to develop, in the secrecy of their collegial council, and without being pressured by the time-limits of prospective elections, a nationally acceptable compromise." He calls consociationalism (*Konkordanzdemokratie*) the "optimum culmination of Swiss political culture."

29. Speaking in particular of black towns in the United States, W. H. Ferry described their goal of participating in the U.S. system on new terms: "The issue is the creation of a new kind of coexistence between blacktown and whitetown since what blacktown wants most whitetown cannot confer. Blacktown wants independence and the authority to run its own affairs. It wants to recover its manhood, its self-love, and develop its ability to conduct a self-reliant community" (W. H. Ferry, "The Case for A New Federalism," *Saturday Review* 51, June 1968, p. 59.

30. For instance, upon his return to the United States from a self-imposed exile (1961-1969) in Cuba and China, Robert Franklin Williams, a black nationalist leader, was referred to by his lawyer (*New York Times*, September 12, 1969) as the "future President of New Africa"—to be created out of Alabama, Mississippi, Louisiana, Georgia, and South Carolina.

31. Jonathan Elliot, *The Debates* (Philadelphia: Lippincott, 1888), vol. 1, pp. 465–466.

5

Ten Yardsticks of Federalism

We are too prone to say that federal constitutions must contain a certain five or eight or ten characteristics and all constitutions lacking any of these are not federal. Such a set of criteria ignores the fundamental fact that institutions are not the same things in different social and cultural situations. . . . The essence of federalism lies not in the institutional or constitutional structure but in the society itself. Federal government is a device by which the federal qualities of society are articulated and protected.

—William S. Livingston
("A Note on the Nature of Federalism," 1952)

We propose that any federation be regarded as an institutional arrangement . . . distinguished from other [sovereign] states solely by the fact that its central government incorporates regional units into its decision procedure on some constitutionally entrenched basis.

—Preston King
(*Federalism and Federation,* 1982)

Nowhere before has so close a union been combined with so much freedom (or autonomy) of the component parts.

—Alexis de Tocqueville
(*Democracy in America,* 1835)

The Union of Soviet Socialist Republics is an integral, federal, multinational state formed on the principle of socialist federalism as a result of the free self-determination of nations and the voluntary association of equal Soviet Socialist Republics. The USSR embodies the state unity of the Soviet people and draws all its nations and nationalities together for the purpose of jointly building communism.

—Constitution of the Soviet Union
(October 7, 1977; Article 70)

For heuristic purposes let us draw a scale (see Figure 5.1) on which one extreme point is a loose *temporary* association of sovereign states for the purpose of defense or economic advantage. Alliances, trade agreements, and common markets would fit this category. The opposite pole presents a tightly centralized totalitarian state. From these two extreme points we may

Figure 5.1

<u>Territorial Organization Scale</u>

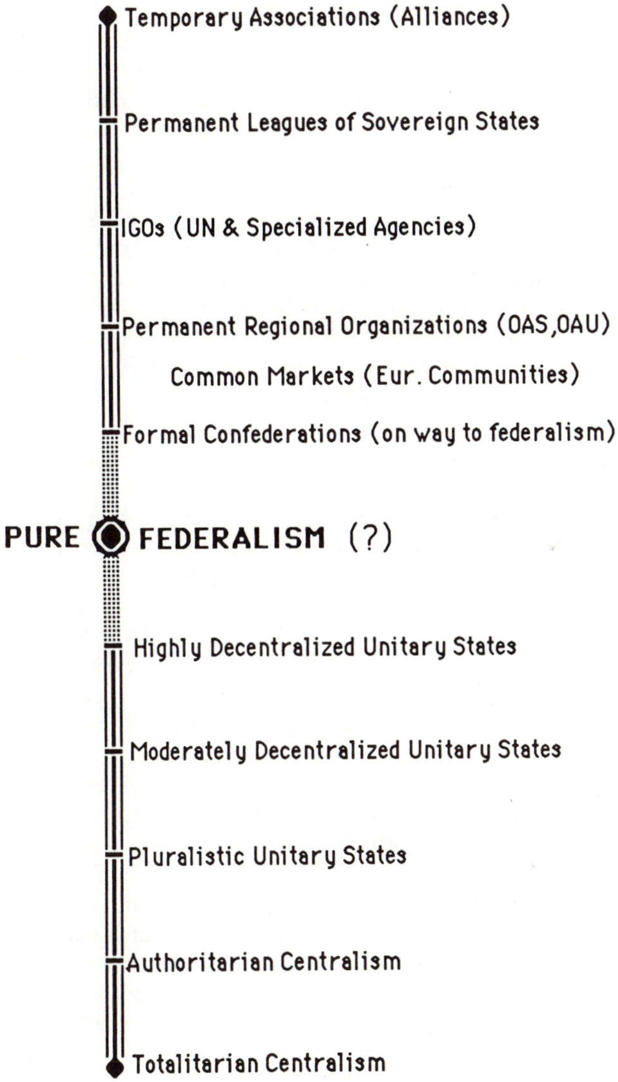

● Temporary Associations (Alliances)

Permanent Leagues of Sovereign States

IGOs (UN & Specialized Agencies)

Permanent Regional Organizations (OAS,OAU)
Common Markets (Eur. Communities)
Formal Confederations (on way to federalism)

PURE ◉ **FEDERALISM** (?)

Highly Decentralized Unitary States

Moderately Decentralized Unitary States

Pluralistic Unitary States

Authoritarian Centralism

● Totalitarian Centralism

proceed to the middle point—true federalism (?)—by successive gradation: proceeding from the loose associational point, we pass through permanent leagues, international intergovernmental organizations (IGOs) in the political and functional fields (UN specialized agencies), and common market communities to reach confederal consociations that are on their way to federalism (the United States in the spring of 1787 but not yet Western Europe in the 1980s). The gradation is a series of concepts, *not* a succession in time and growth.

From the unitary (authoritarian or democratic) pole, the gradation takes us successively to pluralistic, moderately decentralized, and highly territorially decentralized unitary states, shading off toward the federal middle point. Blurred rather than solid lines separate the middle point of federalism from its neighbors above and below. Hence, the difficulties in finding an acceptable definition of federalism and the resulting contrasting scholarly classification of nations according to their claim and practice of federalism.

Some years ago, in my book on comparative federalism, two entire chapters were devoted to an experimental testing of ten basic characteristics that various scholars, particularly students of U.S. federalism, had ascribed to true federal unions. Somewhat ambitiously, these criteria, couched in the form of questions, were labeled by me as *yardsticks*.[1] They represented a deliberate mixture of various ingredients in unequal quantities—a federal "daiquiri" of sorts. They were more or less all based on the U.S. Constitution and practices, because those bases were the most familiar to my readers. Also, the U.S. system, the federal nature of which has practically never been denied, has had the longest continuous existence and has acquired the reputation of being a model.

Using U.S. measuring rods, however, is far from suggesting that U.S. federalism should be considered the only "true" or "pure" federalism. Neither do I suggest that its birth and evolution are relevant for other countries that may contemplate the adoption of a federal system in the twentieth century. Some of the characteristics and aspects of U.S. federalism are so anchored in the country's soil and history that its experience and lessons can hardly be transplanted elsewhere. Furthermore, its record of preserving unity with diversity is much less impressive than some texts on U.S. government would have one believe.

Before proceeding further, we should remind ourselves of some of the specific historical and local reasons for the success and crisis of the U.S. federal system. Unlike many other countries that have tried their hands at federalism in the present century, the thirteen original states had been aware of their collective background, identity, and common interest *before* adopting the federal constitution. They had indeed been a community before they became a federal nation (Chapter 6 discusses this point in more detail).

External factors, too, favored the process of interlocking unity with diversity in the United States. While engaged in their federal experiment, the new states were able to remain relatively isolated from world tensions and wars and their corrosive or subversive domestic consequences. Today,

"Remember, gentlemen, we aren't here just to draft a constitution. We're here to draft the best damned constitution in the world."

Source: Drawing by P. Steiner; copyright 1982 by The New Yorker Magazine, Inc. Reprinted by permission.

none of the new and developing nations can enjoy the luxury of isolation that the young U.S. federation was able to maintain for so long. Also, there was no population explosion or pressure of excessive expectations on the initially meager resources. On the contrary, a dynamic immigrant population began to move into a rich and an underpopulated continent as individual pioneers rather than as a mass anticipating social welfare from cradle to grave to be assured by government plans, funds, and actions. In a word, it was a different century, a different physical, political, and international environment—an era marked by individual and local self-reliance and self-discipline in empty spaces rather than the present-day ferment of excessive expectations in the midst of our overcrowded world. As Valerie Earle perceptively noted: "Where statehood in any but the most formal or legalistic sense scarcely exists, a discussion of federalism seems highly irrelevant and a federal system a venture beyond the reach of leaders who must struggle to stay in power and to begin to feed their people."[2]

The U.S. Model: Negative Aspects

A negative aspect of the U.S. experience should be noted too. Even though the collective identity and common interests of the initial thirteen states with regard to England was a decisive factor in the seventeenth and early eighteenth centuries, the social and economic issue of slavery subsequently split the federal union into two hostile regions; the North and the South became two potential nations. Their frontal collision in the 1860s was tragic and costly in terms of both economic and human losses. "If the cost of the Civil War in terms of casualties alone is calculated as part of the price of national unity," wrote Henry Teune, "then perhaps the cost of national unity in the American experience is not one that many national leaders would be willing to pay today."[3]

On the negative side of the ledger, cost other than civil war casualties should also be considered: for example, the uneven economic and social development and the uneven progress in terms of civil rights, liberties and education in the various autonomous states. Finally, a twentieth century issue should be added: How can the initial federal territorial formula accommodate newly emerging communities—dispersed or partly territorial (urban or rural "ghettos")—that either split some states or superimpose themselves across the boundaries of the fifty states? The conflicting interests of these newer communities have necessarily become a subject of concern, recognition, and action on the part of national and state governments, in both cases in a manner characteristic of a unitary delegation of authority and responsibility. Should unity and uniformity of development or diversity be promoted as the highest value per se?

Whatever the relevance of the 200 year-old U.S. federal experience for other nations, it should be recognized that the rejection of a unitary system in favor of some variant of a federal formula is rarely a matter of free choice on the part of a handful of constitutional lawyers gathered in an

Figure 5.3. The United States

(Courtesy of the Advisory Commission on Intergovernmental Relations)

ivory-tower seminar on comparative constitutional law. There is often simply no practical alternative to the adoption of federalism—as, we may assume, there really was no practical unitary alternative to the system devised in Philadelphia in 1787.

Similarly, in many countries that are composed of different territorial, ethnic, tribal, lingual, racial, or religious communities, a unitary centralized system would cause such resentment and opposition as to jeopardize both the nation-building and the economic progress. Thus, the drafters of a constitution may reluctantly favor the federal formula, even though they initially preferred a unitary system, on the strength of their belief that federalism might more directly lead to unity and progress. Of course, their choice may be wrong. There is really no reliable way of answering the question as to when the constitutional federal recognition and guarantee of diversity may ultimately contribute to a sense of satisfaction and unity or when, on the contrary, the federal formula may reinforce the sense of a separate territorial destiny, including the possibility of going it alone. Occasionally the road to territorial disintegration has been paved with the best of federal intentions.

Despite these and similar warnings concerning either the purity or applicability of U.S. federalism (see Figure 5.3) as a universal model, my ten measuring rods, for purely practical reasons of comparison, remain heavily based on the U.S. federal theory, practice, and constitution (bearing in mind that, actually, the term *federal* never occurs in the text of the U.S. Constitution, and *confederation* occurs only once in Article 1, section 10, where states are prohibited from entering into any confederation).

The ten yardsticks of federalism that I will now discuss follow in order of suggested importance:

1. Has the central authority exclusive control over international relations as befits a nation-state in its relations with other nation-states?
2. Is the exercise of the central authority as it directly reaches all citizens (taxation, federal elections, federal enforcement) independent of individual approval by and resources of the component units?
3. Is the jurisdictional division between the two orders of government clear and unambiguous?
4. Is the federal union constitutionally immune to dissolution by secession?
5. Are the component units immune to central elimination of their autonomous jurisdiction and identity (predating and postdating the union)?
6. Have the component units retained or acquired an independent jurisdiction in significant issue-areas? Have the components retained all the residual powers that the constitution has not given the central authority?
7. Is the components' share in federal lawmaking adequately secured by equal representation of unequal states/provinces/cantons in a truly bicameral system, that is, one in which both chambers are equal in both legislative and political power? Is there any provision for federal-subnational cooperation and coordination on the executive level such as the yearly federal-provincial conferences in Canada, which, occurring on a more or less regular basis since 1984, consist of the federal prime minister and ten provincial premiers?
8. Are the territorial units sufficiently protected against constitutional amendments affecting the original consociational compact?
9. Are there two sets of courts?
10. Is there judicial review in matters concerning the constitutional division of or overlaps between federal and nonfederal jurisdictions?

I shall now proceed with a speculative testing of these ten yardsticks.

Yardstick 1: Control over Foreign Relations

Establishing a separate, sovereign, and identifiable unit in relation to other nation-states is the avowed goal of a federal process, which tries either to establish a new (federal) nation to replace preceding separate sovereignties or to preserve a unitary system by federalization as a timely response to a threat of secession or other revolt against excessive unitary centralism.

The first yardstick of federalism, with its emphasis on the control of national defense and diplomacy, does not and is not intended to distinguish a federal from a unitary system; it is meant to draw a line between a federation, on the one hand, and a league of states or an alliance in which the component units retain a decisive influence on common foreign policy and defense, on the other. Just as any unitary state, a federated state (despite its composite national nature) tries to present itself on the international scene as possessing the capacity to speak on behalf of its component units with a single legitimate voice (as we shall see later, this image of a single authoritative voice of a nation-state in international affairs must be qualified; see Chapter 8, section entitled "Nation-State as a Multivocal Actor").

A fear of the national center that its subunits might engage in their own diplomatic relations is, of course, as old as the territorial state itself. In 1796, postrevolutionary France, for example, issued a decree (Arrêté du 22 messidor, an VII) that stated:

> Foreigners accredited in whatever manner to the Government [of the French Republic] and those who occasionally find themselves on the territory of the Republic on account of their political activities, may have direct relations only with the Minister of External Relations. They may communicate with the government only through his intermediary.

Similarly, in 1810, another decree prohibited all the members of the French cabinet from receiving any communications from foreign embassies or responding to them. Again, all correspondence had to be transmitted and handled by the minister of foreign affairs.[4]

Diplomatic Monopoly of the Center

Let us first look at what is assumed in the national constitutions of nations about whose federal quality there is no controversy. The U.S. Constitution of 1789 (Article 1, section 10) sternly warned the thirteen federal components, "No State shall, without the consent of the Congress . . . keep troops, or ships of war in time of peace, enter into any agreement or compact with another State, or with a foreign power, or engage in war, unless actually invaded, or in such imminent danger as will not admit of delay." The preceding Articles of Confederation had endowed the central authority with a quasi-federal monopoly right to conduct war and diplomacy. Its Article 6 had decreed that the thirteen states could not "send any embassy to, or receive any embassy from, or enter into any conference, agreement, alliance, or treaty with any king, prince, or state." The Indian Constitution includes in its Union List (a list of powers given to the federal center) a similar provision for diplomacy and defense, war and peace, treaties, the United Nations, pilgrimages outside India, piracies and crimes committed on the high seas or in the air, and offenses against international law.

The Swiss Constitution of 1848, however, while giving the federal government the sole right to declare war and conclude peace and to make alliances and treaties, particularly customs and commercial treaties, with foreign nations, permits the Swiss noncentral governments (cantons) to engage in direct, though marginal, transborder negotiations with neighboring noncentral authorities (Chapter 9 discusses transborder microdiplomacy in more detail).

A limited initiative has been also given to the component units of the Federal Republic of Germany by the country's constitution (Article 32, section 3): "Insofar as the *Länder* have power to legislate, they may, with the consent of the federal government, conclude treaties with foreign states." This statement echoes the German confederal and imperial traditions. In imperial Germany, the twenty-three monarchies and three city-republics had the right of separate diplomatic relations with foreign states, and the monarchies that could afford to do so had diplomatic representation abroad. Bavaria had direct diplomatic relations with the Vatican, and a French representative resided in Munich, Bavaria's capital. In the Weimar Republic, the central power reserved the right of final approval and ratification of the treaties that the *Länder* were constitutionally authorized to conclude with foreign states.

In Canada, not only Québec but also anglophone provinces have established a paradiplomatic network abroad to promote their provincial interests in those issue-areas that are more or less clearly under the jurisdiction of provincial governments. The Québec legislature set up a Ministry of Intergovernmental Affairs on April 14, 1967 (since 1984 called the Ministry of International Relations and Foreign Trade) for the purpose of promoting the interests of Québec not only with regard to the federal government in Ottawa but also in negotiations with foreign governments, which initially meant primarily France (the special case of Québec is analyzed in Chapter 10).

Subnational Sharing in Foreign Policy

Using the first yardstick, I now turn to the Soviet Union, a nation-state that claims to be federal without really being so owing to its undiluted one-party totalitarian system. In 1944, on the eve of the Yalta Summit (February 1945), Stalin amended his 1936 Constitution to include Articles 18a and 18b, which granted the constituent republics the right to conduct their own foreign policy and have their own republican military formations. The two articles read as if the Soviet federal union had been transformed into a confederal one: "Each Union Republic has the right to enter into direct relations with foreign States and conclude agreements with foreign States and exchange representatives with them. Each Union Republic has its own Republican military formations." The Soviet Constitution of October 7, 1977 (Brezhnev's) omitted the provision for "territorial armies" but its Article 80 states, "A Union Republic has the right to enter into relations with other states, conclude treaties with them, exchange diplomatic and

consular representatives, and take part in the work of international organizations."

The 1944 amendment represented a complete reversal of Stalin's attitude
voiced at the Twelfth Congress of the party in 1923, when he condemned
confederal tendencies (mostly Ukrainian) in unmistakable terms:

> What becomes of the single union state if each republic retains its own
> People's Commissariat [Ministry] of Foreign Affairs? . . . We are creating not
> a confederation, but a federation of republics, single union state, uniting
> military, foreign, trade, and other affairs, a state which in no way diminishes
> the sovereignty of the individual republics. If the Union is to have a People's
> Commissariat of Foreign Affairs, a People's Commissariat of Foreign Trade,
> and so forth, and the republics constituting the Union are also to have all
> these Commissariats, it is obvious that it will be impossible for the Union as
> a whole to come before the outside world as a single state. One thing or the
> other: either we merge these apparatuses and face the external enemy as a
> single Union, or we do not merge them and create, not a union state, but
> a conglomeration of republics, in which case every republic must have its
> own parallel apparatus.[5]

A. Y. Vyshinsky, who was later to become the Soviet prosecutor and foreign
minister, then accused the Ukrainians who wanted to preserve their own
Ministry of Foreign Affairs of planning to betray their people and the union
by preserving the legal possibility of contact with the big imperialist powers
and with Poland.

Stalin's reversal of his 1923 attitude in 1944 could be interpreted as a
reflection of a changed situation inside the Soviet Union, which, after
twenty-one years of federal life, was able to overcome its earlier centrifugal
forces. Such an interpretation would be exaggerated in light of the fact
that Stalin's 1944 "confederal" amendment has remained to the present day
largely unimplemented in practice. The amendment—and this was probably
its only purpose—allowed Stalin to ask a few months later at Yalta for
sixteen votes in the United Nations General Assembly on behalf of the
then sixteen union republics. Somewhat surprisingly, he was finally satisfied
when he obtained international recognition for the Ukrainian and Byelorussian Republics, whose separate national and diplomatic identities are
expressed by their membership in the United Nations.

It should be noted that this arrangement, which gives the Soviet Union
three votes in the General Assembly, does not make sense at all. The Soviet
Union as a union of now fifteen socialist republics (see Figure 5.4)[6] should
have either fifteen votes in the General Assembly or only one as any other
federal union (the United States, Canada, India, Australia, Argentina, and
Mexico). As matters stand, the largest Soviet republic, the Russian Republic,
is represented in the United Nations only through the Soviet federal
government, as are the other Soviet republics such as Estonia, Tadzhikistan,
and Stalin's own Georgia. On the other hand, the Ukrainian and Byelorussian
Republics, which are members of the United Nations, have not been allowed
to establish direct diplomatic relations with any other nation, not even

Figure 5.4. The Soviet Union: Federal Divisions and Subdivisions

International Boundaries
Boundaries of Union Republics
Boundaries of Regions, Territories
    and Autonomous Republics
Boundaries of National Areas
° Capitals of Union Republics

1. ADIGEI AR
2. CHERKESS AR
3. KABARDIN ASSR
4. N. OSETIN ASSR
5. S. OSETIN AR
6. NAGORNO-KARABAKH AR

Union Republics
Other than RSFSR

Autonomous Republics
within RSFSR

Union and Autonomous Republics within the Russian Republic are shaded;
the Russian Soviet Federated Socialist Republic (RSFSR) is unshaded,
internally divided into provinces on a unitary-delegation basis.

Source: Ivo D. Duchacek, *Comparative Federalism: The Territorial Dimension of Politics* (New York: Holt, Rinehart and Winston, 1970).

with neighboring socialist states such as Poland, Rumania, Bulgaria, or Czechoslovakia.

When the curious deal was made at Yalta in 1945, Stalin's main argument was more "sentimental" than constitutional (although he did point to the fact that the British Commonwealth at that time had more votes than the one vote of its leading member, the United Kingdom): He pleaded that the Ukraine and Byelorussia be granted the right to UN membership because of their sacrifices in the common struggle against nazism. In the Ukrainian capital of Kiev, a visitor can indeed find a Ukrainian foreign ministry housed in an office building of respectable proportions; he or she will have some difficulty in finding the ministries of foreign affairs in other republics. "The Georgian Foreign Ministry has its headquarters in a dilapidated structure in a dark corner of Tbilisi (1958) and consists only of a single reception chamber."[7]

In the communist federation of Yugoslavia (see Figure 5.5), a trend developed in the late 1960's, to create special commissions for foreign affairs in all six federal republics (Bosnia and Herzegovina, Croatia, Macedonia, Montenegro, Serbia, and Slovenia) as well as in the two autonomous regions (Kosovo-Metohija and Vojvodina) for the purpose of influencing the national Ministry of Foreign Affairs (located in Serbian Belgrade) to pursue foreign policies that would be "brought into line with [their] internal policies."[8] The argument in Yugoslavia is twofold: First, decentralization of foreign policy is only part of the need to decentralize communism; second, individual republics have some special problems with regard to their neighbors and have some economic interests that may not call for an overall national commitment. This latter argument is further underlined by the suspicion that foreign trade policy in particular was excessively determined by the interests as perceived by Serbia and its capital, Belgrade.[9] The republics of Croatia and Slovenia tend to translate their ancient links with their Catholic West European neighbors into favorable economic arrangements. On the other hand, the republic of Macedonia seeks additional protection against potential threats coming from neighboring Bulgaria and Greece, which both, at one time or another, voiced territorial claims with regard to Macedonia.

Whereas the Soviet implementation of its own constitutional provisions for "federalization" (that is, territorial segmentation) of the conduct of foreign policy is a patent sham, there is, in our interdependent world, some logic in allowing or even encouraging federal components to participate in the shaping of foreign policy in issue-areas *other than national security*. A major portion of national foreign policy today is concerned with matters of better-or-worse-life issues rather than life-or-death issues to be settled by either war or surrender. (Chapters 9 and 10 discuss the advantages and disadvantages of microdiplomatic encounters of a new kind that are practiced today by noncentral governments, especially in North America and Western Europe.)

To sum up: The first yardstick of federalism—central government monopoly in diplomacy and national security in the traditional sense—does not clearly distinguish a federal system from either unitary or confederal

Figure 5.5. The Federal Divisions of Yugoslavia

Source: Ivo D. Duchacek, *Comparative Federalism: The Territorial Dimension of Politics* (New York: Holt, Rinehart and Winston, 1970).

systems. In some federated states, the component units encroach on the central conduct of international relations in matters pertaining to other than security matters, partly as a reaction to the central government's encroachment on subnational autonomous jurisdictions by means of its international treaty-making power.

Yardstick 2: Independent Sphere
of Central Authority

If a central authority is politically and financially dependent upon the component units, such an arrangement is an *alliance* or a *confederation*, not a federal union. In a federal system, powers are so divided "that the general regional governments are each within a sphere, co-ordinate and independent,"[10] not subordinate. How can some of the "true" federal states pass this test, which aims at differentiating a confederal from a federal system on other than the foreign policy monopoly level?

First, there is the issue of financial resources. Federal constitutions make federal government's independent of their constituent units by granting them the right to levy direct taxes and enforce the federal laws. A federal government must be able to finance its operations, especially in view of the fact that it is in charge of national security and status; in modern times, responsibility for general welfare has been added to the two traditional responsibilities. The U.S. Constitution gives the Congress the power "to lay and collect taxes, duties, imposts, and excises" (Article 1, section 8), but in principle, direct taxes were to be apportioned among the several states according to population until 1913. In that year, the Sixteenth Amendment gave the Congress the right to impose income taxes "without apportionment among the several States, and without regard to any census or enumeration."

In 1985, the fifteen U.S. states that impose income taxes on their citizens led a virulent campaign against President Reagan's tax reform proposal because it had proposed to eliminate deductions of state and local taxes from the federal tax bill. The main argument, voiced by New York and New Jersey in particular, was that the proposed measure was in conflict with constitutional federal principles since it would further weaken the states in favor of the national government. The counterargument was that thirty-five states that do not impose state income taxes should not be expected to contribute indirectly to the well-being of those fifteen states that do impose taxes.

Is the financial independence of the center impaired by an obligation of tax sharing, which is characteristic of modern federalism (for example, in Canada)? According to the Indian Constitution, all revenues received and all loans raised by the central government form the Consolidated Fund of India (Article 266).[11] The constitution also contains very detailed and specific provisions on how to divide some excise duties (Article 268 deals with "medicinal and toilet preparations") and how to channel back to the states some centrally levied and collected duties and taxes.[12]

There may also be an opposite view that perceives the tremendous taxing power of the central government as an impetus toward centralization and transformation of territorial communities and their governments into either branches of the center or humble beggars. Or as a Canadian analyst, Edmond Orban, expressed it more mercifully, centralization of revenues is usually followed by decentralization in spending them.[13]

Another form of dependence of the central authority on local units may be seen in constitutional provisions for indirect elections of one of the two houses of a federal legislature. Such a dependence existed in the United States until 1913, when the Seventeenth Amendment replaced the choice of senators by state legislatures by direct popular election. In other federal systems, such selection is still the practice. In Switzerland, for instance, the upper house of the Swiss federal assembly (the Council of States) is composed of two representatives from each canton; each canton determines the period of the representatives' service, their salary (to be paid from the cantonal treasury), and the method of their selection (in most cases direct election, in other cases by cantonal legislatures). This arrangement reminds us of a confederal assembly of "ambassadors."

In West Germany, the members of the federal upper house are not elected nor do they serve a fixed term. (These provisions also applied in imperial Germany and the Weimar Republic.) They are members or officials of the cabinet in each of the twelve *Länder*. They vote on behalf of their territorial executive en bloc (three to five votes, depending on the size of their *Land*) and according to the instructions given by their respective *Länder* cabinets. The consent of the federal upper chamber is required for all matters involving the federal distribution of power and affecting the administration of federal laws by the *Länder*.[14] In India, the members of the Council of States are "elected by the elected members of the Legislative Assembly of the State in accordance with the system of proportional representation by means of a single transferable vote."[15]

It may be argued that in a different sphere a near-confederal dependence on the component units existed in the United States, when the states had the right to determine unilaterally qualifications for the exercise of the federal right to vote. It is true that constitutional amendments extending the right to vote regardless of race and sex as well as subsequent judicial interpretations have limited the power of the states to distort the right to participate in federal elections. It should be recalled that the founding fathers in Philadelphia assigned to the states the right to determine qualifications for voters because the members of the Constitutional Convention could not agree as to what these qualifications for "free males with property" should be. The Voting Rights Act of 1965, enacted in response to the Selma, Alabama, famous protest march, largely eliminated the southern states' various limitations on the federal right to vote.

Yardstick 3: Clear Division of Powers

The principle of an irrevocable and a clear division of substantial power between the two government networks concerning their separate jurisdictions with respect to different issue areas is central to most definitions of true federalism; the graphic diagram of federalism (Figure 4.1) is based on it. Under a closer scrutiny of both the constitutional texts and federal practices, we seem to discover an intrafederal osmosis (an image of a swirled rather than a distinctly layered cake comes to mind), not a precise division between the two spheres of political and legislative activities. The ebullience of political power simply resists confinement in any watertight compartment, and seven principal leaks or overlaps blur the critical line between national and noncentral authorities.

Diplomatic and Defense "Monopoly". The federal monopoly in the field of foreign policy easily spills over into the seemingly exclusive domain of provincial powers. The problem of federal spillover into the provincial sphere lies, first, in the subject matter of the treaties concluded between the national government and foreign powers, dealing with matters that, unlike national security and diplomatic status, are within the jurisdictional spheres of the noncentral governments (protection of human and labor rights, especially of migrant or host workers; provincial ownership of natural resources in Canada; education; drug traffic and transborder criminal links; protection of wildlife and fisheries; pollution; transfers of energy; tourism; and other economic, social, and cultural matters). There is, of course, as noted above, also the opposite problem of provincial encroachments on national foreign policy since provincial initiatives on the international field regarding nonsecurity matters may and do affect the political aspects of the national management of international relations (for a more detailed analysis of this subject, see Chapters 8–10).

Second, another challenge to the seeming monopoly of the center in international affairs is the need for provincial/state legislation to bring treaties into effect. If the component units of a federal union have the right to prevent international treaties or their implementation, the national government cannot be effective on the international scene and may therefore fail in protecting or promoting the collective interest of the composite whole. If, on the other hand, the component units have no practical choice but to bow to international treaties or their implementing legislation, the so-called exclusive powers of the component units may become ones of concurrence at best or nil at worst. Here, again, we observe how federal constitutions point to a dilemma rather than to an unequivocal solution. At any rate, the seemingly monopolistic power of the central government to make friends and enemies abroad is not as monopolistic as textbooks on federalism and diplomacy would make us believe.

The Emergency Provisions. Emergency provisions in connection with the defense of the federal nation-state against external and internal enemies represent the second major avenue through which the federal authority is encouraged or authorized to cross the federal-state Rubicon and to curb temporarily or totally eliminate local autonomy in the name of the survival and the security of the federal collective whole. We cannot imagine federal constitutions without such provisions, but they necessarily raise the question, How real is the third yardstick of federalism, a clear division of federal and local powers?

The determination of the existence and gravity of an external or internal threat to the federal way of life is in the hands of the central executive; its power is usually limited by a requirement that the central legislature has subsequently to approve a proclamation of emergency or martial law within a determined period of time. In practice, this limitation is less of an impediment to the federal executive than it seems, especially in federations in which the bicameral parliament is tilted to the advantage of the popular lower chamber (in a cabinet system) or in which the dominant party in the executive and legislative center is tempted to use federal power to curb state-based opposition parties.

Furthermore, there is the well-known problem of *objective* measurement of the seriousness or imminence of an external or internal danger to peace and security. Even if we rule out an evil intent on the part of the central authority—which, in practice, we cannot do—there remains, as the familiar controversy concerning the subject of the freedom of expression and its permissible curbs has taught us, an honest disagreement as to whether federal intervention is indeed warranted by a "clear and present," "imminent and grave," nebulous and distant, or wrongly perceived danger.

The Indian Constitution, for instance, authorizes the central government to supersede a state government and assume to itself all the executive and legislative powers of the state government concerned when a state of emergency is proclaimed. The portions of the Indian Constitution that deal with the federal division of powers may be suspended (Article 356). Although, in principle, the emergency powers are granted for a limited period of time (they are supposed to "cease to operate at the expiration of two months unless before the expiration of that period it has been approved by resolutions of both houses of Parliament—Article 352, section 2c), the experience under Prime Minister Indira Gandhi showed that suspension of civil rights and preventive detention may last as long as a decade. The constitution, which unmistakably authorizes the central authority to take over a state government that is found incapable of satisfactory performance, has also been invoked quite frequently by the ruling Congress party, which has used the federal powers against the extreme left or the extreme right, both insignificant forces on the national level but often enjoying mass support in some Indian states.

"Guardian" Powers. From clear cases of national emergency caused by an external attack or by an internal insurrection, we now move into a twilight zone in which federal intervention in the affairs of the component states may be justified simply because the "republican" (whatever that means) institutions are threatened, the political situation seems unstable, the financial administration is irresponsible,[16] or—the most permissive of such clauses—to ensure that federal laws are faithfully executed locally.

The Indian Constitution, for instance, gives the federal government the power to issue administrative directives to the states when necessary to "ensure compliance with the laws made by Parliament" (Article 256) and to guarantee that "the executive power of every State shall be so exercised as not to impede or prejudice the exercise of the executive power of the Union" (Article 257, section 1). Furthermore, the federal center is represented in each of the twenty-two Indian states by a federally appointed governor who, according to the constitution, is supposed to be only a ceremonial figurehead under normal conditions, the real power being in the hands of each state's chief ministers (that is, prime ministers and their cabinets). An amendment (Article 258A) passed in 1957 transformed the governors into powerful extensions of the national center (party and government) in the various states of the Indian union. It reads as follows: "Notwithstanding anything in this Constitution the Governor of a State may, with the consent of the Government of India, entrust either conditionally or unconditionally to that Government or its officers functions in relation to any matter to which the executive power of the State extends."

The federal overlap in India appears so predominant that in 1967, long before the period of Indira Gandhi's centralist rule, a scholar-observer of Indian theory and practice, S.A.H. Haqqi of Aligarh Muslim University, concluded that

> notwithstanding [a] formidable testimony to the federal character of the constitution, one cannot, on a closer scrutiny, help agreeing with those who hold that the Indian Union is not a true federation, an indestructible Union of indestructible States but a unitary state with subsidiary federal features. ... The Indian Constitution vests in the Union Government such formidable powers that, not only in times of war or during an emergency but even in times of peace, it can, if it so wishes, superintend, direct and control the activities of the State Governments.[17]

Latin-American federations may be similarly characterized as unitary states with only subsidiary federal features on account of the constitutionally legalized and frequently used practice of federal intervention (in fact, central/autocratic). The Mexican Constitution authorizes the national government (that is, the one-party leadership) to see that democratic governments prevail in the states and that the constitution and federal laws are executed by the state officers. Similar constitutional authorizations and practice characterize the federal states of Argentina, Brazil, and Venezuela.

In Canada the constitution authorizes the central government to veto or disallow provincial bills (a power that is rarely used) and to appoint provincial lieutenant governors (largely ceremonial figureheads), and provincial judges. In Switzerland, it is within the competence of the central legislature (Federal Assembly) to guarantee the constitutions and the territories of the cantons and, in consequence of this guarantee, to intervene as well as to take measures for the internal security of Switzerland and for the maintenance of peace and order. The executive branch (Federal Council) is empowered to examine the laws and ordinances of the cantons, which must be submitted for approval, and it is also empowered to supervise the branches of cantonal administration that are placed under executive control.

In contrast with the just-mentioned, sometimes detailed, and often sweeping general authorizations for federal intervention, the provisions of the U.S. Constitution appear laconic and are dispersed among several articles. Each state is guaranteed a "republican" form of government and federal protection against invasion and "on application of the legislature or of the executive (when the legislature cannot be convened) against domestic violence" (Article 4, section 4)—which, of course, may take the form of intervention. Another article makes the federal executive responsible for a faithful execution of laws (Article 2, section 3); and Article 1, section 8, provides for "calling forth the militia [now the National Guard] to execute the laws of the Union, suppress insurrections and repel invasions."

In combination with the defense powers of the president as commander in chief, the provisions just mentioned represent a potentially wide open door for federal interference because the request of the state authorities for action is not necessary when the issue is local resistance to federal laws or a serious threat to internal peace in the United States. In 1842, President Tyler was ready to send troops to Rhode Island to protect one of the two governments there, each of which claimed to be the legitimate one. In 1960, President Eisenhower sent federal troops to Little Rock, Arkansas, to enforce a court order for school desegregation. "The action at Little Rock affected the balance of forces in the Federal system because it proved that in an eventual confrontation between the national government and the state on the question of civil rights, the state must comply."[18]

The Concurrent Power. Another type of overlap between federal and state powers is the provision for a sharing or a reciprocal delegation of powers, often in the form of a "concurrent list," found in modern constitutions. Such provisions represent, as it were, a bridge for a two-way traffic between the otherwise exclusive shores of federal and state powers. The concurrent lists usually contain a clause that makes the federal law prevail over the provincial law when the federal authority chooses to legislate on any matter in the concurrent list. The length of the list varies greatly from very brief (Canada) to very long (India). The Indian Concurrent List contains forty-seven items, starting with some portions of the criminal law and procedure, family law, contracts, and bankruptcy and trust and ending with price controls, social security, trade unions, newspapers, electricity, boilers, prevention of cruelty to animals, and vagrancy.

A related constitutional overlap between federal and state powers may be seen in the reciprocal delegation of authority and in federal-state subdivisions of one shared power so that a portion of it is given to the federal government while another part of the same power is kept in the hands of the local authorities. Examples are the shared federal and state control of the National Guard in the United States; controls over banking, trade, and railroads in Australia; and control over family law or alcoholic beverages in Switzerland.

Delegation of the execution of federal laws to local units is a frequent feature in many federations. In Switzerland, for instance, the federal penal code is adjudicated by the cantonal courts; their organization and procedures are also cantonal. Laws concerning the organization of the Swiss army are enacted by the federal legislature, but the execution of the military laws is cantonal (Article 20). The same is true with regard to the modern welfare provisions of the Swiss Constitution (the utilization of water power, the welfare of the people, the economic security during economic crises, and the relief of unemployment);[19] the constitution requires that cantons be consulted before the enactment of federal regulations and that as a rule, the execution of the federal regulations be entrusted to the cantons.

Such a formula of concurrence of otherwise divided powers is also clearly present in the German tradition and practice of federalism, which leaves the bulk of the legislative power to the federal center while largely transferring administrative and judicial powers to the states, with the exception of foreign affairs, defense, and the mail. Thus, in the absence of federal field agencies, the *Länder* administer the rules that are initiated by the federal cabinet and enacted by the federal parliament through their own local agencies, personnel, and funds. Such a practice, dating back to the empire, entails minimum interference in the long-established administrative structures and practices of the member units; for the average German citizen, the establishment of the federal union "brought about no changes in the government officials with whom he had to deal."[20] One of the consequences of this federal-legislative federalism is that it acts as a brake on the growth of the federal administrative apparatus. The German variant of federalism differs substantially from the U.S. concept because, as Arnold Brecht described it, the former provides for a "horizontal" division of powers in contrast to the "vertical" division in the United States.[21]

Concurrent lists as well as constitutional provisions for cooperation, mutual dependence, and a reciprocal delegation or sharing of powers between federal and state governments are viewed by some observers as logical, inevitable, and desirable but are deplored by others as possibly contrary to, or at least harmful for, federalism. In defense of concurrent lists and provisions for the delegation of authority, it may also be said that sometimes such provisions represent a transitional solution on the part of the founding fathers, who are not and cannot be certain which powers would be best given to the central authority and which to local governments. The existence of concurrent powers and concurrent lists is simply another reflection of the fundamental impossibility, and perhaps also the undesirability, of dividing political powers neatly or permanently.

Elastic or Coefficient Clauses. The next possible channel for federal-state/provincial/cantonal osmosis is known in the United States as the "necessary and proper," "elastic," or "coefficient" clause. This is the last, eighteenth grant of exclusive powers to the federal center (Article 1, section 8), which, in addition to the previous seventeen specific grants of power, authorizes the Congress "to make all laws which shall be *necessary* and *proper* for carrying into execution the foregoing" seventeen federal powers (italics added). The problem evidently is who interprets—and with what bias—the meaning of the two crucial but controversial adjectives "necessary" and "proper." In 1819, in the famous case of *McCulloch v. Maryland*, Chief Justice John Marshall interpreted these words as meaning "useful and convenient" rather than "absolutely indispensable."

Lack of Verbal Precision in All Federal Constitutions. A sixth problem that underscores all the previously discussed overlaps is simply the lack of verbal precision in any text written by humans, including a constitutional description of the territorial distribution of authority. However finely chiseled a constitutional text may be, the federal needle always seems to have a sufficiently big eye for the unitary camel to go through.

There are several reasons for the problem. One is basically semantic: The significance of terms tends to change with time and space. The legal language is only somewhat more accurate than that of the orators; if this were not the case, the profession of law would not have been so profitable through the centuries. The lack of verbal precision in federal constitutions also reflects the previously mentioned difficulty of quantifying political power. Determining what are central and national matters as distinct from what are peripheral or provincial matters proves quite resistant to an exact specification or a neat division into permanent compartments of separate jurisdiction. The lack of verbal precision may, of course, sometimes also be deliberate; some founders simply wish to conceal a unitary hope in a federal wrapping.

Impact of Extraconstitutional Changes. The seventh problem was depicted in the simplified diagram of a federal system (see Figure 4.1) in the form of a broad channel marked "Extraconstitutional Links" and "Centralist Tendencies," potentially emerging from among the elites and/or their publics. Four causes of such tendencies that challenge constitutional federal provisions as well as intrafederal boundaries are:

1. Central economic planning, technological innovation, and costly projects or social welfare programs often call for national financing and controls. In addition, the growth of various corporations (manufacturing, financial, insurance, labor and farm organizations, and mass media) challenge the intrafederal boundaries which, drawn in earlier eras, cannot be justified on modern grounds of rational efficiency, organization, and communication.

2. Population shifts affect the initial distribution of power especially by the growth of big cities and the emergence of new regions which are superimposed not only on intrafederal but also national boundaries (U.S. Mexican borderlands with their twin cities or the cooperative trinational regions along the Rhine).

3. External threats necessarily erode local and provincial powers by extending the federal powers as required by crisis mobilization of resources and people.

4. The emergence of new parties, leaders, ideologies or orientations of the cadres may introduce novel centralist or secessionist elements into the formerly prevailing federal political culture and practice.

Movement up and down through the extraconstitutional channel is conditioned by the perceived (resented or accepted) intrafederal asymmetries. There is obviously no federal system in the world whose components could be equal in size, population, ideological and cultural traditions (even when a federal union is monoethnic), climatic conditions, natural resources, development, administrative skill, political clout, social structure, predominance of either rural or urban interests, and relative geographic location (near a national border, distant from the nation's center, etc.). As a result, the federal components may vary in their attachment to the federal union and in their readiness to contribute to various federal programs aiming at standardization of economic, social, and cultural conditions throughout the whole federal nation. Many a separatist movement has been sparked by federal or wealthy provincial Scrooges who are unwilling to contribute to any improvement of conditions in the less fortunate of the components.

Figure 5.6. Canada

(Courtesy of the Advisory Commission on Intergovernmental Relations)

The diagram of federalism (Figure 4.1) can only suggest the intrafederal asymmetry by depicting the *unequal* size of the federal components, despite their equal or nearly equal strength in some federal upper chambers. As to the importance of population asymmetry and its effect on political influence in lower legislative chambers let us consider, for example, the disparity between Switzerland's two populous cantons of Zurich and Bern, which have almost one-third of the 196 seats in the Swiss federal legislature, and the seven cantons of Uri, Schwyz, Underwalden, Glarus, Zug, Appenzell, and Schaffhausen, which, combined, have only fourteen seats. In the Canadian all-powerful House of Commons, two provinces, Ontario (nearly 9 million people) and Québec (over 6.5 million) have 160 members out of the total of 265—a fact of political asymmetry that is resented by the much less populous province of British Columbia (2.8 million), Alberta (2.3 million), Saskatchewan (991,000), Manitoba (over 1 million), and the smallest province Prince Edward Island, with a total population of 124,000.

Disparity in size, population, wealth, and development in Latin American federations is usually cited as one of the reasons (besides the ideological orientations of the various juntas and one-man or one-party political systems) for their unitary/centralist practices despite their constitutional federal pledges. Extreme disparity in size, population, and economic development also characterizes the United States, yet, since 1860, its political pluralism and equalization efforts coupled with a maturing national consciousness have not created any effort to even flirt with separatism, which is present in many other nation-states, federal or not.

Yardstick 4: Immunity Against Secession

Clearly, no nation-state is, or can be, really immune against territorial secession. Nevertheless, some federal and confederal constitutions solemnly proclaim the permanency or even *eternity* of the union (how foolish founding fathers can be!). The German interdynastic confederation of 1871 (Bismarck Constitution), for example, proclaimed that the various kings and grand-dukes concluded "an eternal federation to protect the federal territory . . . as well as to promote the welfare of the German people. This federation shall be known by the name of German Reich."

The text of the U.S. Constitution does not contain any explicit interdiction of secession. Implicitly, it may be argued that the Preamble's first sentence, which stresses a "more perfect union," should be read in conjunction with the Articles of Confederation, which it amended and which had committed the thirteen states to a "perpetual union."

The Soviet, Yugoslav, and the first Burmese Constitutions, on the other hand, contain provisions recognizing the right of territorial self-determination and therefore secession. The authoritarian regimes pay lip service to national self-determination, knowing full well that neither a territory nor an individual citizen is allowed to leave a "socialist paradise to enter a capitalist hell." The Soviet Constitution reserves "the right freely to secede from the USSR" to every union republic (Article 17 in the Stalin constitution; Article 72 in the current charter). All union republics have a portion of their boundaries contiguous with those of the Soviet Union, allegedly to be able to go it alone if any of them wishes to do so without being an encircled island somewhere in the middle of the Soviet subcontinent. In reality, of course, the right of secession cannot be exercised since, according to official doctrine, such a territorial transfer would weaken the cause of communism and strengthen the cause of capitalism. As Stalin expressed it in 1920, "Of course, the border regions of Russia, the nations and the tribes, which inhabit these regions . . . possess the inalienable right to secede from Russia . . . but the demand for secession . . . at the present stage of the revolution is a profoundly counterrevolutionary one."[22]

As the Soviet military invasion of Hungary in 1956 and the Soviet occupation of Czechoslovakia in 1968 demonstrated, even allied sovereign countries have no right to secede from the Soviet bloc if they occupy strategic geographic positions in the framework of the Warsaw Pact. It may actually be argued that one of the many reasons for the Soviet overreaction to both the Hungarian and the Czechoslovak desires for self-determination was the fear that secession by an ally might trigger secessionist tendencies within the western portions of the Soviet Union.

The right of secession was also subordinated to the cause of socialism in the Yugoslav Constitutions of 1963 and 1974, whose Basic Principles, Part 1, read in part as follows: "The peoples of Yugoslavia, on the basis of the right of every people to self-determination, including the right of secession, . . . aware that the further consolidation of their brotherhood and unity is to their common interest."

The first constitution of the Union of Burma[23] was coauthored by British constitutional experts (who despite their constitutionless and unitary background seem to have had a predilection for a federal aftermath to their imperial rule—from Canada and India to Australia and Nigeria) and guaranteed "the right to secede from the Union in accordance with the conditions hereinafter prescribed" (Articles 201 and 202). The constitution prescribed the procedure for an orderly secession including a plebiscite "for the purpose of ascertaining the will of the people of the state concerned." The right of secession was not to be exercised at all within the first ten years of the federation. The reason for this unusual provision was to give federalism in polyethnic Burma a chance—a decade-long trial period. In practice, however, the constitutional and federal government in Burma was of extremely brief duration, if it started at all. A military dictatorship quickly replaced the federal democracy, and tribal secession attempts by means of jungle warfare made the elaborate constitutional provisions concerning the tribal and frontier areas useless.[24]

Although federal and unitary systems assume unity and its permanency, in both cases the grant of ethnoterritorial autonomy may be perceived as a guarantee of unity as well as an invitation for secession. Factors other than unitary decentralization or federal noncentralization determine whether or not the unity, desired by the central elites, finally turns out to be quite impermanent. The problem of national self-determination and secession is far beyond the scope of this present discussion; it has been adequately covered by several authors whose selected contributions are listed in the Bibliography.

Yardstick 5: Component Units
Indestructible by Centralist Absorption

With the fifth yardstick, our concern shifts from the union and its center to the federal components, whether predating or postdating the federal union. Two points qualify the fifth yardstick. As noted in the preceding chapter, unitary systems, even the authoritarian ones, in theory can curb, suspend, and even totally eliminate noncentral governments and all units of self-rule but almost never do so. The reason is either political wisdom, that is, respect for territorial pluralism, especially if buttressed by longevity, or simply concern for greater administrative efficiency and a desire for local inputs and participation. In some instances, the constitutions of unitary governments (France, China, Italy) actually guarantee the scope and function of territorial self-rule. The existence of units of local self-rule is simply not a proof of federalism, only of decentralization.

Second, although most federal systems are indeed born from the consociational bottom up, the opposite "creation" is also conceivable: As noted, a timely yielding to the federalist bottom by the unitary top may transform unitary decentralization into true federal noncentralization. In many cases the federal components predate the federal union, but in other cases they postdate its birth. All federations have to provide for possible territorial extension, the creation of additional units of self-rule, and new intrafederal groupings in response to new needs or dissatisfactions however consociational their beginnings might have been.

The oldest successful federation, Switzerland, is a good example not only of a step-by-step growth of twenty-two cantons to a federal union, built around the original cluster of the first three allied cantons (Uri, Schwyz, and Unterwalden) but also of subsequent subdivisions reflecting the new interests of subcommunities. Three of the cantons, for example, have been divided into half-cantons. Unterwalden, one of the three constituting cantons, was divided in the fifteenth century into Obwalden and Nidwalden; the main reason was the difficulty of communication between the two major valleys that constitute the canton. In 1597, Appenzell broke into two half-cantons because of the religious issue (Ausser Rhoden, Protestant, and Inner Rhoden, Catholic). In 1833, the canton of Basel split into its urban and rural components (Basel-Stadt and Basel-Land), a result of rural resentment accompanied by violence against urban dominance. In 1978, the new French-speaking canton of Jura was carved out of the otherwise dominantly German-speaking canton of Bern (Figure 5.7).

The growth of the United States from the original league of thirteen colonies into a federal union of fifty states is another example of mixing territorial communities that had preceded the federal nation with new ones (created, as it were, from "above"—that is, by transformation of federal territories into new states by their admission into the Union). Initially, some of the territories and states were perhaps as artificial as the *départements* established by Napoleon in France; but subsequently, they too acquired a true territorial identity (the case of the two Dakotas was mentioned previously) based on their separate existence over a considerable span of time and buttressed by habit, tradition, local pride, and vested interest. The need for adjustment to future territorial changes requires that all federal systems provide constitutional means not only for possible new territorial accessions but also for regrouping, division of existing units, and possible internal boundary changes.

Is the creation or regrouping of federal components subsequent to the birth of a federal union contrary to the spirit of its consociational conception? I do not believe so, provided that the federal principle of indestructibility of the component units is satisfied by interdicting any change or extinction of territorial identity without the consent of the territorial units directly

Figure 5.7. Names of the Swiss Cantons

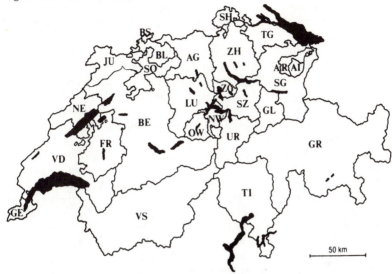

NAMES OF THE SWISS CANTONS

French	Map Abbreviation	German
Appenzell-Rhodes Intérieures	AI	Appenzell-Inner Rhoden
Appenzell-Rhodes Extérieures	AR	Appenzell-Ausser Rhoden
Argovie	AG	Aargau
Bâle-Ville	BS	Basel-Stadt
Bâle-Campagne	BL	Basel-Land
Berne	BE	Bern
Fribourg	FR	Freiburg
Genève	GE	Genf
Glaris	GL	Glarus
Grisons	GR	Graubünden
Jura	JU	Jura
Lucerne	LU	Luzern
Neuchâtel	NE	Neuenburg
Schaffhouse	SH	Schaffhausen
Schwytz	SZ	Schwyz
Soleure	SO	Solothurn
St.Gall	SG	St. Gallen
Tessin (Ticino in Italian)	TI	Tessin
Thurgovie	TG	Thurgau
Unterwald-Nidwald	NW	Unterwalden-Nidwalden
Unterwald-Obwald	OW	Unterwalden-Obwalden
Uri	UR	Uri
Valais	VS	Wallis
Vaud	VD	Waadt
Zurich	ZH	Zürich
Zoug	ZO	Zug

concerned.[25] Or, to express it colloquially: A state, province, canton, *Land* may commit territorial suicide, but it cannot be halved, quartered, or otherwise slaughtered by any other component or the nation as a composite whole.

A somewhat debatable position is put forward in an ambiguous provision in the Indian federal constitution which requires that the opinion of the state legislatures of the states directly concerned with the creation of a new state or a regrouping of the old ones be *expressed*. It is not clear whether the expression of opinion is really binding upon the central government. Conceivably, the state legislatures' expression of opinion could be overruled by the national Parliament.

When India emerged as an independent federal state, it was composed of nine fully autonomous states (labeled by the constitution as Category A), eight somewhat less autonomous states, because they were more backward (Category B), and ten minor states (Category C), which were to become federally administered territories—such as Delhi, Himachal Pradesh, Manipur, Tripura, and other strategically located areas (Figure 5.8). These divisions are constantly being altered, mostly in response to linguistic nationalism, expressed in the slogan One language, one state. Finally, in the 1960s, the state of Punjab was divided on the religious issue between the Hindus and the noncaste Sikhs. By 1980, federal India consisted of 22 states and 9 union territories (including Delhi).

The principles of linguistic nationalism and religious antagonisms (Muslim/Hindu and Hindu/Sikh) imposed a substantial revision of territorial boundaries within India, which had been drawn by the British;[26] further revisions were made by Indian nationalists for the sake of administrative efficiency but without much regard for local linguistic or cultural sensitivities. Thus, forty years after its birth as an independent and federal nation, India still remains, as it were, an unfinished nation, time and again torn asunder by new secessionism and intercommunal strife—as was the case again in November 1984 following the assassination of Indira Gandhi by Sikh separatist radicals.

In the four South American federations (Brazil, Argentina, Venezuela, and Mexico), most of the component units followed rather than preceded those nations' federal institutions. The Mexican Constitution of 1917 permits the transformation of federal territories into states when (Article 73, sections 2 and 3) they have a population of 80,000 inhabitants and the "resources" necessary to provide for their political existence. When a state is to be carved out of an existing one, it must have a population of at least 120,000 inhabitants and must prove before the national legislature that it has the necessary resources to provide for their political existence. A subsequent ratification by the states is also necessary. A simple majority is required if the consent of the legislature of the state involved has been secured; ratification by a two-thirds majority of the states is required when the state involved refuses to give its consent.

In West Germany, only Bavaria and the two city-states of Hamburg and Bremen coincide with previously existing *Länder* (Figure 5.9). Other *Länder*

Figure 5.8. Federal India (the initial postliberation map)

Source: Ivo D. Duchacek, *Comparative Federalism: The Territorial Dimension of Politics* (New York: Holt, Rinehart and Winston, 1970).

5.9. Federal Republic of Germany (map)

(Courtesy of the Advisory Commission on Intergovernmental Relations)

represent aggregates of former provinces, and two, Rhineland-Palatinate and Baden-Württemberg, are entirely new. The *Länder* were carved out of German territory with a marked disregard for traditional internal boundaries. Thus, with the exception of Bavaria and the two city-states, the *Länder* at first commanded little genuine attachment, but "the cake of custom by now has endowed the ten *Länder* structure with some kind of general recognition."[27]

Yardstick 6: Residual and Significant Powers

The Tenth Amendment to the U.S. Constitution states, "The powers not delegated to the United States by the Constitution, nor prohibited by it to the States, are reserved to the States respectively, or to the people." Federal Australia follows a similar principle.

Some U.S. citizens too readily assume that this principle should apply if federalism is to be prevented from slipping into centralism. Yet, in the majority of federal systems today, we find opposite constitutional provisions: Powers given to the provinces are enumerated; the rest of the power is reserved by the central authority. This situation exists, for instance, in Canada, whose basic initial federal constitutional act (the British North American Act of 1867) was prepared in the period following the U.S. Civil War. It was then generally believed that the residual powers of the U.S. states were one of the main reasons for political confusion and civil war. The federal constitution of India contains long and detailed lists of powers reserved for the central authority (Union List), powers reserved for the component units (State List), and powers exercised by both elements (Concurrent List)—the last usually with the provision that if the central authority chooses to exercise some of the concurrent powers, it thus preempts the state's powers.

More important than the location of residual powers in one or the other level of government is the requirement that in a true federation "there must be some matter, if only one matter, which comes under the exclusive control, actual or potential, of the general government and something likewise under the regional government. If there were not, that would be the end of federalism."[28]

Here one question must be posed: Does it matter what kind of power is left to the exclusive domain of one or the other level of government? Territorial distribution of authority in a federal system has never been intended to be on a fifty-fifty basis; a federal system, by definition, favors the national power by placing in its hands defense, war, and taxing powers. But if through a constitutional division of power the federal center were to retain 99 percent of the power, leaving the territorial components with 1 percent, would it still be correct to speak of a federal system? "The matters entrusted to the constituent units (whether their powers are residual or delegated) must be substantial, and not merely trivial" is the answer of one prominent student of federalism, Arthur W. Macmahon.[29] If, on the other hand, the central authority were left with only some symbolic or ceremonial powers, it would not be a nation-state at all, only an alliance or a loose league. Evidently, the old problem of quantitative measurement of political power appears here again. Is it indeed possible to quantify power so as to speak in terms of 99 percent and 1 percent? Furthermore, because power is only a means to an end, there arises the problem of also measuring the value of the various ends that one or the other level of government may desire to attain. What seems provincially or locally vital may be viewed nationally as marginal, and vice versa.

Yardstick 7: Bicameralism and Equal Representation of Unequal Units

The Connecticut Compromise is often viewed by U.S. citizens as an essential yardstick of federalism as, on July 5, 1787, the founding fathers agreed to a proportional representation of unequal states in the lower house of the Congress and an equal representation of unequal states (two senators per state) in the upper house (the Senate, a federal chamber to replace the British concept of a hereditary, aristocratic one). The U.S. bicameralism is a true and full one because both houses are equal in matters of legislation: No law can be enacted unless both houses agree on the same text. This situation contrasts with many other bicameral systems in which the upper house enjoys only a limited or suspensive veto over legislation.

Furthermore, unlike the parliamentary system, the lower house in the United States does not create the national executive branch (the cabinet), and the executive branch is not directly responsible to the lower house. The Senate's advice and consent to executive appointments and treaties make that body, with its 100 senators, a powerful one and a partner of the national executive; this arrangement contrasts with parliamentary systems, in which this role is exercised by the lower house. We should note, of course, that the former awesome powers and prestige of the U.S. Senate are no longer what they used to be. A series of four articles published by the *New York Times* (between November 25 and 29, 1984), entitled "Senate Deplores Disarray in New Chamber of Equals," opened its lengthy analysis with the following words:

> The United States Senate was created as a legislative aristocracy whose members six-year terms would insulate them from passing political passions. In the view of many senators, however, it has degenerated into a raucous town meeting, focusing on narrow issues of the moment rather than the broad policy decisions envisioned by the founding fathers.

We are witnessing the disintegration of the U.S. Senate," said Senator Dan Quayle, Republican of Indiana. "Something very elusive has gotten away from us," added Senator John C. Stennis, a Mississippi Democrat, then the dean of the Senate. And the majority leader from 1980 to 1984, Senator

Howard Baker, Jr., a Tennessee Republican added, "The biggest problem is a diminution of the value of the Senate as the nation's first and premiere public forum."

Curiously, neither the senators nor the *New York Times*, while deploring the decline of the Senate, cared to mention the initial and now also diminished role of the Senate as a *federal* chamber based on an equal representation of unequal components. The intrafederal bargaining has, in part, shifted to the House and other forums and institutions.

Originally, the Senate could have been viewed as a guarantee of and a channel for the decisive influence of the states on the shape and direction of national policy. Because the practice of instructing senators disappeared more than a century ago and because their election has passed from the hands of the state legislatures into the hands of the people, it is debatable whether a senator today still represents primarily his or her own state interests, multistate regional interests (the South, the Midwest, the West, or the East), functional divisions (agriculture, cities), or his or her party. A similar observation can be made about the Australian Senate, created to safeguard and represent state interests, which has now "become a body in which divisions are along strict party lines."[30]

The principle of equal representation of unequal component units has been adopted by many federations. Australia's six unequal states are represented equally in the Senate; in Switzerland, too, forty-six councillors represent the twenty-three cantons (actually, twenty-six units because three cantons have been subdivided into half-cantons, each of which is represented by one councillor). The principle of equal representation is also present in all Latin-American constitutions as well as in the communist federations. In federal Czechoslovakia now, the highest legislative organ is the Federal Assembly composed of the House of the People and the House of the Nations. The House of the People is composed of 200 deputies whereas the House of the Nations is composed of 150 members, half of whom are elected in Bohemia-Moravia and the other half in Slovakia. In the Soviet Union, each union republic is represented by twenty-five deputies in the Soviet of Nationalities, the federal chamber of the Supreme Soviet, the highest legislative organ (the other house is called the Soviet of the Union).

Furthermore, the Soviet Constitution provides that each of the fifteen union republics be represented by one deputy in the Presidium of the Supreme Soviet, the parliament in miniature that fulfills a dual role: to act as a permanent standing committee on behalf of the national legislature when that is not in session and to act as a collegial president, a ceremonial head of the Soviet Union. The Presidium is composed of one chairman, one secretary, fifteen members elected by the Soviet of the Union, and fifteen vice-chairmen representing the constituent units of the Soviet Union.

Soviet federalism is multilayered. Its largest unit, the Russian Republic, for instance, is itself a federation. In addition, in the territories of some of the union republics, federal or not, there are autonomous republics, autonomous regions, and national districts with the right to direct representation in the central legislature. Unequal autonomous republics are equally represented by eleven deputies each, autonomous regions by five deputies each, and national districts by one deputy each. The degree of direct representation in the national legislature is related to the degree of autonomy granted by the constitution.

This seventh criterion of a federal structure calls, like all the other yardsticks, for several qualifications:

1. Some systems that claim to be federal have not adopted the principle of equal representation of unequal units but a compromise between size and equality. In India, for instance, the less populous states are favored, but not to the point of equality with the populous ones. The allocation of seats in the Indian federal chamber, the Council of States, was determined by the Fourth Schedule, which assigned a maximum of thirty-four seats to the most populous state, Uttar Pradesh, but only one to Nagaland; the federal capital of New Delhi is represented by three, and other federal territories by two or one.

In Canada, the principle of equal representation of unequal units has been applied with ingenious modifications that reflect the very uneven population density of the country's vast territory. In 1867, the then nine provinces were arranged into four groupings, each of which was entitled to twenty-four senators; within the third and fourth groupings which are composed of several provinces, the provincial representation is roughly proportionate to the population.[31] Newfoundland, which voted to join Canada in 1949, is in a separate category with six senators. In 1975, Northwest and Yukon federal territories were assigned one senator each. All 104 Canadian senators are appointed to serve until the age of 75 by the governor general in the name of the sovereign, that is, by the Canadian Cabinet, and have only advisory power—politically speaking, they are powerless. The Canadians themselves sometimes refer to their Senate as a "wax museum" or an "asylum for dodos."

Following the patriation of the Canadian Constitution in 1982, the role of the Senate in the Canadian federation became once more a matter of controversy and debate. The first question evidently was whether its role should be further enlarged to make it a truly federal chamber receptive to provincial inputs into the rule-making processes or whether it should be further curbed in accordance with the Westminster concept of the lower house as a fountain of political and legislative near-omnipotence. In 1985, Prime Minister Brian Mulroney (as reported by the *Globe and Mail* on May 10, 1985) suggested that the Senate's power to delay money bills from the House of Commons be limited to thirty days and other legislation to forty-five days. All Senate amendments to bills from the lower house would simply die after fifteen days unless acted upon by the House of Commons. The proposal clearly reflected the then new prime minister's impatience with the Senate's delay in approving government spending in winter of 1984-1985.

A more substantial reform of the Canadian Senate, postponed to 1988, naturally links its political role with the method of its members' selection.

Possible methods are appointment (by provincial legislatures or by federal and/or state cabinets), provincial elections (as in Australia), or a combination of the various modes mentioned.

It should be admitted that all cabinet systems, in which the power of the lower house to make and unmake cabinets is based on strict party discipline, find it inherently difficult to find an appropriate role for a second chamber. At best, the second chamber is made into a house of second thought, provided the senators do not think about and debate public policy too long. When in the unitary system of France, during the Third Republic, the senate had power equal to the Chamber of Deputies to unseat cabinets, the effect was clearly destabilizing. Yet in a federal system, the second chamber is usually not needed as a cabinet maker but as an echo chamber for regional interests; a federal upper chamber is expected to reflect, not the will of the majority of the moment, but the territorially delineated interests of provincial, state, or cantonal majorities.

In federal Canada, a possible reform of the presently nearly powerless Senate is closely connected with interprovincial harmony, or the lack of it. A Canadian analyst, Roger Gibbins from Alberta, suggested that Canada would venture on the "slippery slop of a true Senate reform" only when it finds itself on "the verge of regional dismemberment."[32] According to Gibbins an interregional crisis may come following the Conservative victory in 1984 and the subsequent realization on the part of the provinces that a change of the governing party, from Trudeau's Liberals to Mulroney's Conservatives, did not and could not provide a sufficient response to regional conflicts and alienation. In his analysis, Gibbins referred to the alienation of the western provinces, not Québec.

2. Is bicameralism, normally associated with federalism, really needed in federations consisting of only two territorial communities? Equal representation of unequal components as a protection against tyranny by a numerical majority might be implemented in one single legislative body. Such was the case in once-federal bicommunal Pakistan whose western and eastern provinces each elected seventy-five representatives to a unicameral National Assembly in 1971. However, East Pakistan seceded and with the help of India, which separated East and West Pakistan by 1,000 miles, became Bangladesh.

The question must be raised whether federalism is at all an appropriate formula to manage problems arising from the coexistence and confrontation of only two ethnoterritorial communities facing each other in a potentially explosive situation, such as is found in Northern Ireland, Cyprus, the West Bank, Sri Lanka, Surinam, Malaysia, Guyana, Fiji, and, with some qualification, Belgium.

In communist Czechoslovakia, for example, is it really the federal constitution of 1968 and the federal institutions and structures based on it that hold the bicommunal federal state of Czechoslovakia together in relative biethnic harmony? Or is it the basic cultural and linguistic (Slavic) affinity that is primarily responsible for the absence of interethnic tension? Or is

Figure 5.10. Czechoslovakia

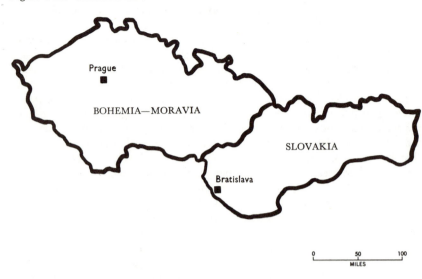

it simply the monolithic single-party system and the presence of a Soviet occupation army that prevent any separatist tendencies from surfacing?

3. The third qualification of the federal yardstick under discussion is the nature of bicameralism itself in a given system. By *bicameralism* I mean coequality not only of the legislative but also of the political powers of the two chambers of the central legislature. Yet many federal systems that have adopted the British (Westminster) cabinet system of government make the prime minister and the cabinet responsible to the lower house only. In the Commonwealth federations of Canada, Australia, and India, only the popularly elected *nonfederal* lower house makes and unmakes cabinets.

Furthermore, in a cabinet system, it is usually the lower house that has the last word in legislative matters because the refusal of the upper house to go along may be overridden after a prescribed period of time. In India, for instance, a money bill can be delayed by the federal chamber for only two weeks, and it is the Speaker of the House who may determine which bill is a money bill. At best, the federal upper houses in British-inspired federal systems have a suspensive veto.

In West Germany, where the component units are represented by three to five delegates each, the federal upper house (the Bundesrat) has only a suspensive veto on many subjects of legislation except in any in matter affecting the federal distribution of power, in which case its veto power is absolute and annuls the measure. In theory, it was assumed that the number of bills potentially subject to the absolute veto would be small. In practice, this has not been the case, partly because of the Bundesrat's insistence that it can veto a whole bill when a portion of it is subject to absolute veto. The lower house (the Bundestag), however, performs the decisive political role of a national cabinet maker.

4. Finally, a fourth dimension of bicameralism should be mentioned: the problem of a possibly desirable "federalization of the national executive," which today has so much power. The initial concentration of the federal founding fathers on bicameralism was in accordance with the then-accepted concept of the primary importance of parliaments as rule makers; they were to be the central fountain of all decisions to be implemented by the executive branch and interpreted by the judiciary. In fact, however, the legislative rule-making monopoly has been replaced now almost everywhere by the rule-making activities of both the executive and the judicial branches of the government. In the modern era, some of the most important rules have been made either by executive order or by the judicial creative interpretation of the existing laws and the constitution. The question should then be asked whether and how the principle of equal representation of unequal component units can be reflected in the executive branch and in the judicial branch. In both Canada and the United States, attempts have been made to add a federal dimension to the executive level: The Canadian now-regular federal/provincial conferences of the eleven premiers and the U.S. meetings and research staff of the National Governors' Association represent extra-constitutional attempts to ensure regular provincial/state inputs into the national/federal decision-making processes.

In conclusion, it is necessary to point to the inevitable difficulty of attempting to have a federal structure faithfully mirrored at the top of the political pyramid where the decision-making body tends to be less numerous than the number of groups it desires to represent. In federations that are composed of a small number of units, the cabinet may succeed in reflecting the component units on a roughly proportional basis. In Australia, all of the six states are usually represented in the national cabinet (Figure 5.11), and in Canada, every province usually has at least one cabinet member with several ministerial posts often being so assigned as to be representative of territorial economic interests (agriculture to the prairie states, fisheries to the Maritime Provinces). The result is a guarantee of federal represen-tativeness, not necessarily of competence.[33] In Switzerland, the seven-member Swiss cabinet (Federal Council) is composed of five Germans (two of whom come from Bern and Zurich), two Frenchmen (one from the largest French canton of Vaud), and one Italian (from Ticino). But how can a cabinet faithfully reflect the component units in federations composed of thirty-one (Mexico) or fifty states?

When we consider the executive in terms of real concentration of power, even a federation composed of two units (Czechoslovakia), six units (Australia and Yugoslavia), nine units (Austria), or eleven units (Germany's ten *Länder* and West Berlin) has a serious problem because what finally matters is the power held in the hands of one person, whether a president, a prime minister, or a party chairman. How can one "federalize" the body and brain of a single person? What is left is an extraconstitutional hope that the

Figure 5.11. Australia

(Courtesy of the Advisory Commission on Intergovernmental Relations)

chief executive will have a federally segmented brain or a "federal soul," and be capable of tolerance and justice toward all the component units and generally immune against any particular subnational pull, be it his or her birthplace (South, East, or West in the United States), religion (Muslim or Sikh in India), language (Québécois in Canada), color of skin (Chinese in brown-race Malaysia), or ethnic origin (a Ukrainian in the Soviet Union, a Croatian in Yugoslavia, or a Slovak in Czechoslovakia).

The composition of other federal institutions poses problems similar to those of a national legislature and a chief executive because bureaucrats, managers, and judges not only interpret or adjudicate federal rules but also partly create them. Should, for instance, the principle of equal representation of unequal units be applied to the civil service, managers of the national economy, and federal judgeships, or would that mean a change from a federal system to a confederal one?

Yardstick 8: Amending
the Federal Constitution

If the U.S. model of federalism were viewed as the only pure one, the eighth yardstick could be expressed as a protection of the component units against a constitutional amendment (affecting the original consociational compact) by something less than veto but much more than a majority in the national legislature. According to many experts, this is by far the most reliable yardstick of federalism when the *text* of a constitution is analyzed. If the ultimate control over constitutional changes is in the hands of *all* the component units, such a system, based on unanimity, seems not to have moved from a confederal association of states to a new federal nation. A new supraterritorial identity, institutions, and power have not really been created if for any amendment the consent of every single component unit is required.

If, on the other hand, only a vote of the central parliament is required (without a subsequent plebiscite or referendum), such a system, based on a national majoritarian principle, makes the amendatory process indistinguishable from that in a unitary system. Such is the case, for instance, in the Soviet Union when a two-thirds majority in both houses of the central parliament is sufficient to adopt any type of amendment, including one that would transform the Soviet federation into a unitary state and eliminate all fifteen union republics completely.

Some federal constitutions distinguish between amendments that affect the federal distribution of power and those that do not; only in the first case is ratification by the component units required. The problem with such a differentiation between federal and nonfederal amendments is that a constitutional change that does not seem to affect the federal division of powers may ultimately, in conjunction with environmental changes, do so in the future. By contrast, in the United States all amendments even those that do not affect the federal distribution of power, require ratification by three-fourths of the states, and one type of amendment cannot be passed and ratified by even forty-nine states out of the fifty: The last sentence of Article 5 states that "no State, without its consent, shall be deprived of its equal suffrage in the Senate." This is considered the basic point of the whole federal bargain expressed in the Connecticut Compromise at Philadelphia in 1787.

In Canada, following the patriation of the constitution in 1982, amendments must have the assent of Parliament and two-thirds of the provinces containing at least 50 percent of Canada's population. This arrangement gives the two populous provinces, Québec and Ontario, quite a bit of clout in regard to amendments. Furthermore, a dissenting province may refuse to apply a new amendment to its territory (the Canadian term is to "opt out") if the amendment (Article 38.2) "derogates from the legislative [provincial] powers, the proprietary rights or any other rights or privileges of the legislature or government"—in European terminology, used in Canada, "government" means the executive. And if an amendment transfers powers relating to education or other cultural matters to Ottawa (an important issue in francophone Québec), any province will receive "reasonable compensation" from the central government so as to be able to continue the exercise of those provincial powers.

In view of the size and population of francophone Québec, the last provision amounts to a practical veto, yet in 1985, both the ruling and the opposition parties in Québec included the constitutional veto as one of the basic conditions for Québec's accession to the Constitutional Act of 1981. The Liberal party working document (published by *Le Devoir* on February 6, 1985) as well as the Québec party platform of May 27 presented the right to veto as another part of the constitutional recognition of the Québec community as one of the two founding polities. In terms of the terminology as used in this book, granting a broad veto power to Québec Province would transform the Canadian federation into a dyadic (bicephalic) confederation.

Yardstick 9: Two Sets of Courts

Two sets of courts—federal and nonfederal—may seem a minor criterion, but some authors find it important. Commenting on the nationally controlled judicial system in Venezuela, for example, one author wrote, "In 1945 the states surrendered their last major power when they ratified a constitutional amendment which conferred upon the national government exclusive control of the judicial system."[34] Herman Finer listed the absence of a dual, that is national and provincial, judicial system as one of his six criteria that do not qualify the Soviet Union as a federation.[35]

Actually, only a few federations—the United States and, with modifications, Mexico and Brazil—have developed two parallel networks of courts: federal courts to adjudicate national laws and provincial courts to adjudicate local laws. The United States, for instance, has established a complete judicial hierarchy on both the federal and the state levels. In the federal court structure, there are, in ascending order, district courts, circuit courts of appeal, and, at the top of the federal judicial pyramid, the Supreme Court. In each state, another judicial pyramid of state courts culminates with the state's highest court of appeal. The two systems, however, are not federally fully separate; not only is the federal Supreme Court the highest court of appeal from both networks, but the two systems actually interlock by a degree of *concurrent* jurisdiction (jurisdiction that is shared by both the federal and the state courts). Only some matters are reserved for the exclusive jurisdiction of the federal courts, such as crimes and offenses against the United States; prize, patent, copyright, and some bankruptcy cases; civil cases of admiralty and maritime jurisdiction; cases to which a state is a party; and cases involving foreign ambassadors.

In all the other federal systems, we find different variants of a single integrated court system, usually provincial or state courts topped by a federal highest court of appeal. For special cases, a federal court is sometimes added to the system. In Switzerland, the "organization of the judiciary, legal procedures and administration of justice remain in the cantons" (Article 64A); the cantonal courts adjudicate both federal and cantonal laws. A Federal Tribunal stands above the whole system as a court of appeal over the cantonal courts and as a court of original jurisdiction in some federal matters. West Germany, too, has a single integrated system of state courts with a Federal Supreme Court at the top. The state courts and their procedures are, however, regulated and made uniform by federal codes.

The Indian Constitution (Article 247) authorizes Parliament to establish "any additional courts for the better administration of federal laws," but it has chosen not to do so. There are only state courts supervised by India's federal Supreme Court. A similar situation has developed in Australia, as that country's constitution (Article 73) provides that the federal supreme court (the High Court of Australia) shall "hear appeals . . . from all judgments of any other federal court . . . or any other court of any State"; yet the Australian Parliament has so far not established a complete federal judicial hierarchy but has mostly employed the state courts for federal purposes.[36] In Canada, the provinces have established their own judicial systems, which regulate procedure in civil matters. The central government, however, appoints and pays all the judges, regulates the procedure in criminal matters, and has conferred upon provincial courts jurisdiction in most matters of national law. The whole system, again, is topped by a supreme court, which has an appellate jurisdiction in civil and criminal matters from the provincial courts.

If a fully developed, parallel federal and state court system were a decisive yardstick of federalism, only the United States (and, with some qualification, Mexico and Brazil) could pass the test.

Yardstick 10: Judicial Arbiter of Federalism

In all systems, federal as well as unitary, there is a need for an impartial agency that can ascertain the meaning of the nation's supreme law, the constitution, and that, in light of its findings, can determine the compatibility of any given law or official act, national or local, with the constitution. This need may lead and has led to a broad conception of judicial review, the right of the courts to annul or confirm the validity of laws passed by national or local legislatures.

Because the U.S. practice of judicial review, as exercised by the Supreme Court, has been characterized in modern times by the Court's support of civil rights and liberties, many unitary and federal constitutions, in one form or another, have now imitated that theory and practice to some extent. There have been brave attempts to transplant the U.S. institution of judicial review from its native soil to areas that are somewhat less hospitable to the power of the judges to decide issues that often are political and social in nature, although presented in legalistic garb. As yet, in no country is there a real counterpart to the awesome power of the U.S. Supreme Court. Especially in Europe, there is some doubt about placing the wisdom or folly of a few judges above the people and their elected representatives when it comes to the interpretation of the nation's fundamental law, which expresses the political and social compact of the founders.

In a federal system, there seems to be an acute need for an impartial agency, because the interpretation of the meaning of the constitution includes also the delicate original political agreement between territorial communities from which the whole federal system issued. In its role of protector and interpreter of the federal compact and arbitrator of possible disputes about the division of power between two jurisdictional spheres, such an agency should be, ideally, independent of both the federal and the provincial governments and should stand sublimely above both.

Only Switzerland seems to be near the ideal. Not judges, but only the sovereign people of Switzerland can question the validity of federal laws (the courts may question the validity of cantonal laws): Either 30,000 voters or eight cantons can challenge any law passed by the federal legislature and so either confirm its constitutional validity or annul it. A simple majority of the voters decides the issue in a legislative referendum; a majority on the part of cantons is not required. This arrangement is in contrast with a formal amendment of the Swiss Constitution, which requires, in addition to the majority of voters in a constitutional referendum, approval by the majority of voters in the majority of cantons.

Until 1949, Canada had another impartial constitutional agency, independent of both the national and the provincial governments, the Judiciary Committee of the Privy Council (composed mostly of the law lords of the British House of Lords) located in London. For Canada this committee has been replaced by Canada's Supreme Court, which is now the only final court of appeal in the federation, and since the adoption of the new Canadian Constitution of 1982 and its novel Charter of Rights and Freedoms, Canada's Supreme Court may well be on its way to acquiring step-by-step and appeal-to-appeal, the "quasi-legislative" power of its U.S. counterpart. As noted by a Canadian expert on constitutional law, Edward McWhinney:

> It is likely that the Supreme Court of Canada . . . will play a major role in implementing the new Charter of Rights and translating its abstract norms into concrete reality . . . the sheer volume of case law from the new civil rights jurisdiction is likely to produce a quantitative, and ultimately a qualitative, change in the Court's work and function.[37]

In all other federal systems except the Soviet Union, but including communist Yugoslavia, a judicial agency has the role of interpreting the original federal consensus and, therefore, is the arbitrator in potential jurisdictional disputes between the federal and provincial governments. In most cases, this function is given to the highest federal court of appeal; in West Germany, however, a special constitutional court has been established. In contrast to most German courts, its members are elected by the parliament; half are elected by the federal chamber, the Bundesrat, and half by a special committee of electors that reflect the proportional strength of political parties in the popularly elected chamber, the Bundestag.[38]

Such a judicial agency, whether it is the highest court of appeal or a special constitutional court as in West Germany, is not, and clearly cannot be viewed as, independent of one or the other party involved in a potential jurisdictional dispute; these agencies are, as a rule, created and can be dismissed (by impeachment) by the national government with the concurrence of the national legislature. "The result has been," as noted by K. C. Wheare, "that Supreme Courts or their equivalent have been accused from time to time of undue partiality to the general government"[39]—their creator.

It is possible that the national (federal) selection of the judiciary for the role of supreme arbitrator may not be ideal. But what is the alternative?—except perhaps the legislative and constitutional referenda that Switzerland has had. The judiciary may indeed be assumed to be more impartial than any other institution. One should not, for instance, too readily assume that a supreme court created by a national government will necessarily prove partial to that government. In Canada, the judicial interpretation of the federal constitution has finally resulted in curbing rather than extending the powers of the national government in relation to the provinces. Before the contrary happened in the United States, the difficulties that President Franklin D. Roosevelt experienced with the Supreme Court during the period of the New Deal amply demonstrated that judges, although appointed federally, may prove quite partial to states' rights because of their political and social philosophy. In conclusion, let me add that even the highest court of all is composed only of individuals—and individuals, including the Supreme Court justices, have their political and social preferences.

Controversial Results of Testing

Any yardsticks chosen to test federalism are necessarily of unequal weight and, therefore, of different relevance. The national center's independence of the component territorial communities in rule making seems more important than a constitutional guarantee of two separate, federal and provincial, sets of courts; dependence on the component units for amending the constitutional division of powers seems more essential than equal representation of unequal units in the federal chamber (or the other way around?); and a neat and precise division of authority appears more fundamental than such questions as where the residual powers are kept.

Even if we assign a very approximate greater or lesser weight to the ten yardsticks (as we have done by listing them in order of importance), we still cannot convincingly demonstrate that the absence of a very important criterion can be compensated for by five or six less-important criteria. Taking the example of West German federalism, which is, in the final analysis, more important: (1) the federal supervision of local administration and adjudication of federal laws, federal regulation of the selection and training of civil servants and judges, federal prescription of uniform administrative and judicial procedure throughout all the *Länder*, and the federal powers concerning defense, foreign policy, mail, and the railroads or (2) the dependence of the federal upper chamber (Bundesrat) on the component units that determine both its members/delegates and their votes, the local administration and adjudication of federal rules, and even the local collection of taxes?[40]

Having now, after a lapse of many years, reapplied my ten yardsticks of federalism, I should be close to an acceptable answer to the question what constitutes pure federalism—*but I am not.* Yet I feel justified in flexing again my definitional muscles, as it were, because the exercise has at least demonstrated that, over time, the federal theme in different national environments has diversified even more and so we are cautioned even more emphatically against a possible ethnocentric tendency to equate the U.S. experience with "true federalism."

The tests, I believe, also demonstrate that many federal constitutions and their new amendments deliberately, and sometimes unwittingly, tend to transmute the definitional boundaries among unitary, federal, and confederal systems into a mesh that permits mutual interpenetration. Hybrid rather than purebred systems are the result. There are unitary constitutions that emphasize that—God forbid!—they are not federal, and yet they guarantee the identity, future, rights, and territorial self-rule of various communities. On the other hand, all federal constitutions authorize some degree of central interference in the domestic affairs of the component units by various implicit or explicit grants of emergency or potential powers. These range from the "elastic clause" and the federal right to preserve a republican or democratic form of government in each state to the implied tendency toward centralization that may result from the federal monopoly to make war, engage in international economic politics, and promote the general welfare.

Many modern federal systems have also deliberately bridged the "great divide" by authorizing or encouraging mutual dependence and reciprocal delegation of fiscal and administrative authority between the national and subnational governments. To describe this phenomenon the term "unitary federalism" was used by one German author,[41] one of the truly explosive metaphors among the 326 previously mentioned. This study tends to use the image of intrafederal *osmosis* also to describe fiscal and political centralization interlaced by administrative decentralization—bearing in mind the old dictum that "administration is often half the policy." The main issue, of course, is still whether a system of territorial and political pluralism works, not whether it fits most or all of the yardsticks of federalism, and so qualifies as *foederalismus purissimus.*

The controversial results of the preceding testing are therefore presented here with a great deal of humility—which, by itself, is a controversial statement since, as we all know, a proclamation of humility may be a sign of a lack of it. As the apocryphal story about the competitive argument between four religious orders appropriately tells us: "We're clearly the best when it comes to teaching," said the Jesuit. "When it comes to preaching, we surely are the best," argued the Dominican. "As to good works, since Assisi we have always been the best," said the Franciscan. "Brothers, when it comes to humility, we beat you all," said a Trappist—and with him, many a student of comparative federalism.

Notes

1. The segment dealing with the ten yardsticks of federalism contains several updated portions of Chapters 7 and 8, of Ivo D. Duchacek, *Comparative Federalism: The Territorial Dimension of Politics* (New York: Holt, Rinehart and Winston, 1970) pp. 188–310.

2. Valerie Earle, ed., *Federalism: Infinite Variety in Theory and Practice* (Itasca, Ill.: F. E. Peacock, 1968), p. 212.

3. Henry Teune, "The Future of Federalism: Federalism and Political Integration," in Earle, *Federalism*, p. 228.

4. Quoted by Marcel Merle, *Sociologie des relations internationales*, 3d ed. (Paris: Dalloz, 1982), p. 311 (author's translation).

5. J. V. Stalin, *Works*, vol. 5. (Moscow: Government Publishers, 1955), pp. 341–344.

6. The Soviet Constitution enumerates the fifteen major nationalities that constitute the component units of the Soviet federal union in the order of their numerical importance: the Russian Soviet Federated Socialist Republic (the RSFSR, extending from Leningrad and the Baltic Sea to Vladivostok and Alaska, is itself federated; the Russians constitute 50 percent of the total Soviet population), Ukraine, Byelorussia, Uzbek, Kazakh, Georgia, Azerbaijan, Lithuania, Moldavia, Latvia, Kirghiz, Armenia, Turkmenistan, and Estonia. In addition, within the boundaries of these union republics there are autonomous republics (ASSRs), autonomous regions (ARs) and national districts (NRs).

7. Vernon A. Aspaturian, "The Union Republics and Soviet Diplomacy: Concepts, Institutions, and Practices," *American Political Science Review* vol. 53:2 (June 1959), p. 404. See also Aspaturian's fully documented and thoroughly researched book *The Union Republics and Soviet Diplomacy* (Geneva: Librairie Droz, 1960).

8. *Politika* (Belgrade), October 19, 1966, reporting on a speech by the Muslim leader of the Communist party of Bosnia, Refik Hulic.

9. *Borba* (Belgrade), January 28, 1968: "Of course, these new institutions (Commissions for Foreign Affairs) are in no way republican foreign ministries. However, there is no doubt that there is an increasing feeling that we need a more decisive course aimed at overcoming old practices in the pursuit of foreign policy, which thus far has been the exclusive prerogative of the central state organs [in Serbia]."

10. K. C. Wheare, *Federal Government* (New York: Oxford University Press, 1964), p. 10.

11. Article 273 of the Indian Constitution also states, "There shall be charged on the Consolidated Fund of India in each year as grants-in-aid of the revenues of the States of Assam, Bihar, Orissa, and West Bengal, in lieu of assignment of any share of the net proceeds in each year of export duty on jute and jute products to those States, such sums as may be prescribed."

12. Article 269 enumerates seven such categories of taxes, including taxes on railway fares and freight, the sale or purchase of newspapers and the advertisements therein.

13. See Part II (p. 211-475) of Edmond Orban, *La dynamique de la centralisation, dans l'Etat fédéral: un processus irréversible?* (Montréal: Québec/Amérique). In his study, Orban identified three causes of centralization in federal systems: the role of the state as a welfare agency (*etat-providence*), technological innovation, and complex

interdependence. He saw, however, that such centralization is softened by a concomitant decentralization in administering central social, economic, and fiscal programs.

14. Peter H. Merkl, *Political Continuity and Change* (New York: Harper and Row, 1967), p. 402. The author concludes that in the German type of federalism, the Bundesrat "allows the Länder governments a degree of direct participation in all aspects of national politics which no American state or Canadian province can boast."

15. Article 80 speaks of election by the *elected* members because in India, a small number of the members of the upper houses, on both the union and the state level, are not elected but are appointed by the president or the state governor, respectively.

16. Article 360 of the Indian Constitution permits such a superseding of state authority by the central authority when "the President is satisfied that a situation has arisen whereby the financial stability or credit of India or of any part of the territory thereof is threatened."

17. S.A.H. Haqqi, "Federalism, Single Dominant Party, and the Problem of Linguistic Autonomy in India" (Paper presented at the Sixth World Congress of the International Political Science Association, Geneva, September 21-25, 1964), pp. 2-3.

18. Harry Lazer, *The American Political System in Transition* (New York: Crowell, 1967), p. 79.

19. Articles 24A, 31A, 31C, and 31D, respectively.

20. Karl H. Cerny, "Federalism in the West German Republic," in Earle, *Federalism*, p. 145.

21. Arnold Brecht, *Federalism and Regionalism in Germany: The Division of Prussia* (New York: Oxford, 1945), chap. 6.

22. *Pravda* (Moscow), October 20, 1920.

23. The ethnic composition of Burma is Burmese, 75 percent; Indians (nonterritorial), 9 percent; Karens, Chins, Shans, and Kachins (territorial ethnic groups), 7 percent; Chinese (nonterritorial), 5 percent; others (including Europeans), 4 percent.

24. The constitution provided for a bicameral national legislature. In its upper house, called the Chamber of Nationalities, the non-Burmese were to have a majority (seventy-two to fifty-three) composed as follows: Karens, twenty-five representatives; Shans, twenty-four; Kachins, twelve; Chin division, eight; and Karenni states, three.

25. The U.S. Constitution states in Article 4, section 3, that "new States may be admitted by the Congress into this Union; but no new State shall be formed or erected within the jurisdiction of any other State; nor any State be formed by the junction of two or more States, or parts of States, without the consent of the legislatures of the States concerned as well as the Congress."

26. Until 1947, the British administered some provinces on the Indian subcontinent directly while other territories, about 500 princely states, were administered indirectly.

27. John H. Herz, "The Government of Germany," in G. M. Carter and J. H. Herz, *Major Foreign Powers* (New York: Harcourt Brace Jovanovich, 1967), pp. 441-442.

28. Wheare, *Federal Government*, p. 75.

29. Arthur W. Macmahon, *Federalism: Mature and Emergent* (New York: Russell and Russell, 1962), p. 4.

30. Louise Overacker, *The Australian Party System* (New Haven: Yale University Press, 1952), p. 328.

31. The Canadian constitution act of 1867 (the British North America Act as amended in 1915 and modified in 1949) contains the following provisions: Article

21, "The Senate shall . . . consist of One Hundred and Two Members, who shall be styled Senators"; Article 22 (the numbers in brackets indicate the number of senators assigned), "In relation to the Constitution of the Senate Canada shall be deemed to consist of Four Divisions: 1. Ontario [24]; 2. Quebec [24]; 3. The Maritime Provinces (Nova Scotia [10], New Brunswick [10], and Prince Edward Island [4]); 4. The Western Provinces of Manitoba [6], British Columbia [6], Saskatchewan [6], and Alberta [6]."

32. Roger Gibbins, *Senate Reform: Moving Towards the Slippery Slope* (Kingston, Ont: Institute of Intergovernmental Relations, 1983), pp. 45–47.

33. Alexander Brady, *Democracy in the Dominions* (Toronto: University of Toronto Press, 1958) p. 83. Compare also William S. Livingston, "Canada, Australia and the United States: Variations on a Theme," in Earle, *Federalism*, 112.

34. M. C. Needler ed., *Political Systems of Latin America* (Princeton, N.J.: Van Nostrand, 1964), p. 255.

35. Herman Finer, *Theory and Practice of Modern Government* (New York: Holt, Rinehart and Winston, 1949), p. 820.

36. Geoffrey Sawer, "Judicial Power Under the Constitution," in M. Else-Mitchel ed., *Essays on the Australian Constitution* (Sydney: Law Book Company, 1961), p. 71.

37. Edward McWhinney, *Canada and the Constitution 1979-1982: Patriation and the Charter of Rights* (Toronto: University of Toronto Press, 1982), p. 17.

38. Herz, "Government of Germany," pp. 449–450.

39. Wheare, *Federal Government*, p. 59.

40. Peter H. Merkl, *Political Continuity and Change* p. 736, calls the role of the Bundesrat pivotal and traces its peculiar character back to the confederal congress which consisted of the instructed representatives of the princes. See also p. 401 in the same work.

41. Gunter Kisker, *Kooperation im Bundestaat: Eine Untersuchung zum Kooperativen Föderalismus in der Bundesrepublik Deutschland* (Tübingen: Mohr, 1971).

Part 3
Confederal Associations

6

The American Confederal Experience and the World Today

The English colonies [in America] were as badly divided as Christian and Turk.
—Benjamin Fletcher,
British governor of New York (1693)

Early settlers in America discovered the advantages of cooperation for mutual succor and defense. But they also learned that unification of settlements over a broad area required a sustained common interest and an ideological underpinning as well. Although the colonies shied away from the idea of union as the seventeenth century drew to a close, they still sensed the need for some cooperation in meeting common perils and solving problems of intercolonial rivalry. Beyond cooperation for limited emergencies, however, they would not care to go.
—Henry M. Ward
(*"Unite or Die"*:
Intercolony Relations, 1690–1763, 1971)

Mr. Chairman, whether the Constitution be good or bad, the present clause clearly discovers that it is a national government, and no longer a Confederation. I mean that clause which gives the first hint of the general government laying direct taxes. The assumption of this power . . . does . . . entirely change the confederation of the states into one consolidated government.
—George Mason
(Speech in the Virginia Convention, 1788)

None of the Ten, of course, came to [the European Community's summit at] Maastricht with optimism. They left, however, even more disappointed, some concerned with their fishermen, others with their farmers, and still others with their steel workers. There may be a subtle nuance between national interest and national egoism—but Tuesday evening (March 24, 1981) there was no doubt: The European Summit was clearly dominated by national egoisms.
—Le Monde (Paris, March 26, 1981)

The socialization of the nation for the first time brings the economic claims of the masses into the forefront of the picture. The defence of wages and employment becomes a concern of national policy and must be asserted, if necessary, against the national policies of other countries; and this in turn gives the worker an intimate practical interest in the policy and power of his nation.
—E. H. Carr (*Nationalism and After*, 1945)

Never before have so many nations and their leaders so frequently and so openly admitted their complex interdependence; never before have they created so many cooperative frameworks and elaborate mechanisms to manage their growing interdependence and its consequences. Simultaneously, however, national leaders and their supporters continue to insist on the sovereign independence of their states with the expectation that the intricate web of regional or global cooperative links will serve their separate interests.

Today there are over 1,000 intergovernmental cooperative associations in addition to the United Nations Organization; before World War I, there were only 37 such organizations. Since 1951, the number of intersovereign associations has increased by about 150 percent. In the 1980s nearly every nation belonged to more than 60 international intergovernmental organizations (IGOs), some nations were members of more than 100 IGOs, and Denmark headed the list by belonging to 164.[1] In addition, the *Yearbook of International Organizations* (1981) lists over 2,600 transnational, nongovernmental organizations, including transnational corporations, transnational associations of trade unions, and world religious organizations.

Can the contemporary world of sovereign, yet intertwined, nations learn from the history and experience of Confederal America? As this and the following chapter will suggest, the 200-year-old Articles of Confederation have, paradoxically, a contemporary relevance for the very reasons that many historians, constitutional lawyers, and political scientists have tended to malign them: for not having been bold enough; for having mirrored, without much imagination, the then-prevailing parochial priorities; and for having failed to produce an effective union with a central authority possessing adequate taxing and executive powers.

Could it, or should it, have been otherwise? Clinton Rossiter, for example, noted that the prevailing mood among the political leaders of the various states simply could not give "a faraway, central regime in the United States what they were busy denying to a faraway, central regime in Britain." He concluded that the Articles of Confederation "seem to have been just about as viable a form of government as could have been offered to the American people" at that time.[2]

Before the Declaration of Independence, only a few people saw beyond these devices and, deploring the parochial interests of the various states, tried to place the concept of an emerging American national unity above the centrifugal interests of the thirteen states. The others, while collectively opposing England, shifted their primary allegiance from the "mother country" (England) to the thirteen "mother states." In practical terms, according to Daniel J. Boorstin, "there was less national unity after the adoption of the Articles of Confederation in 1781 than before."[3] Even in 1792, three years after the adoption of the federal constitution, an ardent Federalist, Fisher Ames, was still to complain: "Instead of feeling as a Nation, a State is our country. We look with indifference, often with hatred, fear, and aversion to the other States."[4] Charles de Gaulle would have probably nicknamed confederal America, "*l'Amérique de treize patries.* Under the Articles, the U.S. community was indeed an imperfect union of homelands.

Similarly imperfect—and for similar reasons—are today's intergovernmental cooperative associations established among sovereign nations. Although aware of their growing interdependence and the benefits to be derived from coordinated policies and actions, sovereign nations still look at each other "with indifference, often with hatred, fear, and aversion"—as did, according to Fisher Ames, the U.S. states in the eighteenth century. National leaders today seem ready to pursue in common only some clearly defined objectives and, for these specific purposes, delegate some limited powers to a common institution provided that their national interests are preserved and promoted. What Henry Ward wrote (see one of the epigraphs to this chapter) about the British colonies in America at the end of the seventeenth century can be largely applied to nation-states at the end of the twentieth century. They, too, do not wish to go, in Ward's words, beyond "cooperation for limited emergencies,"[5] that is, beyond their present international frameworks—military alliances, economic communities, common markets, and the various networks of rules, norms, and procedures, the so-called international regimes. Except for occasional rhetoric and reformist manifestos, there is no emotional allegiance to a higher, supranational community. There is no European, Asian, or African counterpart to the regional "Americanization" of the British and other settlers in the separate colonies and then the states of confederal America.

An example of the contemporary preference for the confederal rather than the federal formula are the ups and downs in the progress of the European Community toward a closer political, and possibly federal, union. The regional unification of Western Europe began in 1951 with the truly ground-breaking Coal and Steel Community. This group was followed, relatively quickly, by the European Atomic Energy Community and the European Economic Community (Treaty of Rome, March 25, 1957), but so far, the West European nations have been reluctant to move further toward the kind of common foreign policy and defense that characterized confederal America. Consisting originally of six nations (West Germany, France, Italy, Belgium, The Netherlands, and Luxembourg), the European Economic Community was subsequently increased to twelve (England, Ireland, and Denmark in 1973, Greece in 1981 and Spain and Portugal in 1985). The increase in the number of members has so far meant a diluted rather than a closer union, although European Parliament, whose members were initially selected by delegation from national legislative assemblies of the member states, was for the first time in 1980 formed on the basis of direct elections within the various nations of the Community. In its uphill struggle, the European Parliament has not yet been able to transform its previously purely consultative role into real budgetary and legislative powers. The interest and participation of European voters in the second elections in 1984 was minimal. Those who did vote were guided by local (that is, national) rather than all-European concerns.

Even more important, as Ilan Greilsammer noted, "the Community institutions, probably because of their highly technical and narrowly specialized character, have not succeeded in diffusing a 'European spirit,'[6] which would weaken the component nationalisms. When, in a 1974 public opinion poll (*Allensbach Archives*) German adults were asked, Do you think that you will live to see the day when the West European countries join together to form the United States of Europe? 51 percent answered no and 29 percent answered yes. Twenty years before (in 1953) 41 percent had said yes and only 29 percent no. A similar decline was reflected in answers to the question, Would you approve or disapprove if the German flag were no longer raised at major official ceremonies but a European flag instead? Another blow to the idea of European integration was administered by the annual conference of the British Labour party (October 1, 1981) when it voted more than five to one in favor of British withdrawal from the European Economic Community when the British socialists return to power.

Falling behind in competition with the United States and Japan, the nations of Western Europe—including now the Mediterranean tier extending from the Iberian peninsula to Greece—have found it extremely difficult to reconcile their various national priorities even in such routine matters as respective fishing quotas and farm prices. In the words of the former president of the European Parliament, Simone Veil of France, the Community tends to become "a scapegoat for national difficulties" instead of being a cradle of a "United States of Europe," the dream of the Community's founders and once a popular term that is rarely heard today. The general mood of Western Europe was summed up by the vogue term "Euro-pessimism" (as reported by the *New York Times*, July 7, 1985).

In Western Europe, and even more so in the rest of the world, humanity basically remains, as it has always been, fenced into separate corrals. Although recommendations, analyses, and prophecies concerning the desirability, if not inevitability, of common, continental, or global approaches to common problems abound, there are no indications that the fences of national sovereignty are soon to be dismantled in favor of some supranational—global, continental, or even regional—federal union.

Participatory and Nationalist Arguments Against Integration

In eighteenth-century America, the primary objection to a concentration of decisive powers in the hands of a national authority was based on the political elites' concern with democratic controls and participation, deemed possible only on a local or state scale. In his study of the Articles of Confederation, Harry W. Jones pointed to the interesting link between the idealization of localism then and now. In both cases, citizen participation in decision making is the main issue.

It was local government they trusted, and the more local the better. Like the "participatory democracy" theorists of our own day, the colonists idealized small-unit decision making: the village was the best, the county almost as good, the state acceptable. But nation-wide government was to them inherently incompatible with democracy.[7]

Although participatory democracy was a central issue in eighteenth-century America, among contemporary nations—the overwhelming majority being subject to various military, socialist, or fascist dictatorships—citizen participation and control is not the issue: *nationalism* is, especially its basic distrust and suspicion of all foreigners, democratic or not. To paraphrase Jones, a continentwide or global federal government is today inherently incompatible with perceptions of national-territorial interest. Thus, both democracies and dictatorships, primarily as national and nationalist entities, manifest an identical reluctance or outright hostility toward any truly supranational unification.

In our "internationalist" world, given the asymmetry of nations in terms of their size, wealth, development, and military power, nations dread regional or world government in which more or less ill-intentioned foreigners would have the majority. World government could become a tyranny by majority or, even worse, a tyranny by minority if, for example, the superpowers were to gang up against the rest of humankind. From the nationalist view, dictatorship imposed by foreigners is worse than dictatorship exercised by one's own kind. Many a Third World leader may well view a plan for a world federal structure as only an attractively disguised return to world imperialism. As we will see in Chapter 10, the contemporary vigorous reassertion of anglophone Canada's separate cultural identity vis-à-vis the United States, Mexico's anxieties or irritations with regard to the United States, and Québec's direct linkages with France to compensate for the isolation of the French-speaking North Americans in the midst of an Anglo-Saxon ocean indicate the difficulty, if not the impossibility, of thinking of North America in terms of an integrated common market in ideas, products, and technology.

In the 1780s, as Clinton Rossiter argued, Americans "were not ready to submit to the commands of an American government which could not, they were convinced, extend its sway over half a continent without destroying the states and turning away from republican principles."[8] But emotionally, as Rossiter maintained, they were ready to be Americans.

Nothing distantly similar can be said about nations today. The West Europeans are not emotionally ready to be Europeans, only some reformist dreamers and scholars are. This observation applies even more to Asians, Africans, South Americans, East Europeans, and North Americans. None of the 160-odd nations today is ready to submerge itself into some regional, continental, or global pool so as to be human or "earthian" first and national second.

Yet, despite these nationalist objections to a supranational federal unification, or because of them, the number of the various cooperative organizations or frameworks among sovereign nations have grown spectacularly since the 1950s. These organizations as well as other cooperative frameworks both reflect and cause an unprecedented cross-boundary move-ment of persons, goods, knowledge, and ideas.

As perceived by the central elites, the primary purpose of intersovereign cooperative systems is to help national governments service their respective publics better—not an abstract "humanity." External cooperation is expected to sustain or enhance internal national power. As Wolfram Hanrieder expressed it:

> The tremendous power of modern welfare-state vis-à-vis its "subjects—its impressive modern power to give, take, and withhold vertically—is obligated to accept the logic of interdependence and so compelled to interact with other states, to cooperate horizontally, to turn to external sources to meet their people's demands.[9]

In other words, while publics turn to their national governments for the solution of social and economic problems, these governments must look to foreign governments in order to satisfy the demands of their citizens. It is this mixture of reluctant internationalism grafted onto welfare-oriented nationalism that endows the contemporary intergovernmental associations and international regimes with loose confederal features. Like the thirteen hesitant American states, the nation-members of modern "confederal" associations "go it" with others in order to go it—simultaneously and successfully—alone. Geoffrey L. Goodwin described such "international nationalism" succinctly: "By providing instruments of collaboration which have helped their member states to respond better to the demands of external environment, international functional agencies are perpetuating and strengthening the sovereignty of these states rather than eroding or di-minishing it."[10]

Such goals and consequences represent confederal rather than federal themes.

Regional and Functional Cooperatives

There is a great variety among modern cooperative associations of nation-states in terms of their importance, success, duration, number of nations involved, geographic area covered, functional scope, specificity of issues to be handled collectively, and chance of further progress toward greater federal unity. Many of these associations overlie each other functionally or territorially and are unavoidably or deliberately interlaced. This intertwining is present, for example, in the specialized agencies and the Economic and Social Council of the United National Organization.

The names of these intergovernmental associations also vary greatly, ranging from *agency* to *union*. Their modest or ambitious titles rarely indicate the extent of their commitment to and practice of international cooperation. For illustrative purposes, some of the terms currently used are listed below:

International Atomic Energy Agency (IAEA)
General Agreement on Tariffs and Trade (GATT)
Association of Southeast Asian Nations (ASEAN)
International Bank for Reconstruction and Development (IBRD or World Bank)
Economic Commission for Europe (ECE)
Commonwealth of Nations (formerly the British Empire)
European Economic Community (NEC)
Conference on Trade and Development (UNCTAD)
International Finance Corporation (IFC)
Council for the Cooperation of the States of Gulf (CCG or Common Market of the six Arab states on the Indian Ocean)
United Nations Children Fund (UNICEF)
United Nations Institute for Training and Research (UNITAR)
East African Common Market (potential)
North Atlantic Treaty Organization (NATO)
Warsaw Pact (sometimes referred to as Socialist Commonwealth)
International Telecommunication Union (ITU)

One intergovernmental organization, the United Nations, claims to be universal and all-inclusive in terms of both its purposes and its membership—although, because of its strict concept of neutrality, Switzerland refuses to become a member of the political portion of the United Nations Organization. The U.S. term "United Nations", which by omitting the word "organization" seems to parallel the United States, is a misnomer since by a wishful grammatical trick it has endowed the world organization with a false aggregative personality. In other languages—French, German, Spanish, Russian, Italian (and Czech)—the grammar as well as realism dictates the use of "organization." In German, the United Nations (die Vereinte Nationen) requires, as it were, a "confederal" plural rather than "federal" singular verb (e.g., the United Nations fail, not fails, to act). In fact, the United Nations is an organization of disunited nations and certainly not an entity separate from or above its national components.

Is there a convenient term that could be applied to all these systems of cooperation and regulation among sovereign nations? Consociation is an obvious possibility dating back to Johannes Althusius (1557-1638) and Hugo Grotius (1583-1645); the title of the next chapter has borrowed this unfamiliar term from these medieval authors. International regime is another possible term. Contemporary scholars in international and comparative politics have begun increasingly to use this term to describe and analyze the various intersovereign cooperative frameworks built around specific, frequently technical, international issues. Regimes represent sets of norms, rules, and procedures that are based on a perceived convergence of national interests and are proclaimed (by a treaty, for example) and often institutionalized (by the creation of appropriate agencies) to regulate some specific issue-areas. In other words, international regimes are sets of arrangements that are meant to affect relationships of perceived interdependence.[11]

For the purpose of this analysis—and given the ambiguous meaning of "regime"—I have found it useful to refer to the various cooperative systems of sovereignties as *confederal associations* (or "consociations of sovereignties"). The cooperative frameworks created and managed by *noncentral* governments across national boundaries are referred to in Chapters 9 and 10 as "transborder cooperatives."

Some of the modern confederal intersovereign associations are primarily *regional.* Their aim is to coordinate policies and actions of sovereign territorial states within a geographically delineated area. Examples include the European Communities and the Organization of American States with its Alliance for Progress mechanism. Other intergovernmental associations are primarily *functional.* They group a number of nations, contiguous and noncontiguous, around such specific issues as common defense; ideology (communism); religious creed (Islam); trade; finance; food; raw materials production and distribution; technology transfers; peaceful uses of atomic energy; communication satellites; travel; cultural exchanges; standardization of weights, measures, and statistical data; regulation of transnational corporations; fisheries; conservation; and exploration of space and Antarctica.

The line between regional and functional organizations is often blurred. Geographic proximity may encourage a common approach to a cluster of functional or technical issues and a common function may merge distant and noncontiguous territorial communities into a quasi-territorial community. One of the oldest intergovernmental associations, the Universal Postal Union, for example, has created, as it were, a single "postal territory" consisting of both contiguous and noncontiguous nations. The Treaty of Berne states, "The countries between which the present Convention has been concluded form, under the designation of Universal Postal Union, a single territory for the reciprocal exchange of correspondence."[12]

Despite the great variety in their specific goals and corresponding situations, all of the above associations have two characteristic confederal features: (a) an avowed need for cross-boundary regulation and cooperation and (b) opposition to a federal merger that would result in a delegation of significant taxing and executive powers to a common authority. An important ingredient of this opposition is the fear that the common authority might fall under the domination of the most powerful components of the system.

Contemporary Relevance of Old Concepts

It is always tempting and occasionally rewarding to read new relevance into old documents such as the Articles of Confederation and the records of the debates that preceded as well as followed the belated ratification of the Articles on March 1, 1781. There are, of course, some serious analytical risks involved when we intermingle eighteenth-century Massachusetts with twentieth-century France, old Virginia with modern India, and Benjamin Franklin's Pennsylvania with Julius Nyerere's Tanzania. When major confederal themes are extrapolated from the political and social turmoil of postcolonial

America and projected onto the current world scene, some particular hazards should be noted.

One hazard—and a constant *compagnon de route*, so to speak—is the tendency to engage in predetermined thinking, either wishful or Cassandra-like. Under its spell, a researcher may unwittingly, though sometimes deliberately, rearrange the past—or the present—to make it fit his or her thesis. Thus, the researcher may look for and therefore selectively find those encouragements or caveats in the past that he or she hopes or fears the present or future may require. In this connection, it is useful to recall that during the period of the Marshall Plan and its explicit encouragement of European unification, some U.S. leaders and even scholars tended to urge their West European counterparts to imitate as speedily as possible the successful model of the U.S. federal unification as anchored in the federal constitution of 1789. Conveniently overlooking the disheartening lesson of the 1860s, these federalist sermons directed at the West Europeans were sometimes glib and, what is worse, based on false analogies.

With regard to the more applicable U.S. confederal model, there is another potential hazard: the tendency to view any contemporary "consociation of homelands" as a prologue to a full federal union that will follow as speedily as it did in the case of the original American states in the 1780s. Jones rightly reminds us that in the United States, the confederation has usually been evaluated as "a way-station on the road to American federalism" rather than a "self-contained episode."[13]

The U.S. experience with the "confederal-federal" scenario is a frequent cause of wishful thinking about the European Communities and other confederal frameworks. If, in the United States, confederation was the second act of a political drama whose first act was the Declaration of Independence and whose third act was the federal constitution of 1789, it certainly does not follow that this sequence will occur elsewhere. The most promising and most advanced confederal associations, such as the European Economic Community, may have no federal future. Some confederal associations may remain self-contained episodes of either much longer or much shorter duration than confederal America. Still other associations may never move beyond their planning stage. Conceivably, instead of being a prologue to federal union, a confederal system may be its epilogue or even close-to-last act: a federal state (*Bundesstaat*) may devolve into an association of states (*Staatenbund*) to be then followed by the last act of the drama, the dissolution of the system into secessionist components. In fact, as this study suggests (see Chapters 8 and 9), confederal themes tend to appear in some federal unions, especially in the area of international or transborder regional contacts among the various territorial components of federal states and their foreign counterparts.

The transformation from a federal to a confederal system could conceivably be, for example, the future fate of federal Canada not only on account of Québec's quest for associate (confederal) status—if not outright secession—but also as a possible reaction to Québec's new status on the part of the centrifugal western provinces. As Donald Smiley noted, the evolution of Canadian federalism "is likely to bring about constitutional reforms enhancing the powers of the provinces and their fiscal administrative autonomy vis-à-vis the central government. . . . An extreme extension of provincial power and the more effective constitutional guarantees of such powers is necessary if Québec separatism is to be defeated."[14]

Three features of the American experience, predating the Declaration of Independence and the Articles of Confederation, diminish the relevance of American confederation for our era: common colonial experience, common sacrifice and victory, and common language.

Awareness of Common Colonial Experience

Initially, the thirteen British colonies in America were founded as well as governed as separate entities. The result was a mutual lack of knowledge of and interest in the affairs of both neighboring and distant colonies. Given the then-existing communications, the other colonies seemed distant. Andrew C. McLaughlin described the situation as follows:

> When the people were thinking of themselves and not of Europe, they must have felt their differences more keenly than their similarities. . . . A Georgian knew little of New York or Massachusetts. Life on the plantations of Virginia was far different from life in the little settlements of New England. When John Adams, leaving his fireside in Braintree, went to Philadelphia as a delegate in Congress, the letters which he sent home were welcomed as tidings from a "far country." "Of affairs of Georgia," wrote Madison to Jefferson in 1786, "I know as little as those of Kamskatska." When we add to all this the fact that the colonies were established at different times and from different motives, and that climate, soil, and industrial life varied greatly from Maine to Georgia . . . union seems almost beyond the verge of possibility.[15]

Yet, by the 1760s, political leaders in the colonies had become increasingly aware of a basic similarity in their respective destinies because of the overarching imperial authority (which also made several attempts to impose some form of imperial unity on the thirteen colonies, as it were "from the top down").

An interesting study by Richard L. Merritt[16] indicates that for a major portion of the years from 1735 to 1775 attention to the colonies as a whole in the colonial press was negligible. In contrast, references to the home colony were prominent in the various journals. Merritt used a quantitative analysis of references to home colonies as opposed to references to their collective sum total in colonial newspapers (922 issues between 1735 and 1775) in five urban centers: Boston, New York, Philadelphia, Williamsburg, and Charleston, South Carolina. The analysis showed first a slow, then a dramatic, increase in colonial press references to America: "By 1766, the year in which the colonists rejoiced that their resistance had effected the repeal of the odious Stamp Act, the continental share of the American symbol count has risen to 37.3 per cent—an increase of almost 1000 per cent over the level of 1761."[17]

There were relative differences among the colonies in their respective attention to other colonies. Massachusetts, for instance, remained quite self-centered. It "was not particularly prone to be attentive to other colonies, and was the least interested in the collective concept," wrote Merritt. However:

> Despite differences, the colonies had a remarkably congruent image of their country. . . . Generally speaking, the attention patterns in the newspapers of the different colonies presaged positions toward the American Union taken during the last quarter of the 18th century. . . . In the exceptional year of 1775 the colonist paid an unprecedented attention to the continent as a whole.[18]

The continental experience of the thirteen colonies, as reflected in the colonial press and written in the common language of the elites, does not easily transfer to other continents subject to British or other European rule. In African and Asian colonies, there was no free press written in a language common to all the separate colonies and the imperial overlord. In Africa, for example, the colonial powers—England, France, Portugal, Spain, Germany, Italy, and Belgium—not only kept their respective imperial domains separate but, guided by strategic, commercial, navigational, and administrative considerations, imposed further territorial compartmentalization on their respective domains. The colonial powers drew their intra-imperial boundaries without regard to preexisting ethnic, linguistic, tribal, or religious lines.

In Africa, the calls for a Pan-African union, while heard here and there, followed rather than preceded the achievement of independence. Although appealing to many Africans in principle, Kwame Nkrumah's plan for a Pan-African federal union was, more often than not, suspected by many African leaders as leading to Pan-Ghanaism rather than to Pan-Africanism. In this context of mutual suspicion and conflicting national interests, the Organization of African Unity (OAU, created in 1963) has so far remained a rather loose association of sovereignties. The OAU is only occasionally able to coordinate African policies with regard to South Africa and some outsiders but is rarely capable of regulating intra-African conflicts such as Libya versus Chad, Morocco versus Algeria, and Ethiopia versus Somalia. Similarly, within the Arab League (organized in 1945), territorial-political divisions have so far proved stronger than basic ethnic and religious unity.

In Central and South America—though unlike Africa quite homogeneous in terms of culture, faith, and language (except for Brazil)—the former Spanish colonial empire finally split, and has remained split, into many more territorial segments than there were colonial units (vice-royalties under the rule of royal governors). The Organization of American States is a loose "confederal" system in which the dominant power of the United States is both the condition for and an obstacle to collective success. Despite the postimperial British support of various attempts at federal unions of former British island colonies in the Caribbean, all the attempts have ended in failure: "Balkanization" of the Caribbean has become the dominant pattern.[19]

As to Asian nations, their common colonial and then anticolonial experiences have led even less to any significant attempts at any continental or subcontinental confederal system. Except for the prewar Japanese imperial concept of an "Asian coprosperity zone" and postwar ASEAN (Association of Southeast Asian Nations, formed in 1967), one rarely finds, even in precolonial or postcolonial rhetoric, any Pan-Asian counterpart to Nkrumah's passionate appeals for a Pan-African continental union. When the colonial lid in Asia, superimposed on preexisting ancient nations and their territorial systems, was at long last lifted after World War II, further fragmentation rather than unification set in, dissolving entities that either predated colonial imperialism or had been maintained under it. One example is the two-phase division of India into Pakistan and India first and later of Pakistan into East and West Pakistan (now Bangladesh and Pakistan). In Asia, of course, the colonial experience includes attempts at imperial expansion by Asian nations themselves, such as Japan, China, and more recently, Vietnam with its colonial ambitions in Laos, Kampuchea, and possibly Thailand.

In terms of a prenatal predisposition for unity, the United States stands therefore quite apart from other nations, including those of Europe whose recent collective experience with the Nazi imperial rule was too short to count significantly as a unifying factor—even though the experience of the French and German antifascists under nazism certainly played an important role in the French-German reconciliation, the cornerstone of the European Communities.

Common Sacrifice and Victory

The second special American experience was the practical as well as emotional impact of a common victorious continental war against a powerful enemy. This highly cementing factor was largely absent in Latin America, Asia, and Africa where sovereign statehoods were acquired by the various colonies territory by territory rather than by means of a joint continental war effort. Also, unlike America, independence on other continents was often achieved by diplomatic negotiation rather than by war at a time when the European colonial powers, weakened by intra-European war, had lost both the power and the ambition to continue their colonial domination. On the whole, diplomatic decolonization was the rule, military confrontation an exception. The Sepoy Rebellion in India in 1857, the Indonesian-Dutch and Indochina-French wars, and Algeria's violent struggle for independence were one-colony, and not one-continent, wars.

When the Articles of Confederation are criticized today for their inadequacy in terms of providing an effective national government, it is sometimes overlooked, as a recent study by Gerald M. Galluci has rightly noted, "that the thirteen States so [imperfectly] united were able to defeat the chief world power of the age."[20] Ernest Renan emphasized the "heritage of glory and of grief to be shared; to have suffered, rejoiced, and hoped together . . . indeed common suffering unites more strongly than common rejoicing."[21] In contrast to the decolonization processes on other continents, territory by territory, the first decolonization in North America made the thirteen colonies suffer, rejoice, and hope collectively in a common war effort. Thus, there were memories and blood spilled together to form an emotional base for a common political future.

Common Language and Cultural Heritage

The third special characteristic of the American evolution from thirteen separate entities through confederation to federal union was the common British cultural heritage, unparalleled in potentially preconfederal and pre-federal situations elsewhere. The English colonies shared a common culture, political tradition, legal concepts, and language not only among themselves but also with their imperial "mother-country." For this reason, foreign scholars as well as statesmen often dismiss the relevance of the American experience for their respective continents, which are deeply divided by ancient linguistic, cultural, political, religious, or ideological barriers. Complaining about the "vanity, touchiness, and national pride" of West European nations, Chancellor Helmut Schmidt, for example, noted, "It will be a long time before Europe, *without a common language*, could even approach America's hope for a united continent."[22]

Moreover, scholars, particularly those in Europe, have traditionally tended to analyze nationalism and its integrative and disintegrative effects in terms of *linguistic* communities ("ethnies"), taking only marginally into account factors of geography, history, and ideology as determinants of national sentiments that may sometimes be more important than language. This certainly was the case of the English-speaking North American community which first asserted and finally fought for its territorial economic and ideological goals against another English-speaking nation. With equal ease, passion, and anger, both English-speaking adversaries garnished their hostile rhetoric with quotes from identical sources such as the King James Bible, Shakespeare, and English translations of Montesquieu and Greek philosophers and historians. As Winston Churchill once quipped, the British and the Americans became two peoples separated by a common language. For students of nationalism and ethnicity, the birth of the thirteen American "nations" first, and one federal nation afterward, represents an instructive example of nationalism dominantly determined by ideology ("ideoethnicity") and territorial-economic interests (assisted by geographic distance) and not by separate language and culture.

Although the ideological, cultural, and linguistic unity of the thirteen states has been emphasized in contradistinction to deep divisions on all other continents, the contrast should now be qualified by the previously mentioned record of hostility and suspicion among the various states and regions. Despite their common provenience and heritage, the American states and regions profoundly differed in their political concepts, economic interests, climate, topography, and resulting habits and morals. As the British governor of New York, Benjamin Fletcher, quoted in one of the epigraphs to this chapter, said, "The English colonies were as badly divided as Christian and Turk."

As among sovereign nations today, there were conflicts of major economic interests between the eight trade-oriented states in the north and the five agricultural states in the south, there was mistrust and suspicion between small and large states; and there was explosive competition concerning territorial expansion into lands west of Virginia as well as other rival territorial claims. As one writer put it in 1696, "the colonies had become, and did in a manner treat each other, as foreigners."[23] More than a century and a half before the Civil War, armed conflicts among the mutually unfriendly states could not be ruled out. In pursuit of its territorial claims, Connecticut, for example, sent troops into the Wyoming Valley of Pennsylvania, which, in turn, had a boundary dispute with Virginia; New York engaged in a dispute with the people who had settled Vermont under grants from New Hampshire. Actual warfare among the colonies, as Merrill Jensen observed, "had been prevented only by the external power of Britain which subdued them but did not eliminate their animosity toward each other. . . . Economic disputes, political theories, and the inherited prejudices of one state against the other—all worked in the direction of separatism and the complete independence of each state."[24]

Even when war against the British rule began and unity of policy and action against the common enemy became the first priority, old intercolonial tensions resurfaced when the form of common government was under discussion. "Longstanding intercolonial antagonisms were exacerbated," Jones wrote, "in the early attempts to arrive at collective American decisions, and particularly during congressional consideration of the Articles of Confederation."[25]

Prenatal Unity and Disunity

The prenatal unity of the thirteen American states—resulting from their common heritage of language, law, and government, their shared negative experience with imperial governance over a long period of time, and their subsequent common revolt against England as well as their geographic situation and relative isolation—distinguishes the American experience in several important aspects from contemporary attempts at confederal associations undertaken by sovereign nations. On the other hand, the prenatal and postnatal disunity, asymmetric diversity, distrust, and hostility among the thirteen states and the two major regions, north and south, as well as their elites' suspicious attitude toward any delegation of substantial powers to a suprasovereign central authority make a comparative examination of confederal themes in 1781 and 1981 possible and useful.

One reservation concerning any possible relevance of the American confederal theme seems justified: How can the assumptions, principles, goals, and practices of a confederal system that was found inadequate and outdated by some of the best minds of the country at the time of the belated ratification of the Articles of Confederation in 1781 possibly be relevant? A mere eight years later, the confederal system was discarded and replaced by the more perfect union of 1789. One possible answer may be suggested: Even if the inadequacy of the Articles in the American context and the ensuing chaos were beyond any doubt or dispute—which is not the case[26]— one can argue that a scheme that did not work under one set of circumstances at a particular time for one set of territorial communities, and had to be replaced by a more appropriate system, may yet prove workable and useful under a different set of circumstances, in another time frame, in another environment, and with a different set of participating communities.

A shared perception of some external or internal challenge—military or nonmilitary—that confronts a group of territorial communities both singly and collectively is the self-evident precondition for any coalescence of sovereign units. Associating communities have to view the gains, current or future, to be obtained by joining with others as clearly outweighing the satisfaction and advantages of remaining alone. Such a view and calculation undergirded the city leagues of ancient Greece and formed the background for the decision of the thirteen colonies in North America to form a "league of friendship" and a confederal "perpetual" union. A similar perception of separate advantages to be secured by joint action characterizes the contemporary defensive, functional, and regional associations of territorial states. Today, these confederal associations are usually established for a limited though renewable period of time rather than for eternity—which perhaps reflects the accumulated wisdom of the centuries concerning the fragility of all political arrangements.

Notes

1. Harold K. Jacobson, William Reisinger, and Todd Mathers, "States and IGOs: A Multiplying Entanglement" (Paper presented at the American Political Science Association Annual Meeting in Washington D.C., August 20–September 2, 1984), p. 1.

2. Clinton Rossiter, *1787, The Grand Convention* (New York: Macmillan, 1966), pp. 47–48.

3. Daniel J. Boorstin, *The Americans: The National Experience* (New York: Random House, 1965), p. 403.

4. Fisher Ames to George Minot, February 16, 1792, in *Works of Fisher Ames*, ed., Seth Ames (Boston, 1854), vol. 1, page 112, quoted by Merrill Jensen, *The Articles of Confederation: An Interpretation of the Social-Constitutional History of the American Revolution, 1774–1781* (Madison: University of Wisconsin Press, 1940), p. 164.

5. Henry M. Ward, *"Unite or Die": Intercolony Relations, 1690-1763* (Port Washington, N.Y.: Kennikat Press, 1971), p. 3.

6. Ilan Greilsammer, "Some Observations on European Federalism," in *Federalism and Political Integration*, ed., Daniel J. Elazar, (Ramat Gan, Israel: Turtledove, 1979), p. 127. Cf. Marcel Merle: "It is easier to mobilize the French against the anonymous dictatorship of fatherlandless technocrats as de Gaulle has expressed it (technocrates apatrides) or against the danger of supranationalism than to persuade them to dilute their sovereignty (Marcel Merle, *Forces et enjeux dans les relations internationales* [Paris: Economica, 1981], p. 114).

7. Harry W. Jones, "The Articles of Confederation and the Creation of a Federal System," in *Aspects of American Liberty: Philosophical, Historical, and Political* (Philadelphia: American Philosophical Society, 1976), p. 132.

8. Rossiter, *The Grand Convention*, p. 38.

9. Wolfram F. Hanrieder, "Dissolving International Politics: Reflections on the Nation-State," *American Political Science Review* 72 (December 1978), p. 1276.

10. Geoffrey L. Goodwin, "The Erosion of External Sovereignty," *Government and Opposition* 9 (Winter 1974), p. 70.

11. This working definition, adapted to the needs of this comparative analysis, is based on Ernst B. Haas's study "Why Collaborate? Issue-Linkage and International Regimes," *World Politics* 32 (April 1980), pp. 357-405. Further insights into the workings of contemporary international regimes are contained in Oran R. Young, "International Regimes: Problems of Concept Formation," *World Politics* 32 (April 1986), pp. 331-356.

12. Treaty of Berne (October 9, 1874), Article 33, section 1.

13. Jones, "Articles of Confederation" p. 130.

14. Donald V. Smiley, "The Canadian Federation and the Challenge of Québec Independence," *Publius* 8 (Winter 1978), pp. 199-224.

15. Andrew C. McLaughlin, *The Confederation and the Constitution* (New York: Harper, 1905), pp. 44-45.

16. Richard L. Merritt, "Perceptions of Unity and Diversity in Colonial America, 1725-1775" (Paper presented at the Sixth World Congress of the International Political Science Association, Geneva, September 21-25, 1964). Subsequently part of Richard L. Merritt, *Symbols of American Community (1735-1775)* (New Haven: Yale University Press, 1966), p. 125.

17. Merritt, "Perceptions of Unity," p. 5.

18. Ibid., pp. 6, 18. A 1695 plan would have subdivided colonial America into regions by combining, for example, South Carolina with Barbados, Virginia with North Carolina, Massachusetts with Rhode Island, and New York with Connecticut.

19. The failure of the West Indian federation is analyzed by Gisbert H. Flanz, "The West Indies" in Thomas M. Franck ed., *Why Federations Fail—An Inquiry into the Requisites for Successful Federalism* (New York: New York University Press, 1968), pp. 91-124.

20. Gerald M. Galluci, "The Articles Amended: The American Confederal Tradition Restated" (Paper presented at the American Political Science Association Annual Meeting, Washington D.C., August 28-31, 1980), p. 6. By permission of the author.

21. Ernest Renan, "Qu'est ce qu'une nation?" *Discours et Conférences* (Paris: Ancienne Maison Michel Lévy Frères, 1887), p. 186 (Translation by Sir Alfred Zimmern, ed., *Modern Political Doctrines* (Oxford: Clarendon Press, 1939).

22. Interview with columnist James Reston, *New York Times*, March 6, 1981 (italics added).

23. Quoted in Evarts B. Greene, *Provincial America* (New York: Holt, 1905), pp. 117-118.

24. Jensen, "The Articles of Confederation," pp. 116–117, 124.
25. Jones, "The Articles of Confederation," p. 131.
26. Jackson Turner Main, *The Antifederalists: Critics of the Constitution, 1781–1789* (Chapel Hill: University of North Carolina Press, 1961), p. 281: "The Antifederalists, who lost their only major battle, are forgotten while the victors are remembered, but it is not certain which is the more memorable."

7

Consociations of Sovereignties: Myth and Reality of International Organizations

Tocqueville failed to take account of the human capacity for contact without communication, for knowledge without understanding. Far from leading to a community of mankind, the economic and technological unification of the world has in fact aggravated, and made far more dangerous, the animosities of national communities that continue to value their separate sovereignty over their common humanity and even their security.

—James W. Fulbright
(*The Atlantic Community: Progress and Prospects,* 1963)

[International integration] involves the gradual politicization of the actors' purposes, which were initially considered "technical" or "non-controversial."

—Ernst B. Haas and Philippe C. Schmitter
(*International Organization,* 1964)

International organization functions now less to deprive governments of their domestic functions than to assist them in acquiring the competence to do their jobs more effectively.

—Inis L. Claude, Jr.
(*Swords into Plowshares,* 1956)

The evolving web of international governmental organizations has modified the global political system . . . but it has not yet radically transformed this system . . . international governmental organizations institutionalize aspects of traditional international politics.

—Harold K. Jacobson, William Reisinger, and Todd Mathers
("States and IGOs: A Multiplying Entanglement," 1984)

The ever-growing number of international organizations represents collective responses to three basic types of challenges to territorial nation-states: (1) military threats, (2) regional peace and cooperation, and (3) various economic, technical, and environmental issues, usually of a global rather than a regional nature. In the preceding chapter such organizations are labeled "consociations of homelands" on account of their dominantly confederal emphasis on the preservation of their members' sovereignty and the consociational mode of their decision making, befitting intersovereign associations that are reluctant to accept a supranational framework and any central authority with the power to tax and enforce rules.

When a group of territorial communities perceives an outside military challenge as a clear, present, and future danger for each of them separately as well as collectively, the response since time immemorial, has taken the form of bilateral or multilateral alliance.

Under the pressure of war against the British, confederal America, though internally divided into separate, often unfriendly states, achieved a remarkable degree of unity against the common foe by transferring military and foreign policies from the member states to the confederation. Article 9 of the Articles of Confederation assigned to "the united states in congress assembled . . . the sole and exclusive right and power of determining on peace and war . . . of sending and receiving ambassadors, entering into treaties and alliances . . . managing all affairs with the Indians, not members of any of the states." Concomitantly, Article 4 forbade the thirteen states to engage in diplomatic relations, conclude any treaty of alliance with foreign powers or among themselves, or engage in military action unless actually invaded. Moreover, the diplomatic and military decisions did not require unanimity; a nine-state majority was required.

Even though the execution of these powers depended on separate contributions in human resources and money by the member states, such a concentration of diplomatic and military powers in the hands of a confederal assembly was greater than in any military alliance or regional association today. Only the Warsaw Pact Organization of May 14, 1955, valid until 2005, could be presented as an example of a thoroughly integrated "military federation." In reality, the Warsaw Pact Organization, sometimes referred to as a Socialist Commonwealth, is a rigid imperial union imposed by the Soviet Union on minor communist states: East Germany, Poland, Czechoslovakia, Hungary, Bulgaria and, to a much lesser extent, Rumania. Through its economic institution, the Council for Mutual Economic Assistance (Comecon or CMEA), Mongolia and Cuba became associated members in 1962 and 1977, respectively.

External challenge based on a common perception of a military threat by an identifiable outside power has so far proved to be more effective in producing closely knit confederal systems than the other two possible challenges: disorder originating from within the association or nonmilitary external challenges. This observation, emphasizing the *external* nature of the threat, applies paradoxically even to the contemporary threat of an atomic holocaust since it originates from within the world system of states, not from without it. This situation is why the doctrine of mutual assured destruction has failed to produce an irresistible impetus for a global intersovereign fusion. As Reinhold Niebuhr warned a quarter of a century ago; "Fear of mutual destruction easily degenerates into a fear of a particular foe."[1]

Peace Within Associations

The second challenge may come from within the association itself. The purpose of such a confederal association is to maintain peace and order among its members and to settle their anticipated differences and conflicts by peaceful means. In order to promote and preserve intraconfederal peace and harmony, the Articles of Confederation provided for rather complex arbitral procedures. Article 9 made "the united states in congress assembled . . . the last resort of appeal in all disputes and differences now subsisting or that hereafter may arise between two or more states concerning boundary, jurisdiction, or any other case whatever."

One of the most explosive issues threatening peace and order in confederal America—the acquisition of new lands west of Virginia—was removed by consociational accommodation prior to the adoption of the Articles. Actually, Maryland made the settlement of this territorial issue a condition for its ratification of the Articles. Only after Virginia, New York, Connecticut, and other states agreed to cede their western land claims to the confederation did Maryland at long last ratify the Articles and so made possible their adoption on March 1, 1781.

Subjecting particular territorial claims to an unsettled area to collective controls and decisions has some partial modern counterparts. The international agreement on Antarctica (1959) prohibited the use of Antarctica for other than peaceful purposes and guaranteed "freedom of scientific investigation" to all nations. Similarly, ten years later, the Soviet Union and the United States removed the ocean floor from nuclear competition by making it a nuclear-free area at a time when new technology made it possible to place nuclear missiles on the seabed.

Other examples of the promotion of peace and order within an association of sovereign states may be found in the United Nations Charter. In fact, its primary concern is to prevent violent international conflicts. Chapter 6 of the Charter suggests various peaceful procedures to settle disputes among nations. First and above all, it recommends diplomatic negotiations—consensual (consociational) accommodation. Chapter 6 enumerates other procedures that place a third party between the rivals; the so-called third-party techniques include fact-finding and good offices, mediation, conciliation, arbitration, and judicial settlement at the International Court of Justice (World Court) in the Hague.

All of these procedures are naturally only optional, none is compulsory—which is only consonant with the concept of sovereignty. Sovereign nations cannot be forced to submit to any rule or procedure against their will. The jurisdiction of the World Court, for example, can be established only by voluntary agreement between the plaintiff and the defendant to accept the Court's jurisdiction as binding in a particular dispute or in some or all future disputes. No sovereign nation can be subpoenaed by the Court. The Court has no right to deal with the so-called international criminal offenses; nor can it handle political as opposed to legal disputes among nations. The preliminary question, whether a dispute is legal or political, is also a matter of sovereign interpretation by the nations concerned. Thus, political disputes that concern vital security interests of nations remain excluded—that is, precisely those disputes that could seriously impair peace and order among nations.

The Organization of American States (OAS) and the European Economic Community have both introduced procedures for handling regional disputes. The Rio Pact (Inter-American Treaty of Reciprocal Assistance, December 9, 1948, Article 2), obligates the member nations "to submit every controversy which may arise between them to methods of peaceful settlement and to endeavor to settle any such controversy among themselves by means of the procedures in force in the Inter-American System" before referring any controversy to the United Nations. Article 6 of the Rio Pact provides for an immediate meeting of the Organ of Consultation (an assembly of foreign ministers representing the member states) if the integrity of the territory or the sovereignty of any American state is affected by an aggression that is not an armed attack (for instance, infiltration and guerrilla warfare) or by an intracontinental conflict. Article 7 further provides that "in the case of a conflict between two or more American States . . . the High Contracting Parties, meeting in consultation shall call upon the contending States to suspend hostilities and restore matters to the *status quo ante bellum*."

The North Atlantic Treaty Organization is solely directed against an external (Soviet) threat and contains no provision for the maintenance of intra-Atlantic peace and order. In contrast, the European Economic Community, which is not an alliance, is primarily innerdirected. The European Court of Justice in Luxembourg is the final arbiter of Common Market law. In 1981, for example, it was called upon to settle a dispute between the continent-oriented European Parliament in Strasbourg and Luxembourg, on the one hand, and the "own-nation-oriented" governments of France, West Germany, and Belgium, on the other. Those three countries refused to pay their full share of the Community's 1981 budget because it was fractionally increased by the new, directly elected European Parliament without the approval of the three governments.

Threats to Collective Welfare

The third large group of challenges, all external to individual territorial states but affecting them directly, consists of nonmilitary threats to "mutual and general welfare"—to use the confederal terminology of 1781. These functional, dominantly technical challenges have so far proved even less effective in producing closely knit unions than threats to peace from without or within the confederal group. In the eyes of political elites and their publics, these various economic, technological, demographic, or environmental challenges, while serious, constitute relatively distant threats; they are also not perceived as menacing all of the members equally and immediately. Nevertheless, nonmilitary challenges have produced an ever-increasing number of intergovernmental, rather loosely organized functional organizations. The problems calling for such collective responses include:

1. *Economic and financial matters* (international trade, tariffs, currency flow and stability, credit, unequal distribution of resources and development, depletion of energy, peaceful uses of atomic energy, etc.)
2. *Social and health problems* (population explosion, famines, illiteracy, infant mortality, epidemics disregarding sovereign boundaries, drug traffic, etc.)
3. *Ecological issues* (pollution and depletion of planetary resources, protection of some animals, conservation of the ozone layer, tampering with world climate, etc.)
4. *Free movement* of persons, news, views and art (cooperation in the use of communication satellites, distribution of radio wavelengths, extradition of criminals, and prosecution of terrorism across national boundaries)
5. *Standardization needs* (statistical data and procedures, measures and weights, safety rules in air transportation, shipping registration rules and many other highly technical issues that result from the present rapid and multiple contacts among people and nations through their porous territorial boundaries)

Agreements among nations that these problems are indeed pressing and that something should be done about them collectively form the basis for such global functional associations as the UN specialized agencies and other international functional organizations. Even the most egocentric national governments contribute financially to the maintenance of these organizations and provide them with expert knowledge and personnel. Governments would not do so if they did not expect some benefits in return.

At the time of the Articles of Confederation, the number and importance of nonmilitary functional issues subject to government regulation and therefore to potential international controls were much more limited than is the case in the last third of the twentieth century. The present-day proliferation of functional international associations reflects not only an awareness of global and regional interdependence but, to an even larger extent, the leading role modern governments have assumed in the economic, ecological, social, communication, and cultural fields. Such a concentration of regulatory powers in the hands of contemporary democratic, socialist, and fascist governments was naturally unknown to and unanticipated by confederal America.

Nevertheless, even in the Articles of Confederation, there are provisions that subjected some of the regulatory, functional powers to the confederal whole—in addition to the military and diplomatic ones. Examples are the power to regulate the alloy and value of coin (although not bank notes); establish and regulate post offices from one state to another; fix the standards of weights and measures; provide for mutual recognition of official records, acts, and judicial proceedings; and guarantee all privileges and immunities of free citizens in each of the thirteen states, their free ingress and regress to and from any state, and their right to enjoy everywhere all the privileges of trade and commerce.

Modern counterparts to these 200-year-old confederal provisions may be found, at least partially, in the various intergovernmental agencies related to the United Nations such as the International Monetary Fund, Universal Postal Union, International Communication Agency, World Meteorological Organization, and International Civil Aviation Organization.

The list of common tasks as reflected in the titles of these agencies is impressive, and so is the accumulated expertise and experience of most of them. But have these cooperative associations reduced tensions among nations and brought them to a closer unity? To answer this question it is necessary to examine the relationships among the security and functional issues that preoccupy nations singly and collectively.

Functional Contributions to Peace

In contrast to the preceding separate listing of the various tasks and agencies, in real life the various types of external challenges to territorial communities do not occur in isolation one from the other; they overlap. As internal politics (central and noncentral) cannot be separated from foreign and military policies, so politics in general cannot be separated from economics, technological changes, social concerns, ideological considerations, and environmental imperatives. More often than not a confederal association has to be a multipurpose one to better serve its central purpose.

In the eighteenth century, for example, Article 2 of the Articles of Confederation listed "common defence" as the first reason for the confederal union but also included, as reasons two and three, "the security of their liberties" and "mutual and general welfare"—quite modern terminology. Similarly, confederal associations of sovereign states today try to enhance their economic, social, or cultural cooperation by stressing external military or ideological challenges. European unity has sometimes been promoted by asserting its uniqueness vis-à-vis the two non-European superpowers, the United States and Soviet Union. In the late 1950s, a prominent French writer, François Mauriac, argued that Europe need not fear that which divides Russia from the United States but rather that which these two giants have in common.

Whereas economic and functional associations strengthen themselves by dealing also with external cultural, ideological, or military challenges, obversely, military alliances try to strengthen their mutual bonds by a coordinated promotion of economic and cultural cooperation. Article 2 of the North Atlantic Treaty, for example, pledges that parties will "seek to eliminate conflict in their international economic policies and will encourage economic collaboration between any or all of them" and "promote conditions of stability and well-being."

Since the Inter-American Alliance (the Rio Pact of 1947) did not establish any agencies, organs, or common institutions, they were subsequently established at the Ninth International Conference of American States at Bogotá, Colombia, in 1948, which adopted the Charter of the Organization of American States and designated the Pan American Union as its permanent secretariat. The charter established various common organs and agencies such as the Inter-American Conference, which meets every five years, the Council of the Organization in Washington, which meets at frequent intervals, the Organ of Consultation, which is composed of foreign ministers and meets in any emergency, the Inter-American Peace Committee, the Inter-American Defence Committee and Defence Board, the Inter-American Economic and Social Council, the Inter-American Cultural Council, the Inter-American Council of Jurists, and various specialized functional agencies (Pan-American Health Organization, the Commission of Women, the Inter-American Institute of Geography and History, the Indian Institute, and the Children's Institute).

In 1961, this elaborate machinery was expanded by an ambitious economic and social development program with the label, Alliance for Progress. Its charter was signed by the sponsor, the United States, and all the other Latin American states (except Cuba) on August 17, 1961, at Punta del Este (Uruguay). The purpose of the alliance was to narrow the economic and social gap between the United States and the rest of the Western Hemisphere, presented in nearly revolutionary terms of economic and social changes (land reform) and political changes (anti-authoritarian). According to the U.S. Agency for International Development, the Alliance for Progress sought to change ways of life that were rooted in 400 years of custom and tradition by means of a huge revolution of peaceful reform, self-help construction, and development. Today, we may note that global strategic considerations and the status quo orientation of the United States, coupled with Latin American suspicion of the interventionist nature of the giant in the north (even when it chooses to be generous), have so far frustrated many of the early hopes raised by the machinery and developmental plan for a closely knit confederal association of Latin American countries and the United States.

The Warsaw Pact Organization (Treaty of Friendship, Cooperation and Mutual Assistance signed on May 14, 1955, in Warsaw and extended for another twenty-year period on April 26, 1985) provides for mutual military assistance of the European communist nations in case of armed attack (Article 4) and prohibits the member nations from participating in any other coalition or alliance (Article 7); it too has been extended far and wide into economic, technical, and financial fields. In addition to the Political Consultative Committee and the Joint Command of communist armed forces in Warsaw, both firmly in Soviet hands, there is Comecon (CMEA-Council for Mutual Economic Assistance) in Moscow. One of its tasks is to coordinate the flow of investment, technology, and skills throughout the communist bloc as well as various joint ventures such as the joint electricity grid that links the Soviet electrical system with systems in Eastern Europe and the "friendship oil pipelines," which feed oil from the Urals to Poland, Czechoslovakia, and Hungary and transport oil to Western Europe via Eastern Europe.

Another supervisory task of Comecon is to coordinate the communist planned economies and harmonize their five-year plans with that of the Soviet Union, allegedly on the basis of the "socialist division of labor." This seemingly sound principle (according to which each country is to concentrate on producing what it can produce best) has become, in the hands of the mighty Soviet Union, an instrument of imperial control. Less developed communist countries—Rumania in particular—have resented and objected to being assigned the role of being raw material bases for the industrially more advanced comrade republics. Similar to the leaders of the developing countries of the Third World, the communist national elites would prefer a balanced development of their respective national economies rather than a one-sided development that favors the Soviet Union economically and ensures its political dominance.

On January 10, 1964, the ideological journal of the Chinese Communist party, *Hongqui*, described the problem succinctly and bitterly accused the Soviet Union of a policy whose aim was "to force fraternal countries to abandon industrialization and become sources of raw materials and markets for Soviet surplus products." The editorial also equated the "socialist division of labor" with colonialism: "In the name of the international division of labor, the leaders of the Soviet Union oppose the adoption by fraternal countries of the policy of building Socialism by their own effort and developing their economies on an independent basis. They attempt to turn them into economic appendages."

On paper, the so-called Socialist Commonwealth looks like a substantially integrated defense *and* economic community. In fact, it is neither a confederal nor a federal combination of unity with diversity but an imperial union imposed on diversity: not *e pluribus unum* but *unus supra plures*. Moreover, since the Russian invasion of Czechoslovakia in 1968, the Brezhnev doctrine has tried to perpetuate and justify Soviet political, military, and economic dominance of the whole system by granting Moscow the right to intervene—in the name of the Warsaw Pact Organization—in the domestic affairs of member republics for the purpose of protecting the common interest of the communist bloc. Moscow monopolizes the interpretation of that collective interest.

Nonmilitary provisions contained in or added to military alliances reflect the modern experience with total war, which cannot be prepared for or conducted without a total mobilization of all nonmilitary resources—ranging from steel production to the media—long before the actual outbreak of hostilities. Sometimes, of course, these nonmilitary provisions and institutions represent their drafters' hopes that the alliance or loose confederal association will evolve into a real federation. During the cold war in the fifties, for instance, some enthusiastic "Atlantists" on both sides of the ocean promoted NATO as a possible first step toward a federal union of the United States with a federated Western Europe.

When, on the other hand, we examine modern emphatically nonmilitary and purely functional associations, however specific and technical their task, their charters or personnel often affirm that their functional activities contribute to the maintenance of peace and order among sovereign nations. The charter of the United Nations Educational, Scientific, and Cultural Organization (UNESCO) in Paris expresses the hope that it will "contribute to peace and security by promoting collaboration among the nations through education, science, and culture." The plausible argument is that wars start in the minds of people. The International Labour Organisation (ILO) in Geneva aims, according to its charter, at contributing to the establishment of universal and lasting peace through the promotion of social justice.

The Charter of the World Health Organization (WHO) in Geneva describes its objective as "the attainment by all peoples of a level of health that—as the General Assembly expressed it in 1977—will permit them to lead a socially and economically productive life." When a blueprint for "health for all by the year 2000" was drawn up, nutrition, safe water supply, communicable disease control, and research in applying the existing knowledge to health problems of developing countries were identified as priority areas. The various programs and activities of WHO are expected to contribute to the maintenance of international social and political peace. The Preamble of the Food and Agriculture Organization (FAO) in Rome wishes "to raise levels of nutrition and standards of living, the efficiency of production and distribution of all agricultural products and thus to contribute towards an expanding world economy"—and so, as an economic determinist may believe, to peace.

The International Atomic Energy Agency (IAEA) in Vienna has the tasks of furthering peaceful uses of nuclear energy and radioisotopes in various fields and of ensuring that the assistance it provides is not used for military purposes. The commencement on March 5, 1970, of the Treaty on the Non-Proliferation of Nuclear Weapons (NPT) gave additional support to the application of international safeguards. In order to detect diversion of nuclear materials for military purposes, the agency has set up a safeguard system that is based on material accountancy as verified by IAEA inspectors.

In summary, whether explicitly (as in the case of UNESCO) or implicitly (as in some other cases), the charters and working resolutions of all international functional organizations express the hope that cooperation among nations in functional fields is not only beneficial for its own sake, but bound to have important political by-products. Worldwide progress in education, science, culture, social justice, health, standards of living, and peaceful uses of nuclear energy is expected not only to improve the life and well-being of billions but also to favorably influence the behavior of national governments on the diplomatic and military levels. The expected transfer of the habits of cooperation in functional fields onto the political level—the so-called functional spill-overs—is a central assumption of "functionalism," a popular approach to peace among sovereign nations. In Louis A. McCall's words, "functionalism is basically a strategy to subvert the resistance of the nation-state to a massive surrender of sovereignty through a program of integration by stealth."[2]

The foremost believer in a beneficial politicization of the various, initially seemingly noncontroversial, technical issues was David Mitrany.[3] Mitrany explicitly linked the pragmatic development of special-purpose functional organizations to the promotion of peace and prevention of wars. In his view:

> The problem of our time is not how to keep nations peacefully apart but how to bring them together. . . . Sovereignty cannot in fact be transferred effectively through a formula, only through a function. By entrusting an authority with a certain task, carrying with it command over the requisite powers and means, a slice of sovereignty is transferred from the old authority to the new; and the accumulation of such partial transfers in time brings about a translation of the true seat of authority.[4]

Mitrany hypothesized that the development of successive webs of intersovereign functional activities and agencies—and the resulting habits of international cooperation—would overlay political and ideological divisions among nations and lead to their gradual integration, or as Mitrany called it, "federalism by installments."[5] The growing usefulness of functional agencies would thus transfer both national sovereignties and loyalties to the world community. In Mitrany's opinion, international cooperation is "more likely to grow through doing things together in workshop and market place than signing pacts in chancelleries."[6]

Do functional associations of sovereign states fit Mitrany's thesis? The hopes associated with their potential for a transformation into federations could endow comparative analysis with a great deal of optimism—*provided*, of course, that the functional approach to international peace is valid, especially in its central expectation that international functional activities will reduce or eliminate political conflicts among nations instead of being curtailed or eliminated by such conflicts. As the present experience with the various functional organizations indicates, it is usually politics that determines the scope and intensity of functional activities, not the other way around. In his critical examination of functionalism, Inis L. Claude, Jr., expressed his doubts about functionalist hopes for "peace by pieces" as follows:

> The record to date indicates that functional activity is, at least in the short run, more dependent upon the political weather than determinative of political weather. . . . Is it in fact possible to segregate a group of problems and subject them to treatment in an international workshop where the nations

shed their conflicts at the door and busy themselves only with the cooperative use of the tools of mutual interest? Does not this assumption fly in the face of the evidence that a trend toward the politicization of all issues is operative in the twentieth century? . . . We may ask whether states can in fact be induced to join hands in functional endeavor before they have settled the outstanding political and security issues which divide them. Functionalism's insistence upon putting first things first does not settle the matter of what things are first.[7].

Furthermore, new economic and social problems and their international dimensions cause new tensions and conflicts that require nontechnical, political solutions and accommodation.

The phenomenal growth of functional associations since World War II, which group sovereign nations into cooperative frameworks around specific economic, social, and technical issues *despite* their political conflicts, suggests that perhaps the question, Functionalism or politics first? has been too inflexibly posed since it limits the answer to one or the other of the two mutually exclusive alternatives. As the record of the past decades shows, functional cooperation in some areas does not exclude simultaneous political conflicts in other areas—just as political harmony among some nations does not exclude new conflicts in the economic, social, and technical fields. The simultaneity and inevitability of *both* conflict and cooperation deprive the overall picture of clarity and neatness—but after all, this is how life among men and nations has always been. It has always resisted geometrically precise delineations.

Explicit Retention of Territorial Sovereignty

A major confederal theme that characterizes all associations of territorial states is their emphatic assertion of sovereign self-rule to be protected against any interference in domestic affairs by the common institutions. The guarantees of territorial sovereignty are usually contained in the introductory articles of a confederal compact and precede all the other stipulations concerning the goals and operations of the association. Article 2 of the American confederation stated: "Each State retains its sovereignty, freedom and independence, and every Power, Jurisdiction and right, which is not by this confederation expressly delegated to the United States in Congress assembled." This article, which was first presented in the form of an amendment of the draft of the Articles of Confederation by Thomas Burke, was clearly meant to qualify and limit Article 3, which proclaimed the need for a firm league for the purposes of common defense and mutual and general welfare—the last broad term potentially permitting an extension of delegated powers by imaginative interpretation.

In the context of eighteenth-century America, the fear of any extension of centralized power reflected the preceding colonial experience with a royal power that had enforced its will on separate colonial governments by vetoing local legislation and reviewing judicial decisions. As already noted, there was a widely held conviction that any governing authority could be made truly responsive and responsible to the people only within the confines of a *small* community. In addition, there apparently was also a conservative assumption that there is a streak of evil in all sinful men in our fallen world, especially in those engaged in the pursuit and exercise of political power: The greater and the more concentrated the power, the greater the potential for corruption. In his letter to Governor Richard Carswell of North Carolina (March 11, 1777), Thomas Burke the author of the key confederal article on sovereignty, expressed his "devil theory" of political power with eloquence: "Power of all kinds has an Irresistible propensity to increase a desire for itself. It gives the Passion of ambition a Velocity which Increases in its progress, and this is a passion which grows in proportion as it is gratified.[8] According to this view, neither the states nor the confederation could be expected to be governed by angels. The provisions for annual elections, short terms of office, and frequent rotations of office were all manifestations of this basic fear of unchecked power.

If ambitions and intents of fellow Americans in charge of the confederation were so dreaded, even at the time of their common struggle against the former homeland, what can we expect from nations and their leaders who have to fend against foreign and often malicious or voracious adversaries? Thus, even in 1945, in the wake of their common struggle against their enemies, the founding members of the United Nations—initially a fighting alliance against a common foe and not yet a universal association of states— placed the guarantees of sovereignty and non-interference ahead of all the other operational provisions of the charter. Article 2 (on principles of the United Nations) states, "Nothing contained in the present Charter shall authorize the United Nations to intervene in matters which are essentially within the domestic jurisdiction of any state."

This provision placed a broad limitation on the authority of the United Nations Organization. In a way similar to the Articles of Confederation, certain matters were to be excluded from the competence of the United Nations. The term "essentially" (not "exclusively") is ambiguous; ever since the charter was written, the member nations have tended to interpret the article rather narrowly in terms of the UN jurisdiction and rather broadly in terms of their territorial autonomy and sovereignty, which today extends also to adjacent sea and air space above territories and territorial waters. The interdiction of interference applies also to the jurisdiction of the functional organizations of the United Nations. UNESCO, for example, can make recommendations to its members, but they are not required to abide by them. UNESCO's Convention prohibits the organization from interfering in the domestic educational, scientific, and cultural policies and practices of a member state. UNESCO cannot even carry on a survey or establish a cultural or on educational project in a country except at the explicit request and with the cooperation of the government of that state.

The principle of noninterference is only an operational extension of the central concept of sovereignty. Article 2 of the United Nations Charter begins: "The Organization and its Members, in pursuit of the Purposes stated in Article 1, shall act in accordance with the following Principles. 1. The Organization is based on the principle of the sovereign equality of all its Members."

The combination of the terms "sovereign" and "equality" is not fortuitous. In spite of their inequality in power, wealth, size, and population, nations claim to be legally equal because, in principle, they are all equally sovereign. But are they really? Is a small and weak nation, dependent for its survival on trade with (or lack of territorial ambitions on the part of) a mighty neighbor really independent in framing its foreign and domestic policies? A superpower casts a shadow on the line that separates the fiction of sovereign equality in law from dependence owing to inequality in fact. In his comments on the issue of independence and mutual dependence of the thirteen united states, Andrew C. McLaughlin expressed an opinion that, to a large extent, applies to present-day nation-states.

> One cannot very well ignore the word "sovereignty" in the Articles; but one cannot be absolutely sure of the meaning of the word in the minds of men that used it; and one cannot, on the other hand, blind one's eyes to the fact that the states announcing their sovereignty were incompetent to act individually as completely self-reliant members of the family of nations.[9]

Today, in our era of complex interdependence, few, if any, nations are *completely* self-reliant and competent.

Starting with the principle of sovereign equality, political leaders and their legal advisers have developed and successfully promoted another general principle, *equal votes by unequal units*—an important issue in confederal America and ever since. The concept of equal votes by unequal territorial communities only partly reflects democratic idealism; it also partly reflects territorial sovereignty or nationalism and the often justified suspicion of voting by foreigners. Article 18 of the UN Charter therefore provides that "each member of the General Assembly shall have one vote." (Similarly, Article 5 of the Articles of Confederation stipulated that "in determining questions in the united states, in Congress assembled, each state shall have one vote.")

In some cases, the principle of sovereign equality has produced the requirement of unanimous decisions. The ensuing paralyzing effect of a veto power thus being granted to every unit could be overcome—as in practice it often is—by consociational procedures, that is, a search for consensus by means of interelite negotiations. If such a consensus cannot be obtained, the paralyzing effect of a single veto applies fully. Under the Articles of Confederation, for example, unanimity was required to amend the original compact. In 1782, the then smallest state of the confederation, Rhode Island, blocked an amendment that would have given the union the right to levy and collect a 5 percent duty on foreign imports and thus, by a limited direct taxation, help the financial state of the confederation. Four years later, in 1786, a New York veto prevented a new version of the same amendment from being accepted by the confederation.

As is true with any other myth, the fiction of sovereign equality can become operative if all concerned decide to agree on the principle—even though they know better—because they consider it preferable to any other alternative. Indeed, if the principle of equality of all nations is rejected, what other yardsticks of their relative power and voting rights would they agree on? Can sovereign units decide sovereignly to be less sovereign and pass on a slice of their sovereignty by agreeing to accept collective decisions made by the majority? Can territorial communities also sovereignly decide to submit even to unequal, that is, weighted, votes in some issues and so, in regard to these issues, become less equal? Many studies have been written on the subject of the indivisibility or divisibility of sovereignty and on supreme power that can become less than supreme, but there is no legal or philosophical consensus on this issue among sovereign nations. A modern international counterpart to the Connecticut Compromise is hard to imagine.

Nevertheless, whatever the final answers to these questions, in practice, sovereign nations have sometimes found it either convenient or unavoidable to submit to the majority or even weighted votes and accept their morally or legally binding character. In decisions concerning vital issues of national security and well-being, such an acceptance has been quite rare, reluctant, and usually replete with decisive reservations or escape valves.

In the American confederation, important questions were decided by a majority of nine states while procedural and routine matters were decided by a simple majority. Similarly, in the Organization of American States, a two-thirds majority on the vital issues of war or peace is required and accepted, although military sanctions can never be made obligatory. In principle, therefore, the United States (a veto-holding superpower in the United Nations) could be obligated in the OAS by a two-thirds majority decision to adopt a position that it had opposed by words and vote—quite an unusual provision subjecting a superpower to a numerical majority of minor states. Optimists might see in it a beginning of democratic voting procedures among sovereign nations with a federal potential. Skeptics might argue that the United States, in accepting such a majoritarian limitation on its sovereignty, has risked very little since it would always be able to combine with at least one-third of the Latin American states and so defeat a decision it deemed contrary to its national interests. And, of course, withdrawal is always a possibility.

The United Nations and Its Pseudoconfederal Features

The term "pseudoconfederal" is used here in order to contrast the United Nations organization with other loose confederations whose true aim it is to solve inter-member conflicts. At the United Nations many members do not primarily participate to solve but to publicize, and so exacerbate conflicts.

Many member states do so by speech-making and vote-taking. To paraphrase Walter Lippman, voting with such an offensive goal is indeed "war" by ballots instead of bullets—usually leading to a stalemate, which, of course, is still better than "solution" by violent means.

In the United Nations General Assembly, decisions on important questions are made by a two-thirds majority of the members present and voting (Article 18). According to the charter, important questions are recommendations with respect to the maintenance of international peace and security; the admission of new member states; suspension of membership; expulsion of members; budgetary questions; and election of ten members to the Security Council (the other five are permanent members who need not be elected, that is, the five great powers), all members of the Economic and Social Council, and nonadministering members of the Trusteeship Council. All other questions, deemed procedural, require only a simple majority—including the determination whether some questions should require a two-thirds majority.

In the General Assembly, then, the difference between superpowers and microstates apparently disappears; all have but one vote (with the exception of the Soviet Union and its three votes: the USSR, Ukraine, and Byelorussia). So, for example, the People's Republic of China, with more than a billion people can be outvoted by the two votes of Bahrain and Barbados, even though the combined population of these two voting members of the United Nations (Bahrain 200,000 and Barbados 260,000 inhabitants) corresponds to less than one-fifth of one of New York City's boroughs, Brooklyn. The seemingly idyllic image of a democratic majority of votes cast by unequal member nations entitled to one vote each has to be qualified by two observations.

First, except for some "housekeeping" issues, such as acceptance of the budget and instructions to the Secretariat, the decisions of the General Assembly are not *legally* binding—they are not deemed binding even upon those countries who voted for them. In fact, they are not decisions at all, but (strong) recommendations, resolutions, permissions, legitimizations (for example, approvals of an "observer" status for nonsovereign communities such as the P.L.O.), or authorizations. These "decisions" cannot therefore affect the sovereign power of any voting nation to determine for itself what is and what is not in its national interest. The resolutions and recommendations of the General Assembly have, at best, some moral value, which in our world does not mean very much. Recent attempts on the part of Third World nations to endow the resolutions of the General Assembly with legal significance—as additions to the body of customary and written international law—have produced more controversy than acceptance.

Second, even if the resolutions were to be considered legally binding, they could not be enforced except by a decision of the Security Council, in which the principle of equal voting powers of unequal nations has been replaced by a voting formula that combines a weighted vote with the majoritarian principle. According to Article 27 of the charter, decisions of

Figure 7.1.

"*I have grave doubts about the success of this conference.*"

Source: Drawing by Richter; copyright 1983 by The New Yorker Magazine, Inc. Reprinted by permission.

the Security Council on substantive matters must be made by an affirmative vote of nine member states out of fifteen, and the nine votes must include the concurring vote of the five great powers (the United States, USSR, China, England, and France). The concurrent vote of the five great powers is also necessary for any amendment of the charter, including the question of who, in addition to the original five, is also "great."

Substantive matters that require unanimity of the five great powers include the decisive powers to determine an act of aggression, the identity of its perpetrator, the nature and scope of economic or military sanctions, and other forms of international enforcement. The negative vote of one great power (the so-called veto power) nullifies a decision, even if agreed to by fourteen of the fifteen members of the Security Council. To express it in less procedural terms: Basically, the UN Charter provides for a world dictatorship by five great powers if and when they are in agreement and for only a permanent diplomatic conference (which may be quite useful) if they are not in agreement. Article 1 aptly describes the world organization as "a center for harmonizing the actions of nations."

Except for Switzerland and the two Koreas, all nations have joined the United Nations and have agreed "to accept and carry out the decisions of the Security Council" (Article 25). Why have they done so? Why have they, though reluctantly, agreed to be treated as less than equal and sovereign in the only organ of the United Nations that can make enforceable decisions?

One reason is they did not have any other choice in 1945, and they do not have one now. None of the five great powers would have joined or remained in the U.N. unless their possible defeats by a bevy of inferior powers had been clearly excluded. Rather than violating an unacceptable decision (or seceding from the United Nations), the great powers evidently preferred to be able to prevent by a negative vote any decision that could adversely affect their major national interests. It is a cold war myth to assert that in 1945 only the Soviet Union insisted on the veto guarantee; the United States and the other great powers insisted on it too.

A second reason is that at that time, and ever since, the possibility of the five great powers ganging up against and imposing a collective dictatorship over the rest of the world seemed remote. If ever the five great powers were to be in full agreement for a prolonged period, they could indeed dictate to the world—through or without the UN Charter. But if they were in conflict, member nations risked very little by agreeing to the great powers' weighted votes. As medium and small nations concluded in 1945, the potential usefulness of a permanent framework for multilateral diplomacy clearly outweighed the remote risk of a five-great-power dictatorship. Only the strictly neutral and legalistically minded Switzerland did not join the world organization, fearing that unanimity on the part of the five great powers could one day force that country to abandon its neutrality by ordering a collective action that would discriminate against the aggressor and favor the victim. Other neutrals did not and do not seem troubled by such a possibility.[10]

In the UN Charter, sovereign nations, ready to accept a limited degree of constant contact and cooperation ("a place to tug the world by the sleeve," a diplomat referred to the UN at the time of its fortieth anniversary in 1985), expressed those facts of international life that they were and are unwilling or unable to alter, hence, the contradictions. The charter simply could not bridge the gap between the claim of the sovereign equality of all nations, as expressed in the General Assembly, and the fact of their extreme inequality, as reflected in the Security Council. From a constitutional point of view, as Hans J. Morgenthau argued, the United Nations system is

> a monstrosity. The United Nations may speak with respect to the same issue with two voices—the General Assembly's and the Security Council's—and between these two there is no organic connection. Two-thirds or more of the total membership of the United Nations may recommend one thing, and nine of the fifteen members of the Security Council may disregard the recommendation and decide something else.[11]

And, one may add, enforce it. By comparison, the American confederation, at its inefficient and insolvent worst, was far more ahead in terms of its unity of purpose and action two centuries ago than the United Nations Organization and its functional affiliates are today.

Other examples of weighted votes in international organizations can be found in the International Monetary Fund (IMF) and the World Bank, in which voting powers are related to the contributions of the participating nations. The largest contributors are the financially powerful Western nations—a situation that medium and small nations, particularly those of the Third World, resent and try to alter with minimal hope for success. If the recipient poor nations were to insist on equal voting rights, the result would be an empty treasury since the financial superpowers would refuse to be subject to "taxation" without adequate representation. The unavoidable, though quite unpleasant, alternative for poor nations is to have the treasury replenished and accept the proposition that those nations that contribute the most have a proportionate influence on the flow of the money. In the IMF, for example, where all decisive power is basically vested in the board of governors, voting powers are approximately in proportion to the size of the quota of the member states the governors represent.

The authorized capital of the International Bank for Reconstruction and Development (World Bank) is $10 billion. The capital stock is divided into shares of $100,000 each, available for subscription only to members and transferable only to the World Bank. The smallest subscription is for 2 shares of stock; that of the United States is the largest, 31,750 shares. As everywhere else, financial supremacy translates easily into a political and managerial one. Similarly, in the European Economic Community, the smaller nations (Belgium, Denmark, Greece, Ireland, Luxembourg, and the Netherlands) had to agree that the four major powers—Great Britain, France, West Germany and Italy—will have more votes than the smaller ones.

Weighted votes in international associations are in fact more frequent than the national leaders' rhetoric on the subject of sovereignty and equality would suggest.

Limited Delegation of Powers—Absence of Direct Taxation

Two other confederal themes are present in intergovernmental organizations. When sovereign nations become aware of their common interests yet insist on their territorial sovereignty and independent self-rule, they agree to delegate only so much power to the common pool as the common handling of selected specific issues and coordination of component actions may require. Generally, nations prefer to err on the side of caution. Powers that are not expressly delegated are retained by the territorial components. A general "elastic clause," such as is found in Article 1, section 8 of the U.S. Constitution, is unacceptable to a confederalist. The federal elastic clause in the 1789 Constitution follows the enumeration of seventeen grants of power to the federal government and authorizes the Congress "to make all laws which shall be necessary and proper for carrying into execution the foregoing powers." The terms "necessary" and "proper" can be understood and interpreted as meaning "convenient and useful," which would run contrary to the confederal principles of functional specificity and inviolable sovereignty of the territorial components.

The Articles of Confederation of 1781 did transfer to the assembly of state delegates a number of significant powers, the most important of which was the power to conduct defense and foreign policies, including the appointment of all superior army and naval officers in the service of the United States. The confederal assembly (the united states in Congress assembled) had no executive branch and had to handle these various confederal tasks through cumbersome congressional committees. Even before the Articles were ratified, however, a rudimentary executive machinery began to emerge to manage confederal affairs such as diplomacy, military affairs, and finance. For example, the Congress created a department of foreign affairs in January 1781, and in February, the departments of war and finance—each run by one person responsible to Congress and holding office during its pleasure.[12]

Despite these deviations in practice (deviations anticipating, as it were, the future federal structures), confederal decisions were implemented by the enforcement agencies of the component units on the basis of their apportioned contribution ("quotas of men and charges" of the various states). Confederal decisions could not be imposed on the inhabitants of the component states; nor could their inhabitants be taxed directly by the confederation. These provisions were also directly related to the absence of a common confederal citizenship.

The absence of direct taxation—which so decisively undermined the confederation—has similarly plagued all contemporary international associations. Whether global, regional, or functional, they all experience constant budgetary crises. Of course, one may ask, Who doesn't? Budgetary crises are certainly not unique to confederal systems. Nor is the intimate relationship between finance and politics unique. Technical financial arrangements tend to become politicized, and political issues acquire financial dimensions. Nevertheless, in confederal systems, budgetary problems have two characteristic features: One is the right of the confederal components not to be assessed without their consent; second is the effective resistance of the rich and large to making contributions that, in some ways, would not be proportionate to their political or administrative clout in the organization (for example, proportionate to the number of nationals employed in the confederal structure). Tensions surrounding collective expenditures are regular features of the confederal way of life in the United Nations, NATO, the European Community, and the Warsaw Pact Organization.

In terms similar to the Articles of Confederation, the UN Charter (Article 17, section 2) states that "the expenses of the Organization shall be borne by the Members as apportioned by the General Assembly." In the United Nations Organization, member states contribute to the general budget and working capital fund on a scale determined by the General Assembly *with the assent of members concerned* (a typical confederal feature) on the recommendation of the Administrative and Budgetary (Fifth) Committee. Since 1974, the United Nations Organization has had a biennial program budget, which is drafted in the framework of a four-year plan in order to provide the member nations with a comprehensive picture of its nature, scope, and objectives. The budget is essentially financed from assessed contributions of member states following a scale of assessment that ranges from less than 1 percent of the budget for the overwhelming majority of nations (142) to more than 1 percent (18 nations). The United States contributes most of all (25 percent); the Soviet Union is second (11.6 percent). When it comes to financial contributions to the United Nations, the Soviet Union exhibits an atypical modesty: It has never claimed that its socialist economic system was superior to, more productive—and therefore internationally more "taxable"—than U.S. capitalism.

In the European Communities, the cost of running the institutions is subject to approval by the European Parliament. In 1981, the Parliament voted some additional spending, thus apparently exceeding its limited powers in budgetary matters. Jealous of its sovereignty, France blocked the parliamentary action, fearing that it would be a precedent that would lead to a federal union and direct taxing powers. Another example of a highly politicized budgetary crisis is the annual NATO ritual in which West Europeans keep on pleading, singly or collectively, poverty or domestic electoral difficulty in order to resist U.S. prodding for them to contribute more money, arms, and men against the common Soviet threat.

Similar arguments could be, of course, heard in both colonial and then confederal America. In colonial times, for example, with regard to a common action against the French, Virginia pleaded poverty and argued that its security was not dependent on that of New York, which had pressed the other colonies for a common stand and larger contributions. In reply to similar New York pressures, Connecticut intimated that New York alone ought to carry the burden of opposing the French: "You have a large trade; we have not. We live by hard labour at the earth."[13]

In 1781, the finally ratified Articles of Confederation denied the Congress the right to raise any money by direct taxation and kept that decisive financial and political power in the hands of the individual states. This decision reflected the then (and presently still valid) recognition that the power to direct public money is "the center of gravity, for it will eventually draw into its vortex all the other powers"—thus wrote Abraham Yates in the *New York Packet*, April 21, 1785.[14]

If one listened attentively, one could perhaps detect a distant echo of this statement during the final phases of the Law of the Sea Conference in 1980. The purpose of the conference was to establish a new international regime concerning the navigation and exploitation of oceans and seas. Over 150 nations strenuously negotiated a tax code down to the decimal place to finance the proposed new International Seabed Authority to license and regulate seabed mining. This detailed and time-consuming work was done to prevent the future central authority from assuming any discretionary taxing power. To be on the safe side, Reagan's government decided in 1984 not to ratify the treaty, the main objection being not only the taxing power but the general jurisdiction of the Seabed Authority.

As mentioned previously, the right to leave a confederal association is characteristic of any intersovereign framework. What else can sovereignty, the supreme authority to either accede or secede, mean? By contrast, a federation is deemed perpetual since it is committed to building and maintaining a union, a "federal nation." Many comparative studies actually distinguish between confederal and federal systems on the basis of the "secession" criterion. Nevertheless, history and contemporary practice offer blurred evidence on this point.[15]

Collective Rights of Self-Definition,
Self-Determination, and Secession

In contrast to individual rights and liberties, *group* rights and the concept of territorial interest groups as "rights-and-duties bearing communities" have been somewhat less studied, articulated, and defended—except, of course, in the studies of federalism, confederalism, and interest groups.[16] In the traditional liberal framework, the emphasis is on the protection of individual rights *against* the state in the areas of personal liberties or on active protection *by* the state in the area of economic, social, and educational guarantees. Any analysis of consociational, confederal, or federal systems necessarily includes the protection of *collective* dignity and *collective* political and economic rights of territorial communities found in contact, conflict, and cooperation with other territorial units. The group right to be collectively free, secure, and respected is an integral part of the right of national self-definition, self-determination, and self-rule. On the international scene, it simply means the right to determine one's own place in the system of sovereign states, that is, the right to independent statehood by means of secession or the right to an associated status by means of accession to a federation or a confederation.

Article 13 of the confederation, grouped the former colonies, then sovereign states, into a "perpetual union." This explicit constitutional commitment to perpetuity does not appear *verbatim* in the federal constitution, which, however, promises "a more perfect union"; Appomattox in 1865 rather than any specific article in the constitution settled the right of secession in the U.S. context. Some other federal systems, however, have recognized, at least on paper, the right of secession. Such was the case in the first Burmese federal constitution of 1947 and still is the case in the Soviet Constitution (in both the Stalin and Brezhnev versions as discussed in Chapter 5).

In contemporary alliance treaties, whether their duration is deemed permanent or limited, there are provisions permitting withdrawal by member nations, following some prescribed procedures. In the Organization of American States, for example, Article 112 proclaims that the "present Charter shall remain in force indefinitely, but may be denounced by any Member State upon written notification to the Pan-American Union [which serves as a Permanent Secretariat of the Organization]." No nation has as yet left the OAS voluntarily; Cuba was suspended in 1962.

In the North Atlantic Treaty Organization, Article 13 provides for a twenty-year renewable duration after which "any Party may cease to be a party one year after its notice of denunciation has been given to the Government of the United States." In 1966, France withdrew its military forces from NATO and forced the removal of NATO headquarters and facilities from its soil in 1967. These actions were taken under President Charles de Gaulle, who had feared a U.S. domination of Western Europe through NATO. In 1981, the British Labour party committed itself to withdrawal from the European Community in case the British socialists accede to power.

The Warsaw Pact Organization (Article 11) which is supposed to remain in force until May 15, 2005, stipulates the condition for withdrawal as follows: "For such Contracting Parties as do not at least one year before the expiration of this period present to the Government of the Polish People's Republic a statement of denunciation of the Treaty, it shall remain in force for the next twenty years." Although the military alliance of the communist states is the most tightly organized system, in 1961 Albania, then an ally of China, withdrew from the Warsaw Pact in protest against the Soviet domination of the "Socialist Commonwealth." There is no evidence that anyone bothered to follow the above-quoted procedures prescribed by Article 11 of the treaty.

In the United Nations Organization and its related specialized agencies, withdrawals are quite simple though not frequent. In 1965, Indonesia became the first nation to announce its withdrawal from the world organization on account of a dispute with its neighbor, Malaysia, another member nation. Two years later, following a military coup d'etat and a change in its foreign policy, Indonesia rejoined the United Nations. A very permissive provision for withdrawal may be found in Article 10 of the Treaty on the Non-Proliferation of Nuclear Weapons (1970): "Each Party shall in exercising its national sovereignty have the right to withdraw from the Treaty if it decided that *extraordinary* events, related to the subject matter of this Treaty, have jeopardized the supreme interests of its country" (italics added). Is there any yardstick that can tell us what is extraordinary, exceptional, off the beaten track, unordinary, uncustomary, unprecedented, out of the ordinary, weird, inusitate, beyond the pale—or any other nuance?

Conflicting Impacts of Interdependence

Do the elites and their supporters remain stubbornly nationalist by inertia *in spite of* their awareness of the interlocking nature of their and other nations' interests? Or do they reassert their self-centered nationalism because of their awareness of interdependence among nations and its possible consequences? Both inertia and new fears play their role. Although mutual dependence should, in principle, lead to closer regional or global cooperation, it also induces fears of possible domination and exploitation. These fears are often quite justified since interdependence among nations is so asymmetric. Asymmetry in an anarchic, that is, an unorganized, system of states invites economic or strategic ambitions and so necessarily provokes corresponding fears and anticipatory defenses.

As the preceding analysis indicates, there is not much hope that the constitutional history of the United States, with its two-act confederal-to-federal scenario, could repeat itself soon on the global scene. If it contains any valid lessons for the future, it shows that livable life—not a utopian paradise, of course—has never been the result of a single sweeping formula or a single revolutionary stroke. Within national communities, consensus and order have been built, step by step, by constant, patient, often tedious accommodation, ever so often interrupted by passion, irrationality, or violence. It cannot be otherwise on a larger than national scale. In this slow and gradual process of attempting to achieve a higher degree of mutuality, confederal associations of states represent, not a solution but some of the necessary steps in the right direction. For the time being, nations and their leaders seem ready to support international cooperative structures only insofar as they are deemed directly helpful in achieving their own national objectives: nothing more and nothing less. There is no evidence of any significant emergence of a supranational spirit or global mystique.

Present-day cooperative associations among sovereign nations represent a contemporary balance between globalism and territorialism, and between the desire for smallness and the imperatives of large-scale perspectives.

Modern consociations of sovereignties reflect what today is feasible, not what ultimately may be desirable.

Notes

1. Reinhold Niebuhr, "The Myth of World Government," *Nation* 152 (March 16, 1946), p. 314.

2. Louis A. McCall, *Regional Integration: A Comparison of European and Central American Dynamics* (Beverly Hills, Calif.: Sage, 1976), p. 8.

3. David Mitrany, *A Working Peace System* (Chicago: Quadrangle Books, 1966).

4. Ibid., p. 25.

5. Ibid., p. 83.

6. Ibid., p. 7.

7. Inis L. Claude, Jr., *Swords into Plowshares: The Problems and Progress of International Organization* (New York: Random House, 1970), pp. 353–354, 367.

8. Edmund C. Burnett, ed., *Letters of Members of the Continental Congress*, 8 vol. (Washington, D.C., 1921–1936) 2:294.

9. Andrew C. McLaughlin, *A Constitutional History of the United States* (New York: Appleton-Century, 1935), pp. 134–135.

10. A more detailed analysis of these issues may be found in Ivo D. Duchacek, *Nations and Men: An Introduction to International Politics*, 3d ed. (New York: Holt, Rinehart and Winston, 1975), pp. 22–23, 363–366.

11. Hans J. Morgenthau, *Politics Among Nations*, 5th ed. (New York: Knopf, 1973), p. 458.

12. For details, see Edmund S. Morgan, *The Birth of the Republic 1763–1789* (Chicago: University of Chicago Press, 1956), pp. 113–118.

13. Herbert Osgood, *The American Colonies in the Eighteenth Century*, 1924 reprint (Gloucester, Mass.: Peter Smith, 1958), vol. 1, pp. 233–234, 345.

14. As quoted by Jackson Turner Main, *The Antifederalists: Critics of the Constitution, 1781–1789* (Chapel Hill: University of North Carolina Press, 1961) p. 79.

15. Portions of this and the preceding chapter are substantially revised versions of Ivo D. Duchacek, "Consociations of Fatherlands: The Revival of Confederal Principles and Practices" (Paper presented at conference, The Continuing Legacy of Articles of Confederation, sponsored by the Liberty Fund and Center for the Study of Federalism, Temple University, Philadelphia, August 30–September 2, 1981); a shorter version was published in *Publius* 12 (Fall 1982), pp. 129–177.

16. A controversy concerning the very existence of group rights emerged in Québec in connection with the decision of the High Court of Québec that declared Québec Law 101 on the French language unconstitutional insofar as it prohibited bilingual advertisements (December 28, 1984). The then-Québec minister of intergovernmental affairs, Pierre-Marc Johnson, opposed the judgment and declared that the Court had to deal not only with a conflict of two laws but also with a clash between group rights (Law 101) and individual rights (promoted by the Québec Charter of Rights and Liberties). Johnson added that the anglophone society devoted to individual rights found itself in conflict with the group-rights-oriented francophones. This statement led to a controversy in which a member of the Québec legislature,

Pierre de Bellefeuille, opposed the very concept of collective rights since, as he argued, even a minority right is necessarily addressed to the individuals composing that community. Bellefeuille also expressed his fear that the emphasis on group rights would prove harmful to individual rights promoted since the French Revolution began in 1789 (*Le Devoir* [February 22, 1985]).

Part 4
Permeable Sovereignties

8

Percolation of Sovereign Boundaries

Sieve: a device with meshes or perforations through which finer particles of a mixture (as of ashes, flour, or sand) of various sizes are passed to separate them from coarser ones.
—Webster's New Collegiate Dictionary

Technical achievements, which a previous generation had believed capable of solving every ill to which the human flesh is heir, have created, or at least accentuated, our insecurity . . . technics have established a rudimentary world community but have not integrated it organically, morally, or politically. They have created a community of mutual dependence, but not one of mutual trust and respect. Without this higher integration, advancing technics tend to sharpen economic rivalries within a general framework of economic interdependence; they change the ocean barriers of yesterday into the battlegrounds of today.
—Reinhold Niebuhr
(Christian Realism and Political Problems, 1953)

The phenomenon of states seeking to intensify efforts at peaceful, joint management of national concerns is certainly alive, if not always well. Moreover, these efforts continue to take place in organizations and communities which define themselves as "regional." . . . They take the place of the previous order of competitive states within their regions. . . . If the institutional outcome is but a greater state subsuming the states it replaces, regional entities will not constitute a new order in world politics.
—Ernst B. Haas ("Turbulent Fields
and the Theory of Regional Integration," 1975)

The confluence of new structures and old patterns has resulted in self-generating and far-reaching dimensions of global life that are so recurrent as to amount to an overall pattern of disorder, one that can usefully be called Cascading Interdependence. . . . Gone is the relative tidiness provided by historic jurisdictions and stable polities, by legal precedents and accepted procedures, by shared values and cultural continuities. . . . Shortages in energy, food, water, lumber, and other resources now routinely and quickly make their way . . . along the causal chains that link the structures of world politics. . . . Direct and unavoidable conflicts between internal and external demands are now surfacing in new arenas far removed from guns-or-butter issues.
—James N. Rosenau
("A Pre-Theory Revisited: World Politics
in an Era of Cascading Interdependence," 1985)

The territorial compartmentalization of humanity is now being—and has always been—challenged frontally by two alternative propositions and ideals: globalism and regionalism. Their aim is basically, in the name of humanity and peace, to tear the territorial fences down either globally or regionally. Always present in reformist rhetoric, and occasionally attempted, neither globalism nor regionalism has significantly eroded the territorial segmentation of our planet.

By *globalism*, or universalism, I mean the various doctrines, movements, and organizations that promote world unity to replace the millennia-old divisions and subdivisions of the planet into mutually suspicious and competing territorial compartments. Supranational (one-world) themes have been articulated by religious bodies and their leaders, anational ideologies and their idealistic adherents, messianic reformers, gurus, and professors of international law who have already written detailed texts of future world constitutions.[1]

The cumulative effect over time of such supranational exhortations on various audiences, fenced into their respective territorial habitats, is difficult to gauge, but it seems that even in our era of global interdependence, nearly instant communications and universal fear of nuclear homicide/suicide have not succeeded in transposing the concept of global supranationalism from the pulpits and academic periphery onto the desks of political decision makers and into the minds of the general public. More than thirty years ago a Protestant theologian, Reinhold Niebuhr (also quoted in one of the epigraphs to this chapter) wisely noted:

> Virtually all arguments for world government rest upon the simple presupposition that the desirability of world order proves the attainability of world government. . . . While a single sovereignty may be the final and indispensable instrument of a common community, it is not possible to achieve unity by the power of the government alone. Government may be the head of the body, which without a single head could not be, or become, a single body, but it is not possible for a head to create a body.[2]

Chapter 2, dealing with the domestication of supranational creeds, notes with melancholy that religious doctrines as well as internationalist ideologies have been subject to various degrees of territorial expropriation and transmutation. By immigration westward, the Greek Zeus and Ares became Roman Jupiter and Mars, respectively, and with them, the whole Greek pantheon was latinized; neither have Jesus Christ or Allah (and even less so Marx and Lenin) quite avoided territorial/national attempts at expropriation.

Universalistic challenges to the territorial framework of politics and creeds have to be necessarily promoted from within particular territorial states and not by some supranational outer-space station, unblemished by territorial habit, practice, ambition, and suspicion. As a consequence, territorial authorities and their publics often tend to treat many a supranational enthusiast as either a naive tool or a crafty agent of a territorial government that may use universal themes for territorial or expansionist purposes (for example, the Nazi and then Soviet support of disarmament and peace movements). We may well be here in the presence of a planetary Catch 22: Every antiterritorial exhortation carries with it its territorial imprint and may therefore be suspected and resisted on this account—sometimes correctly so.

Regionalism, when considered as a doctrine "has been closely tied," as Richard Falk and Saul Mendlovitz expressed it, "with the idea of an association of states, linked above all, by a condition of geographic proximity"[3]— and, it should be added, an awareness of cultural/economic affinity that conditions the will of separate sovereignties to become, within regional limits, less separate. Common markets, transborder cooperative zones, and defense communities are examples of such regional attempts at integration of territorial sovereignties. As noted in the preceding chapter, West European communities and their elaborate institutional frameworks, based on common cultural heritage and developed economies, well illustrate the achievements and hopes as well as the limits of regionalism. The ups and downs of West European regional integration have demonstrated how difficult it is to overcome territorial fission and replace it with regional fusion.

In the framework of this study, as Ernst B. Haas warns us in one of the epigraphs to this chapter, a suprasovereign regional community, even if it were to attain its goal, would basically challenge only the *size* of the existing territorial units, not the principle of territorial delineation itself. A regional union is rarely, if ever, viewed by its architects as a stepping-stone to global unity. Every so often an aggregate power and intraregional integration are asserted and buttressed against other regional blocs (for example, Western Europe against both the Soviet bloc and the United States). At the end of World War II, the English historian, Edward H. Carr, correctly warned us: "A division of the world into a small number of large multinational units . . . would be simply the old [territorial] nationalism writ large."[4]

A world divided into five or ten regions may, in fact or in Orwellian fiction, become more dangerous on account of the inflexibility of an interregional world system in which a limited number of actors may face each other in a few narrow, zero-sum alleys. It remains, of course, still to be proved that the more flexible shifts of alliances and counteralliances in a 160-unit system, with its labyrinth of confrontational alleys, are really safer.

In his studies of regionalism in general and West European communities in particular, Ernst B. Haas, pointed also to the inevitable competition between regionalism and globalism in an era of universal (not only regional) interdependence:

Integration processes clearly continue, diffused and sidetracked, by the competing process of growing extra-regional enmeshment which may not be integrative in the same sense, or which may lead to a different focus for integration. . . . The paradox of all this is that as we increasingly subordinate the discussion of regional integration to the consideration of overall inter-dependence, we undermine the theoretical and ideological tenets which in the past seemed to point toward increasing regional integration.[5]

Egressive and Ingressive Transborder Flows

Whereas the two frontal challenges to the territorial fragmentation of humanity (with their aim of tearing down sovereign boundaries either globally or at least regionally) have not made much headway, there is another pair of challenges that have affected territorial divisions and practices laterally, as it were, but significantly. For lack of a better term, this study calls these two challenges egressive and ingressive transborder flows.

An *ingressive* flow represents a movement of ideas, persons, products, and pollutants across national boundaries from the inside out; an *egressive* stream of challenges and opportunities—economic, environmental, ideolog-ical, and cultural—flows from the outside in. Neither aims at tearing territorial boundaries down, only at piercing them, leaving them otherwise intact. Thus, while political authority everywhere remains solidly territory-bound, its spatial limits are being perforated by these two inbound and outbound flows, which intermingle, at times reinforcing each other, at times slowing one another down occasionally to a standstill. Both streams, battering at the territorial boundaries separating one national community from another, are only sometimes compatible or cumulative. Quite often, they are com-petitive or mutually intolerant as, for example, the activities of transnational corporations that find themselves in conflict with transborder environmental movements or national governments that sometimes compete with subnational communities and noncentral governments for foreign contacts and support.

Although, in contrast to the frontal challenges of globalism and regionalism, these cross-frontier flows do not aim at eliminating intersovereign barriers, they have caused porosity in such barriers; even the contemporary successors to the ancient Chinese Wall—the Iron and Bamboo Curtains and the Berlin Wall—are no longer what they used to be. The term "sieve" (see first epigraph to this chapter) seems often quite appropriate to describe territorial boundaries in the free world in general and in North America in particular, if I may be allowed to apply a cooking-utensil term to describe such a sacrosanct and time-honored concept as sovereign frontiers. The concept of territorial impermeability has combined with the facts of permeability to produce what may be called international relations among perforated sov-ereignties.[6]

The flow of ideas, products, persons, and pollutants from the inside out represents, in part, responses to external lures or threats; in part, it also reflects internal insufficiencies and needs for which there is no intraterritorial remedy, including the need to satisfy an increase in demands for social and health services and environmental protection as well as keenly experienced contemporary "shortages in energy, food, water, lumber and other resources" as Rosenau points out in one of the epigraphs to this chapter. Thus, welfare expectations in combination with various fiscal and resource shortages induce subnational communities, private enterprises, interest groups, and noncentral governments in democratic federal systems (a new development) to venture into the international arena.

Subnational percolation of national boundaries represents part of the change that James Rosenau called "a world crisis of authority," "cascading interdependence," and "subgroupism." In Rosenau's words:

> The explosion of *subgroupism*, of individuals redefining their loyalties in favor of more close-at-hand collectivities is . . . rooted in a substantial enlargement of the analytic aptitude of citizens throughout the world which, along with a diminished sense of control over the course of their lives, has led individuals to heighten the salience of subgroup affiliations and lessen the relevance of whole system ties, thereby precipitating the authority crisis.[7]

An external flow goes across national boundaries from the outside in and consists of foreign governments' policies and actions—threats and opportunities—that result from and mirror contemporary global and regional interdependence in a highly asymmetric world. Trade opportunities; investment offers; and energy, water, technology, or cultural transfers as well as a migrating labor force, drug traffic, health problems, and air and water pollution are the usual ingredients of ingress streams crossing sovereign boundaries, sometimes at the invitation of, at other times without the permission of, territorial authorities. One way of expressing the contemporary cross-frontier movement is to call the flows: "4-I + 4-P flows"—Ideas-Information-Innovation-Incitement + Products-Persons-Pollutants-Power.

Messages, goods, and persons did get, of course, around the world, crossing many a border on their way long before Johann Gutenberg, Marshal McLuhan, communication satellites, cassettes, and laser beams: Twelve apostles marching on foot and without any electronic equipment proved to be quite an effective group of transborder communicators despite Roman "jamming." Neither did the Westphalian Peace of 1648, which has been credited with the conception and birth of the modern territorial state, prevent various transplants of religious differences across all borders onto other continents.

The present percolations of intersovereign boundaries differ from past ones mostly in terms of intensity and velocity. On the other hand, one should not even today overstate the political impact of the mechanical improvements in and rapidity of cross-frontier communications. The same technology that has facilitated and accelerated transborder communication of messages has also provided territorial authorities with new electronic means of jamming, intercepting, and censoring incoming and outgoing messages; electronic surveillance can effectively impede transnational circulation of news and views. In addition, we should warn against the automatic placing of an equal sign between the technical aspects or contents of signals and messages and understanding among individuals and groups. For example, knowing our neighbors much better and communicating with them more frequently may, in fact, induce us to love them less. Empathy is not necessarily the result of more frequent and intensive contacts.

After the steam engine was invented so that railways began to circle the world and steamships shortened distances between continents, many a brilliant mind forecast a universal love of humankind rising from the smoke of the new locomotives rushing across the borders to their foreign destinations at the astonishing speed of over thirty miles per hour. In the revolutionary year of 1848, Victor Hugo expressed the hope that technical innovations, and in particular the revolution in transportation, might soon bring about a loving commonwealth between a united Europe and a united America, "facing each other and stretching out their hands across the seas in close cooperation." To the thunderous applause of the delegates to the 1849 peace congress in Paris (yes, they had such congresses over 140 years ago), the famous French writer Hugo concluded in the same way that many a speaker at a peace rally concludes today: "What do we need? To love each other."[8] Karl Marx and Friedrich Engels, too, seemed mesmerized by the railroads and incorporated their hopes for the beneficial effects of the locomotives on proletarian unity in their Communist Manifesto of 1848:

> The ever expanding union of the workers . . . is furthered by the improved means of communication which are created by modern industry, and which place the workers of different localities in contact with one another. . . . And that union, to attain which the burghers of the Middle Ages, with their miserable highways, required centuries, the modern proletarians, thanks to railways, achieve in a few years.

(What would have been Marx's and Engels's estimate of the time needed to achieve proletarian unity had they composed their manifesto in our age of jet travel and computers?)

The Curse of Asymmetry

In a world consisting of economic, technological, and military giants and dwarfs, nations overfed and underfed, well led and poorly led, with open and closed systems, ideologically radical and ideologically placid, relatively cohesive and explosively heterogeneous, reasonably secure geographically and highly vulnerable, with temperate and murderous climates, landlocked and with direct access to sea routes and resources, national leaders invoke and occasionally even believe in the legal principles of sovereignty, equality, and independence, but in practice they constantly experience the consequences of asymmetric interdependence. In these multiple asymmetries, only some units can compensate for their deficiencies with other riches; thus, lack of oil may be balanced with food, bauxite with technology, or fertilizers with tourists. But usually, giants are giants on nearly all levels, and dwarfs are dwarfs; it is an unjust world in which the uneven distribution of resources and climate has not been reduced over the centuries but accentuated by human ingenuity.

In such a context of natural and human-induced global inequalities, interdependence (unaccompanied by a radical redistribution of the world's wealth) evokes fears and suspicions of dependence, neocolonialism or "social imperialism" as China calls the promotion and practice of socialist imperial dominance of East Central Europe by Soviet multinational joint enterprises. Interdependence that is so highly asymmetric in terms of resistance to external pressures or blackmail induces territorial states to remain "the most rigid defenders of the principle of national sovereignty."[9] Or, as Samuel P. Huntington cogently argued, "An increase in the number, functions, and scope of transnational organizations will increase the demand for access to national territories and hence also increase the value of the one resource (access) almost exclusively under the control of national governments."[10]

If we were to assume there is a direct causal connection between economic and technological imperatives and the decline of territorial political exclusivity, we would be trapped into wishful thinking like that of the early functionalists who tended to assume an automatic spillover effect of cooperation on the nonpolitical level onto the political level.[11] Economic and technological interaction among nations, though often managed by nonpolitical experts or scientists, experiences considerable difficulty in escaping the magnetic pull of the security, political, and prestige concerns of territorial states, especially those that practice socialist nationalism and have centrally planned and directed economies with their five-year plans. The big "security-brother" watches over the external activities and contacts of his little brethren, the specialists in the economic, ecological, and technological fields.

In the nineteenth century, trade and financial interdependence among the major powers could develop more independently of political rivalries. As Carr argued, there was then a parallelism or a coexistence between a universal "closely knit world economic system," on the one hand, and an "unqualified recognition of the political diversity and independence of nations," on the other. This parallelism was made possible by "two subtle and valuable pieces of make-believe which were largely unconscious and contained sufficient elements of reality to make them plausible." These two helpful illusions were, first, that the world economic system was truly international and, second, that "the economic and political systems were entirely separate and operated independently of each other."[12] In that laissez-faire century, according to Carr, traders, manufacturers, and bankers co-operated transnationally and globally almost free of political motives or constraints; only in extremis were they called to order by their respective national "security managers."

Today, a socialist-authoritarian or military regime can hardly be expected to separate its foreign "high policy" (concerned with defense) from its foreign "low policy" (concerned with such seemingly nonpolitical matters as economy, technology, and ecology). Only if we assume some overwhelming global pressures, resulting from a catastrophic denuding of our planet, may we anticipate a decline in the decisive influence of both socialist and capitalist "security managers" and a corresponding increase of businesslike intimacy between socialist technocrats and directors of socialist enterprises, on the one hand, and their capitalist counterparts, on the other. However important the socialism-capitalism dichotomy may to be, it is not and has never been the only problem in the development of "depoliticized" and strictly functional independence. Even a uniformly socialist but still asymmetric world could not dissipate fears of major-power selfishness, as the Albanian-Soviet, Yugoslav-Soviet, and Rumanian-Soviet tensions demonstrate. Would, for example, the Third World socialist countries dread a socialized General Motors, Exxon, and IBM as instruments of a communist United States less than they do now?

Transnational Corporations

The number, variety, and financial power of contemporary transnational corporations form only one, albeit vehement, ingredient of what is called transborder flows. By transnational corporations, I mean enterprises that control assets—factories, mines, or sales offices—in two or more territorial states. According to the first UN study, completed in 1970, there were 7,500 such corporations; although almost half of them had affiliates in one country only, nearly 200 of the multinational corporations, among the largest in the world, had affiliates in twenty or more countries. As to their financial power, 211 perhaps deserved the label of transnational *gigacorporations* as their annual sales were over $1 billion.[13]

How significant their impact on the territorial divisions of humanity has already been or will eventually be is a matter of controversy. This study has already noted the national-territorial capacity to capture and fence in transnational ideological and religious movements and organizations. Similarly, despite their tremendous transnational wealth, even corporate giants may occasionally become "blackmailable" captives of territorial dwarfs. Once investment has been made locally and corporate activities have begun, the initial bargaining power of a corporate giant—to invest or not to invest— has been curtailed.[14] Some oppose this view and speak of transnational corporations as new "world powers" or "new sovereigns."[15] Still other analysts stress the intertwining of the corporate profit interests with the national security concerns of their home countries.[16] Furthermore, the multinational character of the enterprises does not quite sever their top managerial elites' links—emotional or subliminal—to their home countries (as was the case of the former colonial administrators and entrepreneurs), and both the host and home countries know it. Thus, many observers anticipate simultaneous tension *and* accommodation between transnational corporations and states—an uneasy coexistence, but not a replacement of one with the other.

There are now several dozen voluminous scholarly and journalistic studies on the subject of transnational corporations; it is beyond the scope of this study to further develop and refine the particular corporate percolation of sovereign barriers. Nevertheless, three general points should be made. First, transnational corporations are similar to many other transnational organizations in their resentment and criticism of the territorial fragmentation of humankind, but, like all other transnational organizations, they adapt themselves flexibly to the facts of (territorial) life.

Second, as mentioned previously, transnational hopes for a frontierless world for the purpose of profit do not coincide with other hopes for an integrated globe. Corporate transnationalism motivated by a search for profit and development often clashes with the transnationalism of those movements and organizations that try to make the world not only unsafe for the corporations but safe for communism, democracy, socialism, the Third World, Islam, or a particular class or race. Transnational associations devoted to the promotion of art and human rights, the salvation of human souls, or protection of the biosphere often oppose economic and business transnationalism and its callous by-products more vehemently than their own national governments do.

Third, in 1970, transnational corporations were mostly referred to as an invention and instrument of Western supremacy. Fifteen years later, *Beijing Review* expressed a moderately positive view of transnationals, stressing that the Third World, too, has established hundreds of transnationals and profited from them. In an article entitled "Third World Transnationals on the Rise," a Chinese communist writer (Zhang Zuqian) explained: "It was not merely luck that gave rise to transnational corporations of developing countries and regions. The growth of these corporations reflects the economic advance made by the developing countries and the changing international social and economic climate."[17]

Zhang used the example of India, which had only 20 enterprises operating abroad in 1970 but a decade later had established and was operating ten times that number (207). The Latin American countries had only 24 corporations abroad in 1977, but had established an additional 65 by 1981. According to statistics compiled by the International Labour Organisation in November 1982, some 2,000 transnationals were then owned by twelve developing countries and regions. Listing 500 of the largest industrial businesses operating outside the United States, *Fortune* magazine (August 1981) identified 41 of them as being owned by developing countries: South Korea led the list with 10, followed by Mexico (7) and Brazil (6). The *Beijing Review* added with obvious satisfaction, "At the same time, these young corporations have grown stronger."

External Interference

By interference or intervention, I mean deliberate, systematic, and organized activities conducted across national boundaries by which government agents and instruments (such as money, weapons,explosives, and communication gadgets) can reach individuals, groups, and processes in a target state, without the consent of its government but with the purpose of affecting its performance, control, policies, or structure. This definition contains elements of Andrew Scott's and James N. Rosenau's definitions of intervention.[18]

In the context of the present study interference (despite a slight difference in tone and time the terms "interference" and "intervention" are used here interchangeably), as a deliberate lateral challenge to the territorial principle, merits attention since its practice and success presuppose the very opposite of traditional concepts of an impermeable sovereignty of a state and its citizens' identification with and loyalty to the state. Interference depends, on the contrary, on the presence of the following two factors: (1) the *porosity* of national boundaries, which permits the unauthorized entry of foreign agents and instruments, and (2) *receptiveness* on the part of individuals and groups within the state to foreign communications, based usually on a perceived coincidence of one's own and foreign interests.

Today, intervention in the domestic affairs of foreign nations is a general practice, although in principle, it is contrary to the universal principle of impermeable sovereign boundaries and therefore forbidden by the UN Charter and condemned by several resolutions of the UN General Assembly. In 1966, for example, the Soviet Union (ten years after its armed intervention in Hungary, two years before the invasion of Czechoslovakia, and fourteen years before the Soviet occupation of Afghanistan), the United States (then engaged in Vietnam), Cuba (interfering in Central and South America and Africa), Libya (interfering in Africa and the Middle East), Eastern European bloc countries, and Syria voted in the UN General Assembly without any embarrassment, nay, with gusto, for the following resolution: "No state has the right to intervene, directly or indirectly, for any reason whatsoever [!], in the internal and external affairs of any other state."[19]

Among the countries voting, only Malta abstained, and its delegate made the following statement:

> The draft declaration on the admissibility of intervention in the domestic affairs of States . . . is being openly violated by several states that voted in favour of it in the First Committee; and it is not likely that these States will modify their policies in accordance with the draft declaration. In these circumstances, my delegation does not believe that the adoption of such a declaration at the present time will increase the prestige of the United Nations. Accordingly, my delegation will not participate in the vote.[20]

This was the only honest stand and therefore a lonely one.

Rhetorical condemnations of intervention have never prevented either its practice or a selective open approval of some interventions while condemning the other "kind." According to some international lawyers and scholars, for example, intervention in self-defense against foreign attack or intervention (that is, intervention to enforce non-intervention) may be justified. As Manfred Halpern argues, "If national sovereignty is threatened, or itself threatens peace, freedom, or justice, wisdom demands intervention."[21]

Interference as a Spin-Off of Interdependence

Some modern writers have argued that contemporary practices, especially of nonmilitary forms, of intervention are consistent with the present era of interdependence in which the former rigid norms of international law (based on the concept of impermeable, self-sufficient, and self-contained territorial states) simply cannot apply anymore. Intervention in economic, ecological, human rights, and cultural spheres is thus deemed to be simply a symptom of worldwide transborder "togetherness." An expert on international law concerned with the need for foreign aid and technology transfers, Richard A. Falk, expressed the link between interdependence and the need to engage in transborder activities as follows: "The rigidity of non-intervention is inappropriate for a world of growing interdependence, where the welfare of nations often depends upon foreign aid, technical assistance programs, guaranteed prices, and military alliances."[22]

Furthermore, in a truly interdependent world, it is sometimes difficult to draw a line between deliberate intervention and unwitting interference, or simply transborder influence. Thus the sheer existence of a powerful nation may become a source of power projection that attracts or antagonizes the neighbors first and the rest of the world second. One could suggest that such an emanation of national power potential would still make the United States and the Soviet Union primary actors on the international scene even if these two nations became isolated hermits by abolishing their respective departments of foreign affairs and defense and all their diplomatic posts.

> We have grown so much that we are today like an awkward young giant in a crowded and cluttered room: whatever we do or do not do—whatever position we place ourselves in—we cannot help affecting others. . . . Our bigness and our economic might have taken us past the happy age of innocence in which we could say of the world around us: "We just work here."[23]

Other authors have praised the principle of foreign intervention when it is allegedly undertaken for a humanitarian or an ecological *good* cause such as prevention of genocide, apartheid practices and other forms of inhumanity, exploitation of migrant workers in foreign lands, environment-polluting practices, and the exporting of dangerous drugs.

Since intervention means foreign meddling in the domestic affairs of a territorial state, on some occasions, another argument in favor of intervention might be heard: Intervention is not only permissible but an actual duty when it comes to relations between territorial states that are viewed as "children" or "brethren" of the same racial, ethnic, or ideological family. In 1958, for example, the spokesman of Saudi Arabia, Ahmad Shukairy, argued that the Western concept of *foreign* intervention in domestic affairs could not apply to the relations among the various Arab territorial states, since "no Arab is an alien to any Arab" and "no Arab country is foreign to another Arab country." If, according to this concept, all Arab states are integral parts of one single Arab nation, an Arab interference in the domestic affairs of another Arab state is apparently inconceivable since all Arab affairs are by this definition domestic, and external relations can be only with non-Arab states. The same theme was repeated in 1985 when the head of the Libyan Arab Brotherliness Bureau (the Libyan equivalent of an embassy) in Khartoum in the Sudan, Jumael Fezzani, argued that relations between Sudan and Libya "are an internal matter within the same Arab nation, just like relations between New York and Florida."[24]

Similarly, the Soviet Union's so-called Brezhnev doctrine of 1968 argued that territorial barriers between brotherly socialist states cannot bar transborder penetration when world socialism is at stake. Under such circumstances, intervention in the domestic affairs of a socialist country is not only permitted but becomes a duty.

> It is impossible to ignore the allegations being heard in some places that the actions [the armed invasion of Czechoslovakia] of the five socialist countries contradict the Marxist-Leninist principle of sovereignty and the right of nations to self-determination. Such arguments are untenable primarily because they are based on an abstract non-class approach to the question of sovereignty and the right of nations to self-determination. . . . The sovereignty of each socialist country cannot be opposed to the world of socialism . . . [which] is indivisible and its defense is the common cause of all Communists. The weakening of any link in the world socialist system has a direct effect on all socialist countries, which cannot be indifferent. . . . Those who speak of the illegality of the allied socialist countries' actions in Czechoslovakia forget that in a class society . . . laws and the norms of law are subordinated to the laws of the class struggle and the laws of social development.[25]

With these words, Moscow justified the tearing down of the political boundaries between the Soviet Union and Czechoslovakia and the subsequent military occupation of that country following the so-called Prague Spring.

A special case of interference is that of transnational terrorists—that is, nongovernmental groups that hope to promote their cause by a spectacular challenge to the governmental authorities of a foreign state whose criminal code and procedure they often succeed in temporarily suspending. Transterritorial in their techniques, many terrorists groups, however, are quite specifically territorial in terms of their final objectives (the PLO, for example).

Frequently, the recipient targets for interfering foreign governments are the individuals and groups opposing the particular rulers or system of the state selected for interference. Opposition to government is, of course, as old as territorial government itself. Although we have no documentary evidence, we may assume that at the dawn of human history, among cavemen a critique of or a revolt against incompetence, tyranny, corruption, lack of foresight, risky expansion, or inadequate defense against ambitious neighbors must have surfaced.

The external support of such internal dissent is also ancient. In India at the time of the Mauryan Empire (300–200 B.C.), Kautilya, an Indian philosopher with practical experience in politics, described the various ways in which a disaffected group in a rival king's territory may be won over to the side of the interfering state through bribery and appeals to their "master-passions that would make the move against their king." According to the 2,200 year old Indian recipe, the four master passions of the disaffected individuals and groups to be externally exploited are "anger, fear, greed, and pride."[26]

In introducing his history of the wars among the Greek city-states (the Peloponnesian War, which began in 431 B.C.), Thucydides described the attempts of the Greek city-state Corcyra to reinstall the exiled leaders of the city of Epidamnus and the opposite efforts on the part of another city-state Corinth.[27] It is indeed clear, as noted by Max Beloff, that "the Greek City-States exploited civil strife to further their own policies and that political parties existed within the Greek states which depended, or came to depend, upon foreign support."[28]

The decision on the part of one government to meddle in the internal affairs of another territorial state depends on a great many variables such as (a) the respective size and power of the states involved (especially the power to retaliate by counterinterference), (b) the international climate, (c) the cost involved, (d) the motives, aims, organization, numbers, and leadership of the opposition group to be supported by foreign help, and (e) their chances of success or at least nuisance value. The list of the most frequent opposition goals includes:

1. Rejection of the territorial principles as such (anarchists, messianic reformers, one-world dreamers); such aims rarely attract foreign interest
2. Splitting the territorial system into two or more parts; ethnoterritorial secession, particularly, invites foreign fishing in ethnically troubled waters
3. Fundamental systemic change (polyarchy to hegemonism; capitalism to socialism, etc.); again, quite a magnet for foreign meddling
4. Structure modification (unitary to federal, parliamentary to presidential, etc.); rarely a cause for foreign involvement
5. Change of domestic policies (including transition from ideological orthodoxy to pragmatism)
6. Change in foreign policy orientation, a very frequent cause of foreign involvement in our era of tacit spheres of influence
7. Pragmatic desire for a better government performance
8. Demotion of the ruling group (without other major changes)
9. Dissent proper (for example, struggle for the freedom to oppose the government and organize for this purpose)[29]

Forms of Interference

The forms of interference range from:

1. Open or clandestine military intervention on the side of the opposition (USSR in Afghanistan, Czechoslovakia, Hungary; United States in Central America; Cuba in Africa).
2. Military movement suggestive of forthcoming military action (U.S. naval maneuvers in the Caribbean or the Mediterranean).
3. Training of personnel from the target or neighboring territories, transfers of advisers, supplying means of transportation, weapons, communication instruments (United States in Central America; Cuba in Africa; the Soviet Union nearly everywhere).
4. Transnational nonmilitary support (such as various technical, health, economic aid, or peace corps programs) undertaken for the purpose of political and military infiltration rather than assistance, or supply of funds for the opposition party and its press. In June 1975, for example, the Swedish Social Democratic party, then in control of the Swedish government, publicly announced its intention of making a monthly contribution of $15,000 to strengthen governmental (anti-Franco) activities of the Spanish Socialist party (PSOE). According to the *New York Times*: "In Western Europe parties increasingly cooperate across the frontiers. . . . The most revealing sign of the evolution is the amount of intervention that goes on in the internal politics of other countries as a matter of course, without criticism or complaint of foreign meddling."[30] The tolerant attitude of Europeans toward interventions on behalf of social democratic parties contrasts with European resentment of the U.S.involvement in intra-European politics and support of parties in Central America.
5. Supportive external agitation (Soviet support of the freeze demonstrations in Western Europe in 1984).
6. Public expressions of moral support and encouragement; the smuggling of leaflets, books, and periodicals; and radio propaganda (Voice of America, Radio Free Europe, Radio Moscow, Radio Vatican, etc.). De Gaulle's "Vive le Québec libre," proclaimed in Montréal in 1967, was an example of a verbal/symbolic interference in the domestic affairs of a foreign country. The Canadian government sharply protested and caused the French president to cut short his official visit.

Mention may be made of a marginal but interesting phenomenon that may be called "phantom intervention." This type of situation occurs when an opposition group within a nation-state anticipates, and so feels emboldened by the expectation of, interference that a foreign government has no intention of initiating. Such an unrealistic anticipation is usually based on either ethnic affinity or ideological reputation. In 1956, for example, some Hungarian freedom fighters seriously believed that, on ideological grounds, the United

States could not permit a defeat of the anti-Stalinist revolution in Budapest—a slow reading of the U.S. Declaration of Independence by a freedom fighter over the Budapest Radio represented a melancholy example of a "phantom," that is, an intervention ardently wished for by the would-be recipients but never seriously contemplated by the "interventionist."[31]

Whether publicized, clandestine, phantom, or unwitting, penetration of territorial boundaries from the outside and the resulting influence on intraterritorial developments has today become a daily occurrence—easily observable though difficult to measure. The various deliberate, systematic, sometimes unwitting and sporadic interferences in domestic affairs by foreign governments well illustrate the permeability of the legally impermeable intersovereign boundaries, and the decline of traditional international law and order. Such unauthorized penetrations of sovereign boundaries may be also viewed as another indication of the shrinking of our world into a global village. And, of course, in any village neighbors and relatives tend to poke their noses into other people's affairs. Constantly.[32]

Nation-State as a Multivocal Actor

In the context of the external and internal streams that perforate but do not eliminate intersovereign barriers separating the 160 nation-states one from the other, it seems useful to qualify and refine the traditional concept of a nation-state's speaking to other nations with a single legitimate voice. In the past, and in writing the texts of national constitutions, national governments and their diplomatic apparatuses were primarily concerned with national security and national status. This is no more so. After World War I, the rubric of international politics began to include issue-areas that previously, especially in the laissez-faire century, had been viewed as being within the domain of private initiative and management (for example, trade or cultural exchanges) or under the jurisdiction of noncentral governments in federal systems (U.S. states, Canadian provinces, Swiss cantons, German *Länder*) such as social, educational, ecological, humanitarian, and criminal matters and minor transborder management.

In shorthand fashion, some authors have referred to the difference between so-called high politics, clearly in the hands of the national center, and low politics, primarily in the hands of private groups or noncentral governments. The problem has always been how reliably can one draw a line between the two types of politics. Purely functional issues—economic, social, ecological, or cultural—easily become highly politicized since they have or may ultimately have a direct effect upon national security. (Chapter 7 points to the limits of the so-called functional approach to international peace depending more on the political climate than on functional workshops.) Security concerns will continue to cast a decisive shadow on what may appear from the local or functional standpoint to be innocent or harmless. Furthermore, compensatory or bargaining links between "pure security" and "pure nonsecurity" issues are frequent. Colloquially, such links can be

Figure 8.1

<u>Cheops Paradigm</u>

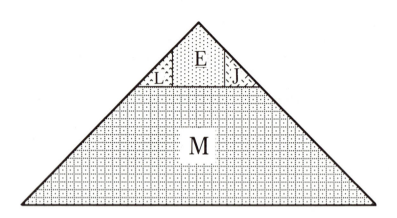

expressed by the formula, "If thou yieldest on Pershing missiles or the USSR-West Europe pipeline, I yield on Jewish emigration or Sakharov." And vice versa, of course. The difficulty of drawing a clear line between security, profit-taking, and human concerns is naturally present also in evaluating and judging the practice of transborder interference.

Paradigms, Diagrams, and Pyramids

In order to illustrate complex political processes in a simplified fashion, diagrams are often useful although, naturally, their static two-dimensionality imposes severe limits. Traditionally (according to the state-centric paradigm), a nation-state appears as a univocal actor speaking to foreign governments with a single authoritative voice only, that of the central government in general and the executive branch in particular.

Cheops Paradigm. This univocal concept has often been depicted in the form of a triangle (See Figure 8.1), a neat Cheops pyramid. The base of the pyramid is the mass public (M), and the apex is formed by the national government—the executive branch (E) in the center laterally monitored and sometimes restricted by the legislative (L) and judiciary (J) branches of government.

The point of contact with the international system is clear: It is the executive branch that protrudes into the external environment, influenced from both sides by the legislative and judiciary branches of government. But our Cheops diagram, a prisoner of geometric lines, distorts the reality in two major ways. Pictorially, it presents the influence of the legislature on foreign policy as being equal to that of the judiciary, which is far from reality. Also, the straight line separating the government from M should

Figure 8.2

Saqqara Paradigm

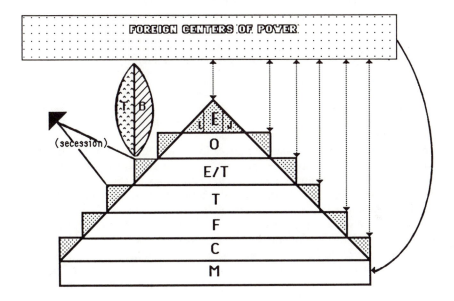

be both porous and undulated to indicate that the link between the mass public and the apex varies; the people's contact with the legislators is more intensive than that between the public and the minister or secretary of external affairs.

Saqqara Paradigm. In the framework of our concern with multiple perforations of intersovereign boundaries, a more fitting symbol-image seems to be the stepped pyramid of Saqqara (see Figure 8.2). In the Saqqara paradigm, each of the successive component layers possesses "apexes" of its own, which protrude into the international system and are therefore capable of establishing contacts (depicted as dotted lines) with foreign governments and other centers of power. The top apex of the pyramid is, of course, again formed by the national government's "troika": the national executive assisted or hindered by the legislative and judiciary branches. Subsequent layers have, of course, two apexes, each of which is not only the result of our captivity in the geometric configuration of a triangle but also an indication of the less centralized nature of the various communities, each speaking with various voices to the external world.

The first layer, O, standing for the opposition, has its own apexes and points of access to the international scene. The opposition party or parties are usually in contact with foreign governments or their ideological counterparts—legally or illegally. The opposition qua a potential top apex of tomorrow is therefore a magnet for foreign interest long before its accession to power. As to the authoritarian socialist or fascist regimes in which the opposition seems to have no chance of becoming the government of tomorrow, foreign governments nevertheless attentively listen to or assist the dissenters, however isolated they appear to be. One reason for such links is the possibility they present to gauge the performance and controls of otherwise closed regimes. The second reason is simply, One never knows.

The second layer, E/T, represents ethnic communities, territorial or dispersed, which often maintain close political and cultural links with their blood relatives abroad and are either targets or initiators of international contacts. Clearly, the clout of dispersed ethnic groups (such as the francophones in Manitoba or Ontario) is usually less than that of ethnoterritorial communities (such as Québec in Canada; Corsica, Alsace, and Brittany in France; or Basque and Catalan provinces in Spain). A diaspora can threaten the center only with trouble, not with secession—which, of course, a *territorial* ethnic community can. The left-hand apex of the ethnoterritorial layer has a line going off to the side to indicate the possibility of movement toward secession.

The third layer T represents a nation's territorial subdivisions other than ethnic ones (federal components such as provinces, states, *Länder*, or cantons). The two curves forming a leaflike shaded area illustrate the potential emergence of a confederal overlap (T and B stand for transborder regional linkage) between two federal systems. I call the regional overlap "confederal" since its goal, in contrast to a federal bargain, is to create not a new transborder supranational community (a new "nation") but only a close cooperative combination or league of two subnational communities, both of which still prefer and maintain their primary membership in their respective sovereign nation-states. A confederal overlap is basically an "intersovereign consociation," and its mode of decision making is negotiation aiming at consensus.

The fourth layer, F, represents organized functional interest groups ranging from business (including transnational corporations) to labor. Robert Keohane and Joseph Nye's world paradigm,[33] which focuses on the role of nongovernmental international actors, has usefully corrected the traditional state-centric paradigm.

The fifth layer, C, is composed of various types of communicators and promoters of nonmaterial values, especially mass media but also universities, churches, scientists, writers, and artists.

The sixth layer, M for mass public, is shown at the base without any protruding apex; the mass public lacks a meaningful lateral propensity to *initiate* contacts with its counterparts abroad. The general public rarely extends its contacts across the national border independently of the government (except partly through tourism); the public usually enters into contacts with foreign communities through one or more of the five other interest communities/groups. On the other hand, the general public may be and often is a recipient target for foreign mass media.

Except for the last layer, the positioning of the layers does not indicate their descending order of importance or numerical strength—this is another limitation of the visual illustration of complex social and political phenomena. Although the diagram depicts the various component layers of a territorial state as having their own apexes as points of entry into the international system, those apexes are also gates through which external lures and threats enter the territorial systems. The apexes should therefore be viewed as both exits and entrances.

The various voices of a multivocal nation-state that are heard abroad may be sharply dissonant—both between the various communities and between the center and the various subnational components—the dissonance may be either confusing for foreign powers or invite their meddling. But these voices may also be mutually complementary and (to use a musical metaphor) produce a nuanced symphony. As we well know, in the matter of foreign and defense policy in its traditional sense, there may even be a general consensus between the government and its opposition in times of crisis. In war, a normally multivocal actor may become impressively univocal— As Churchill's England did during World War II.

Notes

1. One such world constitution was prepared at the University of Chicago in 1948 at the peak of the cold war, marked by the fall of Czechoslovakia and the Berlin blockade. Another world constitution was drafted in 1965 (at the time of full U.S. involvement in Vietnam) at the Center for the Study of Democratic Institutions in Santa Barbara, California. See also Grenville Clark and Louis B. Sohn, *World Peace Through World Law* (Cambridge: Harvard University Press, 1958).

2. Reinhold Niebuhr, *Christian Realism and Political Problems* (New York: Scribner, 1953), p. 33.

3. Richard A. Falk and Saul H. Mendlovitz, eds., *Regional Politics and World Order* (San Francisco: W. H. Freeman, 1973), p. 3.

4. Edward H. Carr, *Nationalism and After* (New York: Macmillan, 1945), p. 53.

5. Ernst B. Haas, "Turbulent Fields and the Theory of Regional Integration," *International Organization* 27:1 (Winter 1973), p. 208.

6. See John H. Herz, "The Territorial State Revisited," *Polity* 1:1 (1968), pp. 11–34, a partial revision of his "Rise and Demise of the Territorial States," *World Politics* 9:4 (1957), pp. 473–493, in which he was the very first to focus systematically on the insecurity and defenselessness of territorial states whose outer shells had ceased to be impermeable to air and nuclear attacks.

7. James N. Rosenau, "A Pre-Theory Revisited: World Politics in an Era of Cascading Interdependence," *International Studies Quarterly* 29 (1984), p. 246.

8. Quoted by Hans Kohn, *The Twentieth Century* (New York: Crowell-Collier-Macmillan, 1950), pp. 5–6.

9. Seyom Brown, *New Forces in World Politics* (Washington, D.C.: Brookings Institution, 1974), p. 188.

10. Samuel P. Huntington, "Transnational Organizations in World Politics," *World Politics* 25:3 (1973), p. 363.

11. K. J. Holsti, "Underdevelopment and the 'Gap' Theory of International Conflict," *American Political Science Review* 69:2 (June 1975), p. 336. Cf. Joseph S. Nye on integration still moving forward by "cultivated spillover"—"package deals not only on the basis of technological necessity but on the basis of political and ideological projection and political possibilities," in Leon N. Lindberg and Stuart A. Scheingold, eds., *Regional Integration: Theory and Research* (Cambridge: Harvard University Press, 1971) p. 202

12. Carr, *Nationalism and After*, p. 13.

13. United Nations, *Multinational Corporations in World Development*, ST/ECA (New York: Department of Economics and Social Affairs, 1970).

14. Theodore H. Moran, *Multinational Corporations and the Politics of Dependence: Copper in Chile* (Princeton N.J.: Princeton University Press, 1974), p. 216.

15. Luiz Simmons and Abdul Said, eds., *The New Sovereigns: Corporations as World Powers* (New York: Praeger, 1974).

16. Richard J. Barnet and Ronald E. Muller, *Global Reach: The Power of Multinational Corporations* (New York: Simon and Schuster, 1974). See also Mira Wilkins, *The Maturing of Multinational Enterprise: American Business Abroad from 1914–1970* (Cambridge: Harvard University Press), p. 438. The latter work emphasizes the coincidence of U.S. business interests and government "political policies," especially vis-à-vis Western European economic and political power.

17. *Beijing Review*, March 18, 1985.

18. Andrew Scott, *The Revolution in Statecraft: Informal Penetration* (New York: Random House, 1965), p. 194, and James N. Rosenau, "The Concept of Intervention," *Journal of International Affairs*, 22:2 (1968), p. 167.

19. "Text of Resolution (A/RES/2131-XX)," *UN Monthly Chronicle* 3:1 (January 1966), p. 29.

20. Ibid.

21. Manfred Halpern, "The Morality and Politics of Intervention," in James N. Rosenau, ed., *International Aspects of Civil Strife* (Princeton, N.J.: Princeton University Press, 1964), p. 286.

22. Richard A. Falk, "The International Law of War," in Rosenau, *International Aspects of Civil Strife*, p. 238.

23. George F. Kennan, "Foreign Aid in the Framework of National Policy," *Proceedings of the American Academy of Political Science* 23 (1950), pp. 104–105.

24. *New York Times*, August 16, 1958, and July 9, 1985.

25. "Sovereignty and International Duties of Socialist Countries," *Pravda*, September 25, 1968.

26. Upendra Nath Goshal, *A History of Indian Political Ideas* (London: Oxford University Press, 1959), p. 133.

27. Thucydides, *History of the Peloponnesian Wars*, trans. Charles Foster Smith (Cambridge: Harvard University Press, 1956), pp. 47–48.

28. Max Beloff, "Reflections on Intervention," *Journal of International Affairs* 22:2 (1968), p. 199.

29. This typology is based on a schema suggested by Vladimir V. Kusin, "Typology of Opposition," *Soviet Studies* 25:1 (July 1973), pp. 125–129, in his critique of Leonard Shapiro, ed., *Political Opposition in One-Party States* (London: Macmillan, 1972); it has been modified by the incorporation of insights and categories found in the writings of Robert A. Dahl, Samuel P. Huntington, Zbigniew Brzezinski, Frederic C. Barghoorn, Jerzy J. Wiatr, William Shapiro, Gordon Skilling, and in particular Otto Kirchheimer who analyzed his distinction between classical opposition within

a general consensus and opposition of principle (i.e. without consensus) in "The Waning of Opposition," *Social Research* 24:2 (Summer 1957), pp. 127–156.

30. *New York Times*, February 9, 1976.

31. This segment on interference has adapted and revised a portion of the author's Chapter 11, "Interventions: Violent and Nonviolent," in Ivo D. Duchacek, *Nations and Men: An Introduction to International Politics*, 3d ed. (New York: Holt, Rinehart and Winston). Copyright 1975 by the Dryden Press, CBS College Publishing, reprint, Washington D.C.: University Press of America in 1982.

32. The argument presented in this chapter was initially developed in Ivo D. Duchacek, "Fusion or Fission: Internal and Lateral Challenges to the Territorial State" (Paper presented at the Congress of the International Political Science Association, Edinburgh, August 16–21, 1976.)

33. Robert O. Keohane and Joseph S. Nye, eds., *Transnational Relations and World Politics* (Cambridge: Harvard University Press, 1972).

9

Encounters of a New Kind: International Competence of Noncentral Governments

The meaner sort of men confine their outlook within the cities where they were born. But those whom God has given a greater light neglect no means of improvement whether it come from near or from afar. . . . The light of nature teaches each of us in his private life to maintain relations with his neighbours because as their near presence enables them to injure so it also enables them to do us service.

—Cardinal de Richelieu (1585-1642)

The economic interdependence of the modern world is more than international. It is also inter-local. . . . Every jiggle in the pattern of the international economy is likely to pinch some local group . . . and convert it immediately into a vocal group.

—Bayless Manning
(*Foreign Affairs*, 1977)

Mazda means thousands of jobs for Michigan workers. . . . Mazda's decision to invest in Michigan's future . . . establishes as fact that cooperation pays. Michigan Mazda is a testimony of cooperation . . . within state government and by state government with local government, industry, and labor.

—James J. Blanchard,
governor of Michigan
(Advertisement in *New York Times*, June 30, 1985)

Shanghai Opens Its Arms to the World: Shanghai, vital to the Chinese economy, is as important to China as New York is to the United States. And for prospective investors, it is truly the Big Apple among the nation's 14 open cities.

—Wei Liming
(*Beijing Review*, January 14, 1985)

Following the 14 coastal cities that opened their doors to outside world, China's inland provinces also began welcoming trade, investment, and advanced technology from overseas. The Sichuan Symposium on Investment held in Chengdu in April [1985] showed that Sichuan is attractive to foreign investors in spite of its distance from the coastal ports.

—*Beijing Review* (July 1, 1985)

Since the early 1970s, as managers of economic, social, and cultural affairs, noncentral governments in North America and Western Europe have been increasingly induced to look for or respond to numerous and very varied contacts with foreign centers of economic, cultural, and political influence. These governments include not only immediate transborder neighbors (which would hardly be novel, except for the contemporary intensity) but also distant centers of industrial or investment power, including national governments that either own or control national economies.

The external activities of noncentral governments naturally presuppose that they possess a considerable degree of real autonomy. For this reason, such external activities are observable and significant primarily in the case of territorial components of *democratic* federal or decentralized systems such as U.S. states, Canadian provinces, Swiss cantons, West German and Austrian *Länder*, Spanish Catalonia, the Walloon and Flemish parts of Belgium, as well as major municipalities as emphasized in some of the epigraphs to this chapter.[1]

Although the samples presented in this chapter, come mostly from the Western world, socialist authoritarian systems too have been tempted to experiment with such potential flexibility and effectiveness (reflecting local needs, interests, and pride); the small size of the noncentral authorities makes them appear less forbidding to the outsiders than a national center. Both federal Yugoslavia and regionalized China, for example, have permitted or encouraged international contacts on the part of their various provinces. In 1981, Xu Dixin wrote in the *Beijing Review* (December 20, 1981), about the new special economic zones in China that "open the door to foreign countries. Take Shenzhen and Zhuhai, for example, their economic ties with Xianggang (Hongkong) and Aomen (Macao) are much closer than with the interior."

In communist Yugoslavia, despite its single-party rule, two of its border provinces (republics), Croatia and Slovenia, are today members of a five-nation Alpine Community (Communauté des régions alpines—ALP-Adria), which associates communist Croatia and Slovenia with the Alpine regions of federal Austria, West Germany, Switzerland, and the northern region of Italy for the purpose of allowing a passport-free circulation of foreign visitors.

That the international acceptability of noncentral governments on account of their small size, geographic location, or ethnic character may, paradoxically, prove useful for tightly centralized authoritarian governments in their interventionist undertakings abroad has become evident in Angola, which is clearly under Soviet and Cuban domination. Angola was, in fact, induced to develop a "sister" relationship with one of the fifteen Soviet ethnoterritorial republics, Azerbaijan, which has exported to Angola air conditioners from Baku (the republic's capital city) and seventeen repair stations for Soviet-made agricultural machinery as well as books and pencils collected by the Azerbaijani children for their Angolan counterparts. Even these centrally ordered subnational contacts add to what I call in this chapter "encounters of a new kind."

International activities of noncentral governments rarely make the first page of national dailies. They are neither alarming nor dramatic—they can hardly compete for the public attention with murder, terrorism, war, or arms talks—they primarily deal, so to speak, with the territorial daily bread. The following ten news items, for example—while significant from our analytical point of view—could be found in the *New York Times*, *Le Monde*, *Globe and Mail*, and other national dailies only many pages after news from abroad and the capital city.

Six Canadian provinces—Alberta, British Columbia, Nova Scotia, Ontario, Quebec, and Saskatchewan—have established forty-six permanent offices in eleven foreign countries.

Twenty-eight U.S. states have established fifty-four permanent offices in seventeen foreign countries; most of them are located in Tokyo (seventeen), in Brussels (eleven), and in West Germany (ten).

The U.S. state missions in Europe have formed a *Council for American States in Europe* (CASE) for the purposes of organizing training seminars for its members in the areas of their major concern: Investment and promotion of trade [in that order]. Though in many ways competitive among themselves, the U.S. state missions abroad cooperate through CASE as a special lobby with regard to the federal government and its embassies and consulates abroad.

In Québec City, the flag of the Belgian French-speaking Walloons, with its red Gallic rooster, is on display throughout the office of the Walloon permanent mission along with the flag of Québec with its blue fleur-de-lis. Nowhere to be seen are the flags of Belgium or Canada.

Business America (May 27, 1985) published an analysis by Dan Pilcher which describes the new state roles in Export Trading Companies [ETC's], Minnesota's and Illinois' plans for state world trade centers, the Oregon law asking Portland State University to run an Institute on International Trade, and Wisconsin's use of foreign nationals who have graduated from Wisconsin universities as "honorary commercial attachés." The article whose subtitle proclaims that "the states have turned a new page in trade development," is symptomatically introduced by the following epigraph: "There is a Japanese saying: 'Ido no naka no kawazu, taikai o shirazu.' The frog in the well never sees the vast ocean beyond."

"The way to China," said the Bavarian Prime Minister Franz Josef Strauss (*German News Service*, October 7, 1985), "is not an economic adventure, but a rewarding task with a future." During his visit Strauss also met for political discussions with Prime Minister Zhao Ziyang and with China's supreme leader, Deng Xiaoping.

Between April 24 and May 12, 1985, Governors of Shandong, Quinghai, Jiangzi, Hunan, and Shanxi provinces visited and negotiated in California, North Dakota, Minnesota, Pennsylvania, Georgia, Florida, Washington, D.C., and New York. The state of Illinois has established a direct link with the

Chinese province of Guangdong and has a permanent representative in its city of Shenzhen.

A trinational region linking the northwestern cantons of Switzerland, a portion of the German *Land* of Baden-Württemberg, and upper Alsace of France celebrated its 20th anniversary on May 20, 1982. The Swiss federal president attended the ceremony (1982). In 1985, the universities of Strasbourg, Basle, Mulhouse (Alsace), and Freiburg (Baden) have formed a multi-campus consortium. It permits the Swiss, French, and German students to take courses and receive credits at any or all the confederated institutions.

The thirteenth annual conference of the five East Canadian premiers and six New England governors and their staffs, was held in New Brunswick in 1985; the previous conference was held in Rhode Island.

The governors of six northern U.S. states and premiers of two Canadian provinces (Ontario and Quebec) signed an agreement in Milwaukee on February 11, 1985, to preserve the Great Lakes water resource against future raids by water-hungry Sun Belt states. In his comment on the nine-page Great Lakes Charter (perhaps controversial from the constitutional interstate point of view), Governor Richard F. Celeste from Ohio wisely noted: "*Most of our tools of government do not fit the problems we have today.*" [italics added]

The last statement elicits general agreement. Neither constitutions nor the traditional procedures derived from them have provided for an adequate handling of the various challenges or opportunities that call for the presence of noncentral governments on the international scene. Whatever the constitutional, conceptual, or practical objections on the part of a central government may be, all democratic systems, and the federal ones in particular, have come to speak with regionally nuanced voices abroad. The issue of constructive coordination of the various signals and activities has been placed on the agenda of all states practicing democracy and federalism, starting with the United States and Canada.

The traditional, seemingly neat division between national security and status handled by the national center, on the one hand, and nonsecurity issue areas, on the other, has been challenged by seven[2] interrelated developments that merit our attention:

1. The imperatives of interdependence (global, continental, and regional)
2. Welfare or service functions of all governments
3. Neighborhood linkages
4. Extension of foreign policy field
5. Opposition from below to the growth of central government
6. "Me-tooism"
7. Separatism (in a few cases)

The Imperatives of Interdependence

Global, continental, and regional interdependence is certainly not a novel fact or concept, but the *subnational* awareness of its pressures and opportunities and the need to react to them is. The awareness of subnational vulnerability to extranational, distant events has now, as it were, trickled from beyond the borders down to subnational elected leaders and their staffs, responsible for the progress and well-being of their respective subnational *territorial* communities—and for their own political survival in them. In order to remain custodians of the living standard of their people, not only nations but also subnational territorial communities have to engage in activities beyond the national frontiers.

The increase in the number and intensity of subnational entries by noncentral authorities onto the international scene is of relatively recent vintage. The list of causes is all too familiar: the world recession in the wake of the global jolt caused by the oil boycott by the Organization of Petroleum Exporting Countries (OPEC) in 1973, astronomical national budget deficits, reflecting the continuing arms race and increased social services; the rise in unemployment; and the export trade decline—their sum total has resulted in national governments' frugality with regard to subnational/ territorial development and welfare programs. Governor Bruce Babbit of Arizona, as chairman of the Advisory Commission on Intergovernmental Relations, expressed the situation succinctly in the fall of 1983: "States will probably have to assert themselves as never before in modern times. . . . The message is clear: *the national government will no longer bail us out*" (italics added).

The dwindling of national resources, earmarked or earmarkable for noncentral authorities, painfully contributed to the awareness of extreme vulnerability in regard to state, provincial, cantonal, and municipal welfare programs and development policies to events beyond the national borders— events about which central national governments apparently could, or cared to, do very little. As Alberta's premier, Peter Lougheed expressed the problem on October 19, 1983, "We remain directly affected in Alberta and in Canada by decisions that are made in Riyadh, Geneva, Tokyo, Beijing, Hong Kong, London, or you name it."

Self-help by means of international links has become the order of the day. If we look at the dates on which Canadian provinces and U.S. states decided to venture abroad and look for new opportunities and to establish or augment their representation abroad, nearly all point to the critical 1970s and early 1980s, that is, they were in the post-oil-embargo era.

In 1977, for example, the province of Ontario, which, for budgetary reasons, had previously disbanded four of its state offices abroad, began establishing new ones. In the United States, the 1980 state expenditures for the promotion of trade and reverse investment abroad represented a fourfold increase over the 1976 allocations. Today, the U.S. states collectively commit only a little less for such promotional activities than the U.S.

Department of Commerce does for the whole United States. Thirty states have established a total of fifty-five foreign trade zones. The statistical backdrop for these initiatives and actions is clear: In 1981, there were nearly 5 million jobs in the United States related to the export of manufactured goods; within the manufacturing sector, exports accounted for 12.8 percent of the total manufacturing employment. Among the states, California had by far the largest number of export-related jobs, New York was second, and Texas, Pennsylvania, and Ohio were next in rank. In terms of civilian export-related jobs, the leading states were Connecticut, Washington, Ohio and Delaware—all four above the 6 percent bracket.[3]

In September 1983, the U.S. National League of Cities (which groups both major and small cities in a cooperative framework) organized a conference in San Antonio, Texas, for the purpose of briefing municipal elected officials and administrators on the way to expand their cities' foreign relations. The theme of the conference, printed in boldface, paralleled the Japanese saying quoted earlier about the frog in a well and its limited view of the ocean: "Can your city afford to continue ignoring the rest of the world? Not if your local economy is going to grow. . . . Maybe it's time to expand your city's horizons." And since 1981, the Conference of Mayors has begun to organize annual shows in Zurich and Hong Kong under the motto: Invest in America's Cities.

In some cases (in the United States and Western Europe more than in Canada where cities, except for Montréal, are jurisdictionally more subject to provincial governments), the initiators of such activities are the governments of large or border cities rather than provincial, state, or cantonal governments. The desire of these metropolitan centers to be treated as "world cities" or "international cities" is particularly characteristic of those cities that host international organizations: New York, Geneva, Strasbourg (seat of the European Parliament and European Council), Montréal (seat of the International Civil Aviation Organization), and such large U.S. centers of international trade and finance as San Francisco, Los Angeles, Chicago, New Orleans, Houston, and Dallas. The last city seems to rejoice that its world reputation is no longer tainted by recollections of the assassination of President John F. Kennedy in 1963 since today the city

> is probably better known worldwide because of the "Dallas" television series, which is shown in several countries, according to those who regularly meet with foreign business leaders. While civic leaders aren't altogether pleased with the serial's business-at-any-cost portrayals, they agree the show generates a substantial amount of free advertising for Dallas.[4]

In practical terms, the well-being of the subnational electorates—and therefore their leaders' own staying power—has clearly begun to depend on their ability to couple their primary links with the national center and its funding agencies with their new lines to foreign sources of economic, financial, and industrial power. Wolfram Hanrieder's perceptive argument about internal power—vertically applied and vertically supported—being sustained by horizontal-external-cooperation has also begun to apply to the territorial components of federal and decentralized unitary states. They too have now been "compelled to turn to external sources in order to meet the demands pressed upon them by their electorates."[5] Or, as Thomas O. Hüglin argued:

> When shrinking resources require greater selectivity in investment planning and the costs of redistributive policies can no longer be well financed, collective centralized problem-solving may very well fail. Starting from general hypotheses about the demerits of centralization . . . a more successful politics of scarcity may require a federal multiplicity of noncentralized institutions for the organization and maintenance of a diversified socioeconomic system.[6]

The often fierce competition of provinces and cities for foreign investment and trade may be sarcastically referred to as "civil wars for foreign dough,"[7] but in more generous terms, all these noncentral initiatives and activities on the international scene simply mirror our era of scarcity and its imperatives of self-help, which the elected noncentral elites perceive as authorized by and consistent with their territorial autonomy.

In the United States, the National Governors' Association concluded recently: "States must maintain and enrich their contacts with foreign governments, industries and citizens. . . . They must be diligent in . . . establishing the need for recognition of their individual and collective interests in international affairs."[8] Similarly, the delegates to the Canadian provincial premiers' conference in St. Andrews, New Brunswick, in 1977 stated with understandable emphasis concerning the United States, Canada's largest trade partner: "The provinces . . . have legitimate interests and concerns in the international arena. Given these legitimate concerns and the large volume of Canadian trade with the United States . . . it is entirely appropriate for the provinces to assume a more prominent role in Canada-United States relations."[9]

The logic of interdependence applies to all: Those states that own and directly manage the production of goods and services (loosely called socialist or welfare states) and those that promote and support free enterprise, yet do so by government regulation, which, at least partly, displaces the market mechanism (loosely called capitalist systems). In the case of Canada, some of the public-owned corporations (federal and provincial)—producers of goods and services for sale in international markets—may develop their own "international relations" in order to seek the best external opportunities to fulfill their profit mandate rather than the mandate of public policy. "The soundness of investment rather than governmental policy has become their performance yardstick" concludes one of the most recent studies.[10]

Welfare Roles

Noncentral governments in federal systems have long preceded the national government in what we now call the welfare or social service roles of modern states ("L'état de bien être" in French; "L'état-providence" in Canadian French). Education, social services, and general welfare were on the agendas of local and provincial authorities long before "national socialism," that is, long before national governments began creating various agencies, ministries, and departments to deal with individual and group welfare. These roles have prompted many a noncentral government to assert its international competence in issue-areas that they view as being under their exclusive, traditional, or shared jurisdiction—or at least not clearly under the exclusive jurisdiction of the national center.

Thus, when self-governing territorial communities project their needs and interests abroad, they do so in such matters as foreign reverse investment; trade; location of job-creating foreign plants; ecology; energy; water; cultural and educational exchanges; transfrontier movement of migrant and commuting workers (an important issue in both the Swiss-German-French and the U.S.-Mexican borderlands) and the protection of their human, labor, educational, cultural, and health rights; international sharing of noncentral planning experiences and technological development and tourism (which, for some territorial communities has become a primary or at least a major source of state, provincial, or cantonal income). Noncentral governments do all these things for their own sake as well as to ensure the fulfillment of their provincial social roles. Even in unitary France, somewhat decentralized under President Mitterand in the 1980s, two regional capitals, Grenoble and Lille, for example, decided in 1985 to send investment and trade missions to the United States, relying on their own devices to get from abroad what they could not expect from Paris.

Neighborhood Linkages

A dictionary definition of an international boundary usually suggests an image of a barrier that "fixes the limits of neighboring sovereignties and national identities." This is also the meaning central governments promote and protect but, as this study suggests, noncentral governments qualify or modify. As Montana Governor Ted Schwinden expressed it in 1984 (*Borderlines* 1:2, p. 1), addressing a delegation of Alberta legislators, "Nowhere is cross-border communication more important than in the area of natural resources." The similarity of social, economic, and environmental problems, resulting from geographic proximity, has always been a reason for border governments to look more often toward their immediate neighbors beyond the intersovereign dividing line than toward their respective national centers. As Cardinal Richelieu wisely said in the seventeenth century, neighborhood can cause both injury and mutual service (see the first epigraph to this chapter).

As discussed in Chapter 8, practical and pressing needs rather than any theory have underlined such inevitable and useful perforations of all boundaries since the Peace of Westphalia in 1648, the alleged date of the birth of the "fenced-off" state. In fact, the constant and natural movement across boundaries has been both the natural consequence and a healthy corrective of the fragmentation of humankind into its many territorial corrals, separated one from the other by either artificial or so-called natural frontiers— though one may indeed ask what, after all, is so natural and "boundarish" about a mountain ridge or a river (often meandering) in our era of rapid and massive movements of persons, goods, and pollutants. Transborder neighborhood linkages—and the ensuing need for their regulation—are probably as old as humanity and my including them in this summary is certainly not done for the purpose of novelty.

A particular vicinity on land, however intimate it may be, cannot be isolated from the larger neighborhood framework and the contemporary reciprocal interlacing of the concern of two northern U.S.-East Canadian neighborhoods with acid rain reaching *both* from the Midwest cannot avoid the magnetic pull or impact of the larger Ottawa-Washington neighborhood. The same statement can be made about the efforts of the northern U.S. states and the Ontario/Québec cooperative framework to protect their Great Lakes water resources against ever-increasing needs for water in the Sun Belt; the four southwestern U.S. states facing the six northern Mexican states must be studied, not in separation from, but within the general U.S.-Mexican context; and this caution naturally applies also to the northwestern Swiss-Alsatian-southern German cooperative framework along the Rhine River, which is both separate from and an integral part of the larger Bern-Bonn-Paris framework.

It seems that complex webs of transborder regional cooperative frameworks have primarily developed in those areas of the developed world where a relative prosperity permits a more relaxed attitude toward territorial boundaries and so encourages what may be called "regional transborder osmosis." A potentially positive aspect of such an osmosis is that it involves neighbors that, regionally, are less asymmetric and therefore less afraid of each other than are nations facing each other in a continental context (such as the United States and Canada, the United States and Mexico, and West Germany, France and Switzerland). On the other hand, cooperative transborder twosomes, even when they consist of relatively compatible and symmetric neighbors, remain necessarily a part and bear the burden of an often grossly asymmetric (and less amicable) intersovereign dyad.

In Western Europe, all nations, including centralist France have ratified the Outline Convention on Transfrontier Cooperation Between Territorial Communities and Authorities, which was negotiated and signed in 1979. That document approves the various steps and procedures for closer transborder cooperation among neighboring noncentral authorities. France signed the Convention last and did so with many reservations to preserve the last word for the national government in Paris—"Paris über alles," as a German-speaking Swiss quipped.

In 1982, federal Switzerland organized a working group of all its cantons that are contiguous with France (Groupe de concentration des cantons frontaliers limitrophes à la France) for the specific purpose of conducting direct negotiations with neighboring French *régions* and *départements*. The Swiss Constitution specifically authorizes the cantons to engage in transborder activities in matters within the cantonal jurisdiction. In Délémont, the capital of the new francophone canton of Jura (clearly, a deliberate choice), the Swiss president and foreign minister, Pierre Aubert, carefully drew the line between the Swiss federal and cantonal "diplomacy": "The Swiss Federation intervenes as soon as there is cantonal contact with a foreign *capital*, but a canton may enter into direct contact with the representatives of those local communities which are comparable to our cantons."[11]

When we read some of the 800 agreements and letters of understanding linking the Canadian provinces with the U.S. counterparts we note in them the appropriate polite bow toward federal Washington and Ottawa, but that is followed by a matter of fact description how the agreement pertains to both sides of the border. The 1969 agreement on civil defense emergency planning between Montana and Alberta reads, for example, in part:

> Subject to review by Federal Authorities of both the United States of America and Canada where federal interests are involved . . . the Civil Defense Organization within the State of Montana and the Emergency Measures Organisation within the Province of Alberta will render all possible help one to the other . . . channels of communication will be between the office of the Director, Montana State Civil Defense Agency, and the office of the Co-ordinator, Alberta Emergency Measures Organisation.

To sum up, in our interdependent world, neighborhood dyads interact not only with their neighbors and their neighbors' neighbors within the national borders but also, through the collective national whole, with other parts of their own and other continents. An analysis of a transborder dyad cannot avoid considering the impact of the three additional layers of conflict or cooperation that proceed (1) from the border (the cross-border region) to (2) the nation, to (3) its continental, and finally to (4) its global connections as well as downward from the world scene to the transborder dyad, from (4) to (1). An interneighbor competition or rivalry may poison the center-to-center (international) relations, and local or transborder provincial politics may be used to affect the conduct of national foreign policy.

Extension of Foreign Policy Field

Since World War I and World War II, national governments have been increasingly called upon (one of the effects of global interdependence) to negotiate, sign, and ratify—and thus, indirectly legislate by means of executive agreements—international compacts dealing with human and labor rights, crime, genocide, fishing limits, energy flows, commodity prices, financial matters, and cultural exchanges—all matters of direct interest for, and within the jurisdictional domain of the noncentral authorities of federal components (or delegated to territorial communities in unitary systems). Constitutional texts generally assume and proclaim that the dividing line between foreign policy and domestic concerns is clear and firm—which it is not. Inevitably, many international agreements negotiated and ratified by national centers affect the various territorial or functional segments of the nation more adversely than others. Yet, national constitutions do not contain any particular provisions or mechanisms to ensure participation of noncentral governments in shaping foreign policy which, as noted above, has now expanded far beyond the traditional fields of defense and diplomacy to include economic, social, ecological, and cultural issues. In such a context noncentral governments have tried to preserve either their jurisdictional domain or ensure their inputs into central policy making. In democracies there is, of course, a general assumption that national government is and will remain responsible and responsive to inputs channelled to it by individuals and groups as well as by noncentral governments; with some justification it is expected that, as the scope of foreign policy expands, so will the formal and informal links between noncentral and central governments expand. (There is not yet sufficient experience to evaluate the practical effects of an amendment to the Austrian federal constitution that prescribes consultation with the federal components—*Länder*—*before* the federal government can conclude international treaties that could affect the provincial jurisdiction.)

In Canada, the provinces have taken the position that they have an undeniable right to act internationally in the areas of their constitutional jurisdiction; on the whole, the federal center has yielded on this issue, as can be documented by the activities of British Columbia and Alberta with regard to the Asian rim and the activities of both Ontario and Québec abroad. In 1985, for example, Québec's minister of international relations and foreign trade, Bernard Landry, presented a government paper, "Québec in the World," in which France and the United States were designated as "primary regions" for Québec's international activities in cultural and economic fields; the second level of priority included the Scandinavian countries and Asia; and Africa, the Middle East, and Latin America constituted the third level of priority. In addition, Minister Landry suggested Québec's direct participation in functional specialized agencies (such as UNESCO and WHO), and argued that it would be "foolish for the federal Government to talk [abroad] about hospitals, emergency wards, and vaccinations . . . it is even misleading to other countries to suggest that all the expertise is centralized in Ottawa."[12]

The Québec government document envisions also the possibility of close cooperative links with communist Czechoslovakia, Hungary, and the Soviet Union. In the case of the last, Québec might encounter some serious problems if it ever tries to extend its diplomatic contacts not only to Moscow, the center of the whole Soviet system, but also to Québec's territorial/federal counterparts such as the Soviet Ukraine, Estonia, Georgia, Kazakhstan, or any of the other fifteen republics, which, as noted previously, were granted the right of full external relations by both the Stalin and Brezhnev constitutions but enjoy none (except for the Ukraine's and

Byelorussia's membership in the United Nations Organization and its specialized agencies).

In the United States, state-elected representatives in Congress have always served as state lobbies with the aim to co-shape those aspects of national foreign policy that could be of direct concern to their constituencies such as tariffs, trade promotion, immigration, and, in modern times, environmental protection, illegal drug traffic, and various intersovereign border problems, ranging from meandering rivers to sewage.[13] What is, however, novel today is not only the state governments' awareness of, and sensitivity to, events abroad but also their contemporary diligent effort to supplement their traditional congressional lobbying by their permanent physical presence and activities abroad. The federal center, on the whole, has reacted positively to these new state initiatives insofar as they seem to be in harmony with the national objectives in matters of trade, investment, and cultural exchanges. But, of course, there were, are, and will bound to be clashes, too.

In the 1950s, for example, the issue of states' opposition to federal encroachments on states' rights by means of international executive agreements became quite an explosive issue in the form of the Bricker Amendment.[14] At the time, the issues were human rights and criminal law, placed on federal and state agendas by the International Convention of Genocide and the need for either federal or state-by-state ratification.

Presently, federal-state dissonances concerning trade and investment policies have created some new problems. In November 1977, for example (that is, eight years after Muammar al-Quaddafi's accession to power in Libya), the Idaho State Farm Bureau promoted the signing of a trade contract involving the government of Libya, North Pacific grain growers, and Lewiston, Idaho, grain growers.[15]

On July 1, 1982, the state of Kentucky began an active campaign to promote trade with South Africa and sent a two-week trade mission there on the basis of findings that, according to Gene Smith, deputy secretary of the Kentucky Department of Commerce, South Africa could be considered as a promising and largely untapped market for U.S. business. The mission was sent soon after the electoral campaign for Atlanta's mayoralty during which Andrew Young promoted the concept of Atlanta as "Africa's gateway to the American supermarket." Obviously, in contrast to Kentucky, Georgia's concept of Africa as a trade partner excludes South Africa.

In September 1983, a problem arose in Dallas when the city's office of protocol and the chamber of commerce arranged a mayor's breakfast to honor a delegation of fourteen South African businessmen from Durban. The ranking black member of the city council, Deputy Mayor Fred Blair, criticized (*Dallas Times Herald*, September 1983) the event as inappropriate as "would be these days (following the shooting down of the Korean plane) a hosting event such as this for the Soviet Union." The South African delegation also visited Houston, Chicago, and Los Angeles at a time when vigorous campaigns in many U.S. states and cities (New York City and Berkeley, in particular) had begun to force various state and municipal pension systems and state universities to divest their holdings in banks and corporations that were still doing business with the apartheid country.[16] In 1985, in the wake of violence and the proclamation of a state of emergency in South Africa, most of the trade policy and diplomacy issues were naturally catapulted from the state to the national level.

Another example of influence wielded by noncentral governments on the conduct of national foreign policy is the otherwise constitutional use of local taxing powers. In the 1980s, for example, several U.S. states began to prescribe "buy American" or to forbid the incorporation of foreign banks and foreign purchases of land, measures hardly consistent with the proclaimed national policies of free trade and competition. Another issue is the so-called unitary tax, which seven U.S. states, including California, have imposed on multinational corporations within their boundaries. These companies are taxed not on the basis of the profit earned within the state, but on an estimate of the local company's share of its parent company's worldwide profit. Canada and other U.S. allies—and the corporations—have strongly protested against these subnational taxes, which they considered to be contrary to both free trade and some GATT regulations.[17]

The missile age, with its ever-present potential for an atomic holocaust (which would have no regard for either national or intrafederal boundaries), has projected noncentral governments in free systems onto the international scene in still another way. In U.S., Canadian, and West European towns, districts, provinces, and regions, local majorities and authorities have become involved in promoting and, through appropriate voting mechanisms, adopting various resolutions in the framework of the nuclear freeze and anti-apartheid movements. For example, as noted by John Kincaid, by December 1984, sixty-one of sixty-nine nuclear freeze propositions had been approved by voters in state or local referenda and seventy-nine towns and cities had declared themselves nuclear-free zones.[18] In June 1984, the Berkeley (California) Settlements Initiative called upon the United States "to reduce its yearly aid to Israel by an amount equal to what it determines to be the most accurate approximation of what Israel spends annually on its settlements in the occupied territories of the West Bank, Gaza Strip, and Golan Heights." The proposal was defeated. In 1985, not only Berkeley, but also Los Angeles (where more Salvadorans live than in the city of San Salvador), and other California cities proclaimed themselves sanctuaries for illegal aliens and political refugees from El Salvador, Nicaragua, and other Central American countries. The attempt to defy federal immigration laws and authorities was legally controversial. They were, however, indicative of a trend: Local majoritarian devices are being mobilized for the purpose of initiating a flow of inputs not only in the so-called "low" but also "high" politics.[19]

Opposition to Big Government

The neopopulist dictum Small is beautiful has its intrafederal counterpart: "Noncentral is beautiful." In addition to the usual criticism of a national government's administrative, economic, legislative, and diplomatic performance or its loss of credibility, subnational leaders and their publics today often oppose the national center on a more general ground, arguing that it is unwieldy, big, overbureaucratized, dehumanized, or under the undue influence of one particular sector of the country. The Quebeckers and west Canadians, for example, often accuse Ottawa of following the principle of "what's good for Ontario, is good for Canada"; similarly, at one time, southerners and westerners in the United States complained about the northeastern establishment and its impact on Washington, D.C. The most common complaint today is simply that national governments and their bureaucracies are distant and therefore ignorant of where the local or regional shoe pinches. The Laredo mayor's often-quoted statement is symptomatic: "We live dangerously here in Laredo. We are subject to floods, droughts, the Mexican government, and the U.S. government." In such a context, extranational remedies appear justified by basically populist (or should I say: neoconfederal?) arguments.

"Me-Tooism"

Copycats sometimes reside in gubernatorial mansions and may engage in international activities for prestige, junketing, or paying political debts from the preceding electoral campaign by sending a local contributor on a mission or as a state/provincial representative to Paris, Tokyo, or Brussels. Some noncentral governments have established foreign contacts simply to emulate other subnational successes in attracting foreign investment or manufacturing plants to their territory. Thirty U.S. states, for example, competed over the location of a Volkswagen assembly plant, with Pennsylvania emerging as the final winner.

Some states, one may suspect, have established state offices abroad as a new status symbol, without heeding the general caution of the National Association of State Development Agencies (NASDA) about the cost and effectiveness of state presence abroad. One of the fifty state governments replying to my questionnaire about its foreign relations stated almost apologetically that it had not yet established a state office abroad (should one add, "As other subnational 'Smiths' have done"?) but added that its state university maintained extensive contacts with several foreign countries (which, by the way, may be a very good long-term investment after all).

Separatism

Although local or provincial resentment toward a distant government that is deemed big, inept, ignorant, or neglectful is one of the causes for external activities undertaken by noncentral governments, in only a few cases has such resentment reached the point at which secession and search for independent statehood have been placed on the political agenda. In such a case, nationalist sentiment rather than economic calculation plays an explosive role: Whenever language, culture, and history—studded with discrimination, economic or other—are involved, the persuasive eloquence of trade statistics is usually secondary.[20]

Such is the case in Québec as that province's external activities have often been motivated by separatism, or at least contain a strong independentist message. Time and again, the Québec case has also confirmed the relative irrelevance of economic data when nationalist emotions are mobilized or are spontaneously present.[21] Since 1974, for example, the federal government of Canada has been spending more in the province of Québec than it collected there in taxes ($48 billion in Québec's favor). This fact has been calculated by Québec government economists themselves and published in the official document *Comptes économiques.*[22] Yet, as seen by an ardent "Québécois" separatist, this is not quite the point—since he tends to insist on the Québec right of national self-determination regardless of some immediate economic cost. In this the *Parti Québécois* differs from its Québec opponent, the Liberal Party, which primarily focuses on building up Québec's economic power and foreign trade to ensure Québec's cultural and linguistic survival and political clout *within* the Canadian federation. Québec "diplomatic" activities abroad, which will be discussed in more detail later, are therefore supported—to use a shorthand formula—for primarily economic reasons with political consequences by the Liberals and for political reasons with economic consequences by the Parti Québécois.

Four Types of Noncentral Diplomacy

The forms, goals, intensity, frequency and importance of noncentral governmental entries onto the international stage vary greatly. They depend on various intervening variables such as coordinating mechanisms, as well as self-confidence of the national center; radical, revolutionary or moderate political climate; the quality and skill of provincial/state elites; ethnic/lingual heterogeneity; and, of course, the nature of the political system—noncentralizing federal, centralizing federal, decentralized unitary, or centralized (as well as the corresponding political cultures, ranging from confederal to "Jacobin-centralist"). Nevertheless, even in such a centralist system as France has always been, foreign lures or opportunities seem to have already attracted the interest of and elicited some international contacts on the part of the recently created French *régions* (for example, between the *région* of Rhône-Alpes and Tokyo). In an interview with me in July 1985, an official at the Quai d'Orsay (Ministry of External Affairs) complained about the lack of any mechanism to coordinate regional transborder initiatives abroad. Usually, the ministry learns about them ex post facto.

The various initiatives taken by noncentral governments on the international scene have so far assumed four distinct yet interconnected forms: (1) transborder regional microdiplomacy, (2) transregional microdiplomacy, (3) global paradiplomacy, (4) protodiplomacy.

Transborder Regional Microdiplomacy

By transborder regional microdiplomacy, I mean transborder formal and, above all, informal contacts, which are dominantly conditioned by geographic proximity and the resulting similarity in the nature of common problems and their possible solutions. Transborder regionalism is probably as old as humankind's divisions and subdivisions into various territorial segments. Currently, transborder regionalism manifests itself by various cooperative contacts across a national boundary in such matters of common interest as technical aspects of border crossings by migrants and immigrants; the legal movement of manufactured goods; the management of water resources; problems of pollution (acid rain, Mediterranean fly etc.); energy transfers (gas and hydro-power as between Québec, New York State, and New England states); prevention of smuggling; shipments of stolen goods; excessive purchases across the border and drug traffic (along the U.S.-Mexican border following the various devaluations of the Mexican peso); civil defense; sewage, prevention of natural disasters, such as fires in border forests or twin cities and flooding; various transfrontier manufacturing ventures (such as the U.S.-Canadian Auto Pact or the assembly or twin plants [*maquiladoras*] in the north of Mexico and the U.S. Southwest); and many other formal and informal arrangements resulting from and reflecting the ever-increasing permeability of intersovereign national boundaries.

Examining transborder regional microdiplomacy and summitry, one is constantly struck by the importance of interelite informal networks that do without any formal institutions yet perform their daily transborder tasks of coordination and adaptation of national policies to borderland realities quite effectively. The telephone (direct-dial diplomacy escapes unnecessary monitoring or meddling by central governments), improvised meetings, and luncheon appointments ("We go for lunch to Mexico," said an official in El Paso) seem to be the most preferred instruments for borderland problem-solving.

The New England states (with the exception of Vermont) actually do without any permanent representation in Canada, which is simply not "foreign" or "abroad" in the same sense as are Tokyo and Brussels where so many U.S. states and Canadian provinces maintain missions. "When I wanted to keep my people warm next winter," as Vermont Governor Richard Snelling told me, "I simply picked up the phone and called René [Lévesque]." The solution to the problem was finally not as simple as that, but the remark well illustrates the emphasis on a push-button conference telephone call and interexpert links (*cf.* the Montana-Alberta civil defense compact mentioned previously) that allows interneighbor contacts and compacts on an informal rather than a formal basis, in an ad hoc fashion rather than institutionally, and discreetly rather than with pomp and circumstance.

In Western Europe, the major preoccupation of both central and non-central governments in the 1980s is with the asymmetric development of regions, some of which are well inside the national boundaries while others lay astride them and engage in regional microdiplomacy. The European

Community and its Parliament as well as the loose association of European nations (including the Scandinavian ones) within the Council of Europe in Strasbourg had a number of conferences and expert workshops in their effort to remove the gross disparities between the prosperous and the underdeveloped regions of Europe.[23] The European Conference of Local Authorities, established in 1957, was also meant to be a counterweight to the European Community based on international agreements among the participating central governments. By 1975, the conference had added Regional to Local in its name and so came to represent all the territorial authorities in Western Europe below the level of the nation-state. It tries to play the role of champion of the "Europe of regions" rather than just nation-states.[24] Some regionalists advocate or hope that the regions will form a second chamber of the European Parliament, a "European Senate" of sorts.

The 1981 Conference of Local and Regional Authorities organized by the Council of Europe in Strasbourg adopted, for example, a final resolution on the regional policies of the member states in which it condemned the dangers "now threatening the very concept of regional planning and regional policy on a genuinely European scale." These threats were identified as coming from

(1) those who deny any need for prospective planning . . . maintaining that free market will in the last resort lead to satisfactory spatial and economic structures in Europe, and (2) politicians who are interested solely in the problems of their own region and thus fail to maintain a comprehensive view of regional development on a national and European scale.[25]

Three years later, the European Conference of Ministers Responsible for Regional Planning (CEMAT) chose as the major themes for its seventh session, held in Holland in 1985, decentralization and transfrontier cooperation in spatial planning.

Today there are twenty-four transborder European regions in operation or in the advanced planning stage. Some of them, like Regio Basiliensis (see Figures 9.1 and 9.2), have been in operation for several decades; others are still in their infancy. Their rather loose frameworks are referred to as transborder working groups.

In addition, there are numerous transborder cooperative arrangements that link up districts and municipalities from the Pyrenees to the Norwegian/Swedish/Finnish far north; these interlocal transfrontier cooperative frameworks operate in a similar way as do the Mexican and U.S. or Canadian and U.S. municipalities and counties in North America, that is, quite effectively, under the relatively benign eyes of their respective central and regional governments. In Europe, too, the focus of these intermunicipal arrangements is primarily on mutual help in emergencies, sewage, water management, air and water pollution, and other curses of modern civilization. In European transfrontier regions, the problem of migrating workers also

Figure 9.1. Regio Basiliensis: The "Basel Trinational Agglomeration"

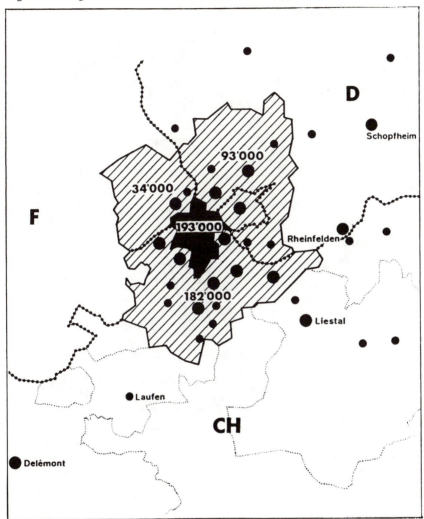

looms large (about 12 million in 1978),[26] especially in the matter of children's education and workers' participation in local politics and labor unions.

Transregional Microdiplomacy

Transregional microdiplomacy is the term used to describe connections and negotiations between noncentral governments that are not contiguous; they are separated by other provincial/state jurisdictions from the international border. One example is Georgia's trade representative who resides in Toronto;

Figure 9.2. Regio Basiliensis

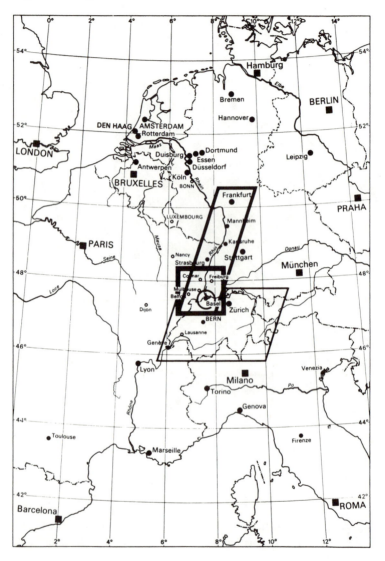

The central square indicates the close transborder "cooperative" between Basel, the northwestern Swiss cantons, south Alsace and the southern portion of the German *land* of Baden-Wurttemberg. The Regio overlaps with other transborder cooperative frameworks extending to Strasbourg and Frankfurt in the north, northern Italy, and western Austria.

other examples are the Canadian provincial trade missions in noncontiguous U.S. states such as those representing Alberta and Québec in Texas; Québec in Louisiana; Alberta, British Columbia, Ontario, and Québec in California; and Alberta, Ontario, and Québec in New York City—from which the three Canadian provinces reach out not only toward the Mid-Atlantic area but also, if not primarily, toward the national government in Washington, D.C.

In contrast to the informality of regional microdiplomacy (with its brief outbursts of formality during the gubernatorial summits), both transregional microdiplomacy and global paradiplomacy have a much more formal pattern. In our era, in which nations have not yet adapted to the international presence of noncentral governments, these forms of diplomacy necessarily raise questions of diplomatic protocol, leading to potential tensions with the diplomatic and consular representatives of a central government abroad, as well as problems of compliance with foreign laws concerning nondiplomatic foreign agents. The Canadian provincial "consulates" (delegations or houses) in the United States, for example, do not enjoy full diplomatic privileges; these are reserved only for the Canadian embassy and consulates. By contrast, in Paris, Québec's special relationship with France means the Québec delegation does have diplomatic privileges—so far denied to the Ontario government representative in Paris. Nevertheless, in contrast to sovereign nations, the Québec limousines in Paris do not have the privilege of flying the Québec blue-and-white flag on the right-hand front fender.

From the point of view of U.S. law the Canadian provincial representatives in the United States are foreign agents and, as such, must file semiannual reports on their activities with the U.S. Department of Justice, which treats these reports as documents open to the public (and therefore open also to this researcher). These reports indicate that, in a significant departure from transborder regional microdiplomacy in its narrow sense, the Canadian provinces target their activities to much larger areas than their geographic location would suggest. The Alberta, Toronto, and Québec[27] missions in New York City, for example, include under their respective "jurisdictions" all the Mid-Atlantic states, a part of the South, and, above all, Washington, D.C. The Québec representation in Boston covers the whole of New England except for southern Connecticut, which is viewed (to quote a Québec official) as a bedroom for New York City rather than an outpost of "yankeedom." The top political officers of the three provincial "consulates" in New York City commute at least once a week to the national capital to meet with and lobby both the federal administrators and the congressmen concerned with economic, ecological, energy, or cultural matters affecting the three provinces.

However incomplete (and deliberately conforming to the U.S. legal requirements concerning foreign agents) the Canadian provincial reports may be, they not only point to the provinces' search for contact with the various territorial U.S. counterparts but they also amply document the provinces' understandable need to monitor and influence the federal scene as managed by Washington, D.C. For example, in a report dated October 20, 1982, the Alberta representative in New York indicated that his main targets were neither New York City nor Albany but the following federal institutions (according to his ranking):

1. U.S. Department of Energy
2. Economic Regulatory Commission
3. Federal Energy Regulatory Commission
4. House of Representatives and its committees
5. Senate and its committees
6. Other such departments, agencies, and autonomous governmental bodies that may, from time to time, be considered a matter of interest to the Government of Alberta.

In the narrative following the list, the report indicates that the Alberta representative attended hearings of the above regulatory agencies and spoke with members of the staffs of various committees of Congress and regulatory agencies. Only at the end of the list can one find the New York-New Jersey Port Authority mentioned as being a target for contact and monitoring by the Alberta "consulate" in New York City.

In answer to a U.S. Department of Justice question as to whom these activities within the United States were to serve, the Alberta representative responded, "Her Majesty the Queen in the right of the Government of Alberta." The New York representative of the province of Ontario answered the same question (Ontario Report, October 11, 1983) simply as, "Government of Ontario, Canada." Any reference to Canada is missing in the Québec Report (June 30, 1983), which states that the delegation in New York served the "Government of Québec—Hon. Prime Minister René Lévesque." To the question whether the provincial agencies in the United States engaged in propaganda,[28] the response of Alberta was positive, but the answers of both Québec and Ontario are negative.

These examples regarding Canadian provinces—which, as it were, leapfrog the "borderlands" to reach more distant yet more important sites of power in the neighboring nation—raise the question as to how significant is land contiguity in today's age of global contacts and interdependence. Perhaps we should not be mesmerized so much by geography (or geographers) when we live in a "global village" in which we all are neighbors of each other. And yet, as I note in Chapter 10 in comparing the Canadian-U.S. and Mexican-U.S. borders, one has to admit in terms of human contacts, "land-is-land-is-land-is-land"—as Gertrude Stein might have put it.

Global Paradiplomacy

Global paradiplomacy, consists of political-functional contacts with distant nations that bring noncentral governments into contact not only with trade, industrial, or cultural centers on other continents (Québec in Dusseldorf or Ontario in Frankfurt) but also with the various branches or agencies of foreign national governments (as Québec, Ontario, and ten U.S. states in Brussels—the European Community headquarters). Noncentral contacts with national governments are, of course, to be expected in our era of welfare/warfare nation-states; they are unavoidable in contacts with socialist authoritarian systems in which one-party and central government authority is fully in charge of all aspects of the national economy. During trade-promotional trips to the People's Republic of China, for example, both the New York City mayor and the British Columbia premier primarily negotiated with the central government and its agencies in Beijing.

Six Canadian provinces (Alberta, British Columbia, Nova Scotia, Ontario, Québec, and Saskatchewan) have established a total of forty-six missions in eleven foreign nations, and twenty-eight U.S. states have fifty-four permanent offices in seventeen foreign countries. In addition, eighteen U.S. port authorities and cities have their own representatives in Western Europe.[29] In 1982, the Delaware River Port Authority proposed to extend its traditional cargo-focused duties by also becoming the U.S. marketing agent for the products of Nigeria and fifteen other African nations, organized as the Economic Community of West Africa.[30]

The federal government of Canada maintains a total of fourteen consulates-general in major U.S. cities. Their promotion of trade and tourism is combined with visa and immigration services. Thus, in some U.S. cities, there are two or three Canadian provincial houses in addition to and in cooperative and sometimes competitive relationships with the consulates of Canada.

The Canadian provincial and U.S. state representatives abroad and their efforts to monitor and influence central governments are nondiplomatic and nonpolitical in the accepted sense of the term, yet it is clear that their activities are bound to have some political dimension as all governments today wish to manage and regulate (if not own outright) so much of private enterprise and to control environmental issues, technology transfers, and cultural and educational exchanges. National ownership of nearly all means of production in communist and some Third World countries makes, as already noted, noncentral governments' contacts with foreign central authorities unavoidable.

Although the establishment and maintenance of permanent provincial and state offices abroad are the visible and expensive signs of the "globalization of provincialism," there are other ways and formulas by which noncentral governments assert their international competence abroad such as trade and investment shows that feature local/provincial/state manufacturing and technological know-how. Of economic significance are the establishment of foreign trade zones by thirty U.S. states; short-term, professional fact-finding missions dispatched abroad by state and provincial governments; and, above all, the well-promoted and well-publicized trips abroad undertaken by the leaders of noncentral governments. A good example is British Columbia's international effort in March 1984 to help its then-ailing economy: Premier William Bennett went to meet government and business leaders in Sacramento, San Francisco, and Los Angeles while the minister of forests, Tom Waterland, went to Germany, France, England, Holland, and Belgium and minister of industry, Don Phillips, went to Hong Kong, Malaysia, and Singapore. The premier then made an official visit to China.

No similar global paradiplomatic contacts seem to have been attempted by the Mexican states. In Europe, West German *Länder*, Bavaria in particular, and French *régions* have now added some global paradiplomatic initiatives to their transborder regional microdiplomacy. One partial exception on the European scene are the two territorial components of Belgium, the Walloon and Flemish communities. Initially, both sent missions to Québec (sometimes nicknamed the "graduate school of microdiplomacy"), and by 1985, both communities had extended their cultural promotional activities into various European countries. Some ethnoterritorial communities in Western Europe such as the Basques, Catalans, Bretons, Corsicans, and Welsh have tried for years to establish some formal links with the Brussels headquarters of the European Community. Scotland is represented in Brussels, and a curious case is that of Madrid, which, as a semiautonomous region, has established formal links with Québec.

Global Protodiplomacy

Global protodiplomacy is a term that may be used to describe those initiatives and activities of a noncentral government abroad that graft a more or less separatist message onto its economic, social, and cultural links with foreign nations. In such a context, the regional/provincial parent authority uses its trade/cultural missions abroad as protoembassies or protoconsulates of a potentially sovereign state. Such missions may be sometimes viewed and treated by the recipient foreign government in a similar fashion. Such was the case of Québec in Paris during the independentist phase of the Parti Québécois, which coincided with Charles de Gaulle's and Valéry Giscard d'Estaing's presidencies.

Why National Centers Worry

The various forms, contents and goals of microdiplomacy in its broadest sense—the international, interregional, and interlocal encounters of a new kind—point to the reasons why international activities of noncentral governments, whether partly political or primarily economic, social, or environmental, arouse both interest and worry on the part of central authorities in charge of national foreign policy. Subnational contacts with foreign centers of political power may be exploited by separatists to achieve their goals, or at least these contacts may whet secessionist appetites.

Even if a separatist potential is truly absent, too many subnational initiatives abroad may lead to chaotic fragmentation and so invite foreign meddling or cause a nation to speak with stridently conflicting voices on the international scene. Cautious or negative attitudes on the part of central national elites toward provincial microdiplomacy reflect also their opposition in the name of constitutional principles concerning the eminent domain of national foreign policy (in the United States, "a single legitimate national voice abroad" was, after all, what the Constitutional Convention in 1787 was partly about), concern for institutional tidiness and efficiency, institutional inertia opposing any change of routine, and fear of provincial egoism at the expense of the national whole as well as the other territorial communities. Perhaps there is also a worry, not entirely unwarranted, about provincial officials' lack of training and experience in the harsh world of international relations.

In one way or another, the problem of appropriate coordination (including harmless duplication) between the national center and the provincial sub-centers (as well as among the latter) has been placed on the federal agenda. (Chapter 10 will deal with some of the issues raised and remedies suggested.)

How Autonomous Territories Negotiate

If by diplomatic negotiation we mean processes by which governments relate their conflicting interests to the common ones, there is, conceptually, no real difference between transborder regional and global paradiplomatic networks of communication and negotiation. In both cases, the goal of regional or global microdiplomacy is the same as that of center-to-center macrodiplomacy: an *agreement* based on conditioned mutuality. Both sides pledge a certain mode of future behavior on the condition that the opposite side act in accordance with its promise. In contrast to domestic law, in international relations (whether on a micro- or a macrodiplomatic level) no common superior authority can be invoked in case of violation. Yet, as we know from international relations, such unenforceable bargains are generally observed since both sides continue to have a very similar interest in (a) preserving the assumed advantage assured by the initial bargain; (b) adhering to their pledges as a reaffirmation of credibility, an essential ingredient for future bargains; and (c) reconfirming the principle of goodwill.

The question to be raised in this framework is the following: How do the subnational authorities (that is, elected provincial/state/cantonal officials, their experts, and their administrative staffs) respond to and operate in a basically anarchic milieu, governmentless in the sense of a total absence of central enforcement, in which conflicting interests may be related to common interests only by a negotiated agreement and its rational, though unen-forceable, implementation? How much of the hierarchical and majoritarian decision-making modes in which these administrators operate in the morning carry across the border in the afternoon when decisions may be reached only by consociational consensus ("talk until you agree")? In other words, here deliberately imitating a Harvard study on diplomacy, How do, in fact, subnations negotiate?[31]

If, as this chapter basically argues, paradiplomacy by noncentral elected officials and their aides is here to stay—here complementing, there challenging, and often duplicating the macrodiplomacy conducted by central governments—several quite practical questions should be posed. Should foreign service officers, who manage the nation's macrodiplomacy, be better informed about the problems and management of the various forms of microdiplomacy? (The U.S. Pearson Program does send about twenty-five foreign service officers per year for training in and exposure to transborder and paradiplomatic relations of state governments.)

Should, on the other hand, noncentral "microdiplomats" have some exposure to center-to-center macrodiplomacy before they are assigned abroad? What should be the criteria for their selection and assignment? Two hundred and fifty years ago a French diplomat had this to say about desirable diplomatic skill:

> There are many qualities which may be developed with practice and the greater part of the necessary knowledge can only be acquired by constant application to the subject. . . . The great secret of negotiation is to bring out prominently the common advantage that they may appear equally balanced to both sides. . . . [A negotiator] should possess an equable humour, a tranquil and patient nature, always ready to listen with attention to those whom he meets.[32]

Do U.S. governors, French prefects, or Canadian premiers—the subnational "princes"—and their respective staffs have an equable humor and a tranquil and patient nature as the French diplomat required in 1716 of his aristocratic princes? Do they speak foreign languages, do they know about foreign political cultures? Maybe we should find out and, if necessary, offer remedial courses in this field.[33]

According to national centers, there may well be another deficiency or error to be corrected: an excessive borderland "chumminess" as a reaction against the two distant capitals whose border policies have to be absorbed by the borderlands although they are policies "formulated far from the border by people unfamiliar . . . with "frontier customs" and regional integrative systems through which daily border activities are coordinated."[34] In addition to such a critical attitude toward distant national centers whose directives are deemed by local authorities to be inappropriate and inapplicable (for example, along the Mexican-U.S. and Swiss-German-French borders), my survey registered what one might call a "transborder professional culture," an interelite shared way of approaching regional/local problems based on an intimate knowledge of and a sensitivity toward transborder interests and the groups promoting them and on frequent personal contacts (sovereign boundaries notwithstanding). Such a cross-frontier professional intimacy resulting from negotiating various border problems is, of course, a close relative of what Keohane and Nye's study identified as "transgovernmental relations," that is, a professional-expert intimacy developed close to but not at the apex of national power.[35] In the case of "cross-frontier transgovernmentalism," it is not proximity but rather distance (in terms of both miles and priorities) of the national apexes that contributes to the emergence and maintenance of what I have colloquially called "transborder chumminess."

It is important to note that neither territorial communities nor other units of political action today can be hermetically sealed out of the conduct of external affairs in the free world, despite the fundamental principle, valid in all territorial states, that assigns the exclusive exercise of foreign policy to the national center. As Daniel J. Elazar wisely noted: "Reality has a way of asserting itself regardless of principle."[36] And one name of that reality, as this study indicates is interdependence.

International Links of Noncentral Governments

Figure 9.3 presents an illustrative diagram based on David Easton's simplified model of a political system that describes the working of a political system in which people's demands and supports—*inputs* into the system—are converted by the authority into actions and policies—*outputs*. The feedback loop indicates the effects of government policies and actions upon further demands and supports that, in part, are shaped by the responses of the central authority. In line with our concern with the *external* dimension of politics conducted by both the national center and noncentral authorities, Easton's model has been modified in two aspects.

First, a foreign state was added to the picture as a potential source of activities that pass through the national boundaries with the aim of inflating demands and pressures upon the national center (line 1) or, on the contrary of undermining and deflating popular or sectional supports (line 2). This is also a graphic illustration of the discussion of foreign interference in the domestic affairs of a nation in Chapter 8.

Second, territorial components (provinces, states, cantons, *Länder*, regions, etc.) were added to both systems (Easton's national system and the added foreign state). Provinces of unequal size (and clout) are represented by various geometric patterns. It is assumed that similar input/output dynamics characterize the inner workings of the various territorial components.

Line 3, representing transborder regional microdiplomacy, symbolizes the informal and formal interactions between provinces on both sides of the border. Line 4 (transregional microdiplomacy) illustrates the provincial "diplomatic leapfrogging" over the frontier into distant areas but still within the neighboring state—such as Alberta's direct links with Texas and New York or Québec's links with Louisiana. Line 5 (paradiplomacy) denotes direct links between provinces and foreign central governments for the purpose of influencing general trade, investment, and other policies and actions (for example, U.S. states' trade negotiations with socialist countries). Line 6 (protodiplomacy) represents a direct link with foreign national governments, as does line 5, but the contents and goals are political (separatist) in support of future independent statehood (e.g., Québec). Line 7 (macrodiplomacy) illustrates traditional center-to-center diplomacy, which is usually concerned with issue-areas that are related to national security and status.

Figure 9.4 is a diagram of the micro- and paradiplomatic relations in the area between Belize and the Bering Sea, a trifederal zone consisting of

252

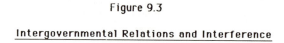

Figure 9.3

Intergovernmental Relations and Interference

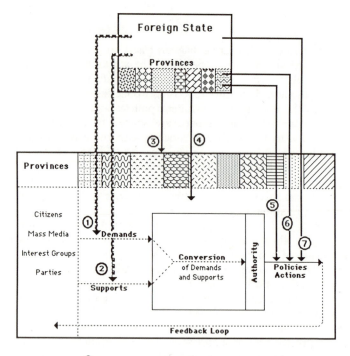

① **Interference** (Aim: Inflating Demands)

② **Interference** (Aim: Deflating Supports)

③ **Transborder Regional Microdiplomacy**

④ **Transregional Microdiplomacy**

⑤ **Paradiplomacy**

⑥ **Secessionist Protodiplomacy**

⑦ **Traditional (center-to-center) Diplomacy**

Figure 9.4

International Links of Noncentral
Governments

(Selected Samples)

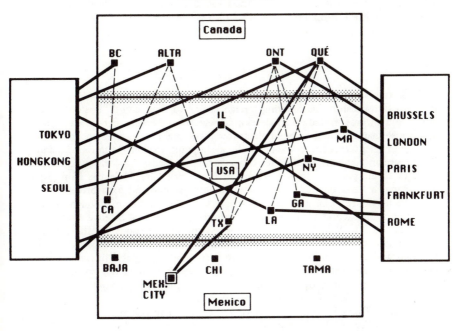

Transborder Regional Diplomacy
(Examples: US/Mexican borderlands and Twin Cities
in the Southwest. East Canadian/New England/New
York transfrontier cooperative frameworks;
West Canadian/US cooperation along the 49th
parallel.)

Transregional Microdiplomacy
Links between noncentral governments whose
jurisdictions are not contiguous.

Para- or Proto-Diplomacy
Contacts of noncentral governments with foreign
central governments.

Mexico, the United States and Canada. The diagram is extremely simplified, and only a few samples of the links are included. If all linkages involving these noncentral governments were to be indicated, the web would be so dense as to be undecipherable.

Northern Mexico, which is contiguous with four U.S. states in the Southwest (California, Arizona, New Mexico, and Texas), consists of seven states (Baja California [Norte and Sur], Sonora, Chihuahua, Coahuila, Nuevo León, and Tamaulipas). Only four of them are noted on the Mexican segment of the diagram (BAJA stands for Baja California, Norte and Sur; CHI stands for Chihuahua; and TAMA stands for Tamaulipas).

Notes

1. Cf. the *New York Times* report, January 19, 1985, that U.S. mayors increasingly travel to Europe and Asia to bring foreign capital to their cities: "Boston recently attracted a Swiss corporation to develop a new hotel, Newark persuaded Japanese and British manufacturers to build plants that make final preparations on automobiles for delivery. A Canadian developer built a shopping mall in Minneapolis, and a West German company built a tire chain factory in Cedar Rapids, Iowa. National Bank of China plans to open a branch in New York City while the Hong Kong and Shanghai Bank opened a skyscraper at Fifth Avenue and 59th Street."

2. In his study, "Constituent Diplomacy: U.S. State Roles in Foreign Affairs," presented at the World Congress of the International Political Science Association, Paris, July 15–20, 1985, John Kincaid grouped the main reasons for the increased participation of the U.S. states in international relations into four causal categories: (1) desire for constituent (federal components) autonomy, (2) global interdependence, (3) international complexity, and (4) the governmentalization of human societies.

3. U.S. Department of Commerce, Bureau of the Census, *Annual Survey of Manufacturers* (Washington, D.C., 1981), p. 1.

4. *Dallas Times Herald*, October 8, 1983. The eight-column article bears the title "World City? Dallas Pressing Effort to Lure Foreign Trade." Commenting on the "Invest in American Cities" trade show in Zurich, October 17–20, 1983, the article says: "It used to be that the Sun Belt cities were on top of the world in terms of economic development. But the recession has hit the Sun Belt . . . and they've found that foreign investments present an opportunity."

5. Wolfram F. Hanrieder, "Dissolving International Politics: Reflections on the Nation-State," *American Political Science Review* 71:4 (December 1978), p. 1277.

6. Thomas O. Hüglin, "Scarcity and Centralization: The Concept of European Integration," *International Political Science Review* 4:3 (1983), p. 345. Like all European scholars, Hüglin—as well as this author—uses the term "federal" in its original sense of noncentralization in contradistinction to the Canadian usage in which "federalization" may often mean "centralization."

7. There are, of course, simultaneous "civil wars for green dough." Within U.S. territory, on February 27, 1985, for example, the *New York Times* reported as follows: "Some states have sent governors, and some towns have sent roses. They are all pursuing what many economic development officials consider the catch of the 1980's: General Motors' $5 billion factory to build the future Saturn car model and the 6,000 to 15,000 jobs it will create." The Saturn plant was finally located in Tennessee.

8. National Governors' Association Committee on International Trade and Foreign Relations, *Export Development and Foreign Investment: The Role of the States and Its Linkage to Federal Action* (Washington, D.C., 1982), p. 115. In the introduction, this volume says: "A large majority of states have developed a range of trade and investment programs paralleling those of the federal government. . . . This explosion in the states' international activities reflects a growing awareness among governors of the degree to which foreign business trends and opportunities can affect the economic health of their communities" (p. 20).

9. Wayne Clifford, the executive director of the International Division of the Alberta Ministry of Federal and Intergovernmental Affairs, noted that this position paralleled one taken by the Canadian Senate Standing Committee on Foreign Affairs that stated: "There needs to be a new awareness at the federal level that a national foreign policy properly includes both federal and provincial activities. . . . There needs to be . . . a greater degree of solicitation by Ottawa of provincial views" (Québec Centre of International Relations, *Le Canada dans le monde* [Québec: XIII Congrès des relations internationales du Québec, 1981], p. 96).

10. Jeanne Kirk Laux, "Public Enterprises and Canadian Foreign Economic Policy," *Publius* 14:4 (1984), p. 78.

11. "La Confédération intervient chaque fois qu'il y a un contact avec une capitale étrangère, alors que le canton peut entrer directement en rapport avec représentants des collectivités locales qui lui sont *comparables*" (October 11, 1982; author's translation, italics added). There exists today an Association of European Border Regions and, since 1975, a European Regional Development Plan, established by the Commission of the European Community. Both Strasbourg and Brussels (as well as Luxembourg) are centers for many of these regional and interregional institutions and programs.

12. *Globe and Mail*, June 7, 1985. For the full text see: Québec, Ministry of International Relations, *Le Québec dans le monde: Le défi de l'interdépendance, Enoncé de politique de relations internationales* (Québec, June 1985), p. 204. The principle of international activities for Québec in the early 1960s was articulated by a Liberal party minister, Paul Gerin-Lajoie, not by the Parti Québécois.

13. Stephen P. Mumme, "State Influence in Foreign Policy Making: Water Related Environmental Disputes Along the United States-Mexico Border," *Western Political Quarterly* 38:4 (December 1985), pp. 620-638. The author recommends (p. 637) that more research be oriented toward vertical "behavioral linkages between subnational governments and 'horizontal' [central] government-to-governments relations in the international political arena."

14. U.S. Senator John Bricker (Republican of Ohio) proposed a constitutional amendment to curb the treaty-making power of the federal government on February 7, 1952. His main purpose was to eliminate self-executing executive agreements, which are often concluded without the concurrence of the Senate, the body empowered to approve international treaties. Legislators considered that these international agreements represented indirect legislation by the federal government encroaching on state jurisdictional domain. Sixty-three senators initially joined in signing the Bricker resolution before the whole amendment (revising the precedent set by the famous *Missouri v. Holland* case in 1920, concerning the shooting of wild birds migrating between Canada and the United States) was defeated by one vote in July of 1953.

15. Earl H. Fry and Gregory A. Raymond, *Idaho's Foreign Relations: The Transgovernmental Linkages of an American State* (Boise, Idaho: Center for Research, 1978), p. 36. See also Earl H. Fry, "The Politics of Investment Incentives and

Restrictions: A Preliminary Analysis of the Transnational Linkages of the U.S. States and Canadian Provincial Governments" (Paper presented at the Western Social Science Association Annual Conference, Albuquerque, April 27–30, 1983).

16. George W. Shepherd, Jr., *Anti-Apartheid: Transnational Conflict and Western Policy in the Liberation of South Africa* (Westport, Conn.: Greenwood Press, 1977).

17. Although the Treasury and the Council of Economic Advisers unanimously recommended a congressional correction of these state practices, a Supreme Court decision in June 1983 upheld the tax, and President Reagan, on September 22, 1982, endorsed the unitary tax in the name of his "new federalism." Thus, global income of some transnational corporations continues to be included in figuring state taxes in seven U.S. states. See also ACIR on the same issue.

18. Kincaid, *Constituent Diplomacy*, pp. 18–19.

19. A specialized municipal lobby for foreign policy was established in 1984 in Palo Alto under the name, Center for Innovative Diplomacy. It seems primarily committed to antinuclear and disarmament causes by means of "citizen diplomacy" and municipal involvement in shaping foreign policy. A 138-page *Action Handbook for Local Elected Officials* (Palo Alto, Calif.: Center for Innovative Diplomacy, 1984), written by the center's founder and director, Michael H. Shuman, contains a legal analysis of the rights and limits of municipalities in the fields of diplomacy and defense as well as border management. The handbook also provides models for municipal ordinances to establish a nuclear-free zone or to reduce national military spending by redirecting tax revenues back to the cities and towns. To make it easy for local leaders, the models provide dotted lines for the municipal officials to fill in their signatures and their towns' and cities' names.

20. Time and again, the nationalist leaders paraphrase either the Filipino message to the United States, "Better a government run like hell by Filipinos than one run like heaven by foreigners," or the Algerian response to the French: "After independence it will be a mess, but it will be our mess."

21. The former Liberal prime minister of Canada, Pierre Elliot Trudeau, demonstrated the difficulty of balancing emotions and dollars. During the patriation of the Canadian Constitution in 1982, he criticized the provincial premiers for lacking a higher purpose and a nonpedestrian vision of Canada, treating their country merely as a "confederation of provincial shopping centers." Québec was sometimes criticized by him for exactly the opposite reason: too much vision and too little concern for the economic facts of Canadian life.

22. *Le Devoir* (Montréal), September 7, 1983: "Les comptes économiques de 1982: Ottawa verse $18 milliards au Québec et y perçoit $13.2 milliards.

23. In Western Europe, where national systems are dominantly unitary, the very terms "regional/spatial planning" (a newly coined English term for the French "aménagement du territoire") and "regional policy" are defined as "measures taken by the central government authorities to promote the socio-economic development of less prosperous regions" (Council of Europe, Standing Conference of Local and Regional Authorities of Europe, "Report on the Regional Policy of the Member States of the Council of Europe and the European Institutions" [Strasbourg, October 18–20, 1983], p. 3).

24. Council of Europe, *The Conference of Local and Regional Authorities of Europe* (Strasbourg: 1980), p. 54, describes the European regional ideology as follows: "To build Europe is an obvious need, but it does not mean building a new, abstract, unitary diagrammatic and technocratic entity. It means federating, developing institutions from the bottom, following the rising order of federalism, in which unity is founded upon diversity. This implies recognition of the *nation*, its institutions

and history, and of the municipalities which are the birth place of civil liberty. Between the municipal primary cell and the nation stands the *region*, an operational intermediary and a living reality. . . . European unity . . . would be all the stronger for being based on local realities."

25. Council of Europe, *Conference of Local and Regional Authorities of Europe* (Strasbourg, October 27–29, 1981), Resolution 122, p. 1.

26. Council of Europe, *Conference of Local and Regional Authorities of Europe*, "Participation of the Individual in Local Public Life" (Strasbourg, June 2–22, 1978), p. 34.

27. An official publication of the Québec government lists eight states and the District of Columbia into which its New York representation ramifies out, namely, Delaware, Kentucky, Maryland, New York, New Jersey, Virginia, West Virginia and Pennsylvania (*Les Carnets du Québec: (1) Les délégations du Québec: action concrète* [1982], p. 9).

28. The U.S. questionnaire, called "Supplemental Statement: Pursuant to Section 2 of Foreign Agents Registration Act of 1938, as Amended" (Washington, D.C.: United States Department of Justice, Internal Security Section, forwarded to foreign agents twice a year since 1939) defined political propaganda as "including any oral, visual, graphic, written, pictorial, or other communication or expression by any person which is reasonably adapted to, or which the person disseminating the same believes will, or which he intends to prevail upon, indoctrinate, convert, induce, or in any other way influence a recipient or any section of the public within the United States with reference to the political or public interests, policies, or relations of a government of a foreign country . . . etc." One can wonder how to distinguish Alberta's self-confessed propaganda (oil and tourism) from the various efforts on the part of Québec and Ontario clearly to "convert . . . or in any other way influence" U.S. recipients in matters of Québec's autonomy/independence, Hydro-Québec, asbestos and acid rain or Ontario's trade, media, and transportation interests.

29. The eighteen port authorities and cities represented in Europe in 1985 were Alabama, Port of Mobile; California, Port of Oakland; Delaware River Port Authority; Florida, Port of Jacksonville; Illinois, Chicago Port Authority; Indiana Port Authority; Louisiana, Port of New Orleans; Maine, city of Bangor; Maryland Port Administration (in England and Belgium); Massachusetts Port Authority; Mississippi Gulf Coast Authority; City of New York; Port Authority of New York and New Jersey (in London and Zurich); Oregon, Port of Portland; Penns Southwest Association; South Carolina, Port of Charleston; Texas, Corpus Christi Business Development Commission and Texas; Port Authority of Corpus Christi; Virginia Port Authority.

30. The West African nations involved were Nigeria, Benin, Cape Verde, Gambia, Ghana, Guinea, Guinea-Bissau, the Ivory Coast, Liberia, Mali, Mauritania, Niger, Senegal, Sierra Leone, Togo and Upper Volta. Interstate competition for West African cargoes involved New York and Norfolk as well as Georgia. At one point, Nigerian officials threatened the Delaware officials that Nigeria might take its cargoes into Georgian ports if the Delaware River Port Authority were not receptive to performing the marketing function.

31. F. C. Iklé, *How Nations Negotiate* (New York: Harper and Row, 1964), pp. 56–57.

32. François de Callières, *On the Manner of Negotiating with Princes* (first published in 1716 under Royal Privilege and Approval; Notre Dame: University of Notre Dame Press, 1963), iii.

33. In a survey conducted by the author in 1985, the twenty-eight U.S. states represented by trade/investment missions abroad were asked whether the state

"microdiplomats" should be assigned for a short time to a U.S. consulate abroad for training or whether the Foreign Service Institute should have a short course for the state representatives on the promotion of trade/investment, tourism, and cultural exchanges. An overwhelming majority of the answers was negative to both questions. Only a few had a mildly positive reaction to a possible short course at the Foreign Service Institute. When asked about help or difficulties emanating from the U.S. Department of State, National Association of State Development Agencies (NASDA), National Governors' Association (NGA), Department of Commerce, or the Office of U.S. Trade Representatives, the answer was almost uniformly, None of the above. As to the criteria for selection of state representatives, knowledge of the target country and foreign language skill were rated as the two most important; foreign trade experience and negotiating skill third and fourth in importance. Civil service experience was viewed as unimportant. Cf Scott Jaschik, "Seeking to Compete in World Economy, State Backed International Education," *The Chronicle of Higher Education - Government and Politics*, December 4, 1985, p. 18. The article quotes Ralph H. Smuckler, president of Administrators of International Education Programs and dean of international studies at Michigan State University as saying, "In the past people worried about the whole country's position abroad; now they worry about their own state's being internationally competitive." And the article adds, "International education is getting more and more attention from state politicians . . . as states place more emphasis on attracting foreign capital and marketing their products abroad."

34. Elwyn R. Stoddard, "Local and Regional Incongruities in Bi-National Diplomacy: Policy for the U.S. Mexico Border," *Policy Perspectives* 2 (1982), p. 126. For a different view of local day-to-day transborder policies practiced in the twin Mexican-U.S. cities along the border, see Paul Callsen, "Informal Transborder Relationships Among Municipal Officials: El Paso, Texas; Ciudad Jurarez, Chihuahua," (Master's thesis, University of Texas at El Paso, May 1985). In that well-researched paper, no evidence could be quoted by the author of federal or state interference with the way municipal authorities run their cross-border affairs. Symptomatically, the author begins his work with Robert Frost's well-known poem "Mending Wall," about something that so dislikes a wall that it makes gaps for two to pass abreast.

35. Robert O. Keohane and Joseph S. Nye, "Transgovernmental Relations and International Organizations," *World Politics* 27:1 (October 1974), p. 44.

36. Daniel J. Elazar, "Federated States and International Relations—Introduction," *Publius* 14:4 (1984), p. 1. The whole issue, edited by Ivo D. Duchacek, elaborates several of the themes of this chapter in greater detail. See in particular John M. Kline, "The International Economic Interests of U.S. States" (pp. 81–94); John Kincaid, "American Governors in International Affairs" (pp. 95–114); and Ivo D. Duchacek, "The International Dimension of Subnational Self-Government" (pp. 5–31). Since the publication of this special issue of *Publius*, several concepts as well as terms have been further elaborated and refined.

10

From Belize
to the Beaufort Sea

Love your neighbor, yet pull not down your hedge.
—George Herbert (1593–1633)

So far from God, so close to the United States.
—Porfirio Díaz, president of Mexico
(1837–1880 and 1884–1911)

*The crucial point is that both [Mexican and U.S.] elites recognize that today
their border cities are more economically and socially integrated with one another
than they are with their respective nations.*
—J. W. Sloane and J. B. West
(*Journal of Interamerican Studies and World Affairs*, 1976)

Federalism has been to us what football is to Britain. It is our blood-sport.
—Joe Clark, Canada's secretary of state
for external affairs (*Globe and Mail*, November 14, 1984)

*It is a notorious fact that Québec is different. It seems to me natural that this
cultural and linguistic richness is recognized and respected within Canada. There
is nothing contradictory in that. Federalism does not aim at uniformity.*
—Brian Mulroney,
Canada's prime minister (January 18, 1985)

*High politics is symbol laden, emotive, and based on attitudes characterized by
greater intensity and duration than "low" politics which is consequently more
susceptible to the rational calculation of benefits associated with economic problems.*
—Joseph S. Nye
(*International Regionalism*, 1968)

*The states of today are not monolithic blocs . . . groups, parties, factions, and
all sorts of other politically organized groups within such states can take a hand
in matters transcending national boundaries. . . . They may exert their influence
as domestic pressure groups so effectively that foreign statesmen would be ill-
advised to ignore them. . . . There are also states, where integration is so poor
that other states must deal with parts, rather than with a fictitious whole, if
diplomacy is to be effective.*
—Arnold Wolfers
("The Actors in International Politics," 1959)

259

Cooperative frameworks astride national land boundaries represent a sub-category of international relations that, paradoxically, combine respect with disrespect for territorial sovereignty. They reflect and implement the imperatives of regional interdependence between two or more nonintegrating territorial segments of sovereign national systems cooperating across the borders. Such transborder regional cooperatives have developed in Western Europe (see Chapter 9) and even more prominently between the three neighboring federal systems in North America, that is, the area extending from the southern borders of Mexico with Belize and Guatemala to the Beaufort and Bering seas and Queen Elizabeth Islands in the Canadian far north. The intended goals of transborder cooperative regionalism are simply to remove obstacles to the mobility of commodities, products, humans, and cultural programs and to seek collectively acceptable solutions to common problems that arise from a neighborhood situation and call for a neighborly solution.

Facing each other across national boundaries, territorial communities have, of course, always found some informal or formal ways of regulating specific border problems. Today, however, under the impact of regional interdependence, the number, urgency, and importance of such transborder issues that are of concern to both sides of an international border have increased exponentially, ranging from relatively prosaic "border-maintenance" problems such as forest fires, which are quite disrespectful of human-drawn frontiers, to electronic data traffic, energy transfers, and various "cultural penetrations"—or "cultural imperialism" in the leftist terminology used by some anglophone Canadians in describing the penetrative power of the U.S. media. Most of these issues involve funds and concerns of both noncentral and central governments as well as those of various interest groups and corporations on both sides of the border.

The number of transborder arrangements along the U.S.-Canadian border is impressive. In 1978, one researcher, Roger Frank Swanson, listed 766 such minor and major transborder arrangements between Canadian provincial and U.S. state authorities.[1] By now the number is much higher. At one point, the Canadian Department of External Affairs planned to update the list of all such understandings between the two sides of the border but finally abandoned that task because of the sheer weight of numbers. Another reason was that most of these transborder "compacts" were thought to deal with what appeared to be marginal, purely local, or technical issues.

Transborder Regional Cooperatives
and Complex Interdependence

The shorthand expression—regional cooperatives—applies to the networks of communication channels, implicit and explicit rules, and informal and formal procedures that permit and regulate (within a transborder region) cooperative interaction between municipal and regional governments as well as individual citizens and private enterprises. Within such transborder regional cooperatives, the mode of common decision making is not—and cannot be—majoritarian; it is consociational. Agreements between territorial segments of two neighboring sovereignties have to be necessarily reached by negotiation and consensus. The term "microdiplomacy" seems appropriate.

The *noncentral* governments represent only one set of actors co-shaping this trinational federal scene. Besides the three general governments, there are several other categories of actors engaged in transborder cooperation or conflicts. Some of them have more clout than provincial and state governments: transnational corporations, polluting industries, and transborder production networks ranging from U.S.-Canadian autopact and data processing to the U.S.-Mexican assembly/twin plants (*maquiladoras*). The constant intermingling of actions and goals of these various sources of transborder initiatives and actions—a silent and segmented integration of a sort—determines what, in matters other than military, is or is not to be done in the borderlands and beyond.

Although engaged in intimate cross-border cooperation, the leaders of the territorial communities do not intend to dissolve their basic links with their respective national systems. A new "zonal" or "borderland" nation, institutionally and emotionally separate from their respective national heartlands is generally not the goal—even though borderland political culture, customs, and linguistic affinity do give the transborder region a distinct flavor. As rudimentary "confederal" overlaps between two contiguous federations, transborder territorial cooperatives remain and are meant to remain intersovereign, that is, they are subnational twosomes within a larger binational dyad. This intention is in contrast to that of federal unions, whose goal it is to create not only a central authority, based on a majoritarian mode of decision making, but a composite federal nation—e pluribus unum. A transborder region's motto could be *Ex duum duet* ("from two-a-twosome"—ancient Greeks would have probably used the verb in dual rather than in singular or plural in referring to such configurations).

In examining the workings of transborder cooperatives, this study applies several insights derived from the concept and study of international regimes by various scholars—Robert O. Keohane and Joseph S. Nye,[2] Ernst B. Haas,[3] and Stephen D. Krasner.[4] In particular, the three basic characteristics of complex interdependence—multiple channels, multiple issues, and nonuse of military force—identified by Keohane and Nye[5] are clearly connected with transborder regionalism in North and North Central America.

1. Multiple channels connect communities on both sides of a national frontier. The inputs and outputs flowing through these channels reinforce each other. Transborder regional cooperatives (regimes) often complement but sometimes conflict with the center-to-center (international) flows. This study focuses on those regimes that primarily involve noncentral authorities.

2. Multiple issues are the second characteristic of complex interdependence. These issues are not ranked either hierarchically or stably; with time and

space their ranking changes. For example, in the 1980s the explosive issue in the eastern part of the United States and Canada was acid rain; in the U.S. Southwest, the flow of undocumented workers, sewage, and water; and along the River Rhine, it was the overheating of the water by intraregional reactors. In regional contexts in the U.S. Southwest and North, military security did not dominate the transborder agendas.

3. Nonuse of military force is the third characteristic of complex interdependence, and it applies to the North and North Central American (Beaufort to Belize) scene. The use or threat of military force is generally perceived as being primarily outerdirected, not innerdirected. When the weaker neighbors of the United States feel they have to react to economic pressures and ambitions, their fears of colonial dependency and exploitation do not acquire a military dimension. (The same applies today in Western Europe where the Rhine is no longer one of the most explosive frontiers in Europe; there too, military preparedness is outer-, not inner-directed.)

In the context of this study, a possible *unintended* effect of transborder regionalism is worth noting, given for example, the highly asymmetric nature of the Mexico-U.S. relationship. Being peripheral and distant from, and quite often critical of their respective national centers—deemed ignorant, neglectful, or unnecessarily meddling—provinces, states, and municipalities (facing and intermingling with each other) more often than not, as noted previously, see themselves as somewhat less asymmetric in terms of power, goals, population, and size than their respective nations. Their equality in their border worries and anxieties makes the components of unequal federal systems somewhat less unequal. In this sense, perhaps, while transborder cooperative zones cannot remove, they may blunt the edges of binational asymmetry.

On the other hand, regardless of symmetry or asymmetry, every so often a neighboring territorial community may be in an acute competition with its opposite number across the border even when a relative harmony prevails between the two national centers. For the Canadian central and economically powerful province of Ontario, for example, the U.S. Midwest is a major competitor whatever goes on between Washington and Ottawa.

When the water dispute between North Dakota and Manitoba was partly resolved in 1985 in favor of the ecological concerns of Canada (the Garrison Dam project), North Dakota retaliated by adopting various bills directed against Manitoba's transborder interests. Defending the fourth retaliatory bill, one legislator said, "Now that we have Manitoba's attention, it would be a bad time to take the pressure off!" The opponents called the retaliatory legislation "petty," and one representative (Orlin Hanson), whose district borders on Canada, read aloud a letter from a Manitoban offended by the four North Dakota bills: "How many slaps in the face can we take in one week?" the letter asked.[6]

One more observation imposes itself. In both the U.S. North and Southwest, transborder regional intimacy (or tension) cannot possibly be equally intensive along the thousands and thousands of miles that make up the borders. The overpopulated bilingual and bicultural twin cities in the U.S. Southwest and the deserts between them and the near-emptiness of the U.S.-Canadian "borderlands" are obviously different. In his analysis of the Mexican-U.S. border economy, Niles Hansen distinguished seven subregions in the area: the San Diego metropolitan area, the Imperial Valley, the Arizona borderlands; the El Paso region, the Middle Rio Grande region of Texas, the South Texas transborder region, and the lower Rio Grande valley. In Hansen's words: "Proximity has had varying subregional consequences. . . . the Southwest borderlands area is not homogeneous and . . . there is little economic interaction among the area's subregions."[7] Along the U.S.-Canadian border the differences between the western/Pacific, central/prairie, eastern/industrial, and Atlantic maritime sectors are obvious, as it were, to the naked eye.

Canadian and Mexican Borders: Similarities and Contrasts

The vast area extending from Belize to the Bering and Beaufort seas represents a unique set of complex relations among noncentral governments across the national (intersovereign) borders. These various relationships reflect our era of complex interdependence in four ways that are special to North and North Central America.

Four Similarities

1. In contrast to the "Balkanization" of other continents into microstates and mininations, North America—from the Arctic Ocean down to the Gulf of Mexico—remains divided under the political and economic management of only three sovereign nation-states.

2. The national boundaries in this continental expanse are extremely long (2,013 miles between Mexico and the United States and 5,255 miles between Canada and the United States to which one has to add the often controversial "saltwater" frontiers as well as the Alaska-Yukon border). In contrast to so many other parts of the world, the two long intersovereign boundaries remain militarily unfortified: No Maginot Line symbolizes the memories of past violent clashes, present tensions, and fears about the future. Despite the overwhelming power of the United States, neither Mexico nor Canada presently dread the use or threat of U.S. military force *within* the Belize-Beaufort region. Whatever fears of colonial dependency, imperial integration (by a mighty United States)—called "continentalism" in the Canadian context—or economic exploitation exist on account of the grossly asymmetric relations among the three nations, none of these fears contains a military dimension. This situation contrasts with fears in the Caribbean, Central American, and South America as well as on other continents. The awesome U.S. military might is generally considered as solely, though not always wisely, *outer*-directed.

There is, of course, tension and argument about the use or misuse of the U.S. military power outside the area. In other words, other than military-security issues dominate the North American and North Central American agendas, such as resources, development, and transborder movement of persons, goods, energy, and pollutants. Looking at the region through federal lenses, we should note that, as emphasized previously, the above named nonsecurity issues have traditionally and constitutionally been considered to be either partly or dominantly within the autonomous jurisdictional powers of noncentral territorial governments (provincial, state, municipal, and local).

3. The three contiguous nations of North America are *federal* states in which one central government and several federal components (thirty-one in Mexico, fifty in the United States, and ten in Canada) have divided and now share power in matters other than national security and diplomatic status. Imperatives of global and regional interdependence confront the three national governments and the ninety-one federal components with new challenges as well as opportunities that call for new problem-solving procedures and mechanisms, especially along the long national borders.

The authors of the three federal constitutions and their amendments (including the British North America Act of 1867 as patriated, amended, and provided with the Canadian Charter of Rights and Freedoms in 1982) did not, and perhaps could not, anticipate these challenges or the need or desire on the part of the noncentral governments to respond to them. Nevertheless, the components of the federal states are being lured or forced into economic/cultural/political ventures across the national borders and into contact with either neighboring or distant centers of political, economic, industrial, technological, or cultural power. These ventures often complement, at times duplicate, and occasionally compete or conflict with national foreign policy in economic, environmental, or cultural fields.

Although the three nations that constitute the contiguous federal zone from Alaska to Guatemala are committed to the federal principle of political pluralism and territorial division of powers, their actual practices greatly differ. In particular, in the context of this study, the elbowroom enjoyed by the leaders of the various noncentral governments varies greatly, ranging from the impressive powers exercised by the Canadian premiers to the minimal independent powers of the Mexican governors, subservient to the one-ruling party yet multifunctional (or multi-interest) system of Mexico. Despite these differences, there has emerged a similar pattern of transborder interactions among the three federal systems: nonintegrative transborder regimes.

4. On both sides of the borders, elites are keenly aware of their respective countries' asymmetric relations to the United States and are sensitive to the penetration of their respective countries by U.S. economic interests, media, popular culture, and life-style. The French-speaking Quebeckers (this study uses the term "Quebeckers" when it refers to all inhabitants of the province [francophone, anglophone, and allophone] and the term Québécois

Figure 10.1. The U.S.-Mexican Border and the Symbolic Overlap of Their Coats of Arms

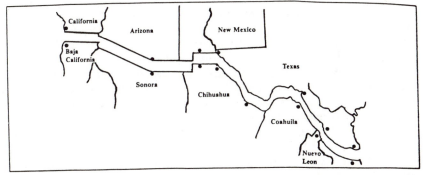

(Courtesy of Governor Bruce Babbitt of Arizona, moderator of the Fourth International Meeting of the Border Governors of the United States and Mexico)

when it refers to the francophone majority of Québec) represent a partial exception as they feel somewhat better protected by their language barrier (in contrast to both English-speaking Canadians and Spanish-speaking Mexicans); nevertheless, in their unguarded moments, even the Québécois seem occasionally ready to repeat and adapt Porfírio Díaz's overquoted statement: "So far from God [and Paris] and so close to the United States."

Nine Contrasts

Nine contrasts between the northern and southwestern U.S. borders merit our attention because of their political consequences.

"*Borderlands.*" This term is used quite comfortably with reference to the 400-mile-wide, 2,000-mile-long belt that is bisected by the U.S.-Mexican border.[8] The same term when applied to the forty-ninth parallel sounds awkward, and few of us would use it. In contrast to Mexico whose six border states repose on the foundation of and links with the other 25 Mexican states, (see figure 10.1), and in contrast to the United States, whose southwestern and northern border states form a "periphery" of a sort to the U.S. heartland, Canada simply has no borderland; its ten provinces are the borderland. (In the case of Canada, the Yukon and Northwest Territories are "hinterlands," in the full sense of the word.) It would be clearly quite unrealistic to speak of the Canadian-U.S. border zone from Victoria to Saint Johns as sharing an identical attitude toward Ottawa and Washington to the same degree as is the case of the border zone from Tijuana/San Diego to Matamoros/Brownsville. The concept of a special border political culture and feeling of transborder affinity or loyalty fits the Alemannic Rhine Valley as well as the biethnic U.S.-Mexican border with its intertwined Hispanic/U.S. cultures but seems misplaced when applied to the U.S. Canadian border.[9]

A U.S.-Mexican borderland scholar, Ellwyn R. Stoddard, expressed the difference succinctly: "Along the more free-flowing Canadian border there is a weak or non-existent border culture whereas a strong border culture extends along the entire length of our southwestern border with Mexico. . . . We depend on one another. To try to separate us [U.S.-Mexico Borderlands] will kill both of the Siamese twins."[10]

Given the nature of international law, the sea-water boundaries are dominantly a matter of concern for national rather than state or provincial governments. Nevertheless, the positive or negative inputs by coastal provinces and states concerned with their respective fishing industries naturally color all international disputes and agreements, such as between Mexico and the United States, and Canada and the United States. This was amply demonstrated in the wake of the new Law of the Sea which the United States refused to ratify in 1982.

A particular issue with no counterpart on the U.S.-Mexican scene is the tension between Canada and the United States concerning the territorial or international status of the Northwest Passage. Basically, Ottawa has opposed the United States assertion that the Northwest Passage represents a body of international waters open to U.S. commercial and military shipping and overflight. Ottawa decided to claim straight baselines drawn in order to demarcate the waters which Canada proposes to maintain and protect as internal waters. Politically, Canada also argues that the Russians would be entitled to sail and overfly the Northwest Passage with naval units, submarines, and warplanes if Washington continued to view and use the Arctic archipelago as international rather than the Canadian national sea route. In September 1985, Ottawa decided to build a super-icebreaker (Polar Class 8) at an estimated cost of $500 million to assert Canadian national control and maintenance over the Arctic waters. On this issue the opposition to any passage by United States icebreakers and other ships through the allegedly Canadian waters was all-Canadian. An editorial in the Québec daily, *Le Devoir* (August 5, 1985), spoke of "l'arrogance américaine" and Ontario's *Globe and Mail* (September 12, 1985) concluded its editorial with: "After all, from Davis Street to the Beaufort Sea, this is our land—and these are our waters."

Federal Differences. Although all three contiguous national systems between Belize and the Beaufort and Bering seas are classified as federal, the commonality of the resulting practices should not be exaggerated. The power of the Canadian premiers has no counterpart in the U.S. states and even less so in Mexico. In the United States, there is no counterpart to the dominant position of the Canadian cabinet and the House of Commons; in Canada, there is no counterpart to the powerful U.S. Senate qua federal chamber. There are, however, predictions that as a result of their confrontation of similar problems as well as some imitation, both of these federal systems change and tend to become more alike. Typically, one recent comparative study concludes:

> Federalism on each side of the forty-ninth parallel is different, but current institutional and constitutional trends, and the problems defining national agendas, are remarkably similar. These trends suggest that both states and provinces are losing autonomy, with Canadian provinces gaining more power at the center, and American states improving their capability to exercise power at home. Thus, it is possible that however unlike the two federal systems may be, they are both changing. Whereas neither would acknowledge imitation, both might recognize resemblance.[11]

In all three federal systems, the party discipline greatly varies; because of its one-party system, Mexican federalism has to be taken with many grains of salt. When the U.S. governors of California, Arizona, New Mexico, and Texas meet their Mexican counterparts from Baja California Norte/Sur, Sonora, Chihuahua, Coahuila, Nuevo León, and Tamaulipas at various gubernatorial summits, the former face a well-disciplined and centrally instructed group of single-party delegates—a situation that, in actual negotiations, seems to cause some problems for the U.S. governors and their staffs, emerging as they do from their respective pluralistic democratic environments.[12] The differences in the negotiating styles and traditions were described by John W. House: "There is a preference for individual contacts at the highest level with U.S. officials in sharp contrast to the fragmented, incrementalist approach favoured by American bureaucrats. Mexicans also prefer 'total package' negotiations rather than piecemeal consideration of issues."[13]

Differences in Microdiplomacy. The differences among the three federal styles and practices have produced another contrast (identified in Chapter 9), that of transregional microdiplomacy and global paradiplomacy practiced by six Canadian provinces and twenty-eight U.S. states but absent from the Mexican federal scene. There seems to be no real possibility that the Mexican states will follow a very probable scenario that Elliot Feldman, discussing the international dimension of federalism in Canada and the United States, described as follows:

> Some Canadian provinces [are] more innovative and experienced, but many states are eager to catch up. States within the union and provinces within

confederation will compete more openly among themselves, on the international stage, for comparative advantage. They will open more offices abroad and populate them with wider-ranging expertise. They likely will conduct foreign policy in all but name and sign commercial agreements that fail to be treaties in name only.[14]

Settlement Contrasts. The thinly populated U.S.-Canadian border contrasts with the U.S. Southwest and its overpopulated and rapidly growing twin cities along the U.S.-Mexican border. (In the east, the density of the population in the "borderlands" between the Canadian provinces and the U.S. states is about 34 people per square mile as opposed to about 606 people per square mile in the Swiss-German-French Regio Basiliensis). Buffalo/Fort Erie, Detroit/Windsor, the two Sault Sainte Maries and Sarnia/ Fort Huron are in no way counterparts of the U.S.-Mexican twin metropolises such as Tijuana/San Diego, Juárez/El Paso, Matamoros/Brownsville, Mexicali/ Calexico, Nuevo Laredo/Laredo, McAllen/Nogales, and Douglas/Agua Prieta.[15] The intermingling of people, culture, and economy in these twin cities endows the whole frontier belt with its special flavor—*ambiente.* Although the U.S. portions of the twin cities attract thousands of Mexicans daily as a near "El Dorado," on the Canadian side of that common border, there is mostly a critical and negative attitude toward the quality of life in the U.S. cities across the border (crime rates, etc.).

Human Traffic. The most painful problem in the U.S. Southwest remains the unmanageable human traffic (in 1983, 1 million illegals were apprehended by the border police, and probably thrice that number succeeded in entering and working in the United States). There is no counterpart for either an illegal or a legal flow of persons across the Canadian border. Although the mass movement across the border in the Southwest is, in its south-north direction, to earn dollars and in its north-south direction to spend them, the human traffic across the U.S.-Canadian border is overwhelmingly directed toward tourists, spending Canadian or U.S. dollars. In 1982, there were over 31 million crossings from Canada to the United States and over 39 million crossings from the United States north toward the Canadian mountains and lakes (the waters of which have not yet been polluted by acid rain coming from the U.S. Midwest).

Contrasting Interface. In northern Mexico, the developing Third World interfaces, physically and directly, with the most developed power of the First World. The per capita income in the United States is eight times that in Mexico. The U.S.-Canada relationship while asymmetric, is between two highly developed and relatively prosperous countries of the First World; their competition inside and outside North America simply belongs to a different class of international and interregional tensions and disputes.

Difference in Historical Bitterness. Psychologically and historically both borders, as stressed in another context, are charged with some bitter memories, including those of violent conflicts and of conquests achieved or contemplated. Nevertheless, the smouldering past, which can be fanned into fire with relative ease along the U.S.-Mexican border, seems to be quite an ash in the United States and Canada.

Contrasts in International Concerns. Since no border zone can really be separated from its domestic neighbors or the national/federal center (short of secession), the difference between the all-Mexican and all-Canadian orientations toward the American continent, the Third World, and the world system in general must also be taken into account. A borderland as a pebble thrown in the middle of a worldwide pond may cause ripples that finally reach the circumference of the continental and world systems, and the reverse movement from distant shore toward a borderland is also normal. The Canadian links with Europe, the Commonwealth, and the Far East have no real counterparts in Mexico, which is constantly concerned with Central and South America as well as with the Third World. For Mexico, the U.S. border is not the only percolated frontier it has to worry about: Its *frontera* with Guatemala has already caused some serious problems and may cause some more in a not too distant future. By contrast, Canada separates the United States from its main enemy, the Soviet Union, and whether the ten provinces want it or not, their sum total, with the Yukon and Northwest Territories, represents either an open gate or an electronic barrier for both rivals—an uncomfortable place for any community to be in the 1980s.

On the other hand, Canada, which is forced by geography to share U.S. concerns about the Soviet Union, has so far resisted any direct involvement south of the U.S. border, especially membership in the Pan-American Union first and the Organization of American States after 1949. Canada participates in the meetings of the OAS by means of a nonvoting observer of ambassadorial rank. So it avoids antagonizing Washington directly by its critical attitude toward U.S. policies in Central and South America; such an avoidance of open conflicts with the United States may be one of the reasons for Ottawa's unwillingness to become a full member of the OAS. Somewhere in the basement of the headquarters of the Pan-American Union in Washington, D.C., there is still a carved chair that was prepared in the 1940s, for Canada's representative to sit on when the OAS was founded and Canada's membership was hoped for. So far, no Canadian posterior has ever honored the precious South American wood, and it is unlikely that one will do so for some time.

Québec. The francophone community, the province of Québec which is right on the U.S.-Canadian border, represents a unique phenomenon. It is an ethnoterritorial community of well over six and a half million people out of which 81.2 percent speak French as their mother tongue (12 percent English and 6.8 percent other). Québec extends far into the Arctic north, its size is enormous: 644 square miles within which France, Spain, both Germanys, Portugal, Switzerland, and Belgium could easily be fitted. Québec's neighbors across the land boundary are New York State and three New England states (Vermont, New Hampshire, and Maine). Initially (since 1608) the cradle of (Royal) New France, Québec is now one of the ten Canadian provinces.

Québec: A Territorial Community
Unlike Any Other

As the only French-speaking ethnoterritorial community in the middle of dominantly anglophone North America, Québec tries to maintain an uneasy balance between its membership in the Canadian federal union, on the one hand, and its two special relationships to the non-Canadian world, on the other. The first intimate link, across the Atlantic with France, is a blood connection that is dominantly emotional, cultural, and political; all Québec car plates remind Quebeckers of their 400-year old history, *je me souviens* ("I remember"). Since 1961, Québec has had a diplomatic mission enjoying nearly full diplomatic privileges in Paris, and a special relationship with France was formally confirmed in 1965.

Québec's second unproclaimed, or tacit, special relationship is with its only foreign neighbor, the United States; this is a nonsentimental, dominantly pragmatic, and commercial relationship. In a transborder *regional* framework, this relationship has been formalized since 1973 by Québec's regular attendance at the annual summit meetings of east Canadian premiers and New England governors. In addition Québec maintains a whole network of Québec delegations (quasi-consulates) in various key cities in the United States.

In a stimulating competition with many traditional French values and cultural orientations, many aspects of the American way of viewing and doing things have become part of the Québec way of life, partly justifying the description of the Quebeckers as "French-speaking North Americans." As such, they enjoy American informality, baseball, television, and hamburgers.

This North American veneer of many a Quebecker easily crumbles at the sheer sight of the Tour Eiffel. Generally speaking, the francophone elites, educated in the often left-oriented humanities at the various universities in Québec, identify with France and often also with West European anti-U.S. themes more ardently than do the general public, technical or commercial elites, and businesspeople. These groups tend to contrast U.S. pragmatism and efficiency with France's legalistic and bureaucratic rigidities, including that country's unyielding bargaining positions in the trade relations between Québec and France, which are rarely softened by a francophone sentiment or political considerations. The French trade connection is often subject to public criticism, for example, in the matter of the French dubbing of American movies or French sales of French-translated American software for use in Québec computers.

The emotionally francophile sector of the Québec elites was particularly hurt in 1985 by the decision of the Renault corporation (owned by the French government) to establish a new automobile factory in anglophone Ontario (at Brampton) rather than in Québec which buys 70 percent of the Renault cars imported to or built in Canada. The French government's answer to the Québec's criticism could hardly have been more devoid of any francophone sentimentality. "Ontario offered a better deal" (*Le Devoir*, June 8, 1985).

The trade statistics indicate that Québec's exports to France amounted to 2.3 percent in 1980 and 1.7 percent in 1981, while Québec's exports to the United States came to 59.9 percent in 1980 and 65 percent in 1961; exports to the Mid-Atlantic states (New York, New Jersey, and Pennsylvania) generally came to 38 percent and those to the six New England states 12 percent.

The Québec-U.S. boundary is one of the most porous in North America. Through it a stream of businesspeople and tourists in both directions and another stream of academics and students in the southern direction continuously flow far and wide to all the corners of the United States, including California and Florida where French-speaking Québec enclaves bear witness to the rigors of Canadian winters. An extrarapid innovation to aid the north-south-north cross-frontier traffic is now in the process of planning: a "bullet train" that would hit speeds of 120 miles an hour between Montréal and New York City with stops at Burlington in Vermont, and Poughkeepsie and Albany in New York State. In 1985, the operating cost was estimated at about $60 million per year and the initial construction cost well over $2 billion—yet it seems that both Québec and the two neighboring U.S. states (New York and Vermont) consider this type of blitzlike percolation of the intersovereign frontier worth implementing.

As mentioned above, the balance between Québec's two special relationships, one across the Atlantic and the other across its southern border, is an uneasy one. Presenting a paper to a Harvard scholarly colloquium in 1983, the then editor in chief of the important Québec daily *Le Devoir*, Lise Bissonnette, described the attitudes of the Québec elites toward their southern neighbor as a mixture of fascination and repulsion and added:

> Among the political elites the reconciliation with the American reality may be measured by means of an eye-dropper (*au compte-gouttes*). This reconciliation is presented as a concession to the real, a sort of survival necessity, which on the American territory one presents in a smiling fashion but inside Québec, as it were, with an apology.[16]

In the middle of a dominantly anglophone North America and with France far away, the French-speaking commonwealth of Québec represents a maverick of sorts: an ethnoterritorial community that, albeit uncertain of its identity, represents a spectacular denial of the North American legend of assimilation and the United States melting pot. This distinction is, of course, one of the reasons why Québec's nonassimilation and insistence on "French only spoken here" (including its crusade against bilingual commercial signs in accordance with the famous Québec Law 101) may irritate some Americans, including those living in Hispanic barrios, Chinatowns, and Polish and Italian neighborhoods, all of which thrive on bilingualism.

Whatever the case for or against Québec's resistance to any assimilation may be, this French-speaking territorial community has not only survived the anglophone encirclement but appears today, after 400 years of hard life—crowned with the last 25 years of radical social transformation ("quiet revolution")—as a relatively self-assured commonwealth. Québec adroitly uses its potential claim for independence either as reserve leverage in its dealings with federal Ottawa or as a real threat to Canadian unity, as was the case in the 1970s when the Parti Québécois was in power and (until 1985) fully adhered to René Lévesque's initial commitment to sovereignty/ association.

The Québec search for a self-confident identity and an appropriate political framework in the middle of an anglophone continent is far from being completed. In the Québec atmosphere, especially among the elites, a pair of questions still lingers on: Are we sons and daughters of France, ("orphans of Louis XV"), only physically separated from the homeland by the Atlantic? Or have we become a separate Québec nation ("French-speaking North Americans"), that is, in the same sense as the people in the United States, New Zealanders, Australians, and anglophone Canadians have become nations with their own separate national identity, which is quite distinct from their homeland despite a common language and a shared history and cultural heritage? Unlike the United States, Canada has never accepted the myth of the melting pot, preferring its own myth of a "harmonious" mosaic.

A good illustration of the difficulty in answering the above questions was given in 1983 when the Québec minister of intergovernmental affairs, Jacques-Yvan Morin, addressed the Académie française in Paris and proposed that, following the attainment of independence, the Québécois should possess dual citizenship, that of Québec and that of France. The Québec prime minister, René Lévesque, was openly critical of his own minister's proposal: "I find it is painful enough [on a assez de misère] to become Québécois completely and authentically. That's all I am interested in. . . . Dual citizenship, that's not serious."[17]

In much less patient terms, Lise Bissonnette suggested with biting irony in *Le Devoir* (June 11, 1983) that she might opt for second citizenship in the culturally related republic of Dominica in the Lesser Antilles rather than in France and criticized the minister for not having consulted anybody in Québec "before heaping ridicule on the Québécois by depicting them in Paris as a nostalgic colonial people." Symptomatically, the article was entitled "The Orphans of Louis XV."

Since 1985, Québec's precondition for its adherence to the newly patriated Canadian Constitution of 1981 has been a constitutional recognition of the distinct character of the Québec people on which the legitimacy of the province's own judicial and institutional instruments has been based. This demand is evidently, an *ethnoterritorial* rather than a purely ethnocultural one. Its corollary is Québec's right to veto constitutional amendments, thus leading to the concept of Canadian federalism as a bicephalic (two-headed, or dyadic) one. Even if granted by the other nine anglophone provinces, the veto power still would not solve the nonterritorial aspects of francophone

Canada. Québec's own attitude toward French-speaking Canadians living in other provinces, especially in officially bilingual New Brunswick as well as in neighboring Ontario, Manitoba, and elsewhere, is, to say the least, hesitant and, in the words of Jean-Louis Roy, the director of *Le Devoir*, "a political scandal."

> Québec's insensitivity—except for a few condescending accolades—toward the French-speaking Canadians outside the Québec territory must cease. . . . A reconciliation between Québec and francophone minorities throughout Canada is absolutely indispensable . . . the absence of Québec policy toward the other francophones in Canada is a historic absurdity and a political scandal.[18]

A student of the territorial dimension of politics easily recognizes here the real dilemma, in a territorially segmented world, that confronts the Québec leadership, which is fully aware of the fact that it derives its political and economic strength precisely from being identified with a self-administering territory within which the francophones constitute a clear majority. The francophone territorial power could be politically diluted by a necessarily costly adherence to a nonterritorial principle of unity with all the other francophones dispersed as ethnic minorities over several provinces. These groups, without possessing territorial institutions, are necessarily left with the task of protecting their identity and rights by means other than territorial self-rule.

The difference in means and methods of action to pursue converging but not identical goals has often been openly admitted by the Québec leaders who are aware of the fact that Canadian francophones do not necessarily consider Québec to be their "homeland," spokesman, and reliable protector. For example, as reported in *Le Devoir* (May 28, 1985), the then-minister of justice, Pierre-Marc Johnson, spoke in Ottawa of the duty of the Québec people "to contribute to the development of the francophone population in Canada, taking into account their own priorities and needs and with due respect to their autonomy." The political and institutional distance between the goals and means of "territorial" Quebeckers, on the one hand, and the roughly 600,000 "nonterritorial" Canadian francophones (still speaking French at home), on the other, could be hardly put in more diplomatic yet clear terms. Students of nationalism could label the Québec position simply as a conflict between two nationalisms: nonmessianic ethnoterritorial versus ethnocultural linguistic.

Québec's Diplomatic Foursome

In the framework of this comparative study of the international dimension of federalism, Québec occupies a special position: Since 1965, it has engaged simultaneously in all four forms of paradiplomacy used by noncentral governments: transborder regional and transregional microdiplomacy, and global paradiplomacy as well as global protodiplomacy. An illustrative diagram

Figure 10.2

Quadruple Triangle

Québec Transborder and International Relations

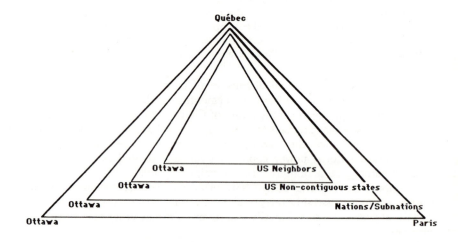

Transborder Regional Microdiplomacy
Québec - Ottawa - New York/New England

Transregional Microdiplomacy
Québec - Ottawa - Non-contiguous US States (CA, GA, IL, LA, TX)

Global Para- and Proto- Diplomacy
Québec - Ottawa - Nations and Nonsovereign Ethnoterritorial Communities
(Capitals or Trade Centers:Brussels, Caracas, Düsseldorf, London,
Mexico City, Milan, Port-au-Prince, Tokyo, Washington-via-NYC;
Regions:Catalonia, Jura, Flemish/Walloon Communities)

Québec - Ottawa - Paris

(Figure 10.2) in the form of a quadruple triangle has the province of Québec at the summit of four interconnected triangles whose left angles are formed by Ottawa, the national government, as a constitutional and political intersection clearly in charge of national security and the general diplomatic status of Canada and watchful when it comes to nonsecurity matters handled by Québec and the other provinces. Nonsecurity matters may have political underpinnings. The federal center generally approves of Québec transborder and transregional microdiplomacy in trade, reverse investment, energy sales, and tourism promotion, but it is somewhat hesitant with respect to global paradiplomacy and suspects that Québec's special relationship with France (expressed in special agreements signed in the turbulent year of 1965) tends to veer toward protodiplomacy and contain a heavy dose of centrifugal tendencies with regard to Canada.

French support of Québec's centrifugal tendencies has often coincided with the low ebb in U.S.-French relations, especially when the Paris government was headed by leaders who simply disliked everything "Anglo-Saxon"—however ill-fitting the term has become today with respect to modern multiethnic, multilingual, and multiracial United States. Thus, when in 1967, de Gaulle visited Québec and proclaimed France's support for Québec secessionism (vive le Québec libre!), many people in the United States could not help seeing in his support not only a sign of sympathy for France's "cousins de campagne" (country cousins) but also a not too subtle jibe at anglophone North America.

It is also clear that since November 1984, when Québec independence was removed from the urgent agenda of the Parti Québécois, French interest in the news from and about Québec considerably declined. The reason seems simple enough: When a French-speaking territorial community in North America interrupts its previously dramatic fight for independence and concentrates on pragmatically improving its way of life by exports of energy and foreign investment, Québec simply becomes less newsworthy from the standpoint of the French media and their public—as, generally, peace and quiet work are less exciting than war or terrorism.

In Figure 10.2, the right angles of the four triangles identify the primary geographic targets of Québec's relations with foreign countries:

1. Neighboring U.S. states
2. Trade, industrial, and cultural centers in various noncontiguous states within the United States
3. Foreign nations
4. France—a category truly apart—and other francophone countries or territories such as the canton of Jura in Switzerland or the francophone (Walloon) portion of Belgium

Transborder Regional Microdiplomacy

Transborder microdiplomacy in the case of Québec has three distinct forms. First, Québec officials, as mentioned before, regularly attend and participate in the work of the annual meetings of eastern Canadian premiers and New England governors. The agenda and work of these regular, well-organized "transborder summits" have changed from the initially social clambakes to workshop sessions on such important regional issue-areas as energy transfers, acid rain, fisheries, and agricultural product trade along the Canadian-U.S. north-south axis.[19]

Second, without any formal pattern or regular schedule, the Québec premier meets with the New York governor whenever an issue recommends doing so, especially in the field of energy transfers. While the Parti Québécois was in power, for example, the nationalized Hydro-Québec and the New York State Power Authority (PASNY) signed a transborder compact providing for the supply of 110,000 gigawatt hours between 1984 and 1987.[20] Subsequently, the leader of the opposition party, Robert Bourassa, based his electoral campaign (leading to an impressive victory and his premiership in December 1985) on his concept of substantially increasing Québec's economic power and prosperity by making it a giant supplier of electric power for the U.S. Northeast in general and New York State in particular with additional gigawatts from a further development of the James Bay hydroelectric project. At that time, export of Québec's water surplus (especially from the James Bay area) to the water-hungry United States entered the phase of concrete planning.[21]

Third, Québec maintains a well-staffed delegation in Boston for New England and another one in New York City, which politically ramifies out to Washington D.C., and in trade and investment promotion covers the Mid-Atlantic states and part of the U.S. South down to Kentucky. Vermont and New York States are occasionally represented in Montréal, but it seems that, on the U.S. side, transborder visits and telephone links are deemed as effective and cheaper than maintaining quasi-consular offices so close to the border.

Transregional Microdiplomacy

Transregional microdiplomacy for Québec means close trade, investment, educational, and cultural contacts with five noncontiguous U.S. states: California, Texas, Illinois, Georgia, and Louisiana; the last is located in Lafayette rather than in New Orleans or the capital city of Baton Rouge because the Louisiana Council for the Development of French in Louisiana (CODFIL) is situated there to preserve the Acadian francophone tradition and culture in western Louisiana. Clearly, in this case the territorial commonwealth of Québec asserts its role as a supporter of dispersed, nonterritorial francophone communities in North America.

Global Paradiplomacy

As to global paradiplomacy Québec has established direct contacts with distant centers of economic power, ranging from Tokyo, Düsseldorf, London, and Caracas to francophone countries where Québec tries to capitalize upon being French without any imperial past. Some of Québec's efforts to capitalize on common latinity (in Italy, Mexico, and even French Jura in Switzerland)[22] contain traces of sentimental "Latin" thinking rather than political or economic reality. A new document issued in 1985 by the Québec government calls for a substantial increase in the number of international links to include Scandinavian countries, the Middle East, francophone Africa, and even the Soviet Union and Eastern Europe.

Writing for the Toronto-based *Globe and Mail* (June 4, 1985), Elliot Feldman opened his article with the question, "Has anyone noticed that the United States is no longer anxious about Québec?" and as the U.S.

expert on Canada, Feldman also offered his answer: "Québec has enlarged and polished its international profile. This remarkable accomplishment is attributable largely to three developments: the redirection of Québec nationalism, the cultivation of policies sympathetic to U.S. interests and the responsible conduct of international affairs."

Global Protodiplomacy

Global protodiplomacy is a term I use in this study to describe those initiatives and activities of a noncentral government abroad that, explicitly or implicitly, endow economic, social, and cultural links with foreign nations with a secessionist potential.

Until 1985, during the rule of the Parti Québécois, the province of Québec engaged in protodiplomacy quite openly; it did not conceal its hope to eventually transform the Québec posts abroad into embassies and consulates of a sovereign Québec nation-state. But when, in 1984, René Lévesque ruled out sovereignty as an immediate objective to be voted on during the next provincial elections, Québec's global protodiplomacy became simply global paradiplomacy, as it had been in the early 1960s when initiated by the Liberal party. When, in 1984, the Progressive Conservative party under Brian Mulroney replaced Trudeau's Liberals, Ottawa's acceptance of Québec's paradiplomacy and special relationship with France and francophone countries became even more pronounced. In 1985, for example, Ottawa toned down its former opposition to the Québec government's membership and participation in the Senegal-inspired and French-directed Council of Francophony.[23]

It should be recognized that all national governments are understandably sensitive to any secessionist potential, implied or openly present, in any international activity that involves their ethnic, cultural, or linguistic communities, especially if located along or outside their borders (as islands, for example). Northern Ireland, Catalonia, and the Basque country are well-known examples. And Paris itself (hence its occasional hesitations toward Québec secessionism) has often proved irritated (marginally or seriously) by separatism in Brittany, Alsace's new assertiveness,[24] by linkages between the French and Spanish Basques, and, of course, by the turbulent Corsican independentists.

We may safely assume that in the foreseeable future, whichever of the two contending political parties in Québec is in power, the Québec microembassies abroad will continue despite the considerable expenditure involved (over $44 million in 1985—which is, of course, much more than any of the twenty-eight U.S. states spends for maintenance of its state offices abroad). Speaking on the subject of future Québec international activities, the Liberal leader Robert Bourassa told me privately, in 1982, and then, following his return to public life, repeated publicly in 1983: "The difference would be in our emphasis on economic relations yet without neglecting the rest [!]. There is no way of going back. Québec is not a province like the others."[25]

Noncentral Governments Go Abroad

The presence of noncentral governments on the international scene in one way or another is a fact—but does it matter? Two questions seem in order. One, do the subnational activities change important outcomes in international relations from what they would have been had the contacts been confined to the traditional center-to-center level? Two, has the national center's effectiveness to speak to the external world with one single clear voice been significantly eroded?

The first question, translated into a contrafactual conditional, points to a problem inherent in all fields of political inquiry: In contrast to the hard sciences, in our "soft" framework we cannot—alas!—repeat the experiments, alternatively adding and/or eliminating various ingredients, and so observe the interplay of independent and dependent variables. We cannot take a test tube, pour into it World War I, the Romanov dynasty's ineptness, the German Imperial Staff, and Lenin, let it bubble into the October Revolution and then repeat the experiment but this time without Lenin (who might have fallen off the train and been run over on his way to Russia) and so prove or disprove that Lenin was essential for the Bolshevik seizure of power.

Similarly, we cannot experimentally pour noncentral governments into a test tube and then filter them out from the international liquid to measure the difference in outcomes. There is also no yardstick by which we could estimate the size of new trade or foreign investment that has resulted from x number of dollars spent by a U.S. state or Canadian provincial representative in Frankfurt or Brussels. And how does one measure foreign responses to the personal charisma, charm, or clout of a governor (e.g., former California Governor Edmund G. Brown's friendship with the governor of Baja California, Roberto de la Madrid, or the unusual position of such mayors of international cities as Jean Drapeau of Montréal, Mayor Edward Koch of New York, or Diane Feinstein of San Francisco)?

In the framework of the second question, there is sufficient evidence of the international audibility of the initiatives taken by noncentral governments on the world scene: in North America, mostly by means of global and transregional paradiplomacy, and in Western Europe, by means of transborder microdiplomacy. Thus, as discussed in Chapter 8, federal or decentralized systems do address the external world with more than one central voice and message: The result may be dissonance, confusing for or exploitable by foreign powers. Often, however, the various voices expressing regional nuances are complementary. To return to the musical metaphor, rather than cacophony the final result may be a complex symphony. As Figure 8.2 illustrates, in intersovereign politics, especially in the free world, national governments have long been accustomed and trained to listen carefully and react cautiously to more than the central voice of foreign nations.

Centralized, Segmented, or "Marbled" Diplomacy

International activities of noncentral governments may conceivably lead to two scenarios: centralization or federal segmentation of foreign policy.

1. Centralization is the first plausible scenario, marked by a new expansion of a national government's power far beyond the traditional/constitutional monopoly of foreign policy (security, diplomacy, and regulation of foreign trade) to encompass all modern economic, social, ecological, cultural, and humanitarian issue-areas. A probable accompanying feature would be a mammoth growth of the national bureaucracy and its subnational branches— all justified in the name of an effective promotion of a balanced sum total of all national and subnational/regional interests by a single legitimate voice abroad.

2. Federal segmentation of foreign policy is the second possible scenario. It presupposes that national concerns with security and status can be separated from other issue-areas and, furthermore, that the federal division of powers between the central and component governments in domestic matters can be replicated in the foreign policy field without creating chaos or returning to a loose confederal system.[26]

Such a federal territorial segmentation of the security and nonsecurity aspects of the conduct of foreign policy should be distinguished from another contemporary change in the actual operation of foreign policy, that is, *functional sectorialization* or functional decentralization. By functional sectorialization I mean a division of international roles among various specialized departments and agencies of the national government along their lines of functional expertise, which permits, among other things, cooperative international contacts "below the foreign policy apex" (Keohane and Nye's "transgovernmentalism"). In all countries today, not only the Ministry of External Affairs (or the Department of State in the United States) but also all the other principal ministries or departments exercise their responsibilities beyond the national borders. At the embassies and consulates abroad, the diplomatic personnel in the traditional sense of the word now often represent, quantitatively, a minority (20 percent in the case of the United States) as opposed to the representatives of the ministries of commerce, finance, foreign trade, agriculture, science, technology, communications, and immigration. Some years ago, Keohane and Nye calculated that forty-four distinct federal bureaucracies were represented at the U.S. embassy in London.[27]

Whereas the presence of commercial or science attachés at a consulate or an embassy abroad is a visible symbol of functional sectorialization of foreign policy, the presence of an officer representing a subnational territorial interest at an all-national embassy[28]—or a separate state or provincial office abroad—is a visible manifestation of a territorial segmentation of foreign policy.

The two sharply differentiated scenarios, centralization and segmentation, are, of course, too clear-cut to fit the facts of real life. If present trends are indicative of probable future developments, they seem to point to a continuing and possibly healthy redundancy, *duplication with coordination*, a scenario representing a middle ground, though a constantly shifting one, between centralization and federal segmentation.

Management of Chaos

Logically, if we speak of duplication with coordination, the coordinative measures constitute a recognition of and a response to actual or potential duplication, which is perceived by the governments concerned as possibly leading to chaos, waste, or friction among subnational and national authorities in the domain of their respective activities abroad. In some cases, duplication with coordination may prepare the way for such a loosening of federal bonds (sovereignty/association, diplomatic federalism,[29] and other confederal formulas) that segmentation may lead to territorial fragmentation and secession.

The concept of duplication with coordination assumes, I think quite realistically, that in our era, the various subnational assertions of territorial interests and needs will continue to seep up to the national and international plateaus while the national perspective and power simultaneously percolate the intrafederal boundaries. The possibility and technique of U.S. states and cities influencing central foreign policy making and its, as it were, horizontal plateau (national government to national government) by vertical means of pressure, lobby, and transmission of local expertise to the state representatives in Congress, was already discussed in Chapter 9. In another context, I referred to this process as intrafederal osmosis ("osmotic federalism").[30] Other scholars (for example Daniel J. Elazar and Morton Grodzins) referred to U.S. federalism as a system of "mild chaos" or "multiple cracks"; Grodzins's popular metaphor, which labeled federalism as a "marble cake" rather than a too neatly designed "layer cake," could be expanded to lead to "marbled" diplomacy.[31]

In a different context, Martin Landau convincingly argued that system redundancy has proved useful not only on an airplane that is in distress but also in a complex organization and in federalism, in which overlaps and duplication with coordination are part of its concept and practice.[32] Landau views "parallel circuits" as partially self-regulating mechanisms in all complex organizations—and a federal nation-state is certainly one of these.

Since the 1970s, both national and subnational governments have taken a number of steps whose aim it was to coordinate the various subnational initiatives and activities. We should note, however, that in a great many cases, no coordinative action has been taken, and no catastrophe has ensued.

One reason for the absence of coordinative concern is simply lack of awareness. National policymakers and administrators often do not know what is actually going on in the borderlands or in other subnational networks abroad. In both Western Europe and North America, I have also found evidence of deliberate efforts on the part of subnational elites not to draw the unnecessary or premature attention of central authorities to local solutions of some local problems by means of informal contacts and good neighbors networks. Often, the efforts were not deliberate deceptions, just avoidance of unnecessary complications. Another reason for the absence of coordinative measures is a frequent conviction on the part of national administrators that most of the subnational contacts and cooperative arrangements are politically quite marginal since, as already noted, they so often deal with complex technical matters of only regional or local importance.

Although I have described the central national attitudes toward micro-diplomacy and transborder regionalism mostly in terms of various centralist anxieties and suspicions, it should be recognized that the national center may, and occasionally does, welcome some degree of federal segmentation of foreign economic, ecological, or cultural policy. Since the 1970s, for the sake of a lively trade, Washington, for example, has encouraged the U.S. states' efforts to promote reverse foreign investment, job-related foreign trade, and cultural exchanges. Partly, such encouragement reflects the belief that national and regionally nuanced objectives, in their broad lines, complement rather than conflict with each other; partly, too, some central policymakers and administrators do take both federalism and its need to adjust to the demands of the contemporary era seriously.

In the United States one can, of course, note some differences at the national center itself. For example, while the U.S. Department of Commerce seems the most encouraging, the Office of the U.S. Trade Representative at the White House is often more cautious for foreign policy reasons, and the Treasury becomes quite alarmed when it comes to U.S. states' power to tax and its potential uses to help the state's export trade and reverse investment—which could lead to trouble with GATT and its rules as well as with the Treasury's concept as to what the taxation is really for. The worries of the U.S. Department of State are political insofar as the states' various commercial initiatives often acquire disturbing political overtones— for example, Idaho's desire for a special relationship with Iran and Libya or Kentucky's enthusiasm for trade with South Africa in 1982. My survey of the activities of the U.S. state representatives in Western Europe (summer 1985) did not record any serious complaint against the federal government and its agencies, except for various visa problems that foreign investors or traders had experienced, notwithstanding strong state endorsements.

In Switzerland, the federal government seems both very cautious (à la Suisse) yet supportive of cantonal transborder activities. In 1982, for example, as noted before, Bern endorsed the creation of a working group of all Swiss cantons contiguous with France for the purpose of conducting *direct* transborder negotiations with the neighboring regions and *départements* of France. The group, however, has remained so far a marginal institution.

In Canada, Ottawa has directed its embassies and consulates to lend support to the trade, investment, and cultural activities of all the provinces abroad, including those of Québec. My survey of provincial activities in

Western Europe (summer 1985) generally confirmed a correct, often cooperative relationship prevailing between Canadian federal representatives, on the one hand, and provincial representatives, on the other. Also, some degree of cooperation abroad was noticeable between two otherwise quite competitive provincial delegations, those of Québec and Ontario in Brussels and Paris. In the Paris office of the latter, a brochure promoting tourism in Québec was on display, though no corresponding brochure was on display in the Québec delegation.

In terms of its political, cultural, and trade activities, the Québec general delegation in Paris, eighty people strong, plays the role of and also physically appears as a medium-size embassy; its handsome building is located in a fashionable district of Paris (rue Pergolèse, near the Arc de Triomphe). The Ontario general delegation there acts and appears like an average consulate; it employs eight people and occupies half a floor in a well-appointed modern office building quite close to the French president's Palais d'Elysée (rue du Faubourg Saint Honoré).

The U.S. state offices in Brussels (there are none in Paris) are much more modest and bear no comparison with the Canadian provincial delegations in Paris, London, and Brussels. The U.S. state offices in Brussels, for example, act and appear as conspicuously apolitical and clearly business oriented. One to three officers are in charge of investment (now priority number one) and trade promotion (the Arkansas representative in Brussels estimated that in 1985, investment promotion constituted 99 percent of his overall effort). Promotion of tourism and cultural or student exchanges is clearly a side issue for all of the U.S. state missions. Two to five West European clerical workers are usually hired locally; they know Europe and its languages well and need no work permit at any European location as they are citizens of countries in the European Community. In a few cases, even the managing director of a U.S. state office abroad (for example, that of Maryland) may be a West European with a good knowledge of the U.S. state she or he represents. The U.S. state offices may be found in buildings located in the business districts of Brussels, and they always contain a conference or seminar room to be used by visiting U.S. businesspeople for their contacts with their local counterparts.

These offices both cooperate and compete. One aspect of their competition is naturally their promotional emphasis on either the labor advantages and general economic resurgence of the Sun Belt (South Carolina, Virginia, Arkansas, and Georgia in Brussels) or their state's central geographic (as in the case of Tennessee which has no permanent representation abroad but was able to surpass many states in attracting a substantial portion of Japanese investment and plants within its borders; its central as well as southern location, largely non-unionized labor force and skillful negotiations by its governor seem to explain Tennessee's success in attracting foreign investment), Illinois and Michigan stress their position on the Great Lakes and closeness to the Canadian market, and Maryland tries to capitalize on its closeness to Washington, D.C.

Figure 10.3. The United States Abroad: Illinois in Europe Promotional Brochure

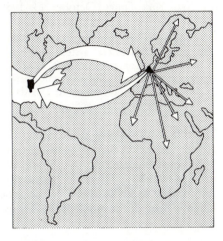

ILLINOIS

And this is Illinois in Europe

In 1968 the Government of the State of Illinois established an office in Brussels, Belgium, to act as a fullfledged business consulting organisation serving the interests of both overseas and Illinois businessmen as a mutually beneficial point of contact.

pliers of industrial and agricultural products ; shipping and transportation to and from Mid-America ; business trips to Illinois exhibitions, conventions and fairs by overseas visitors and arranging on-the-spot contacts with Illinois officials and businessmen.

What the

STATE OF ILLINOIS BRUSSELS OFFICE

can do for you

The Illinois office for Europe and the Middle East is the official representative of the Departments of Agriculture and Business and Economic Development of the State of Illinois - of which it is one of three overseas branches - and is therefore able to call on the resources of private and public organisations throughout the State. The Illinois Brussels office can help with establishing foreign enterprises in Illinois ; finding Illinois sup-

The staff of the Brussels office consists of experienced businessmen with firsthand background in their fields - both in the US and abroad - and they speak the major European languages. Services of the Brussels office are professional, confidential and free of charge.

(Courtesy of the State of Illinois)

The reasons why so many U.S. states have chosen Brussels (second only to Tokyo) as their main base of international activities were listed by the officers in charge as follows: the neutralist reputation of Belgium, the central location of Brussels in Western Europe, a convenient airport close to the city, and availability of relatively inexpensive office space and housing in and around Brussels. The fact that Brussels is also the seat of the European Community and NATO was hardly ever mentioned. Visitors (including this author) cannot help but be impressed by the businesslike and business-liking atmosphere that prevails in these U.S. state missions abroad.

The same is true of Tokyo where seventeen U.S. states maintain permanent missions to compete for Japanese investment. In October 1985, for example, the Illinois governor, James R. Thompson, announced a successful result of preceding negotiations between Chrysler and Japanese Mitsubishi to build a new auto assembly plant on farmland in central Illinois. In its comment the *New York Times* (October 13, 1985) emphasized:

> A few years ago, Illinois, like most other states, was a passive actor in the post-New Deal federal system. But last week, Illinois provided a measure of the intensity of a major shift in which the states have become significant innovators of social and economic change—American federalism seems to have gone full circle, returning to the days before the great Depression, when some states were . . . acting as laboratories for national policy.

The difference, as this study shows, is the international dimension of the U.S. states' new reliance on their own devices.

National endorsement of subnational activities abroad takes various forms, some of which appear to be primarily dictated by the desire of a central government to know about "what's cooking" ab initio and so to ensure a subliminal or direct supervision during the subsequent process.[33]

Instruments of Coordination

Four general types of coordinative measures have either been already adopted or are being considered by national and noncentral governments in order to harmonize their activities abroad. They all affect the practice and institutions of federal systems.

High-Level Channels of Communication and Consultation

New high-level channels of consultation, mutual information, and coordination between national and subnational top echelons either have been or will have to be established. These are to complement the traditional links assured by the territorial representatives in the national legislature (in the U.S. Congress in particular). In Canada, West Germany, and Switzerland, however, the upper chambers have no specifically defined roles in the shaping of foreign policy. In Canada, on account of its lack of power, the Senate does not reflect the federal nature of the country (which is one of many Canadian problems). In my opinion, it is, however, also one of the Canadian myths to believe that the U.S. Senate is *the* place to reconcile regional and state conflicts and tensions. The House of Representatives is certainly another place for interstate contacts and compromises. The very title, "U.S. Senators" (rather than Texan, North Dakotan, or Iowan), illustrates the long way the U.S. federal nation has traveled since the Articles of Confederation with its Congress of state "ambassadors" and subsequent direct elections of senators. Instead, the inter-state and state-federal coordination and reconciliation often take place at the meetings of the National Governors' Association, in its various permanent committees (in particular, the Committee on International Trade and Foreign Relations), and in the work of its permanent staff and researchers.

Other communication and cooperative frameworks are the National Association of Developmental Agencies (NASDA), the National League of Cities, the U.S. Conference of Mayors, the Advisory Commission on Intergovernmental Relations (ACIR),[34] and, of course, the Office of Intergovernmental Affairs in the U.S. Department of Commerce as well as its International Trade Administration with district offices in over fifty locations in the various U.S. states. The Office of Intergovernmental Liaison in the U.S. Department of State is a very modest, almost insignificant, affair—an indirect confirmation of the U.S. central government's general lack of *real* political concern for state activities and initiatives abroad. A more sensitive reaction to U.S. state microdiplomacy seems to be manifested occasionally by the Office of the U.S. Special Trade Representative at the White House.

Similarly, in matters of noncentral microdiplomacy in Canada, the Commerce Department plays a more important role than the intergovernmental administration in the Canadian Department of External Affairs. The provincial offices of the Canadian provinces "accredited" to the central government (a rather unusual feature in Canadian federalism in contrast to the U.S. practice) seem, on the average, to be in contact with the Commerce Department more frequently than with the External Affairs Department. The intergovernmental coordination unit in the External Affairs Department was originally set up as a watchdog for Québec's para- and protodiplomatic activities and only later became an information center for all the provinces.

Although interprovincial meetings on different levels and in different functional sectors abound under the premiers' apex in Canada, the lack of continuity assured on the expert middle levels still seems to represent a problem partly tackled by the establishment of the Federal-Provincial Committee on Trade Relations in 1979 and (following the Conservative party's victory in the 1984 elections) by a plan for regular federal-provincial meetings of premiers, trade, and other ministers.

Another possibility for interexecutive coordination in the nonsecurity fields of foreign policy is the inclusion of state or provincial representatives in various delegations and negotiating teams abroad. This strategy is used quite sparingly. The problem is not only that of intrafederal politics but that of the size and effectiveness of a negotiating team. Nevertheless, appointments of state experts or representatives to be part of a federal negotiating team ad hoc, depending on the issue, have occasionally occurred. One recent recent example is Manitoba's representative at the Canadian embassy in Washington, D.C., concerning the Garrison Dam in North Dakota with potential ecological consequences for neighboring Manitoba. It should be noted that Manitoba obtained a temporary representation at the Canadian embassy in Washington, D.C., only after it had threatened to open a separate office there, a move that Ottawa energetically opposed on account of Québec and its then separatist efforts to establish an official link with Washington, D.C. A New England delegation was associated with the U.S.-Canada negotiations concerning a new fisheries treaty only after the defeat of the East Coast treaty.

Interadministrative Links

The category of interadministrative links represents a great variety of devices, instruments, and channels ranging from liaison offices in the ministries of external affairs to ensure that information and influence flow from the center to noncentral governments and vice versa to the assignments of diplomatic personnel to noncentral governments and vice versa.

In both Canada and the United States, in their respective Departments of External Affairs and State, offices for liaison with state and local governments have been established; also in both countries attempts have been made to sensitize foreign service officers to the provincial problems (and, in Canada, to acquaint provincial officers with international relations and diplomatic procedures). In both cases so far these attempts seem rather halfhearted on both provincial and national sides.

In Canada, the Commerce Department and the Federal-Provincial Coordination Division of the Department of External Affairs monitor, encourage, supply information, and often brief Canadian provincial leaders and their staffs in their international contacts—a task that in the United States seems to be split between the National Governors' Office of States Services and the relatively small Public Liaison Office (PA/IPL) at the U.S. Department of State. During the constitutional crisis of 1981,[35] Ontario's Ministry of Industry and Trade expressed the problem succinctly: "To be effective in the international marketplace, Canada must very clearly be seen to speak with one voice. But for that voice to be credible, there has to be meaningful input from the provinces."[36] It should be recalled that this input obviously includes data and information from Ontario's own diplomatic network abroad; Ontario is second to Québec in the number of paradiplomatic offices and officers maintained abroad.

The Standing Committee on Foreign Affairs of the Canadian Senate further recommended that officials of the Department of External Affairs who are responsible for provincial interests and the flow of information to the provinces spend some time in the capitals of the provinces while provincial bureaucrats be assigned for a week or so to the appropriate embassies or consulates abroad.

In the United States, a partial counterpart is the Pearson Program (so named for Senator James B. Pearson, 1962–1973, from Kansas), which provides for the assignment of U.S. foreign service officers to U.S. state governments for limited periods of time. Currently, only about twenty-five foreign service officers per year are so assigned. There is no counterpart assignment for key state or municipal officials to U.S. posts abroad (as recommended in Canada by the Senate), although they could profit by the experience, especially today when U.S. governors tend to appoint one or two of their aides to serve as main coordinators of the various activities of their states. The question of appropriate training and language qualification for the officers manning state offices abroad will have to be posed sooner or later as well as possible curricular changes in the U.S. Foreign Service Institute. As noted previously, the twenty-eight U.S. state governments that have permanent representatives abroad replied to my questionnaire concerning assignment of their officers to U.S. consulates abroad in the negative, and only a few seemed to favor a specially focused course to be offered by the Foreign Service Institute.

The picture would not be complete if I did not mention an occasional reluctance on the part of noncentral governments to have their officers trained on a national level—I have noted such a reluctance in Switzerland. As mentioned before, there is, on the part of subnational elites, a marked tendency to insist on doing their own "microdiplomatic thing" without involving the national government and its bureaucracy. There is fear lest the federal training and briefing lead to unwanted monitoring and control.

Constitutional Changes and Reinterpretations

It should be emphasized that the constitutional line that separates foreign policy from domestic politics has never been as clear as constitutions, practitioners of politics, and textbooks in government often assert or assume. In the United States, the federal constitution forbade the thirteen federal components "to enter into any treaty, alliance, or confederation" (Article 1, section 9) and clearly gave Congress the right and duty to provide for common defense, regulate commerce with foreign nations, declare war, raise and support armies, provide and maintain a navy, and provide for organizing, arming disciplining, and calling forth state militias. In fact, foreign policy monopoly and diplomatic unity vis-à-vis foreign nations has been one of the reasons why not only the United States but also many other composite nations (Switzerland, Germany, and India) have adopted a federal constitution.

It has been argued, however, that even the U.S. Constitution of 1789 did anticipate significant subnational inputs into national diplomacy and defense by its initial provision (before the Seventeenth Amendment) for the selection of the senators by state legislatures (as is still done today in West Germany), by requiring the majority of the selected senators to nominate ambassadors and approve international treaties (self-executing executive agreements were not anticipated then), and by providing for state militias as the only armed force then in existence.[37] While potential encroachments on state jurisdiction by the federal power to make treaties and executive agreements was the issue in 1952 (the Bricker Amendment mentioned previously), today, a controversy in the opposite direction seems to be in the making—state encroachments on the federal power to "regulate" foreign trade by the "buy American" laws in thirty U.S. states and excessive taxation of transnational corporations in several states (unitary tax) have already been mentioned in another context.

In the United States, a unique suggestion for a possible amendment to the constitution that would favor states' rights in the matter of *foreign* economic policy has come from a state that joined the Union in 1959, Alaska. On January 23, 1982, the Alaska Statehood Commission recommended that Alaska sell its Prudhoe Bay oil directly to Japan, which the federal export ban now prohibits. In the words of the commission:

> We have studied independence . . . secession-unilateral withdrawal of Alaska from the United States. . . . Alaska could support legal independence for as long as its oil and other resource wealth holds out, but independence is neither desirable nor wise. . . . We can conceive of no set of circumstances that would cause us to recommend independence for Alaska. . . . We studied other associations: commonwealth, free association, partition, and a return to territorial status. None, we feel, is preferable to statehood. . . . The Alaska State Legislature [however] should join with other states to apply to Congress under Article V of the U.S. Constitution for the convening of a national constitutional convention, for the sole purpose of defining the procedures that would govern all future constitutional conventions called by the states. As in the Constitutional Convention of 1787, those rules should specify equal votes for each state. . . . The people and the Legislature should consider . . . the wisdom of seeking an amendment to the Constitution that would read: "Except for laws dealing with defense, foreign affairs or civil rights, any act of Congress may be disapproved by a vote of the legislatures of two-thirds of the states [this is a rewritten form of an amendment originally proposed by Arizona's Governor Bruce Babbitt]. . . . We recommend that Alaska pursue its common interests with western Canadian provinces and territories to the full extent allowed a sovereign [?] state under the Constitution. Alaska should invite other western states and the western Canadian provinces to join it in establishing as [sic] conference like the Northeastern Governors and Eastern Canadian Premiers Conference.[38]

Direct Links With International Organizations

A direct link of subnational components with nonpolitical intersovereign organizations is, conceptually, a possibility. As noted previously, Québec requested in 1984 that it be directly represented in such international functional agencies as UNESCO and WHO; analogically, one can imagine a similar request on the part of the food-producing states or provinces in the FAO. In the 1980s the province of Alberta demanded a separate representation in GATT.

In the past Québec experienced substantial difficulties with the central government, then controlled by Trudeau, in its efforts to obtain full membership in the intergovernmental Council of Francophony, organized by the French government. One controversial issue was the previously mentioned, unresolved relationship between the "territorial" Quebeckers and the "nonterritorial" Canadian francophones, especially the Acadians in bilingual New Brunswick, whose participation in the Council of Francophony, separate from that of Québec, was granted by Ottawa and accepted by Paris in 1986.

When it comes to minor territories that are only loosely associated with a nation-state (*federacies*), the practice of autonomous access to the international system of sovereign states is more frequent but, of course, of marginal importance. Thus, microscopic Monaco, associated with unitary France, is a member of several UN specialized agencies (UNESCO, Universal Postal Union, World Health Organization, International Telecommunications Organization, and International Atomic Agency). The Basque province in regionalized Spain has been granted specific power to establish direct cultural relations with states having Basque-speaking communities—which is France (1979 Basque Statute, Article 6.5). In the United Arab Emirate Federation, each emirate has retained its right to join or not to join OPEC (UAE Constitution, Article 123).

The Draft of the Compact of Free Association Between the United States and the Districts of the Trust Territory of the Pacific Islands (sections 121–123) reserves "full authority" to the United States over security and defense matters but grants the districts "the capacity to conduct foreign affairs in their own name and right" and pledges the U.S. support in obtaining "membership and other participation" in international (intersovereign) organizations. Some Puerto Ricans have already argued that separate membership in UN specialized agencies and Caribbean cooperative organizations could be conceivably enjoyed by Puerto Rico as a commonwealth or even as a fifty-first state of the Union. The Vatican has an apostolic delegate (nuncio) to the Dominican Republic who is also accredited to the Conference of Puertorican bishops (Conferencia Episcopal Puertoriqueña).

The only two federal systems that officially grant their components direct access to the international system are Yugoslavia and the Soviet Union. In Yugoslavia, the six federated republics and two autonomous regions have their own secretariats of foreign affairs; the intrafederal balancing of power, interests, and external initiatives among the six single-party units is closer to our definition of a confederal authoritarian system than to that of a federal union.[39] In the Soviet Union, both the Stalin and Brezhnev Constitutions granted all fifteen constituent republics the right to conduct their own foreign policy. In practice, this provision (discussed in Chapter 5) is limited to the symbolic membership of only two republics, the Ukraine and Byelorussia, in both the political organs and specialized agencies of the United Nations Organization.

For a student of federalism, it is fascinating to observe the ways in which federal formulas and terminology have been used for the preservation of imperial links and other unfederal purposes. While insisting on the unitary nature of its own government in Westminster, Great Britain generally favored federalism for its overseas territories such as Canada, Australia, Cyprus, Palestine, India, Pakistan, Burma, and Malaysia. And while opposing federalism in France itself, centralist France seems to have favored it in the Cameroons and in the South Pacific. So did the Netherlands with regard to Indonesia.

In 1981, China began using federal and confederal terminology (and "conceptology") to prepare for its "repatriation" of Hong Kong and, above all, its planned unification with Taiwan. In August 1983, Deng Xiaoping suggested a new "confederal" formula that would exclude complete autonomy for Taiwan, "since it would mean two Chinas," but would recognize "the Taiwan local government's right to follow its own internal policy" as a special administrative region, "different from the other provincial and autonomous regional governments." Deng added that Taiwan could also keep its own forces so long as they do not impair the interests of the unified state, but "the mainland will station neither troops nor administrative personnel in Taiwan. . . . The political [Kuomintang], government, and armed forces in Taiwan will be administered by Taiwan itself. . . . Seats in the Central Government of China will be reserved for Taiwan."[40]

Microdiplomacy: A Blessing or a Curse?

Subnational presence on the international scene has become a fact of life in an interdependent world. It is neither a blessing nor is it a curse. Global microdiplomacy and transborder regionalism reflect and often contribute to harmony among nations; at times, microdiplomacy may also undermine international harmony by introducing local irritants into international re- lations. As we all know, intimate proximity—neighborhood—is not always a source of love and understanding. George Herbert (see the first epigraph to this chapter) spoke about the problem in the seventeenth century; Carl Sandburg paraphrased it in the twentieth.

One aspect of microdiplomacy and transborder regionalism seems self- evident; whatever case we may make either for or against it, there is no reason to expect the concept and practice of pluralistic nation-states to speak with more than one governmental voice abroad to fade away as a passing aberration due only to a temporary recession in North America and Western Europe. Transborder regionalism and subnational microdiplo- macy may be expected to continue to complicate the formulation and conduct of a coherent national policy. In some fields of international economy, ecology, energy, and humanitarian or cultural concerns, we may have to get used to the idea that the world is not only divided into 160-odd nation- states but, in some cases, also into their territorial components. Clearly, it is not and it will not be easy to run such a global double-layer mosaic smoothly.

But then, no serious student of federalism, nationalism, and international relations could have expected otherwise. Life within and among national communities has always been complicated, and, as the evidence suggests, in our era of global and regional interdependence, it will keep on being, not less, but more so.[41]

Notes

1. Roger Frank Swanson, *Intergovernmental Perspectives on the Canada-U.S. Relationship* (New York: New York University Press, 1978).

2. Robert O. Keohane and Joseph S. Nye, *Power and Interdependence: World Politics in Transition* (Boston and Toronto: Little, Brown, 1977), p. 19.

3. Ernst B. Haas, "Regimes Are Norms, Rules, and Procedures Agreed to Regulate an Issue-Area," *International Organization* 36 (1980), p. 358.

4. Stephen D. Krasner, "Structural Causes and Regime Consequences: Regimes as Intervening Variables," *International Organization* 36 (1980), p. 185. "A set of implicit and explicit norms, rules and decision-making procedures around which actors' expectations converge."

5. Keohane and Nye, *Power and Independence*, pp. 24–29.

6. Associated Press, February 21, 1985.

7. Niles Hansen, *The Border Economy: Regional Development in the Southwest* (Austin: University of Texas Press, 1981), p. 33. See also Niles Hansen, "The Rhine and the Rio Grande: A Comparative Study of Transboundary Cooperation," a paper presented as a Symposium on "Problem-Solving Along Borders: Comparative Perspectives," held at the University of Texas at El Paso, March 21, 1984.

8. In its public relations brochure, the Center for Inter-American and Border Studies, University of Texas at El Paso, speaks of the 35 million legal crossings over the five El Paso-Juarez bridges and points to the "30 million people living within a 400-mile wide, 2,000-mile long belt that is bisected by the boundary," which, over time, has produced "a dynamic binational society" with a "highly interdependent regional economy" (El Paso: Center for Inter-American and Border Studies: *El Paso/Juarez: Where Latin America Begins*, 1982), p. 3.

9. There is also no U.S.-Canadian counterpart to the dynamic and productive U.S.-Mexican Association of Borderland Scholars, whose annual meeting in 1984 scheduled nineteen panel sessions at which sixty-two papers were presented. Typically, the meeting began with a panel on "Popular Cultural Expression Along the Border" and a paper on "La Nueva literatura fronteriza." One of the impressive results of the work by borderland scholars is the encyclopedic *Borderlands Sourcebook: A Guide to the Literature in Northern Mexico and the American Southwest*, edited by Ellwyn R. Stoddard, Richard L. Nostrand, and Jonathan P. Smith (Norman: University of Oklahoma Press, 1983), p. 445.

10. Ellwyn R. Stoddard, "Overview," *El Paso Herald/Special Report: The Border*, Summer 1983, p. 97.

11. Elliot J. Feldman, "Federal Systems Are Not All Alike (But That May be Changing . . .)," in Joseph Magnet, *Canadian Constitutional Law: Cases, Notes and Materials* (Toronto: Carswell, 1985), p. 8–14.

12. Stephen P. Mumme, "The Politics of Water Apportionment and Pollution Problems in the United States-Mexico Relations," in Overseas Development Council, *U.S.-Mexico Project Series*, No. 5 (1982), pp. 1–20. Mumme wrote that "the primary obstacle to a new groundwater treaty and resolution of outstanding surface water issues is the decentralization of the treaty-making process [in the United States] of formulating a negotiating position and ratifying water apportionment agreements. Mexico, with centralized management of its domestic policy process, has greater flexibility in developing its negotiating position" (p. 16).

13. John W. House, *Frontier on the Rio Grande: A Political Geography of Development and Social Deprivation* (Oxford: Clarendon Press, 1982), p. 160.

14. Elliot J. Feldman, "Federal Systems Are Not All Alike," p. 88.

15. John A. Price, "Mexican and Canadian Border Comparisons," *Borderlands Sourcebook*, p. 23: "Canada has a much greater economic integration with the United States than Mexico does but this integration is not achieved through border cities." Ellwyn R. Stoddard, "Overview" in *Borderlands Sourcebook*, p. 5, "Borderland

communities traditionally survive by ignoring federal procedures, circumventing them or translating them into border customs that are culturally, historically, and functionally acceptable for daily border intercourse. . . . On a daily basis local border officials carry on foreign policy with their sister cities and counterparts through a network of informal linkages in the public and private sectors." Stoddard calls the border a "permeable membrane."

16. Lise Bissonnette, "La vocation tardive: Perceptions des milieux politiques québécois à l'égard des Etats Unis" (Paper presented at the Colloque Québec-Etats Unis, Harvard University, September 1, 1983).

17. *Le Devoir*, June 4, 1983.

18. Quoted in *Le Devoir*, May 13, 1985. Paul des Rivières, "La reconciliation du Québec et des minorités francophones est indispensable."

19. For a well-researched analytical study of the last ten transborder summits, see Martin Lubin, "The Conference of the New England Governors and the Eastern Canadian Premiers" (Paper presented at the twenty-sixth Annual Meeting of the Western Social Science Association, San Diego, April 26, 1984), p. 86.

20. An agreement between Hydro-Québec and the New England Electric System (NEES) was signed in 1983 to supply 690–2,000 megawatts of electric hydropower to the six New England states.

21. *Le Devoir*, May 21, 1985.

22. The links promoted by some Québécois with the Swiss canton of Jura seem to have been based on a wrong analogy since the Swiss Jurassiens primarily wanted a separation from the German-speaking canton of Bern rather than full independence or accession to France. See also André Donneur, "Le Québec et le Jura," *Le Devoir*, July 12, 1983, in which Donneur critically contrasts the cultural agreement between Québec and Jura with the francophone canton of Geneva's insistence on treating Québec as a part of Canada.

23. *Le Devoir*, May 16, 1985.

24. To voice their regional dissatisfaction with the federal government's centralized socialist planning, in 1984 the Alsatian mayors of Strasbourg and Colmar decided to offend President Mitterand by denying him the traditional reception at their respective city halls. His angry reaction is quoted in an epigraph to Chapter 3.

25. *Le Devoir*, October 13, 1983. This Montréal French daily has also had for many years a weekly column on the contents and forms of Québec's foreign policy, written by a Laval University professor of political science and a well-known expert on federalism, Paul Painchaud.

26. For an in-depth analytical treatment see Elliot Feldman and Lily Feldman, "The Reorganization and Reconstruction of Canadian Foreign Policy," *Publius* 14:4 (1984), pp. 33–39; see also Panayotis Soldatos, "Le Phenomène de fragmentation dans l'activité de politique étrangère d'un état fédéral: le cas particulier du Canada," in *La crise des institutions de l'Etat* (Melanges Phedon: Vegleris, 1984). For a well-documented overview of the close links between Québec and the United States, see Alfred O. Hero, Jr., and Marcel Daneau, eds., *Problems and Opportunities in U.S.-Québec Relations* (Boulder, Colo.: Westview Press, 1984), p. 320.

27. Robert O. Keohane and Joseph S. Nye, "Transgovernmental Relations and International Organizations," *World Politics* 27:1 (October 1974), pp. 39–62.

28. One example was the presence of a Manitoban representative at the U.S. embassy in Washington, D.C. in connection with Canadian-U.S. negotiations concerning the Garrison Dam project between Manitoba and North Dakota. There was, however, no North Dakotan representation at the U.S. embassy in Ottawa. Another example is the presence of a Québec diplomat at the Canadian embassy

in Abidjan (Ivory Coast). The access of these "territorial" officers to all-national classified documents raises some intriguing questions as to their capacity to inform their provincial governments about confidential matters. Except for Nova Scotia, which is represented in London, the Maritime Provinces generally rely on the Canadian Ministry of Foreign Affairs to represent and promote their interests abroad. They do, however, fully participate in New England-eastern Canada gubernatorial summits and the resulting formal and informal transborder regional frameworks.

29. Paul Painchaud, "Territorialization and Internationalism: The Case of Québec," *Publius* 7:4 (1977), pp. 161–175.

30. Ivo D. Duchacek, "Préface," in Edmond Orban, *La Dynamique de la centralisation et l'Etat fédéral: un processus irréversible* (Montréal: Québec/Amérique, 1984.

31. William H. Stewart, "Metaphors, Models, and the Development of Federal Theory," *Publius* 12:2 (1982), pp. 5–24. According to Stewart, the culinary metaphor— the marble cake—though popularized by Morton Grodzins, apparently originated with Joseph McLean who, in 1972, corrected the old image of a federal system as a "layer cake" by suggesting a marble cake on account of the "many combined activities . . . which blend throughout the cake and ignore the layers" (p. 10). This metaphor has become part of a standard vocabulary, as Stewart rightly says.

32. Martin Landau, "Redundancy, Rationality, and the Problem of Duplication and Overlap," *Public Administration Review* 29:4 (July 1969), pp. 346–358, and "Federalism, Redundancy and System Stability," *Publius* 3:2 (1973), pp. 173–196, describes the U.S. federal government as the most redundant government in the world. The constitutional designers not only "engineered feedbacks into the system . . . they multiplexed it at every critical point. . . . Domains overlap, jurisdictions are confused and accountability is dispersed. . . . And for each citizen there is, at the least, two of everything: . . . two constitutions, two executives, two legislatures, two codes of law, two judiciaries . . . two bills of rights, two networks of checks and balances . . . and there are more (188)." I would add, also two types of international contacts: national and subnational.

33. The last nine paragraphs of this section are an expanded version of Ivo D. Duchacek, "International Competence of Subnational Governments: Borderlands and Beyond" (Paper presented at symposium, Problem-Solving Along Borders: Comparative Perspectives, University of Texas at El Paso, March 21, 1984). A revised version will be published in Oscar I. Martinez ed., *Across Boundaries: Transborder Interaction in Comparative Perspective* (El Paso: University of Texas Press, 1986, forthcoming).

34. Cf. Stephen L. Schechter, "Annual Review of American Federalism, 1983," in *Publius* 14 (September 1984). Five articles are devoted to a critical examination of ACIR.

35. For details, see Robert Sheppard and Michael Valpy, *The National Deal: The Fight for a Canadian Constitution* (Toronto: Fleet Books, 1982), and Edward McWhinney, *Canada and the Constitution 1979–1982: Patriation and the Charter of Rights* (Toronto: University of Toronto Press, 1982).

36. Ontario, Ministry of Industry and Trade, *Canadian Trade Policy for the 1980's, An Ontario Perspective* (Toronto, 1982), p. 22.

37. Earl H. Fry and Gregory A. Raymond, *Idaho's Foreign Relations: The Transgovernmental Linkages of An American State* (Boise, Idaho: Center for Research, 1978) p. 25. See also William H. Riker, *Federalism: Origin, Operation, Significance* (Boston: Little, Brown, 1964), p. 58, where Riker writes, "The Second Amendment . . . perpetually guaranteed the right of the states to maintain militia, *presumably*

because they expected it to be the chief military force for the future" (italics added). See also William H. Riker, *Soldiers of the States* (Washington, D.C.: Public Affairs Press, 1957), p. 141.

38. Alaska Statehood Commission, *More Perfect Union: A Preliminary Report*, January 19, 1981, pp. 8–9. The authors of the report, professors Andrea Helms and Gerald McBeath (University of Alaska at Fairbanks) introduced the report by the following statement: "A federation is constantly in a state of tension, always falling apart and simultaneously being forced together toward the center."

39. Pedro Remet, *Nationalism and Federalism in Yugoslavia: 1963–1983* (Bloomington: Indiana University Press, 1985), p. 299.

40. *Beijing Review*, August 8, 1983, p. 5.

41. Parts of this chapter contain revised portions of Ivo D. Duchacek, "The International Dimension of Subnational Self-Government," *Publius* 14:4 (1984), pp. 5–31.

Conclusion

There are no dividing lines between the countries of the Earth like those we see drawn on maps. All the countries and continents blend together as one united planet. So, for a while, you are removed from Earth's problems—the crime, starvation, and overcrowded conditions, and the conflict between nations.
—Dick Scobee,
Commander of space shuttle Challenger,
(talking of the earth as seen from space, 1986)

The fragmentation of humanity into over 160 territorial states and their subdivisions seems to be in conflict with a search for another less territory-oriented system that would mirror and be responsive to the present imperatives of global and regional interdependence. Nonterritorial, that is, global or regional, problems of resources, technology, production, population explosion, and depletion and pollution of our planet are intertwined with the nuclear homicide/suicide dimension of great power politics. Consequently, the search for a different order of interaction and cooperation among territorial nations seems to create a sense of urgency, usually more keenly felt among people who are not at the helm of their territorial domains.

The snail-like progress, if not regression, of the West European unification is depressing. So are the difficulties accompanying the effort to establish a greater U.S.-Canadian economic and political intimacy although the logic of that effort may appear self-evident to many an outsider. Violent conflicts within, among, and across (the case of international terror) territorial nations, rather clearly indicate, as this study has demonstrated, that humanity is not about to alter its fragmented ways of viewing and approaching clearly common problems. Palestinian international terrorism whose violent outbursts systematically pass across so many sovereign boundaries basically aims at the establishment of a geographically delineated, territorial nation-state. The world has physically and technically changed a great deal over the millennia, but not human nature.

Studying human nature and the resulting political action makes one very modest and undemanding. Humans who individually are quite capable of selflessness rarely, if ever, seem capable of adding up their individual capacities for generosity into a collective sum total. All groups, and territorial ones

295

in particular, tend to protect and promote their common interest in an egocentric fashion.

Weighing the various evidences of the territorial way of life on our earth, I have had to remain skeptical of wishful plans for a new global order, a frontierless world or even a regionalized planet, divided into only a few peacefully and constructively integrated regions. This study actually warns that such regionalization might result only in the old territoriality writ large, which is potentially even more dangerous than is the present Balkanization of the planet.

The results of my inquiry clearly caution against the extreme view in which humanity is condemned to perish unless it abandons, now and immediately, its preference for living in territorial corrals and for looking at and interacting with the world through territorial fences. These fences are now meshlike, yet they keep on rigidly delineating the various national and subnational egocentric domains. To paraphrase Mark Twain, the reports of the death of the territorial principle of political organization are greatly exaggerated.

The choice between either territorial fusion (on a global *or* regional basis) or fission is actually wrongly posited; it cannot be expressed in such extreme terms, which practical politics and life have always abhorred. Mutually exclusive alternatives are not as irreconcilable as they appear. As we all know, black and white often seem mutually exclusive, but only until the two opposites intermingle and create various shades of gray. This is, after all, what dialectics teaches us.

Similarly, territorial fragmentation can accommodate mutual interdependence, while global or regional interdependence may continue to be managed, not well, but acceptably by territorial units; in fact, there is no other choice. The human tendencies "to go it alone" *as well as* "to go it with others" can be combined despite their apparent contradiction—actually this combination is what federal political culture is all about. The group tendency to organize its solitude may be combined with partnership; in Canada, for example, the term *deux solitudes* is sometimes used to describe not only a dyadic tension but also the potential for a Québec-Canada near-confederal symbiosis. In my book *Comparative Federalism* several years ago, I expressed the broad themes of federal and confederal political cultures as meaning a combination of subcentral "Leave us alone" with "Let us in," that is, "in" on major decisions affecting the national or collective whole.

This study indicates, therefore, a scenario as untidy and inelegant as life itself: that is, a flexible, nonuniform adaptation to the penetrative flows of various interactions across the territorial divides, a step-by-step rather than an abrupt process. This process is full of duplications, perhaps costly but useful as safety valves (to use Martin Landau's terminology); spotty rather than consistent; proceeding with deliberate speed from issue to issue rather than rapidly and on a large scale, which results in various and changing forms of interactions *across* perforated sovereignties in addition to, but not instead of, traditional politics *within* and *among* nations.

Passing through various transborder channels managed by central, non-central, corporate, or private managers, humanity—here is the long-term optimism of a short-term pessimistic author—will have to, as always, simply muddle through the labyrinthine web of the various levels of local, municipal, regional, national, transnational, intercontinental, and world politics—we all hope without major disaster. It is useful to bear in mind that even the grand scheme of a world government, based on global unity (if such a dream were more than a dream in a foreseeable future), would be no guarantee against either world dictatorship by a few over many or a disastrous global civil war—a possibility that many civil wars within organized territorial states confirm.

A very long process, then, of an intertwining of territorial parochialism and globalism (or regionalism) is to be expected. The process clearly will lack dramatic qualitative changes that could exhilarate a globalist and depress a parochialist—and vice versa. Instead of daring we should anticipate, to paraphrase Max Weber, a slow boring into the brittle walls of territorial sovereignty. The speed with which territorial communities have so far adapted and may be expected to adapt themselves to challenges presented by both external and internal environments suggests the pace of geological changes rather than the velocity of contemporary missiles.

Bibliography

Advisory Commission on Intergovernmental Relations. *The Question of State Government Capability*. Washington, D.C.: ACIR, 1985.
_____ . *Studies in Comparative Federalism: Australia, Canada, the United States, and West Germany*. Washington, D.C.: ACIR, 1981.
_____ . *Studies in Comparative Federalism: Canada*. Washington, D.C.: ACIR, 1981.
Akzin, Benjamin. *States and Nations*. Garden City, N.Y.: Doubleday/Anchor, 1966.
Alliluyeva, Svetlana. "To Boris Leodinovich Pasternak." *Atlantic Monthly* 219 (1966), pp. 133–140.
Allison, Graham T. *Essence of Decision*. Boston: Little, Brown, 1971.
Almond, Gabriel A., and Powell, G. Bingham, Jr. *Comparative Politics: A Developmental Approach*. Boston: Little, Brown, 1966.
Almond, Gabriel A., and Verba, Sidney. *The Civic Culture: Political Attitudes and Democracy in Five Nations*. Boston: Little, Brown, 1963.
Ardrey, Robert. *African Genesis*. New York: Dell Publishing, Laurel Edition, 1967.
_____ . *The Territorial Imperative: A Personal Inquiry into the Animal Origins of Property and Nations*. New York: Dell Publishing, 1966.
Aristotle. *The Politics*. Introduction by Ernest Baker. New York: Oxford University Press, 1962.
Aron, Raymond. *Peace and War: A Theory of International Relations*. New York: Praeger, 1966.
Aspaturian, Vernon A. *The Union Republics and Soviet Diplomacy*. Geneva: Librairie Droz, 1960.
_____ . "The Union Republics and Soviet Diplomacy: Concepts, Institutions, and Practices." *American Political Science Review* (June 1959), pp. 383–411.
Axelrod, Robert. *The Evolution of Cooperation*. New York: Basic Books, 1984.
Bakvis, Herman. "Structure and Processes in Federal and Consociational Arrangements." Paper presented at the American Political Science Association Annual Meeting, Chicago, September 1–4, 1983.
Barnet, Richard J., and Muller, Ronald E. *Global Reach: The Power of Multinational Corporations*. New York: Simon and Schuster, 1974.
Beloff, Max. "Reflections on Intervention." *Journal of International Affairs* 22 (1968), pp. 197–207.
Bergeron, Gerard, and Pelletier, Rejean. *L'Etat du Québec en devenir*. Montréal: Boréal Express, 1980.
Bernard, André. *La politique au Canada et au Québec*. Montréal: Les presses universitaires du Québec, 1980.
Bertelsen, Judy S. *Nonstate Nations in International Politics: Comparative System Analyses*. New York: Praeger, 1977.
Billington, Ray Allen. "History is a Dangerous Subject." *Saturday Review* 49 (January 15, 1966), pp. 59–61 and 80–81.
Bissonnette, Lise. "Orthodoxie fédéraliste et relations régionales trans-frontières, une menace illusoire." *Etudes internationales* 12 (1981), pp. 635–655.
Blackstock, Paul W. *Agents of Deceit: Frauds, Forgeries, and Political Intrigues Among Nations*. Chicago: Quadrangle Books, 1966.
_____ . *The Strategy of Subversion*. Chicago: Quadrangle Books, 1965.

Boorstin, Daniel J. *The Americans: The National Experience.* New York: Random House, 1965.

Boulding, Kenneth E. "National Images and International Systems." *Journal of Conflict Resolution* 3 (1959), pp. 120–131.

Boveri, Margret. *Treason in the Twentieth Century.* New York: G. P. Putnam, 1961.

Boyd, Gavin, ed. *Region Building in the Pacific.* New York: Pergamon Press, 1982.

Brady, Alexander. *Democracy in the Dominions.* Toronto: University of Toronto Press, 1958.

Brecht, Arnold. *Federalism and Regionalism in Germany: The Division of Prussia.* New York: Oxford University Press, 1945.

Brinton, Crane. *The Anatomy of Revolution.* New York: Random House, Vintage Books, 1965.

Brossard, Jacques. *L'Accession à la souveraineté et le cas de Québec.* Montréal: Les presses universitaires de Montréal, 1976.

Brown, Seyom. *New Forces in World Politics.* Washington, D.C.: Brookings Institution, 1974.

Bull, Hedley, ed. *Intervention in World Politics.* New York: Oxford University Press, 1984.

Cairns, Alan C. *From Interstate to Intrastate Federalism.* Kingston: Institute of Intergovernmental Relations, Queen's University, 1979.

Callières, François de. *On the Manner of Negotiating with Princes.* Notre Dame: University of Notre Dame Press, 1963.

Callsen, Paul. "Informal Transborder Relationships Among Municipal Officials: El Paso, Texas; Ciudad Juárez, Chihuahua." Master thesis, University of Texas at El Paso, May 1985.

Carr, Edward H. *Nationalism and After.* London: Macmillan, 1945.

Cerny, Karl H. "Federalism in the West German Republic." In Valerie Earle, *Federalism: Infinite Variety in Theory and Practice.* Itasca, Ill.: F. E. Peacock, 1968.

Clark, Grenville, and Sohn, Louis B. *World Peace Through World Law.* Cambridge: Harvard University Press, 1958.

Claude, Inis L., Jr. *Swords into Plowshares: The Problems and Progress of International Organization.* New York: Random House, 1970.

Coleman, William D. *The Independence Movement in Québec: 1945–1980.* Toronto: University of Toronto Press, 1984.

Collester, J. Bryan. *The European Communities: A Guide to Information Sources.* Detroit, Mich.: Gale Research Company, 1979.

Connor, Walker. *The National Question in Marxist-Leninist Theory and Strategy.* Princeton: Princeton University Press, 1984.

———. "Nation-Building or Nation-Destroying." *World Politics* 24 (1972) pp. 319–355.

———. "Self-Determination: The New Phase." *World Politics* 20 (1967), pp. 28–53.

Cottam, Richard W. *Competitive Interference and Twentieth Century Diplomacy.* Pittsburgh: University of Pittsburgh Press, 1967.

Dahl, Robert A. *Pluralist Democracy in the United States: Conflict and Consent.* Chicago: Rand McNally, 1967.

———. *Polyarchy: Participation and Opposition.* New Haven: Yale University Press, 1971.

———. *Who Governs?* New Haven: Yale University Press, 1961.

Dahl, Robert A., ed. *Regimes and Oppositions*. New Haven: Yale University Press, 1973.

Dahl, Robert A., and Tufte, Edward R. *Size and Democracy*. Stanford: Stanford University Press, 1973.

Davis, Rufus. *The Federal Principle: A Journey Through Time in Quest of Meaning*. Berkeley: University of California Press, 1978.

———. "The Federal Principle Reconsidered," *Australian Journal of Politics and History* 1 (1956), pp. 59–85 (Part 1) and pp. 223–244 (Part 2).

Dawson, Richard E., and Prewitt, Kenneth. *Political Socialization*. Boston: Little, Brown, 1968.

Detton, Hervé. *L'Administration régionale et locale en France*. Paris: Presses Universitaires de France, 1964.

Deutsch, Karl W. *National and Social Communication: An Inquiry Into the Foundations of Nationality*. Cambridge: M.I.T. Press, 1966.

Dinstein, Yoram, ed. *Models of Autonomy*. New Brunswick, N.J.: Transaction Books, 1981.

Djilas, Milovan. *The New Class*. New York: Praeger, 1957.

Doran, Charles F. *Forgotten Partnership: U.S.-Canada Relations Today*. Baltimore: Johns Hopkins University Press, 1984.

Duchacek, Ivo D. "Antagonistic Cooperation: Ethnic and Territorial Communities." *Publius* 7 (1977), pp. 3–29.

———. *Comparative Federalism: The Territorial Dimension of Politics*. New York: Holt, Rinehart and Winston, 1970; reprint, Lanham, Md.: University Press of America, forthcoming.

———. "Consociational Cradle of Federalism." *Publius* 15 (1985), pp. 35–48.

———. "Consociations of Fatherlands: The Revival of Confederal Principles and Practices." *Publius* 12 (1982), pp. 129–177.

———. "Dyadic Federalism." Paper delivered at the Annual Political Science Association Meeting, New Orleans, August 29–September 1, 1985.

———. "Federalist Responses to Ethnic Demands: An Overview." In Daniel J. Elazar, ed., *Federalism and Political Integration*. Ramat Gan, Israel: Turtledove, 1979.

———. "International Competence of Subnational Governments: Borderlands and Beyond." In Oscar J. Martinez, ed., *Across Boundaries: Transborder Interaction in Comparative Perspective*. El Paso: University of Texas Western Press, 1986.

———. "The International Dimension of Subnational Self-Government." *Publius* 14 (1984), pp. 5–31.

———. *Nations and Men: An Introduction to International Politics*, 3d ed. New York: Holt, Rinehart and Winston, 1975; reprint, Washington, D.C.: University Press of America, 1982.

———. "Parliaments: Rule Modification and Controls." *Journal of Constitutional and Parliamentary Studies* (New Delhi) 2 (1968), pp. 55–74.

———. *Power Maps: Comparative Politics of Constitutions*. Santa Barbara, Calif: ABC-Clio, 1973.

———. *Rights and Liberties in the World Today*. Santa Barbara, Calif: ABC-Clio, 1973.

Earle, Valerie. *Federalism: Infinite Variety in Theory and Practice*. Itasca, Ill.: F. E. Peacock, 1968.

Easton, David. *A Framework for Political Analysis*. Englewood Cliffs, N.J.: Prentice-Hall, 1965.

———. *A Systems Analysis of Political Life*. New York: John Wiley, 1965.

Eisenstadt, S. N., and Rokkan, Stein. *Building States and Nations: Models and Data Resources.* Beverly Hills, Calif.: Sage Publications, 1973. Elazar, Daniel J. *American Federalism: A View from the States.* New York: Thomas Y. Crowell, 1966.

──── . "Dialogue on Comparative Federalism." Roundtable discussion held at the Center for the Study of Federalism, Temple University, November 8, 1977.

──── . *Federalism and Political Integration.* Ramat Gan, Israel: Turtledove, 1979.

──── . "Federated States and International Relations—Introduction." *Publius* 14 (1984), pp. 1–4.

Elazar, Daniel J., ed. *Governing People and Territories.* Philadelphia: Institute for the Study of Human Issues, 1982.

Elliot, Jonathan. *The Debates.* Philadelphia: Lippincott (Yates minutes), 1888.

Emerson, Rupert. *From Empire to Nation.* Cambridge: Harvard University Press, 1960.

Enloe, Cynthia. *Ethnic Conflict and Political Development.* Boston: Little, Brown, 1973.

──── . *Ethnicity and Political Development.* Boston: Little, Brown, 1973.

Ericksen, E. Gordon. *The Territorial Experience: Human Ecology as Symbolic Interaction.* Austin: University of Texas Press, 1980.

Eulau, Heinz. "Polarity in Representational Federalism: A Neglected Theme of Political Theory." *Publius* 3 (1973), pp. 153–171.

Europe, Council of. *Colloquy on the Reforms of Local and Regional Authorities in Europe: Theory, Practice, and Critical Appraisal.* Strasbourg: Steering Committee for Regional and Municipal Matters, 1981.

──── . *Reports of the Conference of Local and Regional Authorities of Europe.* Strasbourg: Steering Committee for Regional and Municipal Matters—CDRM, 1976–1985.

──── . *Third European Conference of Frontier Regions—1984.* Strasbourg: Parliamentary Assembly, Standing Conference of Local and Regional Authorities in Europe, 1984.

Fainsod, Merle. *How Russia Is Ruled.* Cambridge: Harvard University Press, 1953.

Falk, Richard A. "The International Law of War." In James N. Rosenau, ed., *International Aspects of Civil Strife.* Princeton: Princeton University Press, 1964.

Falk, Richard A., and Mendlovitz, Saul H., eds. *Regional Politics and World Order.* San Francisco: W. H. Freeman, 1973.

Fanon, Frantz. *The Wretched of the Earth.* New York: Grove Press, 1968.

Farrel, R. Barry, ed. *Approaches to Comparative and International Politics.* Evanston: Northwestern University Press, 1966.

The Federalist Papers: Alexander Hamilton, James Madison, John Jay. Introduction by Clinton Rossiter. New York: New American Library, Mentor, 1961.

Feldman, Elliot J. "Federal Systems Are Not All Alike (But That May be Changing . . .)." In Joseph Magnet, *Canadian Constitutional Law.* Toronto: Carswell, 1985.

Feldman, Elliot, and Feldman, Lily. "The Reorganization and Reconstruction of Canadian Foreign Policy." *Publius* 14 (1984), pp. 33–59.

Feldman, Elliot J., and Nevitte, Neil. *The Future of North America: Canada, the United States and Québec Nationalism.* Cambridge: Center for International Affairs, 1979.

Ferry, W. H. "The Case for a New Federalism." *Saturday Review,* June 15, 1968.

Finer, Herman. *Theory and Practice of Modern Government.* New York: Holt, Rinehart and Winston, 1949.

Foster, Charles R. *Nations Without a State: Ethnic Minorities in Western Europe.* New York: Praeger, 1980.

Franck, Thomas M., ed. *Why Federations Fail—An Inquiry into the Requisites for Successful Federalism.* New York: New York University Press, 1968.

Friedrich, Carl J., ed. *Totalitarianism: Proceedings of a Conference Held at the American Academy of Arts and Science,* March 1953. Cambridge: Harvard University Press, 1954.

———. *Trends of Federalism in Theory and Practice.* New York: Praeger, 1968.

Fry, Earl H. "The Politics of Investment Incentives and Restrictions: A Preliminary Analysis of the Transnational Linkages of the U.S. States and Canadian Provincial Governments." Paper presented at the Western Social Science Association Annual Conference, Albuquerque, April 27-30, 1983.

Fry, Earl H., and Raymond, Gregory A. *Idaho's Foreign Relations: The Transgovernmental Linkages of an American State.* Boise, Idaho: Center for Research, 1978.

Galluci, Gerald M. "The Articles Amended: The American Confederal Tradition Restated." Paper presented at the American Political Science Association Annual Meeting, Washington, D.C., August 28-31, 1980.

Gerson, Lewis L. *The Hyphenate in Recent American Politics.* Lawrence: University of Kansas Press, 1954.

Gerth, H. H., and Mills, C. Wright. *From Max Weber: Essays in Sociology.* New York: Oxford, University Press, 1958.

Gibbins, Roger. *Regionalism: Territorial Politics in Canada and the United States.* Toronto: Butterworth, 1982.

———. *Senate Reform: Moving Towards the Slippery Slope.* Kingston, Ont.: Institute of Intergovernmental Relations, 1983.

Golembiewski, Robert T., and Wildavsky, Aaron, eds. *The Costs of Federalism: Essays in Honor of James W. Fesler.* New Brunswick N.J.: Transaction Books, 1984.

Goodwin, Geoffrey L. "The Erosion of External Sovereignty." *Government and Opposition* 9 (1974), pp. 61-78.

Goshal, Upendra Nath. *A History of Indian Political Ideas.* New York: Oxford University Press, 1959.

Gottmann, Jean. "Geography and International Relations." *World Politics* 3 (1951), pp. 153-173.

———. "The Political Partitioning of our World: An Attempt at Analysis." *World Politics* 4 (1952), pp. 512-519.

———. *La politique des Etats et leur geographie.* Paris: Armand Colin, 1952.

———. *The Significance of Territory.* Charlottesville: University of Virginia Press, 1973.

Gottmann, Jean, ed. *Centre and Periphery: Spatial Variation in Politics.* Beverly Hills, Calif.: Sage, 1980.

Gottmann, Jean, and Laponce, Jean, eds. "Politics and Geography." *International Political Science Review* 1 (1980), pp. 429-577.

Graber, D. A. *Crisis Diplomacy: A History of U.S. Intervention Politics and Practices.* Washington, D.C.: Public Affairs Press, 1959.

Greene, Evarts B. *Provincial America.* New York: Holt, 1905.

Greilsammer, Ilan. "Some Observations on European Federalism." In Daniel J. Elazar, ed., *Federalism and Political Integration.* Ramat Gan, Israel: Turtledove, 1979.

Grodzins, Morton. *The American System: A New View of Government in the United States.* Chicago: Rand McNally, 1966.

———. "The Federal System." In American Assembly, Columbia University, ed, *Goals for Americans.* Englewood Cliffs, N.J.: Prentice-Hall, 1960.

———. *The Loyal and Disloyal: Social Boundaries of Patriotism and Treason.* Chicago: University of Chicago Press, 1956.

Guillaume, Pierre, et al. *Canada et Canadiens.* Bordeaux: Presses universitaires de Bordeaux, 1984.

Gurr, Ted Robert. *Why Men Rebel.* Princeton: Princeton University Press, 1970.

Haas, Ernst B. *Beyond the Nation-State: Functionalism and International Organization.* Stanford: Stanford University Press, 1964.

———. *The Obsolescence of Regional Integration Theory.* Berkeley, Calif.: Institute of International Peace, 1975.

———. "Turbulent Fields and the Theory of Regional Integration." *International Organization* 27 (1971), pp. 173–212.

———. *The Uniting of Europe: Political, Social, and Economic Forces 1950–1967.* Stanford: Stanford University Press, 1958.

———. "Why Collaborate? Issue-Linkage and International Regimes." *World Politics* 32 (1980), pp. 357–405.

———. Words Can Hurt You: Or Who Said What About the Regimes." *International Organization* 36 (1980), pp. 207–243.

Halpern, Manfred. "The Morality and Politics of Intervention." In James N. Rosenau, ed., *International Aspects of Civil Strife.* Princeton: Princeton University Press, 1964.

Hannun, Hurst, and Lillich, Richard B. "The Concept of Autonomy in International Law." *American Journal of International Law* 74 (1980), pp. 858–890.

Hanrieder, Wolfram F. "Dissolving International Politics: Reflections on the Nation-State." *American Political Science Review* 71 (1978), pp. 1276–1287.

Hansen, Niles. *The Border Economy: Regional Development in the Southwest.* Austin: University of Texas Press, 1981.

Haqqi, S.A.H. "Federalism, Single Dominant Party, and the Problem of Linguistic Autonomy in India." Paper presented at the Sixth World Congress of the International Political Science Association, Geneva, September 21–25, 1964.

Harvey, David. *Social Justice and the City.* Baltimore: Johns Hopkins University Press, 1975.

Heisler, Martin. *Politics in Europe: Structure and Processes in Some Postindustrial Democracies.* New York: David McKay, 1974.

Herman, Valentine, and Lodge, Juliet. *The European Parliament and the European Community.* New York: St. Martin's Press, 1978.

Hero, Alfred O., Jr., and Daneau, Marcel, eds., *Problems and Opportunities in U.S.-Québec Relations.* Boulder, Colo: Westview Press, 1984.

Herz, John H. "The Government of Germany." In G. M. Carter and J. H. Herz, *Major Foreign Powers.* New York: Harcourt Brace Jovanovich, 1967.

———. "Ideological Aspects—International Relations." In *International Encyclopedia of Social Sciences.* New York: Crowell-Collier-Macmillan, 1968.

———. *The Nation-State and the Crisis of World Politics: Essays on International Politics in the Twentieth Century.* New York: David McKay, 1976.

Historicus [George Allen Morgan]. "Stalin on Revolution." *Foreign Affairs* 27, (1949), pp. 3–42.

Hoffmann, Stanley. *Duties Beyond Borders.* Syracuse: Syracuse University Press, 1981.

———. "Obstinate or Obsolete? The Fate of the Nation-State and the Case of Western Europe." *Daedalus* 95 (1966), pp. 862–915.

Holmes, Jean, and Sharman, Campbell. *The Australian Federal System.* London: Allen and Unwin, 1977.

Holsti, K. J. "Underdevelopment and the 'Gap' Theory of International Conflict." *The American Political Science Review* 69 (1975), pp. 19-75.

Hooton, E. A. *Apes, Men, and Morons.* New York: Putnam, 1937.

House, J. W. *Frontier on the Rio Grande: A Political Geography of Development and Social Deprivation.* Oxford: Clarendon Press, 1982.

Hüglin, Thomas O. "Scarcity and Centralization: The Concept of European Integration." *International Political Science Review* 4 (1983), pp. 345-360.

Huntington, Samuel P. "Transnational Organizations in World Politics," *World Politics* 25 (1973), pp. 358-362.

Hurwitz, Leon, ed. *Contemporary Perspectives on European Integration: Attitudes, Nongovernmental Behavior and Collective Decision Making.* Westport, Conn.: Greenwood Press, 1980.

Hyman, Herbert. *Political Socialization.* New York: Free Press, 1959.

Iklé, F. C. *How Nations Negotiate.* New York: Harper and Row, 1964.

Isaacs, Harold R. *Idols of the Tribe: Group Identity and Political Change.* New York: Harper and Row, 1975.

Jackson, Robert; Jackson, Doreen; and Baxler-Moore, Nicholas. *Politics in Canada: Culture, Institutions, Behaviour and Public Policy.* Englewood Cliffs, N.J.: Prentice-Hall, 1986.

Jacobson, Harold K. *Networks of Interdependence: International Organizations and the Global Political System.* New York: Knopf, 1984.

Jacobson, Harold K, and Cox, Robert, eds. *The Anatomy of Influence: Decision Making in International Organizations.* New Haven: Yale University Press, 1973.

Jacobson, Harold K.; Reisinger, William; and Mathers, Todd. "States and IGOs: A Multiplying Entanglement." Paper presented at the American Political Science Association Annual Meeting, Washington, D.C., 1984.

Jensen, Merrill. *The Articles of Confederation: An Interpretation of the Social-Constitutional History of the American Revolution, 1774-1781.* Madison: University of Wisconsin Press, 1940.

Jervis, Robert. "Cooperation Under the Security of Dilemma." *World Politics* 30 (1978), pp. 167-214.

————. "From Balance to Concert: A Study of International Security Cooperation." *World Politics* 38 (1985), pp. 58-79.

————. *The Logic of Images in International Relations.* Princeton: Princeton University Press, 1979.

Johnson, Chalmers. *Revolutionary Changes.* Stanford: Stanford University Press, 1982.

Jones, Harry W. "The Articles of Confederation and the Creation of a Federal System." In *Aspects of American Liberty: Philosophical, Historical, and Political.* Philadelphia: American Philosophical Society, 1976.

Kahin, George McTurnan, ed. *Major Governments of Asia.* 2d ed. Ithaca: Cornell University Press, 1963.

Kennan, George F. "Foreign Aid in the Framework of National Policy." *Proceedings of the American Academy of Political Science* 23 (1950), pp. 104-114.

Keohane, Robert O., "The Demand for International Regimes." *International Organization* 36 (1980), pp. 326-352.

Keohane, Robert O., and Nye, Joseph S. *Power and Interdependence: World Politics in Transition.* Boston and Toronto: Little, Brown, 1977.

————. "Transgovernmental Relations and International Organizations." *World Politics* 27 (1974), pp. 39-62.

Keohane, Robert O., and Nye, Joseph S., eds. *Transnational Relations and World Politics.* Cambridge: Harvard University Press, 1972.

Kincaid, John. "American Governors in International Affairs." *Publius* 14 (1984), pp. 95–114.
King, Preston. *Federalism and Federation.* Baltimore: Johns Hopkins University Press, 1982
Kirchheimer, Otto. "The Waning of Opposition." *Social Research* 24 (1957), pp. 127–156.
Kisker, Gunter. *Kooperation im Bundestaat: Eine Untersuchung zum Kooperativen Föderalismus in der Bundesrepublik Deutschland.* Tübingen: Mohr, 1971.
Kline, John M. *State Government Influence in U.S. International Economic Policy.* Lexington, Mass.: Lexington Books, 1983.
Knorr, Klaus. *The Power of Nations: The Political Economy of International Relations.* New York: Basic Books, 1975.
Kogan, Norman. "Impact on the New Italian Regional Governments on the Structure of Power Within the Parties." *Comparative Politics* 7 (1975), pp. 383–406.
Kohn, Hans. *Nationalism: Its Meaning and History.* Princeton: D. Van Nostrand, 1955.
———. *The Twentieth Century.* New York: Crowell-Collier-Macmillan, 1950.
Krasner, Stephen D. "Structural Causes and Regime Consequences: Regimes as Intervening Variables." *International Organization* 36 (1980), pp. 185–205.
Kusin, Valdimir V. "Typology of Opposition." *Soviet Studies* 25 (1973), pp. 30–46.
Landau, Martin. "Federalism, Redundancy, and System Reliability." *Publius* 3 (1973), pp. 173–196.
———. *Political Theory and Political Science: Studies in the Methodology of Political Inquiry.* Atlantic Highlands, N.J.: Humanities Press, 1972.
———. "Redundancy, Rationality, and the Problem of Duplication and Overlap." *Public Administration Review* 29 (1969), pp. 367–380.
Lasok, Dominik, and Soldatos, Panayotis. *Les Communautés européenes en fonctionnement/The European Communities in Action.* Brussels: Bruylant, 1981.
Laux, Jeanne Kirk. "Public Enterprises and Canadian Foreign Economic Policy." *Publius* 14 (1984), pp. 61–80.
Lazer, Harry. *The American Political System in Transition.* New York: Crowell, 1967.
Leach, Richard H. *American Federalism.* New York: W. W. Norton, 1970.
Lehmbruch, Gerhard. *Proporzdemokratie: Politisches System und Politische Kultur in der Schweiz and in Österreich.* Tübingen: Mohr, 1967.
Lenin, V. I. *Collected Works.* Moscow: Foreign Language Publishers, 1960.
———. *Selected Works.* Moscow: Foreign Language Publishers, 1960.
Leurdijk, J. Henk. "From International to Transnational Politics: A Change of Paradigm?" *International Social Science Journal* 26 (1974), pp. 53–69.
Lijphart, Arend. "Consociational Democracy." *World Politics* 21 (1969), pp. 208–255.
———. *Democracies: Patterns of Majoritarian and Consensus Government in Twenty-One Countries.* New Haven: Yale University Press, 1984.
———. *Democracy in Plural Societies: A Comparative Exploration.* New Haven: Yale University Press, 1977.
———. "Non-Majoritarian Democracy: A Comparison of Federal and Consociational Theories." *Publius* 15 (1985), pp. 3–15.
———. *The Politics of Accommodation: Pluralism and Democracy in the Netherlands.* Berkeley: University of California Press, 1965.
Lipson, Leslie. *The Great Issues of Politics.* Englewood Cliffs, N.J.: Prentice-Hall, 1955.
Littlejohn, David. *The Patriotic Traitors: A History of Collaboration in German-Occupied Europe.* London: Heinemann, 1977.

Livingston, William S. "Canada, Australia and the United States:Variations on a Theme." In Valerie Earle, *Federalism: Infinite Variety in Theory and Practice.* Itasca, Ill: F. E. Peacock, 1968.

———. "A Note on the Nature of Federalism." *Political Science Quarterly* 67 (1952), pp. 81–95.

Long, Norton E. "Open and Closed Systems." In R. Barry Farrell, ed., *Approaches to Comparative and International Politics.* Evanston, Ill.: Northwestern University Press, 1966.

Lorwin, Val R. "Segmented Pluralism: Ideological Cleavages and Political Cohesion in the Smaller European Democracies." *Comparative Politics* 3 (1971), pp. 141–175.

Lubin, Martin. "The Conference of the New England Governors and the Eastern Canadian Premiers." Paper presented at the Twenty-Sixth Annual Meeting of the Western Social Science Association, San Diego, April 26, 1984.

Lustick, Ian. "Stability in Deeply Divided Societies: Consociationalism Versus Control." *World Politics* 31 (1979), pp. 325–344.

McCall, Louis A. *Regional Integration: A Comparison of European and Central American Dynamics.* Beverly Hills, Calif.: Sage, 1976.

Machiavelli, Niccolò. *The Prince and the Discourses.* New York: Random House, 1950.

McKenna, Joseph C., S.J. "Ethics and War: A Catholic View." *American Political Science Review* 54 (1960), pp. 647–658.

McLaughlin, Andrew C. *The Confederation and the Constitution.* New York: Harper, 1905.

———. *A Constitutional History of the United States.* New York: Appleton-Century, 1935.

Macmahon, Arthur W. *Federalism: Mature and Emergent.* New York: Russell and Russell, 1962.

McRae, Kenneth D. *Conflict and Compromise in Multilingual Societies.* Vol. 1, *Switzerland.* Vol. 2, *Belgium.* Waterloo: Wilfrid Laurier University Press, 1983–1985.

McWhinney, Edward. *Canada and the Constitution 1979–1982: Patriation and the Charter of Rights.* Toronto: University of Toronto Press, 1982.

Main, Jackson Turner. *The Antifederalists: Critics of the Constitution 1781–1789.* Chapel Hill: University of North Carolina Press, 1961.

Malchus, Viktor Freiherr V. *Partnerschaft an Europäisch Grenzen: Integration durch grenzüeberschreitende Zusammenarbeit.* Bonn: Europa Union Verlag, 1975.

Martinez, Oscar I., ed. *Across Boundaries: Transborder Interaction in Comparative Perspective.* El Paso: University of Texas Press, 1986.

Merkl, Peter H. "Federalism and Social Structure." Paper read at the Sixth World Congress of the International Political Science Association, Geneva, September 21–25, 1964.

———. *Political Continuity and Change.* New York: Harper and Row, 1967.

Merle, Marcel. *Forces et enjeux dans les relations internationales.* Paris: Economica, 1981.

———. *Sociologie des relations internationales.* 3d ed. Paris: Dalloz, 1982.

Merritt, Richard L. "Perceptions of Unity and Diversity in Colonial America, 1725–1775." Paper presented at the Sixth World Congress of the International Political Science Association, Geneva, September 21–25, 1964.

———. *Symbols of American Community (1735–1775).* New Haven: Yale University Press, 1966.

Mitrany, David. A Working Peace System. Chicago: Quadrangle Books, 1966.

Moran, Theodore H. Multinational Corporations and the Politics of Dependence: Copper in Chile. Princeton: Princeton University Press, 1974.

Morgan, Edmund S. The Birth of the Republic: 1763–1789. Chicago: University of Chicago Press, 1956.

Morgan, George Allen. See Historicus.

Morgenthau, Hans J. Politics Among Nations. 5th ed. New York: Knopf, 1973.

Moskvichov, Lev N. The End of Ideology Theory: Illusions and Reality—Critical Notes on a Fashionable Bourgeois Conception. Moscow: Progress Publishers, 1974.

Moulin, Leo. "Le fédéralisme dans l'organisation politique des ordres 'religieux.'" Paper presented at the Sixth World Congress of the International Political Science Association, Geneva, September 21–25, 1964.

Mumme, Stephen P. "The Politics of Water Apportionment and Pollution Problems in the United States-Mexico Relations," in Overseas Development Council, U.S.-Mexico Project Series, No. 5, 1982.

――――. "Regional Power in National Diplomacy: The U.S. Section of the International Boundary and Water Commission." Publius 14 (1984), pp. 115–135.

――――. "State Influence in Foreign Policy Making: Water Related Environmental Disputes Along the United States-Mexico Border." Western Political Quarterly (1985), pp. 1–36.

Murty, Satchidananda. "Ethics and Politics in Hindu Culture." In Harold D. Lasswell and Harlan Cleveland, eds., The Ethic of Power: The Interplay of Religion, Philosophy, and Politics. New York: Harper and Row, 1962.

Nardin, Terry. Law, Morality, and the Relations of States. Princeton, N.J.: Princeton University Press, 1983.

National Governors' Association Committee on International Trade and Foreign Relations. Export Development and Foreign Investment: The Role of the States and its Linkage to Federal Action. Washington, D.C., 1982.

Needler, M. C., ed. Political Systems of Latin America. Princeton, N.J.: Van Nostrand, 1964.

Neuman, Stephanie Glickberg, ed. Small States and Segmented Societies. New York: Praeger, 1976.

Niebuhr, Reinhold. Christian Realism and Political Problems. New York: Scribner, 1953.

――――. "The Myth of World Government." Nation 152 (March 16, 1946).

Nordlinger, Eric. Conflict Regulation in Divided Societies. Center for International Affairs Occasional Papers no. 29. Cambridge: Harvard University, 1971.

Nouvelle Société Helvétique. Anno 709 p.G.: Rapport final de la Conférence de prospective de la nouvelle Société Helvétique. Geneva: Edition Sonor, 1973.

O'Brien, Sharon. "The Medicine Line: A Border Dividing Tribal Sovereignty, Economies, and Families." Fordham Law Review 13:3 (1984), pp. 315–350.

Ontario, Ministry of Industry and Trade. Canadian Trade Policy for the 1980's: An Ontario Perspective. Toronto, 1982.

Orban, Edmond. La dynamique de la centralisation and l'Etat fédéral: un processus irréversible. Montréal: Québec/Amérique, 1984.

Orwell, George. "Reflections on Gandhi." In A Collection of Essays by George Orwell. New York: Harcourt Brace Jovanovich, 1946.

Osgood, Herbert. The American Colonies in the Eighteenth Century (1924 reprint), Gloucester, Mass.: Peter Smith, 1958.

Osgood, Robert Endicott. Ideals and Self-Interest in America's Foreign Relations. Chicago: University of Chicago Press, 1953.

Ostrom, Vincent. *The Political Theory of a Compound Republic.* Blacksburg, Va.: Public Choice, 1971.

Overacker, Louise. *The Australian Party System.* New Haven: Yale University Press, 1952.

Painchaud, Paul. "Territorialization and Internationalism: The Case of Québec." *Publius* 7 (1977), pp. 161–175.

Parti socialiste. *Projet socialiste: pour la France des années 80.* Paris: Club socialiste, 1981.

Pratt, Larry, and Stevenson, Garth. *Western Separatism: The Myths, Realities, and Dangers.* Edmonton, Alberta: Hartig Publishers, 1981.

Putnam, Robert D., et al. "Explaining Institutional Success: The Case of Italian Regional Government." *American Political Science Review* 77 (1983), pp. 55–74.

Pye, Lucian W. *Aspects of Political Development.* Boston: Little, Brown, 1966.

Québec Centre of International Relations. *Le Canada dans le monde: XIII Congrès des relations internationales du Québec.* Québec, 1981.

_____. *Présence internationale du Québec: Chroniques des années 1978–1983.* Québec, 1984.

Québec, Government of. *Bâtir le Québec: Enoncé de politique économique.* Québec: Editeur officiel, 1979.

_____. *Bâtir le Québec: Phase 2—Le virage technologique, 1982–1986.* Québec: Editeur officiel, 1982.

_____. *Challenges for Québec: A Statement on Economic Policy.* Québec: Editeur officiel, 1979.

_____. *La cooperation et relations franco-québécoises: Bilan 1982–1983, 1983–1984, 1984–1985.* Québec: Editeur officiel, 1985.

Québec, Ministry of International Relations. *Le Québec dans le monde: Le défi de l'interdependance, Enoncé de politique de relations internationales.* Québec: Editeur officiel, 1985.

_____. *Les Carnets du Québec: Les délégations du Québec: action concrète.* Québec: Editeur officiel, 1982.

Rabushka, Alvin, and Shepsle, Kenneth A. *Politics in Plural Societies: A Theory of Democratic Instability.* Columbus, Ohio: Charles E. Merrill, 1972.

Rae, Douglas W. "The Limits of Consensual Decision." *The American Political Science Review* 29 (1975), pp. 1265–1271.

Rakove, Jack. "The Legacy of the Articles of Confederation." *Publius* 12 (1982), pp. 45–66.

Ramet, Pedro. *Nationalism and Federalism in Yugoslavia: 1963–1983.* Bloomington: Indiana University Press, 1985.

Rao, P. Kodanda. "Communalism in India." *Current History* 33 (1956), pp. 84–88.

Rejai, Mostafa, ed. *Decline of Ideology.* Chicago: Aldine, Atherton, 1971.

Rémillard, Gil. *Le fédéralisme canadien.* Montréal: Québec/Amérique, 1980.

Renan, Ernest. "What Is a Nation?" In Sir Alfred Zimmern, ed., *Modern Political Doctrines.* Oxford: Clarendon Press, 1939.

Ricq, Charles. *Les travailleurs frontaliers en Europe: Essai de politique sociale et régionale.* Paris: Editions Anthropos, 1981.

Riker, William H. *Federalism: Origin, Operation, Significance.* Boston: Little, Brown, 1964.

_____. *Soldiers of the States.* Washington, D.C.: Public Affairs Press, 1957.

Rokkan, Stein, and Urwin, Derek W. *Economy, Territory, Identity.* Beverly Hills, Calif.: Sage, 1983.

Rose, Richard. *Understanding Big Government.* Beverly Hills, Calif.: Sage, 1984.

Rosenau, James N. "The Concept of Intervention." *Journal of International Affairs* 22 (1968), pp. 165–176.

——— . "Pre-Theories and Theories of Foreign Policy." In R. Barry Farrell, ed. *Approaches to Comparative and International Politics.* Evanston: Northwestern University Press, 1966.

——— . "A Pre-Theory Revisited: World Politics in an Era of Cascading Interdependence." *International Studies Quarterly* 29 (1984), pp. 245–305.

Rosenau, James N., ed. *Linkage Politics: Essays on the Convergence of National and International Systems.* New York: Free Press, 1969.

Rossiter, Clinton. *The Grand Convention.* New York: Macmillan, 1966.

Rothchild, Donald, and Olorunsola, Victor A., eds. *State Versus Ethnic Claims: African Policy Dilemmas.* Boulder, Colo.: Westview Press, 1983.

Rutan, Gerard F. "Two Views of the Concept of Sovereignty: Canadian-Canadien." *Western Political Quarterly* 25 (1971), pp. 456–466.

Sabetti, Filippo. "The Making of Italy as an Experiment in Constitutional Choice." *Publius* 12 (1982), pp. 65–84.

Salisbury, Harrison. *The Long March.* New York: Harper and Row, 1985.

Sauer, Paul. *Württemberg in der Zeit des Nationalsozialismus.* Ulm: Süddeutsche Verlagsgesellschaft 1975.

Sawer, Geoffrey. "Judicial Power under the Constitution." In Else-Mitchel, M., ed., *Essays on the Australian Constitution.* Sydney: Law Book Company, 1961.

Schechter, Stephen L. *Annual Review of American Federalism. Publius* 1980–.

Schmitter, Philippe C., and Lehmbruch, Gerhard, eds. *Trends Toward Corporatist Intermediation.* Beverly Hills, Calif.: Sage, 1979.

Schuetz, Charles F. *Revising the Federal Constitution of Switzerland.* Ottawa: Carleton University, 1983.

Schwartz, Mildred A. *Politics and Territory: The Sociology of Regional Persistence in Canada.* Montréal: McGill-Queen's University Press, 1974.

Schweigler, Gebhard Ludwig. *National Consciousness in Divided Germany.* Beverly Hills, Calif.: Sage, 1975.

Scott, Andrew. *The Revolution in Statecraft: Informal Penetration.* New York: Random House, 1965.

——— . *The Dynamics of Interdependence.* Chapel Hill: University of North Carolina Press, 1982.

Senghor, Leopold Sedar. *African Socialism.* New York: Praeger, 1964.

Sengotta, Hans Jürgen. *Der Reichstatthalter in Lippe 1933 bis 1939: reichsrechtliche Bestimmungen and politische Praxis.* Detmold: Naturwissenschaftlicher and Historischer Verein für das Land Lippe, 1976.

Seton-Watson, Hugh. *Nations and States: An Enquiry into the Origins of Nations and Politics of Nationalism.* Boulder, Colo.: Westview Press, 1977.

Sharpe, L. J. *Decentralist Trends in Western Democracies.* Beverly Hills, Calif.: Sage, 1979.

Shepherd, George W., Jr. *Anti-Apartheid: Transnational Conflict and Western Policy in the Liberation of South Africa.* Westport, Conn.: Greenwood Press, 1977.

Sheppard, Robert, and Valpy, Michael. *The National Deal: The Fight for a Canadian Constitution.* Toronto: Fleet Books, 1982.

Shuman, Michael H. *Action Handbook for Local Elected Officials.* Palo Alto, Calif.: Center for Innovative Diplomacy, 1984.

Simeon, Richard. *Federal-Provincial Diplomacy.* Toronto: University of Toronto Press, 1982.

Simmons, Luiz, and Said, Abdul, eds. *The New Sovereigns: Corporations as World Powers.* New York: Praeger, 1974.

Skilling, Gordon H. *Czechoslovakia's Interrupted Revolution.* Princeton: Princeton University Press, 1976.

Smiley, Donald V., *Canada in Question: Federalism in the Eighties.* 3d ed. Toronto: McGraw-Hill Ryerson, 1980.

_____. *Canada in Question: Federalism in the Seventies.* Toronto: McGraw-Hill Ryerson, 1972.

_____. "The Canadian Federation and the Challenge of Québec Independence." *Publius* 8 (1978), pp. 199–224.

_____. *The Canadian Political Nationality.* Toronto: Methuen, 1967.

_____. "Territorialism and Canadian Political Institutions." *Canadian Public Policy* 3 (1977), pp. 456–476.

Smith, Anthony D. *Nationalism in the Twentieth Century.* New York: New York University Press, 1979.

_____. *Theories of Nationalism.* New York: Holmes and Meier, 1983.

Smith, Anthony, D., ed. *Nationalist Movements.* New York: St. Martin's Press, 1977.

Snyder, Glenn H., and Diesing, Paul. *Conflict Among Nations: Bargaining, Decision Making, and System Structure in International Crises.* Princeton: Princeton University Press, 1977.

Sohn, Louis B., and Buergenthal, Thomas. *International Protection of Human Rights.* Indianapolis: Bobbs-Merrill, 1973.

Soldatos, Panayotis. "La politique de diversification du Canada dans le contexte de ses relations avec les Etats-Unis: La logique du discours et le poids des réalités (The Politics of Diversification in Canadian-United States Relations: The Logic of Discourse and the Importance of Reality)." Paper presented at a meeting of the University Consortium for Research on North America, Harvard University, April 14, 1984.

Stein, Arthur A. "Coordination and Collaboration: Regime in an Anarchic World." *International Organization* 36 (1982), pp. 299–324.

Steiner, Jürg. *Amicable Agreement Versus Majority Rule: Conflict Resolution in Switzerland.* Chapel Hill: University of North Carolina Press, 1974.

_____. "The Consociational Theory and Beyond." *Comparative Politics* 13 (1981), pp. 339–360.

Steiner, Jürg, and Obler, Jeffrey L. *Decision Making in Smaller Democracies: The Consociational Burden.* Beverly Hills, Calif.: Sage, 1977.

Stewart, William H. "Metaphors, Models, and the Development of Federal Theory." *Publius* 12 (1982), pp. 5–24.

Stoddard, Ellwyn R. "Local and Regional Incongruities in Bi-National Diplomacy: Policy for the U.S. Mexico Border." *Policy Perspectives* 2 (1982), pp. 116–126.

Stoddard, Ellwyn R.; Nostrand, Richard L.; and West, Jonathan P., eds. *Borderlands Sourcebook: A Guide to the Literature on Northern Mexico and the American Southwest.* Norman: University of Oklahoma Press, 1983

Swanson, Robert Frank. *Intergovernmental Perspectives on the Canada-U.S. Relationship.* New York: University Press, 1978.

Tarrow, Sidney. "Local Constraints on Regional Reform: A Comparison of Italy and France." *Comparative Politics* 7 (1979), pp. 1–36.

Tarrow, Sidney; Katzenstein, Peter J.; and Graziano, Luigi, eds. *Territorial Politics in Industrial Nations.* New York: Praeger, 1978.

Taylor, Phillip. *Nonstate Actors in International Politics: From Transregional to Substate Organizations.* Boulder, Colo.: Westview Press, 1984.

Teppe, Karl. *Provinze-Partei-Staat: Zur provinziellen Selbstverwaltung im Dritten Reich untersucht am Beispiel Westfalens*. Münster: Aschendorff Verlag, 1977.

Teune, Henry. "The Future of Federalism: Federalism and Political Integration." In Valerie Earle, *Federalism: Infinite Variety in Theory and Practice*. Itasca, Ill.: F. E. Peacock, 1968.

Thucydides. *History of the Peloponnesian Wars*. Trans. Charles Foster Smith. Cambridge: Harvard University Press, 1956.

Tigrid, Pavel. *Why Dubcek Fell*. London: MacDonald, 1971.

Tucker, Robert W. *The Inequality of Nations*. New York: Basic Books, 1976.

Tupper, Allan, and Doern, Bruce G., eds. *Public Corporations and Public Policy in Canada*. Montréal: Institute for Research on Public Policy, 1981.

Union of International Associations. *Yearbook of International Organizations*. 19th ed. Brussels: UIA, 1981.

United Nations. *Multinational Corporations in World Development*. ST/ECA/1970. New York: Department of Economics and Social Affairs, 1970.

Valenta, Jiri. *Soviet Intervention in Czechoslovakia, 1968: Anatomy of a Decision*. Baltimore: Johns Hopkins University Press, 1979.

Vernon, Raymond. *Sovereignty at Bay: The Multinational Spread of U.S. Enterprises*. New York: Basic Books, 1971.

———. *Storm over the Multinationals: The Real Issues*. Cambridge: Harvard University Press, 1977.

Vienna Institute for Comparative Economic Studies, ed. *Comecon Data 1979*. New York: Holmes and Meier Publishers, 1979.

Visscher, Charles de. *Theory and Reality in Public International Law*. Princeton, N.J.: Princeton University Press, 1957.

Wallace, Michael D., and Singer, David J. "Intergovernmental Organization in the Global System, 1815-1964." *International Organization* 24 (1970), pp. 239-287.

Waltz, Kenneth N. *Man, the State, and War: A Theoretical Analysis*. New York: Columbia University Press, 1954.

———. *Theory of International Politics*. Reading, Mass.: Addison-Wesley, 1979.

Ward, Henry M. *"Unite or Die": Intercolony Relations, 1690-1763*. Port Washington, N.Y.: Kennikat Press, 1971.

Watts, R. L. *Administration in Federal Systems*. London: Hutchinson Educational, 1970.

———. *New Federations: Experiments in the Commonwealth*. Oxford: Clarendon Press, 1966.

Weinstein, Brian. "Language Strategists: Redefining Political Frontiers on the Basis of Linguistic Choices." *World Politics* 31 (1979), pp. 345-364.

Wheare, K. C. *Federal Government*. New York: Oxford University Press, 1964.

White, Ralph K. "Images in the Context of International Conflict: Soviet Perceptions of the U.S. and the U.S.S.R." In Herbert C. Kelman, ed., *International Behavior: A Social Psychological Analysis*. New York: Holt, Rinehart and Winston, 1965.

Wildavsky, Aaron, ed. *American Federalism in Perspective*. Boston: Little, Brown, 1967.

Wilkins, Mira. *The Maturing of Multinational Enterprise: American Business Abroad from 1914-1970*. Cambridge: Harvard University Press,

Willoughby, William R. *The Joint Organizations of Canada and the United States*. Toronto: University of Toronto Press, 1979.

Wolfers, Arnold. *Discord and Collaboration: Essays on International Politics*. Baltimore: Johns Hopkins Press, 1962.

Young, Oran R. "International Regimes: Problems of Concept Formation." *World Politics* 32 (1980), pp. 331–356.

Zariski, Raphael. "The Establishment of the Kingdom of Italy as a Unitary State: A Case Study in Regime Formation." *Publius* 13 (1983), pp. 1–19.

_____. *Italy: The Politics of Uneven Development.* Hinsdale, Ill.: Dryden Press, 1972.

Zink, Harold. *Modern Governments.* Princeton, N.J.: Van Nostrand, 1958.

Index